The Responsive Environment

THE RESPONSIVE ENVIRONMENT

DESIGN, AESTHETICS, AND THE HUMAN IN THE 1970s

Larry D. Busbea

MINNESOTA
University of Minnesota Press
Minneapolis
London

This book is supported by a grant from the Graham Foundation for Advanced Studies in the Fine Arts.

Publication of this book has been aided by a grant from the Millard Meiss Publication Fund of the College Art Association.

A portion of chapter 1 was published as "McLuhan's Environment: The End (and *The Beginnings*) of Architecture," *Aggregate,* December 11, 2015. A different version of chapter 4 was previously published as "Soft Control Material: Environment and Design c. 1970," *Journal of Design History* 30, no. 2 (May 2017): 139–56; copyright 2016 Oxford University Press. Different versions of portions of chapter 6 were published in *Repositioning Paolo Soleri: The City Is Nature* (Scottsdale, Ariz.: Scottsdale Museum of Contemporary Art, 2017), in conjunction with the exhibition of the same name, and "Paolo Soleri and the Aesthetics of Irreversibility," *Journal of Architecture* 19, no. 6 (December 2013): 781–808.

Published by the University of Minnesota Press
111 Third Avenue South, Suite 290
Minneapolis, MN 55401-2520
http://www.upress.umn.edu

Printed in Canada on acid-free paper

The University of Minnesota is an equal-opportunity educator and employer.

26 25 24 23 22 21 20 10 9 8 7 6 5 4 3 2 1

Library of Congress Cataloging-in-Publication Data
Names: Busbea, Larry D., author.
Title: The responsive environment : design, aesthetics, and the human in the 1970s / Larry D. Busbea.
Description: Minneapolis : University of Minnesota Press, 2020. | Includes bibliographical references and index.
Identifiers: LCCN 2019017203 (print) | ISBN 978-1-5179-0709-9 (hc) | ISBN 978-1-5179-0710-5 (pb)
Subjects: LCSH: Environment (Aesthetics) | Design—Human factors. | Design—History—20th century. | BISAC: DESIGN / History & Criticism. | ARCHITECTURE / History / Contemporary (1945–). | ART / History / Contemporary (1945–).
Classification: LCC BH301.E58 B87 2019 (print) | DDC 111/.85—dc23
LC record available at https://lccn.loc.gov/2019017203

To my little pattern watchers, Kase and Ramona

Contents

Preface and Acknowledgments ix

Introduction xiii

1 Invisible Environments 1

2 Pattern Watchers 45

3 Responsive Environments 89

4 Soft Control Material 141

5 Cybertecture 167

6 Arcoconsciousness 209

Conclusion 235

Notes 241

Index 279

Preface and Acknowledgments

This is a book about changing conceptions of human–environment interaction and the ways in which these came to be technically and aesthetically modified during the 1970s. My approach is not based on the determinative influence of a particular class of technologies or any stable object. This is not a history of computers in design, "smart" technologies, or even "responsive environments" so much as it is an attempt to track the epistemological and sensible shifts that precipitated or were precipitated by new models of the human subject as a contingent, porous, extended, and attenuated entity.

That this capacious brief might be adequately addressed by the methodological resources of art history is a proposition that I test here but certainly do not resolve. My frequent forays into anthropology, biology, psychology, and various other scientific and humanistic subdisciplines are overreaches. These are not made out of a hubristic belief that I might actually master these fields (specialist readers will recognize my limitations immediately); rather, they are inspired by my research subjects, who understood these same disciplinary distinctions as modern contrivances that would give way to environment in due course.

If I did feel emboldened, though, it was only because of the tremendous support I enjoyed while preparing this material over the past few years. This support arrived in very concrete financial and professional forms, and in much more personal ways. I received travel funding from the University of Arizona's School of Fine Arts Faculty Professional Development Endowment. The UA Provost's Office provided a subvention to underwrite reproduction costs. The book has also received the support of the Millard Meiss Publication Fund administered by the College Art Association. The Graham Foundation for Advanced Studies in the Fine Arts supported this research in its initial stages, and in the form of a publication grant at its conclusion. The foundation not only provided necessary funding for the work but was also present in more existential ways, as many of the projects and individuals I discuss here were funded by the same organization some fifty years ago, and they shared a belief in its mission of placing art, architecture, and design at the center of social discourse.

One of these individuals was Edward T. Hall, who was involved with the foundation on several occasions when he was posted at the Illinois

Institute of Technology in the mid-1960s. Though I never met Hall, I wish here to signal my gratitude to him, for it was the extensive time I spent in his incredible archive at the University of Arizona that convinced me that writing a book about environment in a general sense—a book not about a particular thing or set within a singular discipline, but set in the spaces between these, where all of us exist, after all—was possible. Roger Myer of the UA Libraries' Special Collections was supremely helpful in facilitating my publication of images from the archive, and Karin Bergh Hall kindly gave permission for their use.

I also want to acknowledge the inspiration I derived from the work of William H. Ittelson, one of the founders of the field of environmental psychology. Bill's work transcended disciplinary conventions and truly allowed me to *see* environment in visceral ways. A significant moment in the development of the work presented here came when I was lucky enough to get to meet and spend time with Bill before he passed away in 2018.

I also was able to speak, very briefly, with Paolo Soleri before he passed away in 2013. Arcosanti, which features in chapter 6, is an environment that has continually nourished my historical comprehension and perceptual capacities. My analysis of Soleri and this remarkable place would not have been possible without the help of several people at the Cosanti Foundation: Sue Hertz, Mary Hoadley, Roger Tomalty, and Tomiaki Tamura. I have also received invaluable encouragement from Claire Carter, curator at the Scottsdale Museum of Contemporary Art. Claire was kind enough to involve me in her work on the Soleri retrospective mounted at the museum in 2017, which was a monumental undertaking on her part and a remarkable show. Mere days after we celebrated the opening of that exhibition, however, Soleri's daughter Daniela Soleri published an account of her father's repeated sexual abuse during her youth. This was difficult information to assimilate, and I grappled with what my response should be. Historical amnesia seems just as disingenuous as the endorsement implied by any monographic analysis (no matter how dispassionate or critical). In the end, and with a still unresolved ambivalence, I decided to keep the Soleri material here. I believe Soleri's work is indispensable to an understanding of environmental response circa 1970. But I also acknowledge the compromise this represents.

The other revelations contained in this book were more fortunate, and they would not have been possible without the generosity of several of the theorists and designers I discuss, and that of their families and friends. I thank very sincerely Chris Boutourline, who spoke with me and provided precious archival material about his father, Serge. Susan Buirge was also kind enough to correspond with me about her collaborations with Serge Boutourline. Myron Krueger gave me a bit of his time to speak on the telephone. I had a lovely e-mail exchange with Warren Brodey just after my essay about his work was published; I want to express my appreciation to him for taking the time to read and remark on it. Wolf Hilbertz's family and students were incredibly helpful, and their warmth and enthusiasm made me wish even more that I had been able to meet him. Here I acknowledge the help (and patience) of Derrick and Kai Hilbertz, Newton Fallis, Joe Mathis, and Desmond Fletcher.

While the exchanges noted above led to the creation of a kind of informal archive on which this text relies, established collections were no less significant. I wish to thank Luisa Haddad and Nicholas Meriweather at the University of California, Santa Cruz, where I consulted Gregory Bateson's papers. Phillip Guddemi at the Bateson Idea Group gave permission to quote some of the material gathered there. Nancy Sparrow at the Alexander Architectural Archives at the University of Texas at Austin delivered to me the few items on Wolf Hilbertz scattered among the university's collections. The archivists at the Archives of American Art helped me navigate their Görgy Kepes holdings. Dr. Albert Mueller at the Institut für Zeitgeschichte in Vienna aided me with Gordon Pask materials. I thank Lily Alexander for her help in obtaining permission to publish images by Christopher Alexander.

The raw information gathered in these archival forays was refined as I published and presented some of the material here over the past few years. I thank Monica Amor, Joseph Clark, Ed Dimendberg, Marianne Eggler, James Graham, Maros Krivy, Reinhold Martin, Charles Rice, Olga Touloumi, and Theodora Vardouli for inviting me to speak and publish. Thanks also to Arindam Dutta, John Harwood, and the rest of the Aggregate Architectural History Collaborative for allowing me to republish "McLuhan's Environment" (and for letting me publish it in the first place). To Caroline Maniaque-Benton I offer my warmest regards, not only because she allowed me to present a paper at a panel she organized but also because of her personal support and the inspiration of her work. I emphasize here as well the debt I owe Kjetil Fallan and Finn-Arne Jorgensen, whom I met at their research workshop at the Rachel Carson Center in Munich in 2013. They have subsequently provided professional encouragement and welcome friendship far beyond that single congenial occasion.

Many of these individuals, and a number of others, provided sympathetic and critical readings of this work that greatly improved its quality. I thank Pieter Martin at the University of Minnesota Press, whose validation and concise criticism brought this text from a work in progress to a work. Anne Carter at the Press deftly facilitated the submission of the manuscript and the final sorting of images. I received Judy Selhorst's edited version of the text with what I can only describe as a great sense of relief, for she truly improved it. Jennifer Gabrys reviewed the manuscript for the Press, and I thank her (as well as the second anonymous reader) for her insight.

Other interlocutors have given me time and attention outside the auspices of official peer review and public venues. I thank Chris Fraser for his reading of several chapters and for his work, which is a series of revelatory perceptual environments. (Thanks again, Claire, for introducing us.) Simon Sadler provided incredible insight into a particular chapter and has produced much work that I have drawn from. I could say much the same of many other individuals whom I flatter myself in describing as fellow travelers: Ingrid Halland, Matthew Holt, Kelly Nipper, and Anthony Raynsford all sympathetically read and commented on parts of this text.

Others supported me over the years in myriad ways, and without them I would never have had the wherewithal to compile a second monograph. Rosemarie Bletter and Martin Filler are dear friends and precious connections to the world of architecture culture, which can sometimes feel quite distant from my office here in the desert. Joan Ockman has written letters of support and read some of this material and, moreover, has produced work that has guided me intellectually for twenty years. My colleagues at the University of Arizona have spent years mentoring me and supporting my research endeavors. During that time, I have come into contact with several graduate researchers whose engagement has been inspiring: Brad Derro, Alex von Bergen, Isan Brant, Megan Jackson, David Thomas, and Yanhua Zhou.

My family has been the greatest support. The research for this book began—even if I didn't recognize it at the time—when my partner, Michelle Strier, and I had two children. Kase and Ramona Strier Busbea may not have sped the work here, but they enriched it in ways I can scarcely articulate. Thanks to all of you for making me a little more human.

Introduction

> The air we thoughtlessly breathe; the mood-saturated situations in which we unknowingly exist contained and containing; the atmospheres, so obvious as to be imperceptible, in which we live, move, and have our being. . . . They had to be experienced as fragile, losable, and destructible before they could advance to workable task fields for air and mood phenomenologists, for relationship therapists, for atmosphere engineers and interior designers, and finally for cultural theorists and media technologists. They had to become unbreathable for people to learn to recognize themselves as guardians, reconstructors, and reinventors of what had merely been taken for granted.
>
> —Peter Sloterdijk, *Foams,* 2016

Where do we—as subjects and objects—begin and end? What are our boundaries, and what are the mechanisms that allow them to maintain our spatial identities, each comprising an outside and an inside? Are these boundaries stable and insular for the duration of their existence, or do they transact with their surroundings, extending outward, exchanging particles, energies, and information? Such questions have typically been the purview of biologists and psychologists, not to mention cosmologists and metaphysicians. But after World War II, these and related concerns became very urgent for a certain subset of architects, artists, designers, and theorists. These individuals felt that, in one way or another, aesthetics and design could play pivotal roles in emerging conceptions of humanity and the world in which we exist. They would go on to propose a series of novel spatiotemporal interfaces that promised a new kind of relationship between humanity and its milieu—a new environment sensitive to the smallest input from or modification by its newly sensitized inhabitants.

This is the subject of the current study: the reciprocal production of new theories of *environmental response* across multiple disciplines and the design of architectures and interfaces that would come to be known as *responsive environments.* At the dynamic point of overlap of these two categories of concern was a strangely elusive figure—a hybrid user/designer newly empowered to effect change in humanity's surroundings, even while beginning to perceive the profound conditioning effects of those surroundings. Perhaps it was Edward T. Hall—an anthropologist who found himself at the center of architectural and environmental design cultures in the 1960s and 1970s—who captured this ecological, technological, and existential situation best: "*Man and his environment participate in molding each other*," he wrote. "Man is now in the position of actually creating the total world in which he lives, what the ethologists refer to as his biotope. In creating this world he is actually determining *what kind of organism* he will be."[1]

Hall was not alone in recognizing this new subject who was both endowed with unprecedented technical capabilities and compromised by the interpellative apparatuses of the milieu. Indeed, the attempt to model and optimize the transactional points of contact between these two—subject and environment—became one of the major projects of design and aesthetics by the end of the 1960s. If this claim little resembles the narratives of most histories of art and architecture of this period, that is at least partly because of the qualities of environment itself. Environment was at once ubiquitous and elusive, totalizing yet absolutely localized in its discipline-specific manifestations. In retrospect, this lent the concept its simultaneously banal and obscure characteristics. It functioned at the broadest levels of cultural discourse as the most vacuous of shifters and, on the other hand, as the singular focus of attention in myriad long-forgotten experiments carried out by tinkering scientists, psychological mystics, and holistic designers—or, as the philosopher Peter Sloterdijk so evocatively lists them in the quotation that opens this Introduction, air and mood phenomenologists, relationship therapists, atmosphere engineers, and interior decorators, as well as cultural theorists and media technologists.

The experimental projects of these disciplinarily marginal figures were less technical or aesthetic objects than they were emergent atmospheric affordances for reciprocal interaction. They were responsive environments. In its most concrete sense, the term *responsive environment* denotes a technologically mediated architecture that, through digital or analog means, might alter its own structures or the ambient conditions within them based on any number of user inputs. Such alterations might be made for purposes of convenience (lights switching on as people enter a room), need (extra space for a new family member), wellness and entertainment (soothing light and music), or behavior modification (the deployment of educational systems within a space).

The possibility—the inevitability, frankly—of such systems is a central component of design discourse and popular discourse alike. Such devices and spaces are reflexively assumed to "put the engaging capacities of objects in the forefront."[2] According to the British curator Lucy Bullivant, "The very nature of responsive environments, involving functioning through interfaces that facilitate interaction, is a form of mediation between the inner world of the self and the outside world."[3] Another commentator recently wrote of such projects: "These spaces rely less on traditional architectural effect and more on actively evolving a kind of engagement with space" that might "alter the ways in which we relate to buildings, and ultimately each other."[4] These sanguine appraisals have already been tempered by more critical observations. Alberto Pérez-Gómez reminds us that responsive designs ambivalently call forth the double edge of an architecture/environment that might offer "the gift of psychosomatic completeness, true health and well-being for the social body" or, on the other hand, "the nightmare of so-called 'intelligent' architecture that ostensibly reproduces (and improves) the logical patterns of human reasoning as it interfaces with its inhabitants."[5]

Portents notwithstanding, responsive environments are currently functioning at virtually all levels of cultural discourse and production. We are constantly subjected to the inevitability of "smart" houses and the "internet of things."[6] TED Talks inform us of the coming revolution. At the more rarified end of things, such systems are the main focus of numerous research labs and design schools around the world. Examples include the urban data visualization applications developed by the firm Morphocode, which "explore natural phenomena such as pattern formation, self-organization and emergence"; David Hunter's recent project Data Walking, wherein users outfitted with "environment sensors" strolled through the "data spaces" of various cities; and the many projects of the MIT Media Lab's Responsive Environments section, which seeks to "augment and mediate human experience, interaction and perception, while developing new sensing modalities and enabling technologies that create new forms of interactive experience and expression," as well as the similarly named Responsive Environments and Artifacts Lab (REAL) at the Harvard University Graduate School of Design, which "pursues the design of digital, virtual, and physical worlds as an indivisible whole."[7] A bit of the metaphysics of responsive environments is also beginning to reappear, as in Sha Xin Wei's models of "topological matter." He writes of one installation: "We focus our attention on the amplification of metaphorical gestures by copresent humans performing in a shared responsive medium imbued—by computational means—with alchemical, responsive properties."[8]

This digitally inflected magical thinking was also commonplace half a century ago. Cultural theorist Marshall McLuhan wrote in 1966: "The art object is replaced by participation in the art process. This is the essential meaning of electric circuitry and responsive environments. The artist leaves the Ivory Tower for the Control Tower, and abandons the shaping of art objects in order to program the environment itself as a work of art."[9] Artist and techno-aesthetic guru Gyorgy Kepes implicated architecture explicitly in such developments: "Architecture is making fundamental departures from its traditional position as a discrete, independent, heavy, and solid form catering mainly to the visual sense and is becoming a responding, bodiless, dynamic, interdependent structure answering to man's changing needs and growing controls."[10] Jack Burnham foresaw similar transformations in what he described as "systems-oriented" art:

"Dropping the term 'sculpture,'" he wrote, this art "will deal less with artifacts contrived for their formal value, and increasingly with men enmeshed *with* and *within* purposeful responsive systems."[11] Architect Sean Wellesley-Miller euphorically predicted the imminent arrival of such systems: "We have a long way to go and but little time. But the vision is there: evolutionary domestic eco-systems, responsive environments, a new peace and joy."[12] (These examples will be multiplied in what follows, and also modified and challenged.)

These statements accompanied a number of attempts to implement such systems. They came in the form of interactive educational terminals, DIY construction kits, disco dance floors, pneumatic building systems, and urban data visualization devices, as well as simply work and living environments that might be better suited to the specific cultural needs of inhabitants (or the forgotten universal needs of humanity). Serge Boutourline Jr. sought to turn perceptual activity itself into a kind of environmental production. Kepes installed floor tiles that lit up and changed colors as they were walked on. Myron Krueger developed somatic computer interaction systems in which reactivity was not simply a means to an end; rather, in these systems, as he would say, "response is the medium!"[13] Warren Brodey and cybernetician Avery Johnson launched a start-up that produced a biomimetic material, the core function of which was to deprogram individuals out of their postindustrial stupor. Wolf Hilbertz elaborated a robotic construction system that would not only change environmental structures according to user needs but also facilitate the users' progressive biological evolution. Paolo Soleri sought to extend and orient that evolution toward a cosmic/spiritual event horizon.

It almost goes without saying that the current wave of smart things, responsive technology, intelligent environments, sensory apparatuses, biomimetic materials, and digital atmospherics does not recognize itself as a revival. But it is a revival. There is virtually no theme, practice, or technological advance being addressed today that was not discussed at length at the end of the 1960s and the beginning of the next decade. If I choose here to return to this earlier context, however, it is not to provide a historical corrective; still less is it to construct a stable sociohistorical metanarrative. It is, rather, to identify moments of ideological rupture that were much more explicit then than they are currently.

These ruptures were (and are) located precisely around issues of subject formation, of what it means to be human after the revelation of complete ecological interconnectedness and the identification of the conditioning mechanisms of social and technical milieus. Herein lies the signal difference between that earlier moment and our current one: that designers working fifty years ago were ostensibly more willing than those working today to release their preconceptions about what it meant to be human when faced with an overwhelming, immersive, conditioning environment. They were ostensibly more willing to relinquish the solidity and permanence of things in favor of energetic and behavioral patterns and flows. They were ostensibly more willing to set subjects and objects in motion, allowing them to change as inputs and outputs evolved. In other words, they explicitly embraced the insight recently offered by Beatriz Colomina and Mark Wigley that "the precise context of design is the indeterminacy of the human."[14]

Historically, responsive environments held out hope for new milieus that would no longer impose their stultifying structures on users or inhabitants but would instead become lighter, softer, more flexible, and, indeed, responsive. In this sense, the idea of "response" was itself a shifter, referring to designers, their activities, the resulting objects, and the activities these made possible for a newly conceived user. As such, the elusiveness of response served multiple rhetorical functions—at times the notion was embedded in the physical fabric of a building or room, at others it described metamorphoses in the profession and pedagogy of design, and sometimes new social relations.[15]

The rhetoric of response, and, with it, "participation" and "interactivity," signaled the immanent possibility that the roles of designer and user, producer and consumer, architect and inhabitant would be mixed, reorganized, stacked, or eliminated by new paradigms, technologies, and methods. Despite recent attempts to track the various exclusive characteristics of these concepts—response, participation, interactivity—the common denominator was (and is) a new ethical and political recognition of the need for objects with less finality and, accordingly, subjects with more agency.[16] I do not attempt here to define or isolate these terms systematically, preferring instead to let them slide together metonymically—as they have historically.

Having said this, I must acknowledge that *response* is the term to which I have gravitated most often. This is for the very direct reason that it was used with such consistency by the protagonists I discuss. But I also appreciate its ambiguity. Response hints at a state of uncertainty regarding the locus of agency in complex systems. On the one hand, it recalls the modeling of bleak positivistic, Popperian, or Pavlovian regimes of involuntary behaviors, even as it hints at a new horizon of autonomy for nonhuman systems and actors. Response, in other words, calls forth the subject as much as it is an attribute of the subject. It represents the complex mechanics of getting what is outside into the inside. It indicates the presence of the apparatus as it traces the patterns of overlap among various ecological, behavioral, technical, and perceptual systems.

Accordingly, response, design, and environment were historically inseparable. To be more precise, during the period in question, environment was widely apprehended not just as a problem or an object of design but rather as the very fabric of design activity itself. Another way of saying this is that design can never simply respond to existing environmental circumstances, for it creates new relations—new environments—with every object or interface it produces. It reorients the subject vis-à-vis the networks, systems, and things around her. This new set of relations, this newly formed context, *is* the environment. This explains why the notion of response becomes likewise inseparable from conceptualizations of environment. Environment is radically localized context that solicits and displays various types of response, consciously or otherwise, visibly or otherwise. Thus, by recognizing or revealing an environment's mechanisms, one is also automatically invited to imagine controlling that environment—optimizing it, programming its responses, and so on. Or, to simply invert the proposition again: in seeking to design an interaction in a given situation, one is led inexorably to theorize an environment.

The objects of study presented in the following chapters are highly contingent congelations of discourse, matter, perception, and technology whose shifting patterns effected analogous movements among environment, response, and design activity or thinking. The argument that will play out across these examples is threefold: first, that environment circa 1970 was in a fundamental way understood as a perceptual/aesthetic problem; second, that, once perceived, environment would be subject to the particular manipulations of *design* as that disciplinary and professional category was being reconceived simultaneously; and third, that at the very moment it was made available to these perceptions and activities, environment became more than yet another class of designed objects—it was invested with subjective attributes and lifelike behaviors, qualities that rendered it an active participant in the responsive interactions between subjects and the world around them.

Rather than being categorical or formulaic, however, this argument serves as a contingent frame through which to view the many slippages that actually produced environment and response. It may help us to track the ways in which discourse becomes form and technologies slip into the metaphysical, how extensions become ablations, and hindrances affordances. It may also help us come to terms with the ways in which perception was newly viewed through the lens of environment and the ways in which response was used for human self-design.

The Environmental Research Manifold

Such slippages were intimately linked with the rise of environment as an ethological, ecological, social, political, existential, and aesthetic category circa 1970. But this is not to say that environment had not already been shaping these categories (and many others) well before that date. After all, the notion of environment was not a latecomer to the established fields of biology, psychology, sociology, and anthropology; rather, it was foundational in the consolidations of those disciplines in the nineteenth century. Auguste Comte had to articulate a conception of "climates" to arrive at his notion of positivistic determination for anthropology. Claude Bernard had to develop the notion of milieu in order to articulate his biological conception of the organism as constituting a *milieu intérieur.* Herbert Spencer founded the modern science of psychology on the idea of "circumstances" or "environment" and humanity's interaction with it.[17] Contemporaneous with these scientific uses, such themes were catalytic in romantic aesthetic theory, veritably carving environment or ambience out as what Leo Spitzer so beautifully described in 1948 as "a mid-term between natural and spiritual surroundings."[18] In this regard, the inside/outside dynamics that became the preoccupation of so many in 1970 at times look more like an uncanny repetition of the thermodynamic, evolutionary, and aesthetic debates of a century (or two) prior.[19]

The distinction between the earlier moment and the later one lay, perhaps, in the way environment itself was coming into view in the postwar period—the possibility that the totality of systemic dynamics that comprised the fabric of reality itself might be mapped and modeled. Here we encounter Sloterdijk's observation that a classical conception of nature as a background or backdrop to human activity advanced steadily during modernity, and that a mediumistic or hollow conception of space gave way to a series of techno-aesthetic "explications" that traced the patterns and mechanisms filling the interstices and atmospheres around us. These explications engendered a quite literal "environmental inversion," according to Sloterdijk, a reversal of figure and ground wherein the space of dwelling was brought forward as a material to be measured and manipulated.[20]

During the 1960s and 1970s, this process of environmental explication became quite literal, and its existential possibility took on an operative—at

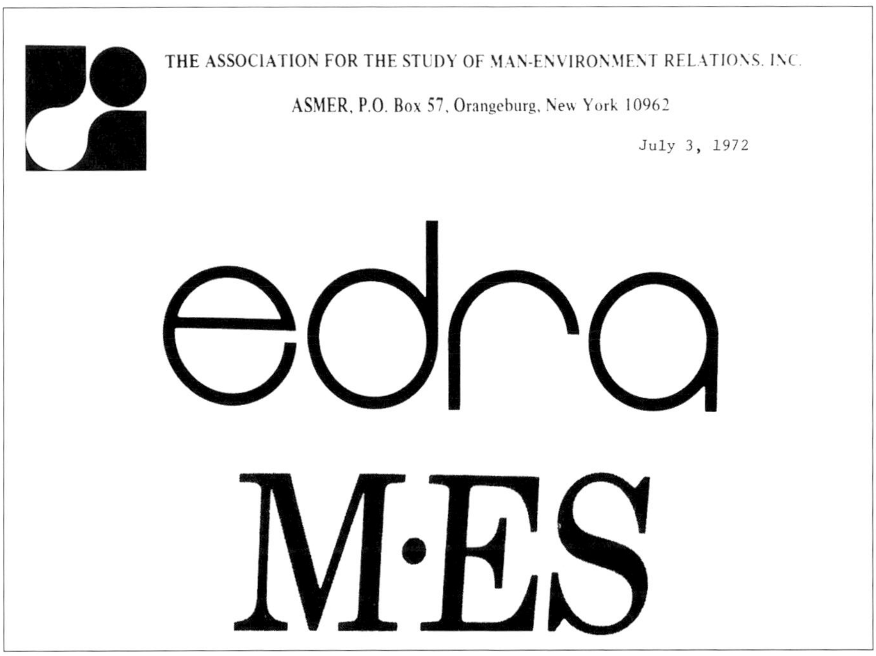

Figure I.1. The Environmental Design Research Association, the Association for the Study of Man–Environment Relations, and ASMER's journal *Man–Environment Systems* were all founded at the end of the 1960s.

times utopian—tinge. Suddenly, the modernist belief in environmental determinism collided with emerging models of social constructionism and ecology, and no area of scientific and humanistic research remained untouched. In this sense, the natural systems traditionally treated in biological ecology, for instance, dovetailed with new models of what came to be known as the "human environment."[21] The polyvalence of this last phrase is interesting, as it suggests a certain ambiguity regarding which term modifies which.[22] This same ambiguity also fueled the formation of multiple subdisciplines and institutions: environmental psychology (and its related fields of architectural psychology, topological psychology, ecological psychology, and the study of environment and behavior), human geography, human ecology, ecological anthropology, general systems theory, and so on.[23]

Significantly, it also gave birth to a multidisciplinary attempt to arrive at an objective approach to new models of the "built environment" known as "design methods."[24] This notion, in turn, would be further consolidated as "environmental design" by the end of the 1960s.[25] These ideas had been percolating throughout the decade, mostly in architecture programs at MIT; the University of California, Berkeley; the University of Texas at Austin; Penn State; and the University of Utah.[26] European institutions underwent similar transformations, as the trend toward environmental integration drove new technological, scientific, and political models of design at Cambridge University, the storied Hochshule für Gestaltung in Ulm, Germany, and the Institut de l'Environnement in Paris.[27]

These academic programs were paralleled by the formation of other types of public and private organizations—advocacy groups, consultancies, and NGOs—that promoted the reform or redesign of particular (or generalized) human environments.[28] For instance, the Association for the Study of Man–Environment Relations (ASMER) was founded in 1966 and published its own transdisciplinary journal, *Man–Environment Systems*, from 1969 to 1973.[29] The commercial publication *Design & Environment* first appeared in 1976 and by 1978 was rebranded as simply *Urban Design* (Plate 1). More famously, in the 1950s Greek architect Constantinos Doxiadis founded Ekistics, an institute devoted to his own method, also named ekistics, of designing human habitations looped into the most inclusive environmental systems. Closest in spirit to the projects featured in this study was the nearly single-handed attempt on the part of Museum of Modern Art curator Emilio Ambasz to found a new environmental design institution ex nihilo in 1972. Provisionally called the Universitas, such an institution, Ambasz maintained, would have to implement new models of design thinking that would "conceive of man as he who creates experiential and conceptual structures in order to satisfy needs and conciliate aspirations, which go from the physical to the cosmological, within the boundaries of the natural and the sociocultural world."[30]

What narrative might account for these disciplinary mutations and design initiatives that could, in the blink of an eye, move from the bodily ergonomics of toilets outward to the boundaries of the cosmos itself?[31] What method could reconcile their empirical assertions with their plainly metaphysical aspirations and their ill-fated attempts to concretize the imperceptible interstices and relations among all objects and subjects? Without claiming to answer such questions, I nonetheless have methodological need of what art historians so casually refer to as a *context* that might contain them or form a background against which their outlines might be perceived. For this problematic purpose I intermittently employ in the chapters that follow the phrase *environmental research manifold.* I use *manifold* here in both the common and specialized senses of the word, in reference to something complex and having a multitude of components whose relationships are not always evident, as well as in reference to a topological figure whose surfaces are curved in such a way that, at any single location, the space looks and acts like a nontopological Euclidean space. I employ the term not to describe an object or a singular locus of research or calculation, but to refer to a virtual object that might substantiate the relations among, or account for the patterns produced by, the disciplinary syntheses and interferences that comprised environment at this moment circa 1970.

I hope, too, that the phrase carries a whiff of frustration, for the environmental research manifold was never able to achieve the grand syntheses of data it sought. This failure was usually blamed on disciplinary and institutional myopia: a desire for immediate results, quantifiable outcomes, and economic verifiability. Seldom was it suggested that the project might be possessed of certain internal ideological contradictions, such as the recognition of the environment as having a conditioning relationship to the subject, on the one hand, and, on the other, the steadfast belief that this same subject would be able to perceive, measure, and, indeed, design the natures and forms of these conditioning mechanisms.

At least such suggestions were not common in the U.S. context. In Europe, a new form of social theory was emerging that would take the invisible nature of these mechanisms and raise it to the level of perhaps the ideological problem of modernity (and postmodernity) itself. France in particular witnessed the formation of this new type of critique, the sources of which lay in the work of Karl Marx, Sigmund Freud, and Friedrich Nietzsche, as filtered through the semiotics of Ferdinand de Saussure. The degree to which this new theory was entangled in notions of environment has been obscured somewhat by an almost exclusive concern with language, the semiotic field, and social institutions. But even these were spatialized in France in the postwar period, when the complex topological interplay of interior and exterior was mapped extensively.[32] And while I cannot fully account for the environmental or responsive implications of the theorization of what Louis Althusser, Michel Foucault, and Gilles Deleuze referred to as *appareils* or *dispositifs*—apparatuses—during the

1970s, I will bring them to bear at certain critical moments on the examples I include in this study.

The Responsive Designer

In all of these disciplinary reorganizations, "environmental response" as framed by the sciences was conflated with "responsive environments" as conceived by designers (every chapter in what follows will demonstrate such conflations).[33] These slippages were made possible, in part, by transformations in the conception of design itself. Indeed, the cross-pollinations, transdisciplinary initiatives, and grand synthetic declarations of these years opened up epistemo-professional gaps in the sciences and humanities that could be filled only by a newly interpellated figure: the designer. Technically capable and aesthetically attuned, qualitatively manipulating quantitative data, perceiving existing patterns and tracing new ones, altruistically empathizing with adverse social conditions with an entrepreneurial spirit, attuning herself to the surrounding totality of existential, physical, and energetic networks—this actor was veritably called forth by the overlapping structures of environment and response.

Jim Burns, a proponent of this new ethos, acknowledged the difficulty in locating this new class of designer professionally and disciplinarily. In one of the exemplary documents of the period, he wrote: "One of the first things we become aware of in examining the activities of these new environmentalists (to use the current—and inadequate—fad expression) is that they are in a state of change in terms of how they practice their own disciplines, be they architects, artists, technologists, or people dealing with psychosocial phenomena."[34]

Before the terms *design* and *designer* became ubiquitous, Susan Sontag likewise understood that the old distinction between what C. P. Snow had so infuriatingly described as the "two cultures" was giving way to a "new sensibility," or "one culture." She characterized this ethos:

> This new establishment includes certain painters, sculptors, architects, social planners, film-makers, TV technicians, neurologists, musicians, electronics engineers, dancers, philosophers, and sociologists. (A few poets and prose writers can be included.) Some of the basic texts for this new cultural alignment are to be found in the writings of Nietzsche, Wittgenstein, Antonin Artaud, C. S. Sherrington, Buckminster Fuller, Marshall McLuhan, John Cage, André Breton, Roland Barthes, Claude Lévi-Strauss, Sigfried Giedion, Norman O. Brown, and Gyorgy Kepes.[35]

This passage resonates nicely with Sloterdijk's list of marginal professionals quoted above. Those listed have in common the fact that they were not isolated specialists working in their respective studios or laboratories; rather, they were "hybrid environmental design researchers."[36] They were individuals uniquely sensitized to the cultural changes of the period. "What other response," Sontag continued,

> than anguish, followed by anesthesia and then by wit and the elevating of intelligence over sentiment, is possible as a response to the social disorder and mass atrocities of our time, and—equally important for our sensibilities, but less often remarked on—to the unprecedented change in *what rules our environment from the intelligible and visible to that which is only with difficulty intelligible, and is invisible*? Art, which I have characterized as an instrument for modifying and educating sensibility and consciousness, *now operates in an environment which cannot be grasped by the senses.*[37]

So, how might these newly recognized designers—TV technicians, electronics engineers, air and mood phenomenologists, neurologists, and relationship therapists, not to mention painters, sculptors, architects, and city planners—be able to "program sensations" via responsive environments?[38] What would be the global impact of such a project?

As Gyorgy Kepes once wrote, in a beautifully tautological formulation, such a project would offer "a sense of freedom to men who can respond to a responsive environment. If it were done well, it could contribute to the development of the two most significant promises of twentieth-century life: the basic new plasticity of the inner and outer environment and the de facto interdependence of our ecological world."[39] I dedicate the chapters that follow to the many ramifications of these questions, the specific design initiatives that were developed to meet them, and the new class of designers charged with implementing them.

Organization of the Book

The various ramifications of these questions, and common themes regarding response and environment, wend their way through this entire text, which I have nonetheless organized in order to give a sense of the disciplinary resonance and dissonance between theories of environmental response and the design of responsive environments. The first chapters are addressed to environmental response. They offer several examples in which the perception of environment became a form of environmental perception, in which the boundaries of inside and outside were transgressed, and in which ecological thinking was brought to bear on the dominant modalities of scientific thinking. They also address the aesthetic conditions of social constructionism and environmental determinism.

Chapter 1, "Invisible Environments," takes up a set of perceptual complexities and the question of why it is so difficult to discern or see environment itself. I profile here several individuals who were instrumental both in establishing a new ontic consideration of the organism's surroundings and in addressing the ramifications of those surroundings for a perceiving, interacting subject. These individuals are Serge Boutourline Jr., James J. Gibson, Erwin Straus, Gregory Bateson, and Marshall McLuhan, who were credentialed, respectively, as a business consultant and machine interaction specialist, a perceptual psychologist, a neurologist and philosopher, a cybernetician, and a media theorist. All of these individuals shared the belief that environmental determinants that had once been occluded (for any number of reasons) were effectively becoming perceptible and visualizable, becoming more intimately integrated with new conceptions of humanity immersed in a conditioning milieu. At some point in their engagement with environment, all of these various researchers were implicated in new modalities of design, from Gibson's articulation of the notion of "affordances," which would be absorbed into operative formulations of interaction design, to McLuhan's speculations about the conditioning functions of existing environments and his explicit (though now forgotten) promotion of electronically mediated responsive environments as a remedy.

Chapter 2 explores the tensions between these two models of environment—a coercive apparatus versus a benevolent affordance—through a particular moment of interaction between the field of design and the social sciences. Titled "Pattern Watchers," the chapter centers on the work of anthropologist Edward T. Hall and his development of the field of proxemics, or the study of the human manipulation of microspace. Proxemics would be emblematic of the ways in which the environmental research manifold would pose challenges to architectural design in the 1960s and 1970s. The elaboration of cultural, behavioral, and environmental *patterns* was central to Hall's work, and after establishing a selective genealogy of that concept, I proceed to contrast Hall's understanding of patterns with that of the most famous architect dealing in a similar currency: Christopher Alexander. What emerges from this exercise is the insight that, though they promised to synthesize the worlds of science and aesthetics, and to ameliorate dire social and political problems, patterns proved insufficient to overcome the ideological dissonance between architecture and environmental design.

The following chapters are addressed more explicitly to the design of responsive environments and the many attempts to redress the coercive mechanics of the modern environment via interventions in their physical and atmospheric structures. Chapter 3, "Responsive Environments," is a select historical overview of the design of activated or responsive environments by designers, artists, and architects from the historic avant-garde to the present (using the 1970s as a kind of historical fulcrum). Here, I trace the many instances in which response has been conceived not only as an attribute of a given class of objects but also as their "medium," to quote Myron Krueger, one of the protagonists of this chapter. The discussion highlights the work of Frederick Kiesler, Gyorgy Kepes, Nicholas Negroponte, and several contemporary design studios, tracking the interplay of aesthetics and techniques as they informed the urgency of designing more flexible and responsive structures as the industrial age gave way to the digital age.

The following three chapters are in-depth studies of specific examples of responsive environments, although, again, they complicate the models posited in chapter 3 as much as they illustrate or validate those models. In chapter 4, I look closely at the collaboration of the psychiatrist Warren M. Brodey and his colleague Avery R. Johnson. The two met in Cambridge thanks to the interlocution of one of the founders of cybernetics, Warren McCulloch. Then, in 1970, they formed their own business to research and design a set of products, one of which was called Soft Control Material. This interactive device was meant to induce in the subject a series of perceptual and haptic exchanges that would deprogram the many psychic and ecological blockages interpellated through the subject by the post-industrial society.

Chapter 5 examines another single (but multifaceted) project: a comprehensive environmental design program formulated by the German American architect Wolf Hilbertz. This program was called Cybertecture, and it included plans for robotically assisted construction, computer-mediated planning, extensive adaptation to changing user inputs, and many more technical features that were virtually impossible circa 1972, when he was elaborating them. Ultimately, for Hilbertz, this system was meant to mediate the relationship of the user with the natural world, forming supple, pliable, sensing structures that could be altered at will; the resulting specific configurations would, in turn, force the subject into new behavioral and interactive patterns that could facilitate a form of conscious evolution. This "environmental evolution," as Hilbertz described it, relied on contemporaneous formulations of "dissipative structures" and emerging theories of human technological "extensions." These were described by Edward T. Hall, Marshall McLuhan, and R. Buckminster Fuller not only as simple tools that allowed the human animal to reach out and manipulate her own environment but also as implements, instruments, and apparatuses that breached the border of that very subject, delving into her "biological particles," as McLuhan would put it.

Chapter 6 concludes my series of case studies of specific architectural and design projects, focusing on Paolo Soleri's architectural, craft, and theoretical production. Among the many designers and theorists profiled here, Soleri had the most explicit interest in the transformative power of aesthetic response and architectural form. I take Soleri's discourse as an occasion to delve more deeply into the topological complexities of the inside/outside dynamics in which the subject was situated at this moment. Here, I argue that the environmental consciousness elaborated throughout this text had more to do specifically with the culture of self-help, consciousness therapy, and productivity sessions of the seventies than with the consciousness expansion of the counterculture in the previous decade. I analyze this model in relation to other architectural conceptions of human consciousness and mysticism that were emerging in the 1970s as part of a "New Age" culture.

I observe in my Conclusion that many of the initiatives discussed here indicated a utopian regime of environmental thinking predicated on the necessity of cybernetic optimization for all systems, inclusive of the environment and the human subject. Within these systems, information would flow freely, mechanisms would efface themselves in favor of pure interaction, and the subject would accordingly find herself in an ethereal space of willful activity in which the environment configured itself automatically around her needs and desires. This is the model that we find resurfacing today, as all of our extensions, all of our spaces, and all of our interactions are increasingly mediated by invisible networks and their ostensible responses to our requirements. But this frictionless, immersive space is perhaps the very embodiment of what the Continental thinkers cited above considered an apparatus. I further observe that what sets my chosen case studies apart from this paradigm is their built-in resistances, which, at some point in the interactive process, entailed the environment *pushing back* against the user, frustrating the ostensibly simple circuits between means and ends, forms and functions, inputs and outputs, or the responses of the environment versus those of the human subject.

1

Invisible Environments

> There is a built-in invisibility in all environments as such, and this is a mysterious thing that I would like to know more about.
>
> —Marshall McLuhan, interview, 1967

> The world that means the most to us, as everyone from Bucky Fuller to Marshall McLuhan has already pointed out, has for the past half century not really been very visible anyway.
>
> —Charles W. Moore, "Plug It in Ramses, and See If It Lights Up, Because We Aren't Going to Keep It Unless It Works," 1967

> So take a look around you. The first step in understanding your environment is to *see* it.
>
> —George Nelson, *How to See,* 1974

What does it mean to observe—as so many did during the 1960s–70s—that environment was not directly perceptible, yet that its presence was felt more intensely than ever before in human history, and that the ramifications of these invisible sensations or conditioning events were primed to increase even more? How to grasp, describe, model, or design a situation that was, as it were, both in front of and behind the senses? The urgency of these observations would both confound and inspire new disciplinary approaches to what would come to be figured as the responsive environment. The sanctioned expressions of these approaches—environmental psychology, ecological perception, human factors design, neuroaesthetics, and other manifestations of the environmental research manifold—opened new perspectives on these problems, even as they foreclosed others. But there were those researchers and designers—many of whom appear in the pages that follow—who attempted to work outside or between these various established fields and whose practices or discourses, in fact, constituted a critique of those fields' compartmentalization and objectivist pretensions. For most of these individuals, these disciplines all failed to *see* environment for what it was—a "totally involving" (to use Marshall McLuhan's term) situational positioning at whose center was a constantly displaced subject.

We can accordingly observe that, around 1970, there were three main reasons environment remained elusive, according to these researchers and designers. One possibility was that the substance of environment was simply not detectable by unaided human senses; for those holding this position, computational technologies and perceptual extensions were appearing immanently that would resolve this in one way or another. Another possibility was that environment was already being perceived, albeit in only partial views or fragments, by various disciplines. In this case, what was needed was a kind of metalanguage that could aggregate all the disparate data from various fields and render a coherent view of the environmental manifold. The third and most challenging issue was the role of the observer, always "inside" and implicated in the very systems she sought to map and describe. How might an environment be held out for observation or design if it was conditioning the very sensorium that sought to observe or design it?

For most of us, the maddening circularity of such quandaries inevitably becomes an obstacle or an abstraction that needs must be put aside so that our praxis might commence or continue. But for many of those involved in the emergence of responsive environments, these structural or formal problems would remain at the center of their intellectual and designerly projects. This chapter examines such instances in the work of several researchers, some famous and others obscure, who would attempt to map, visualize, model, and program this new environment that was paradoxically invisible and yet indelibly sensible: interaction specialist Serge Boutourline Jr., perceptual psychologist James J. Gibson, philosopher and neuroscientist Erwin Straus, cybernetician Gregory Bateson, and so-called media theorist Marshall McLuhan.

In constructing these vignettes, I hope to give a kind of sampling of the various ways environmental perception (or lack thereof) was being theorized and experienced in different fields. But I also hope that characterizing these individuals as having a shared stake in both environmental response and responsive environments illuminates some interesting patterns. Ina Blom has captured the perceptual and ecological complexities of these dynamics: "Environmental responsibility could not be imposed on humans from without, as a moral obligation anchored in transcendental principles, but had to be a function of a heightened sense of involvement in the reflexive continuities that exist between the human sense apparatus and its environment."[1] These patterns were scientifically oriented but also fundamentally aesthetic. Indeed, aesthetics—or, perhaps more accurately, aisthesis—was central to the project of grasping (if not directly seeing) environment.[2] Furthermore, it would be *design* that would come to mediate both the aesthetic and the scientific components of these models of interaction.

The Ballad of Serge Boutourline

I begin with an account of the work of Serge Boutourline Jr. (1932–1982), a figure all but forgotten now, but whose interests, background, and trajectory through this period are, in retrospect, absolutely exemplary of the disciplinary and existential complexities of environment and response. Born in Santa Fe, New Mexico, Boutourline was a business consultant and a theorist of human perception who, according to one source, "developed a signal-oriented approach to the description of human environment."[3] I quote below a short biography published alongside Boutourline's essay "The Concept of Environmental Management," which appeared in Massimo Vignelli's legendary design journal *Dot Zero*:

> A graduate of Harvard University and Harvard Business School, Serge Boutourline has been a consultant on new products to companies like Kimberly-Clark and Arthur D. Little. For the past five years he has been working with professionals in psychology, sociology and psychiatry to develop methods for environmental research. In 1962 he conducted a study with Dr. Robert S. Weiss at the Seattle World's Fair on human behavior in large public spaces. In 1963, as a commercial project, he developed a method for simulating architectural spaces before they are built in order to aid making decisions in design. Currently he is working on the design of responsive environments which enable individual users to control their immediate environments. He is president of a newly formed New York based corporation, Interaction Signal, Inc., specializing in computer controlled interaction devices.[4]

To this deceptively vague overview, we could add that Boutourline conducted the 1962 study in Seattle at the behest of IBM, which would remain his major (perhaps only) client for some time. Boutourline was also an artist of sorts, and he participated in several new media or intermedia projects in New York at the end of the sixties.

Consultant, artist, researcher, theorist, designer, inventor, manager—Boutourline's itinerary left few environmental loci unvisited. This ubiquity notwithstanding, the obsessive object of his attention, his quest to outline "a satisfactory general theory of environment," never became any more real.[5] This criticism, however, would be part of the problem as far as Boutourline was concerned. His "general theory of environment" was not simply a theory *of* some external object or reality but also simultaneously a new understanding of how such a reality might be perceived or theorized in the first place. As such, Boutourline's (and many others') formulations of environment were de facto critiques of any method that sought to analyze *anything* objectively, as if from a distance, or that would maintain a strict distinction between ontology and phenomenology. Environment was both the object and the apparatus of perception.

Writing to the anthropologist Edward T. Hall (to whom chapter 2 is devoted), Boutourline enumerated the paradigms that up until that time had made his general theory untenable:

> The trouble in the past . . . can be laid to two formulations of reality which were useful for the physical sciences (at one point in their history, though not as much now) but which have persisted within the social and architectural sciences to this day. These two formulations are:
>
> > **The assumption of the existence of an Objective Reality**
> > Once one has assumed objective reality, the aim is to find out about "it" as if it existed apart from the observer, user, or other perceiving device. So you have architects trying to find the "essence" of a building and you have social scientists and anthropologists trying to define the "central aspects" of a society or culture.
> >
> > **The assumption of the Separation of "subject" and "object"**
> > Once one has assumed the materialistic notions of objective reality and those of causality then it becomes increasingly necessary to separate the perceiving subject from the "objective world." This then leads to psychologists posing for themselves questions like: "what is the *effect* of x-stimulus on y-subject?"
>
> The trouble with these formulations is that it is impossible to even adequately describe environment within the resulting framework of terms and concepts, and it is impossible to describe the simplest observable "relationship" (I use the term guardedly) of an individual human with that environment.[6]

Already, then, environment was both system and symptom. It was a very real entity whose definition and description were becoming ever more urgent, even as this description was foreclosed by the epistemological systems that had created it. It was not just slipping through the grasp of traditional symbolic systems; it was already structuring those systems and what they were able to symbolize or model. Boutourline's career trajectory would reflect the *mise en abyme* of these implications, as he moved from mere observation and notation to aesthetic theorization and, inevitably, design.

Even as a graduate student, Boutourline was interested in the aesthetics of the emerging milieu of postindustrial technologies and economies. As an MBA candidate, he joined with a cadre of colleagues—Group 25 in the manufacturing course at the Harvard Graduate School of Business Administration—to conduct a study and publish a special report titled *Individual Creativity and the Corporation.*[7] The research involved a review of the existing literature as well as interviews with regional business leaders and managers. In the report, which was published jointly with the Institute of Contemporary Art in Boston, the authors answered in the affirmative the basic question of whether humanistic principles of "creativity" should be applied to production and/or administration. They argued that creativity, rather than being an innate talent, is a kind of trainable practice, the benefits of which would include more innovative products and happier and more productive employees. But, they noted, creativity is not something that can simply be introduced as if from outside. It is a necessary ingredient in the evolution of the worker vis-à-vis new technologies and economies:

> Routine jobs are more and more replaced by machines. Mechanization eliminates not only repetitive jobs on the production line, but even some routine "intellectual" functions.
>
> Many jobs, for example, that required engineers are now handled by computers. Even prototypes can now be made by machines through numerical control. Less and less people are now necessary on routine positions. New skills are required from the individuals in positions created by these technological changes. These are trending toward skills in the preparation, observation and interpretation of data. Progress pushes the individual into jobs where initiative and imagination play a greater role. The individual of today *has* to be more creative.[8]

As these passages demonstrate, Boutourline was one of the original "design thinkers," understanding business and economic issues as being aesthetic and technical in equal measure.

In short order, these concerns became explicitly environmental as well. Going to work for IBM after grad school, Boutourline found himself serving in and around the organization as a kind of aesthetic and ethical consultant, what John Harwood describes as a "behavioral psychologist and ergonomist."[9] The environments in which he found himself were both literal and figurative. Early on, he began work on what would be a constant through line in his life: exhibition design. He began thinking about such design when, at the behest of IBM, he conducted a qualitative study of the perceptual and cognitive experiences of visitors to the 1962 Seattle World's Fair. The official result of this work was a rather dry document produced with Robert S. Weiss (a psychologist who would go on to become one of the leading theoreticians of loneliness in the contemporary world).[10] This report provided practical insights into the best ways to create effective exhibits and pavilions for the emerging category of consumer spectacle, addressing such factors as how long visitors would be willing to wait in line for a given exhibit and whether theater presentations would be superior to walk-through formats for particular kinds of exhibits. These guidelines would enable IBM to maximize the effectiveness of its pavilions at future world's fairs (at which the company's exhibits were indeed very successful). Boutourline and Weiss's approach was able to capture as actionable data certain types of experiences that usually fell beneath the threshold of conscious sensation.

Boutourline never designed an exhibit for IBM, but he worked with Charles and Ray Eames in their Los Angeles office.[11] It seems that the Eameses "made extensive use" of Boutourline's ideas, but it remains unclear what these were, or how they were assimilated into the Eameses' projects.[12] Boutourline's expertise was in providing a kind of environmental metadata. It would be very easy to relegate this work to the status of early consumer research or marketing psychology (and, indeed, this type of data collection would become important in those fields) were it not for Boutourline's later activities. Instead of clarifying his practice and consolidating his techniques into a definable profession, Boutourline continued to broaden the scope of his interests (though exhibition design would remain a central concern). He began this process while still under the employ of IBM, where he was instrumental in positioning IBM computers as personal (as opposed to purely business-oriented) devices.[13] In this sense, he was instrumental in the naturalization of the computer–human interface. Yet he was also unusually prescient regarding the ideological and existential issues raised by this ever-more intimate relationship.

Referring to a landmark internal IBM memo that Boutourline wrote in 1964, Harwood describes the nature of Boutourline's insights as an ethical meditation on the impacts that the computer would have on the everyday lives of users, as well as the various modalities of control that implied.[14] The memo took the form of a position paper addressed to Robert S. Lee, then director of communications at IBM. Boutourline's main focus was on the evolving relationship (commercial and ethical) that IBM would increasingly have with "nonspecialist" computer users.[15] While the memo did not explicitly describe the advent of home or personal computing, it seemed to suggest that possibility through its evocation of millions of nonexpert users in what Boutourline described as "the new business environment." These individuals, Boutourline explained, would need to be addressed in a manner different from that used to communicate with the specialist programmers and operators in those offices where IBM computers were being rented and used. For, as the sheer number of users of computers increased, he wrote, their experiences and issues with the technology would inevitably become more varied and less predictable (compared, with, say, those of a certain small class of engineers who were always using the machines for similar forms of computation). In evoking the potential dangers of this emerging fungible situation, Boutourline expressed a distinctly environmental concern (which he would never relinquish) regarding the tension between an individual's experience of the world and the world's objective reality—what he called a "particular use-interaction."[16]

Boutourline's work for IBM was fascinating, not only in its elucidation of specific issues and problems relating to the emerging technocracy but also because of how he positioned himself, on the borders, so to speak, between production and consumption. Boutourline understood computers as intimately related to how they would perform with and alongside their "users." Thus, in his view, response would be a mutually implicating structure of interactions. And, as is evident from his memo, he saw those interactions as both highly subjective and subject to the ontic properties of the environmental "situation." Just what degree of control does the "user" have at any given moment? How does the user *perceive* (or not) that control or lack thereof?

These questions of situational or environmental perception occupied Boutourline from the outset. A couple of years before the IBM memo, he was secretly immersing himself in the fleeting experiential environments he had been tasked with describing. In an unpublished typescript written around the same time as the 1962 Seattle report, Boutourline began to outline what might constitute the rudiments of his general theory of environment. He described these observations as an integral part of his attempt to formulate a "'grammar of experience' which has its own logic, syntax, and rules."[17] Establishing this grammar placed Boutourline in the position of a postindustrial flaneur, moving through the crowds in the

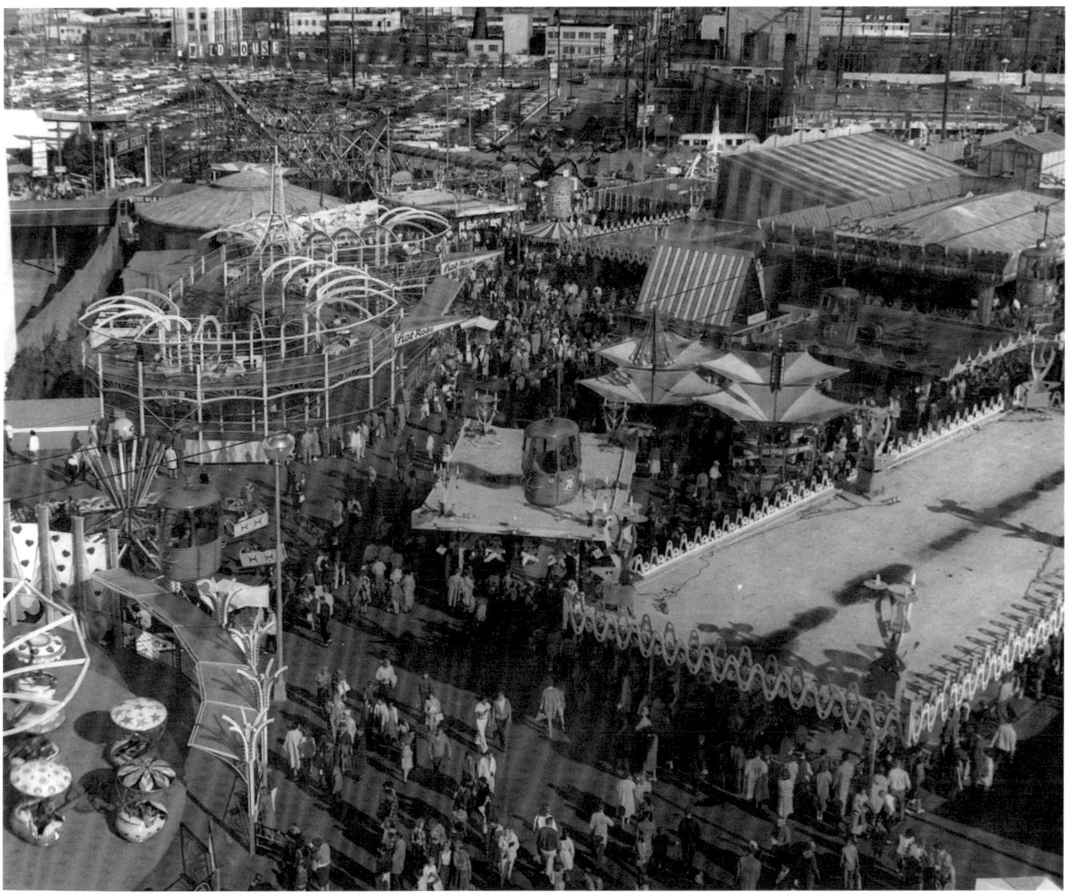

Figure 1.1. View east from the Armory Roof across the Gayway, Seattle World's Fair, 1962. Courtesy of Seattle Public Library.

Seattle Gayway (an outdoor amusement park area of the world's fair that included a section called the Food Circus) while attending to virtually every sensory input: sound and light levels, viewing distances, ratios of architecture to open space, interpersonal interactions with strangers and companions, and so on.

Quantifying these inputs proved surprisingly easy (if Boutourline's notes are to be believed): "For instance one afternoon at 2:45 I counted in the outside spaces around the Food Circus 50 interactions or impulses in 47 seconds. I went inside and got 50 impulses in 51 seconds. I then went outside again and got 50 impulses in 43 seconds."[18] An "impulse" was a definable experience, any meaningful interaction with the environment, which in turn could include anything in one's sensory field: other people, light levels, the sound of carnival barkers or tour guides, movement through the crowds, and so on. A successful place (and the Food Circus was one example) was one that had a nice equilibrium between familiarity and novelty, just the right level of "knowability," the kind of space that stimulated without overloading the perceptual faculties of visitors—without "shooting its wad," as Boutourline said.[19] It bears noting here that Boutourline mentioned nothing in his notes about the formal properties of any architecture, exhibit, or outdoor space. His observations were limited strictly to the perceptual activities engendered in their interstices, the relations established among places by a sensing subject. In this way, he rendered the environment as the sum of a complex series of interactions, and never as a set of tangible, finite objects within a definable spatial container.

It is unclear why Boutourline's work for IBM came to an end, but, in 1967, the company opted not to renew its contract with his consultancy, which by that time was called Interaction Signal, Inc. This change of professional and financial fortune likely precipitated Boutourline's move into freelance "mood phenomenology" and "relationship therapy," as Sloterdijk might describe it. This was motivated by his desire to reconcile the quantitative and technical demands of the new society with the environmental needs of individuals. By the end of the sixties, he had moved to New York, where he participated in the waning counterculture. There, he would independently produce two notable art projects. These attracted the attention of Jud Yalkut, who was interested in Boutourline's work insofar as it intersected with the intermedia and video art scenes of the time.[20] In his legendary manuscript "Electronic Zen," Yalkut describes Boutourline's *Telediscretion*, his collaborations with Susan Buirge, and his invention of a device called Videosketch.

Most of Boutourline's technical/aesthetic projects involved empowering the user of audiovisual technologies through feedback loops and control devices. We see this in *Telediscretion*, an interactive video installation created by Boutourline in 1969 and included in the seminal exhibition *TV as a Creative Medium* at the Howard Wise Gallery the same year. The work no

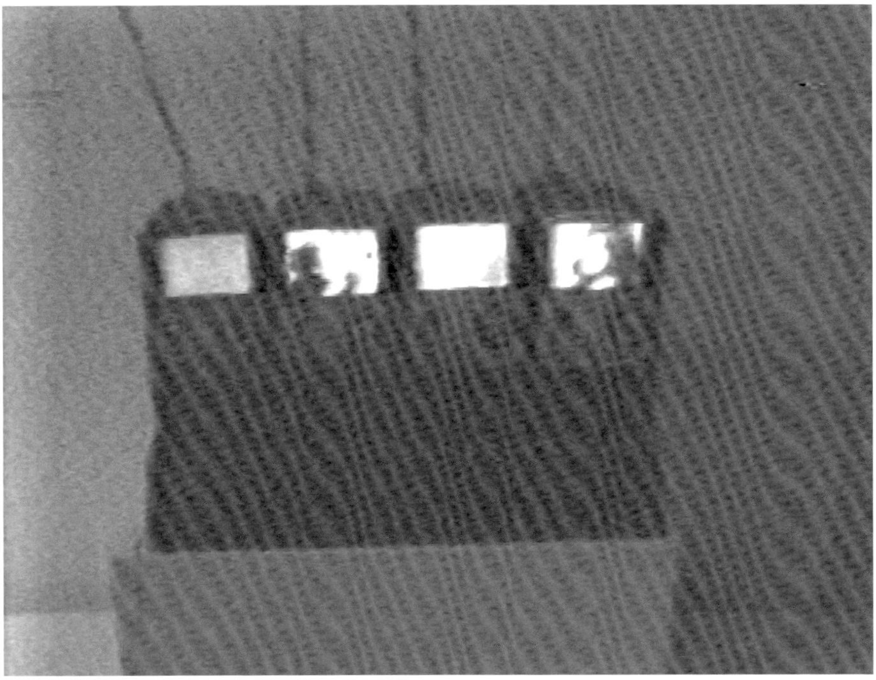

Figure 1.2. Serge Boutourline, *Telediscretion* (1969). Installation view from Ira Schneider, *TV as a Creative Medium* (1969). Courtesy of Chris Boutourline.

longer exists, but the exhibition brochure describes it thus: "Four Mini-TVs with a device for fingertip selection of sound channels. Presentation will include three broadcast channels and one channel playing 'A Commercial for Life,' a video tape conceived and executed by Wynn Chamberlain and Serge Boutourline."[21] Eric Siegel helped Boutourline with the technology for the piece.[22] While historically upstaged by the more enduring pieces in the exhibition—Nam Jun Paik and Charlotte Moorman's *TV Bra for Living Sculpture,* Frank Gillette and Ira Schneider's *Wipe Cycle,* and Paul Ryan's *Everyman's Moebius Strip—Telediscretion* was nonetheless notable for its attempt to give the subject more control over the media environment. A bit like *Wipe Cycle,* the piece utilized broadcast channels in combination with original material. It "contained four television sets lined up on a wall, controlled by a switch which allowed viewers to choose among broadcast programs."[23] The monitors were the Symphonic Radio company's 5050 Mini TV Sets, all mounted on slim pedestals against the gallery wall.[24] The "switch" was a small device with four buttons that allowed for "fingertip selection" of the various "channels," a mechanism that would have allowed the user to create a kind of personal montage of normative and original content. The latter, called for the purposes of the exhibition "A Commercial for Life," was likely what would become Chamberlain's notorious film *Brand X,* which premiered the following year. *Brand X* would become legendary in the New York underground cinema scene as a kind of metacommentary on commercial television. It starred (among others) Taylor Mead, Candy Darling, Abbie Hoffman, and Sam Shepard.

In discussing *Telediscretion,* Yalkut notes that "the interaction and selection of the TV spectator with the transmitted and preprogrammed channels generated levels of feedback, the simultaneous realization of one's ability to program and modulate one's own perceptual inputs, the self-perception of the self as perceiver, in the process of perceiving."[25] Here, the art object becomes a control device that filters the media environment, giving the viewer-cum-user a modicum of agency in the face of overwhelming stimuli or inputs. (We might also note the use of the word *discretion* in the work's title; discretion was something that Boutourline emphasized in the 1964 IBM memo.)

If we read directly from Boutourline's 1962 notes on world's fairs to the premises of *Telediscretion,* one striking feature of environmental discourse becomes clear—that the lines between observation and creation are completely blurred, so that once perceived, the environment is almost automatically rendered available for design manipulation. Boutourline moved directly from his position as a pattern recognizer to that of a pattern designer, or pattern enabler. Videosketch—Boutourline's other contribution to art history—was a composite feedback machine comprising a video camera, processor, and monitor, which together could "see" moving lights and render them graphically as animated lines. The device was used in the *Televanilla* performance that was held at the Martinique Theater in New York. This "intermedia" work, as it was described at the time, involved Buirge dancing in conjunction with various cameras and video monitors that recorded and broadcast her movements.[26] Again, from Yalkut:

> The third piece [in *Televanilla*] utilized the VIDEOSKETCH with Ms. Buirge dancing, lights on each hand and ankle, and one on her head, with the VIDEOSKETCH's receiving eye transferring her lights to the screen "in the form of green blobs, squiggles, fat and thin lines," to the music of Phil Glass. Video images like alpha particles traces *[sic]* in a cloud chamber, the dancer playing against her traces on the screen, like sumi painting strokes, amorphic streaks overlaid, opposing, merging into time passages, with sound arcs surging and bursting about each other, play against play, vision against television.[27]

In this instance, Boutourline's device can be understood as an environmental visualizer, a technical mediator between the proprioceptive subject and her (previously invisible) milieu. It is unclear whether Boutourline marketed Videosketch through Interaction Signal, but nonetheless it appears to be congruent with his company's aim to develop "environments and devices that increase man's capacity to control his own surroundings by direct 'feedback' into the many systems which are aimed at him."[28]

This method of control would underlie Boutourline's statements regarding environmental design, or, as he phrased it, "environmental management." He described this concept in his only published essay, "The Concept of Environmental Management." Here, Boutourline dedicated himself to explaining the type of design activity he felt was appropriate to emerging theories of environment and perception. Again, the essay, though not widely known or influential, uncannily recapitulated many of the themes of design and environment at the end of the sixties.[29] Boutourline's argument moved from the most sweeping social claims to the minutest details of altering microenvironments in the specific circumstances of commercial exhibits. "The dominant situation of modern life is individuals living in a setting which was not designed for them," he wrote in the opening line, recalling, perhaps, the example of the frustrated commuter from the IBM memo.[30] He then acknowledged the efforts of the design community to respond to this exigency via a more holistic and scientifically rigorous method of "environmental design," which entailed

> designing objects systematically so that the designer controls the process of assembling and arranging all the objects in a given system, rather than designing objects individually. The concept of environmental design assumes that *if* a system were designed at one time and *if* researchers were able to provide for designers a knowledge of the effect of the physical environment on people, *then* it would be possible to design essentially optimum human environments by eliminating the problems encountered by designing objects independent of the physical use content.[31]

But even this design approach fell short, according to Boutourline, because while it attempted to work with human parameters and needs, it failed to comprehend the perceptual substance of environment and the temporal experiential sequences that generated it. Ultimately, even environmental design was too static and object oriented.

"Environmental management" was Boutourline's suggested remedy. It represented a design method that would work alongside environmental design but would be oriented more toward the dynamic interaction of the subject with the physical features of a given location. For Boutourline, environment was not a collection of objects in a static space. Rather, it was

> a specific set of measurable physical phenomena existing during a specified period of time at a specified location point. These physical events may be light rays, sound vibrations, chemical particles in the air, measured temperature, measured pressure or any of a number of physical events which are measurable. A room can be thought to be a three dimensional grid consisting of a finite set of points each with its own unique inventory of physical events which change over time.[32]

Environmental management represented a greater awareness of the manipulability of these previously unmapped (but emphatically measurable) perceptual phenomena—changing the lighting, adjusting the volume of ambient music, slightly raising or lowering a particular object of attention (such as a display case). For Boutourline, such ostensibly modest gestures could have profound ramifications in any environmental system. If the limited example of the exhibition venue provided Boutourline specific case studies in the efficacy of such gestures, it was clear that the same principles could easily find application in people's everyday lives, where small "managerial" manipulations could make human environments more meaningful and interactive.

Ultimately, though, the model of environmental management would be replaced by the method of what Boutourline called the "interaction signal." He explored the epistemological and existential implications of this method in an essay titled "Notes on 'Object-Oriented' and 'Signal-Oriented' Approaches to the Definition of the Physical World Which Surrounds Individual Human Beings," the contents of which he presented at a conference of the American Psychological Association and at the Department of Architecture at the University of Washington, Seattle. He then conveyed the essay in a letter to Wynn Chamberlain prior to the pair's work on *Telediscretion*.[33] Just as in his 1964 letter to Hall, Boutourline began his essay with a critique of Western scientific method, which pertained to any model seeking to describe objects *in* space that possess particular "properties." "This process of thinking," he wrote, "creates a fantastic selectivity of events which can be counted as 'real' so long as one sees physical reality as made up of objects and systems of objects."[34] In this paradigm (which had also misled perceptual psychology, according to Boutourline), reality was viewed as a set of nesting dolls—the object sat within a room and had certain properties within itself, intrinsic to it and inseparable from it. This room, in turn, was in a building, which was on a street, and so on; ultimately, these isolates were floating around the great void of the cosmos.

The "signal-oriented approach," on the other hand, replaced the exaggerated selectivity and reification of this view with an understanding that, instead of sitting in rooms and being possessed of verifiable attributes, all things (including people) were immersed in a "sea." This was not a sea of discrete things but rather a field utterly replete with *signals*—no things, just infinite points of contact among environmental factors such as light, air, material, and perception. What mattered were the loci of the points of contact of signals within this four-dimensional field—where a bundle of light passed through a window, or where a pair of corduroy pants rubbed against a couch cushion. Most important was the "envelope" where these signals converged with the perceptual signals of the subject—the "event-at-a-point field." In this schema, objects lost one reality (that of attributes or internal structure) in exchange for another physical reality, one based

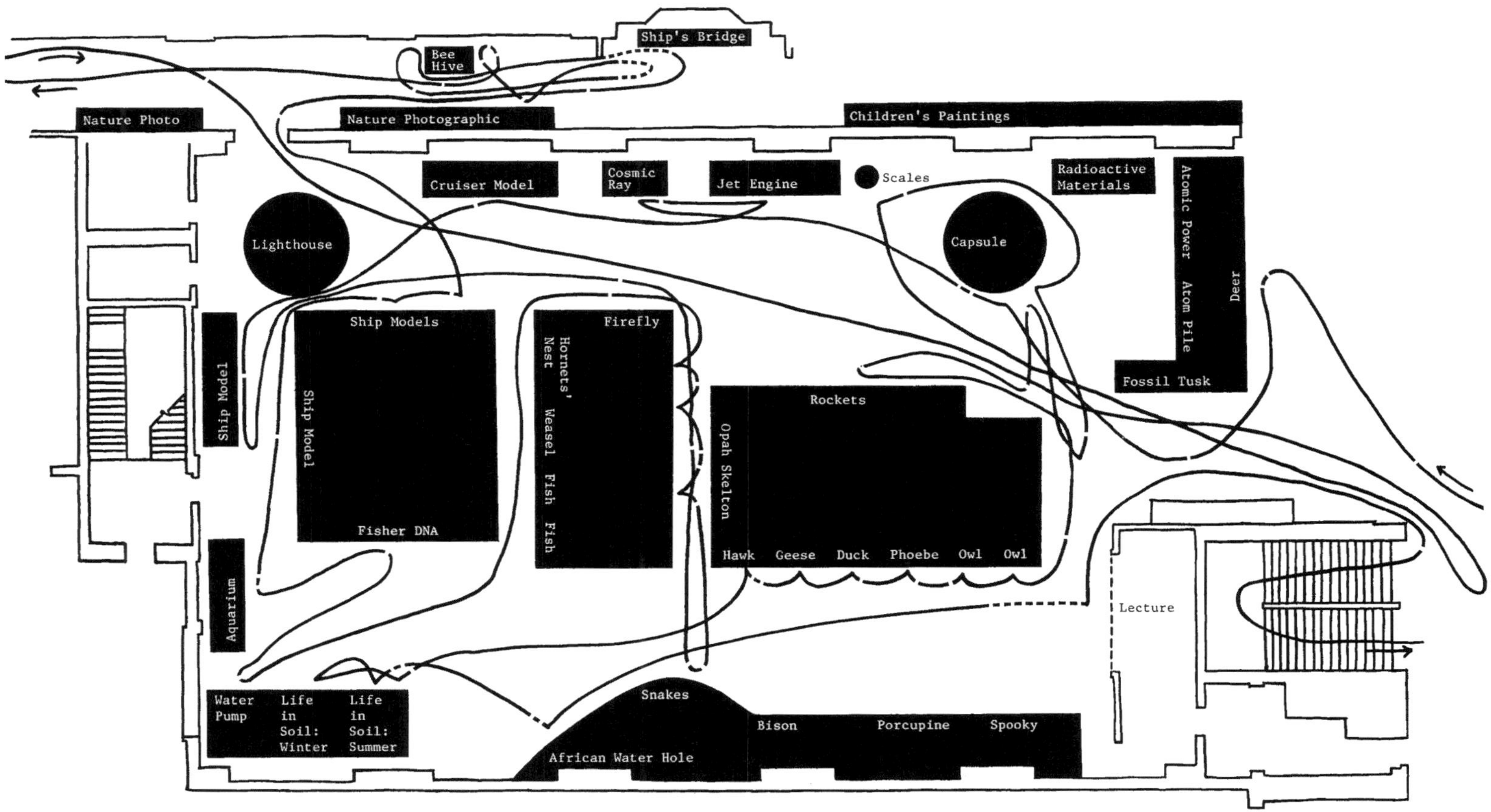

Figure 1.3. "This is an actual record of the movement of a ten year old child in a science museum. The breaks in the lines represent fifteen second time marks. The child can be thought of as developing his own 'exhibit' by choosing where to go, where to stop, for how long and in what sequence. Every visitor to an open exhibition hall develops a sequence of events at his own, moving location. It is this relatively small and in many respects unique subset of events which is 'the exhibit room' for any single visitor, and not the static and total physical form of the exhibit 'system.'" Exhibition plan from Serge Boutourline, "The Concept of Environmental Management" (1967). Courtesy of Chris Boutourline.

on never-ending interactions with other environmental factors. In such a situation, the room invoked above was not a set of objects scattered across a space at particular intervals; it was a sea of infinite centers where signals overlapped and interacted. But, again, I must stress here that this was no mere phenomenology of perception. This was not about a unified body–mind apparatus making its way through a world of sensation. It was an ontology of an environmental fabric of material and immaterial events in a constantly shifting, *but nonetheless objectively measurable,* relationship of interaction. The air really existed. The light really existed. The surface of the fabric really existed, and could be measured as it came into contact with any other signal. These signals—or what many of the people discussed in this study would call patterns—were constantly overlapping and interfering with one another's previous states.

But why insist on the ontic stability of these signals or patterns? Wouldn't an idealist description of the world have been a more efficient way to account for the endless flow of transformation in the environment? Perhaps, but it would have negated the other aspect of interaction signals, which was their *manipulability.* For Boutourline, the sea of signals in which everyone was immersed was highly modifiable. By shifting position on the couch, the corduroy-wearing person physically transformed the event-at-a-point field of corduroy–cushion–skin surface–nerve bundle (or however one chose to delimit this particular envelope). The subject directly effected a change in the environment. Tilt your head to one side. Open a window. Turn the dial on a thermostat. Breathe. These were no longer considered mere gestures that might alter the stable properties or change the position of preexisting things; they were manipulations of reality itself, of the points of contact among myriad signals that constituted the very fabric of physical reality. Boutourline elaborated in conversation with Yalkut:

> Now we're dealing with a set of signals or events, and this is tricky, which exist both because of what I do and because of the "character" of what is out there, again created by what I do because I am selecting "what part" of out there, this rather than this. Like the character of this chair is really the character of a small group of spots that I choose to touch at that moment, which is hardly the chair. That subset of spots is itself defined by what I do. It then becomes hard to postulate the external, extensive object of Newtonian reality which is essentially the common conception of us all.[35]

The terms *creation* and *selection* here are key, as they form the basis for Boutourline's new theory of *production.* In this view, simply living was a never-ending stream of microadjustments to the real fabric of the world. If made into a more conscious activity, this type of production could begin to overtake the contemporary consumer-oriented production of objects.

Here, response itself becomes both the object and the method of designing one's own environment:

> The interconnectedness of events in the sea in which we live makes *operationally* possible the fact of *responsiveness* that perceiving entities experience. That depending upon their contribution to the field of events (that is depending upon how they modify the sets of events which existed before) *that field itself* will change in ways beyond the direct action which the individual has on the shape and content of events at each point in the field itself. The advent of electronic measuring devices and computers capable of complex real-time action through various output devices makes the fact of responsiveness and the particularly strong effect responsiveness is known to have on perceiving humans particularly worth mentioning.[36]

In this single statement we have the rhetoric and fundamental ideas that would define the responsive environment, expressed in the self-reflexive, hallucinatory parlance that seemed unavoidable at that moment. For Boutourline, environment was not simply a perceptual phenomenon, existing in the eye and mind of the subject; it had very real, empirically verifiable (if constantly shifting) attributes that imposed themselves on the bearing and experiences of the subject. It was this interplay that became the focus of so much design thinking around this time.

Nonetheless, there is something undeniably poignant in Boutourline's essay. It is impossible to avoid the feeling that, in evoking the humble environmental manager, optimizing and constantly adjusting a system that someone else designed, he was describing himself: a figure who had somehow become sensitive to the infinite complexity of environmental interaction but lacked the language and agency to fully implement or instrumentalize his newly gained and impossibly nuanced knowledge of the world as a constantly shifting set of interacting signals, never the same from one moment to the next, and never identical for any two individuals. Here, the sensorium became everything and nothing. It coalesced as the very locus at which the subject made contact with the world, but it also disintegrated under the pressure of the ontic and phenomenal realities of that world.

J. J. Gibson: Perception of the Environment/Environmental Perception

As the case of Boutourline demonstrates, the ability to perceive environment was not just a matter of developing a model or apparatus that could unveil a given reality. It was fundamentally a matter of redefining what it meant to perceive, what it meant to have one's senses "stimulated" by "outside" sources. It is therefore unsurprising that specialists in the field of perceptual psychology, for instance, became involved in the debates around environment of this moment. If scientific method had proved inadequate to grasp what an environment was, perhaps the ways in which it understood and replicated observation were at fault. A certain tension thus arose between phenomenology and ontology, between materialism and idealism, inside and outside, and basic and applied research. But more than just a tension, it was the possibility of resolving the paradoxes that had plagued Western philosophy for so long that drove many researchers into the impossibly complex pathways of interaction out of which environmental response emerged. In this sense, environmental theory at this time was always highly self-reflexive. It did not have the luxury of naively denying the epistemological preconditions of its own observations. It was about these very preconditions, the contextual determinants for what could, in fact, be observed, or perceived.

We can observe these complex interactions as they played out precisely in theories of perception itself. In one of Boutourline's rare citations he mentions the work of James J. Gibson. Gibson was important not just for Boutourline but for the design professions writ large.[37] Initially in his 1950 book *The Perception of the Visual World,* then in his 1966 *The Senses Considered as Perceptual Systems,* and finally in his elaboration of the idea of "affordances" in his work of the 1970s, Gibson led a movement away from a near-solipsistic theorization of the human sensorium and toward a more engaged, interactive conception of environmental perception.[38] He did not dwell exclusively on the relationship between eye and brain, as did so many studies of perception, but rather looped in an ontological consideration of the physical environment. Accordingly, his work was a de facto critique of behaviorism, stimulus–response theory, and other linear and mechanistic models of cause and effect that had characterized Enlightenment considerations of the subject.

Grounded partly in his work developing new flight controls for the U.S. Air Force, Gibson's *Perception of the Visual World* concluded that our understanding of perception had to move beyond the specious abstractions of Euclidean space. "In a sense," he wrote, "this is a book about space perception." However, for Gibson, "the space to be considered first is not a void with three lines intersecting at right angles but the space of rooms, streets, and regions, and the space of men who walk, drive, or fly an airplane."[39] Gibson filled space up, as it were, in order to describe the mechanics of perception. He removed its frame but gave it a continuous ground. He privileged objects and their "interspaces" equally, eschewing the traditional biases of gestalt theory (even while relying heavily on its methods).[40]

This model of a replete world was not meant to be a description of physical reality; rather, it explained the function of perception. Gibson called it the "visual world" (thus the title of his book). Indeed, many of the shortcomings of perceptual science, for Gibson, were based on a conflation of what he termed the "visual field" (which, indeed, was very much like a picture rendered in perspective) and this "visual world." The visual field—with a certainty of oversimplifying—comprised those fleeting impressions glancing off of an observer's retina and synthesized or reconciled by some cognitive function. But for all of the illusory effects, afterimages, and general confusion that the human perceptual apparatus engendered in the visual field, the visual world, in contrast, was quite consistent and reliable. Up remained up, and likewise down, the smoothness of an object seldom changed, nor the rigidity of its angles. Gibson's book, therefore, was an attempt to account for the ontological stability of the visual world. "The science of vision, almost from its beginning, has emphasized the errors and inadequacies of vision whereas this conception of the visual world has emphasized just the opposite. . . . The discrepancies between percepts and objects are not difficult to understand; what we need to understand is why there as so *few* discrepancies."[41]

What was the nature of the correspondence between the physical properties of a thing and the image produced on the retina? The common-sense explanation (bequeathed to common sense by the Western scientific tradition) holds that light rays, bouncing through space, are distorted by the physical properties of objects, which distortions then "excite" the surface of rods and cones that constitute the receptive visual apparatus. This activity forms the image. Gibson cautioned, however, that

> it is easy to assume that the retinal image and the retinal excitation are the same thing. But the former, clearly, is a matter of physics while the latter is a matter of physiology. The image is an arrangement of light-points while the excitation is an arrangement of discharging nervous elements. These individual points of the image, it may be noted, together with the rays of light which explain the correspondence to the world, are pure geometrical fictions introduced for purposes of analysis, whereas the spots of the excitation-pattern are anatomical facts.[42]

For Gibson, the key to understanding the correspondences between the physical facts of vision and the fiction of the image were their interlaced patterns: the first anatomical (corresponding to clusters of nerves) and the second "ordinal," or a kind of relative clustering of light spots, whose substance was maintained in consciousness, that could ensure the integrity of the image, even as the eye moved across the visual world: "The ordinal pattern, therefore, is preserved when the eye moves although the anatomical pattern undergoes a complete rearrangement."[43] If the anatomical pattern corresponded to the visual *field,* for Gibson, the extension, uniformity, and boundlessness of the visual *world* were maintained by the peculiar properties of ordinal patterns, structures all the more substantial for not being grounded exclusively in either physics or physiology.

For Gibson, the perceiving subject was not a passive, disembodied recipient of sense data; the eye was not a tablet onto which points of light impressed their indelible shapes. The subject was an activated, kinesthetic register of shifting patterns, and the eye was the field in which those patterns could move and merge, even while maintaining their structural integrity. The patterned visual world was the intermediary between the ontological facticity of objects and the inadequate subjective bundle of apparatuses that was the observer. It was an environment par excellence.[44]

Gibson's subsequent work would revisit these same themes again and again. How does the subject maintain a more or less invariant perception of the world even as her position relative to the things she is perceiving and using is highly variant? As time passed, Gibson would expand his considerations to all the senses and would place even more emphasis on the environmental aspects of his research, which would lead him to an explicitly ecological model of perception. In 1966 he published *The Senses Considered as Perceptual Systems,* a book that would also have a major impact in design circles. The first chapter of this text, titled "The Environment as a Source of Stimulation," contained subheadings that would have sounded incredibly tantalizing to anyone dealing with questions of environmental patterning and design: "The Air as a Medium," "Ambient Information," "The Animate Environment," "The Environment of Emerging Man," and so on. In this and later chapters, Gibson expanded his notion of the senses, describing them not as passive receivers of environmental stimuli but as active agents, working with the ontological properties of the world and the brain to navigate reality. Many of Gibson's propositions here echoed those of his earlier book, but they were stated more forcefully, and the contrast with traditional "receptive" perceptual models was starker. For example: "The pattern of the excited receptors is of no account; what counts is the external pattern that is temporarily occupied by excited receptors as the eyes roam over the world, or as the skin moves over an object."[45] And again: "The perceptual systems, including the nerve centers at various levels up to the brain, are ways of seeking and extracting information about the environment from the flowing array of ambient energy."[46]

This "ambient energy" is worth pausing over. Gibson would continue to develop the concept as the basis for his description of the way perceiver and environment were caught, to use one commentator's phrase, "within a web of movement that spins between" them.[47] This is apparent most explicitly in his landmark text of 1979 *The Ecological Approach to Visual Perception.* In this text, Gibson advanced his theory of the "direct" perception of environmental information via the "ambient optic array," a space replete with the crisscrossing lines of light of the surrounding environment, an array that provided constant, albeit shifting, information that was already structured.[48] Although Gibson certainly knew nothing of Boutourline's notions of signal orientation, the model of the ambient optic array echoed those ideas in eradicating the classic notion of space as empty container for

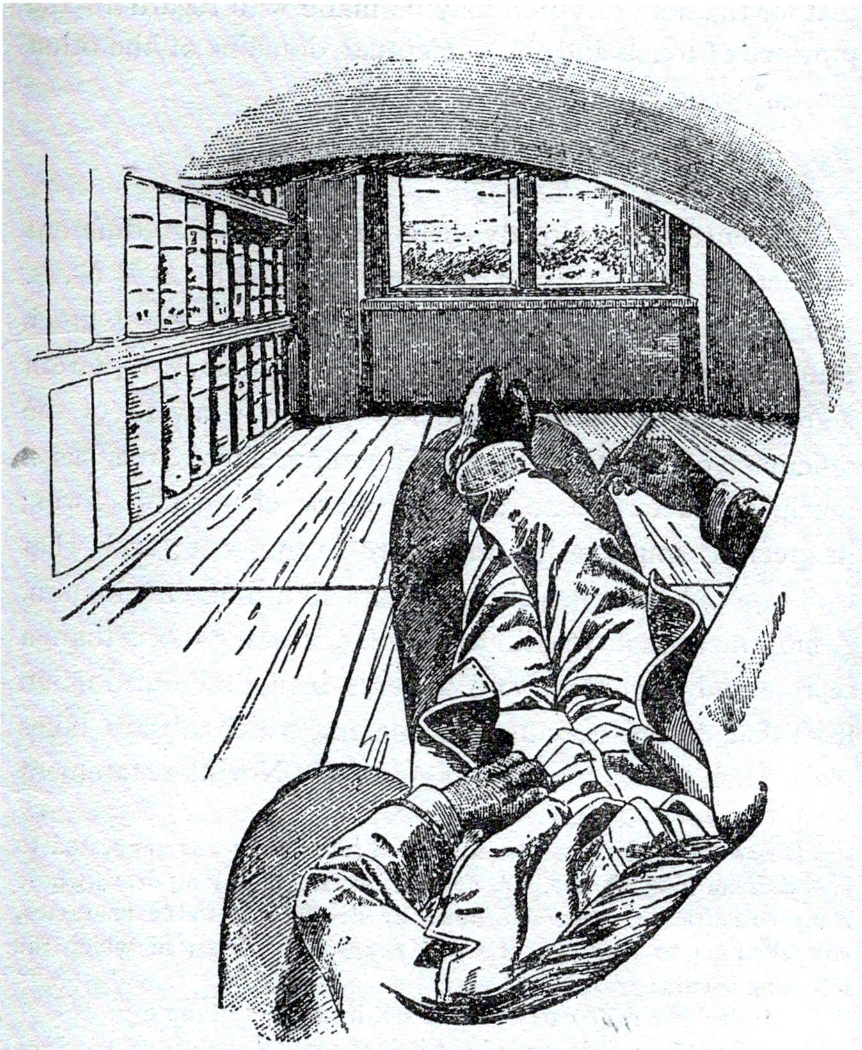

Fig. 1.

Figure 1.4. "In a frame formed by the ridge of my eyebrow, by my nose, and by my moustache, appears part of my body, so far as visible, with its environment." Ernst Mach, from *The Analysis of Sensations* (1886).

extended matter, perceptions of which were carriers of raw sensations to the mediation of the mind. "The concept of space has nothing to do with perception. Geometrical space is pure abstraction. . . . Space is a myth, a ghost, a fiction for geometers."[49] Gibson illustrated this state of affairs by updating Ernst Mach's famous sketch of the visual field with his own version, in which the room maintains its clarity and stability to the very limits of the field observed by the eye. He also stressed here the movement of the head as productive of "deletions and accretions of optical structure." Here, "self-perception and environment perception go together."[50]

But, more than this, here the environment was granted ever greater structure and, almost, agency. If, in *The Senses Considered as Perceptual Systems,* the sense modalities were actively seeking information that

Figure 1.5. "A sequence of overlapping fields of view obtained by turning the head to the right." James J. Gibson, *The Ecological Approach to Visual Perception* (Boston: Houghton Mifflin, 1979).

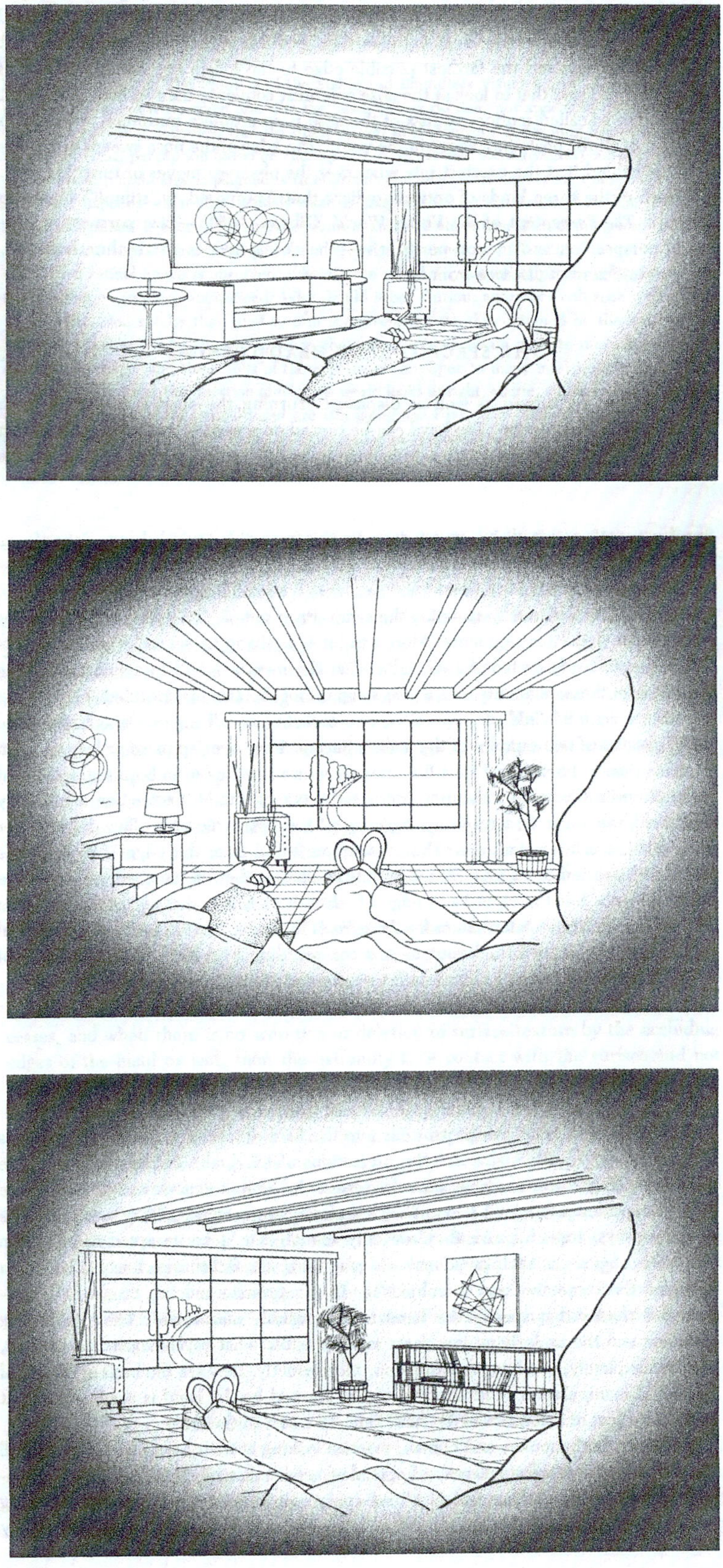

may or may not be in the environment, ten years later, the environment seemed to be offering itself up to those entreaties more actively itself. Environment was space literally networked by direct and reflected light, and this network was real. It had information and meaning embedded in it, as it were, by what Gibson would call "affordances." These affordances were in search of perceptions as much as perceptions were in search of them.

The deceptively complex notion of affordances would perhaps be Gibson's most enduring contribution to the nonspecialist side of perceptual theory. Designers, for instance, took it up in the 1980s and 1990s, but its applications tended to flatten the profound existential stakes of the original formulation of a term that Gibson was inspired to coin based on the connotations of the earlier gestalt postulates of Kurt Koffka and Kurt Lewin.[51] For Gibson, affordances were much more than merely functional clues or cues embedded in a tool or interface that might suggest to a user what manipulations could be made there.[52] They were the raw material of environmental information, transferred through the medium of light/air/perception. Affordances became a conceptual category that allowed Gibson to avoid reductive stimulus–response models, but also what he felt were the idealism, subjectivism, or "mentalism" of the gestalt school. The latter, for instance, understood that the meanings of objects in the world were more or less generated by the subject: a postbox became a significant and meaningful thing only if the subject was desirous of mailing a letter. Thus there was a kind of psychological overlay projected over the world, in which the significance of percepts always dwelled on the interior side of the organism. For Gibson, this simply reinforced the all-too-localized and atomized understanding of the senses as postulated by Descartes and so many generations of empiricists after him.

It is also worth noting here that Gibson distinguished classes of affordances. Objects in the world could afford things like sitting surfaces, missile weight, and aerodynamics: a rock could be thrown; a tree suggested itself as climbable. And perhaps the ultimate or most fundamental affordance was the supporting function of the ground surface, or floor. Could a floor be a floor if it had no subject to which to offer this affordance? Simply: no. It would be an ontic configuration made up of various substances, but no affordance would find its target, and the configuration could not achieve its meaningful status. In addition to the more or less inert objects listed here, Gibson made special mention of tools, which he felt were unique affordances. Also, echoing a larger cultural preoccupation with such objects, Gibson understood the affordance of a hammer or a pair of scissors as an "extension" of the human body into the environment, an extension that might transform the surfaces and structures within that environment.[53] But perhaps the most complex and intriguing class of affordances in the environment was that of other living beings. Our interactions with others were complex, ritualized, physiopsychological interactions wherein the possible range of affordances was constantly shifting from the sexual to

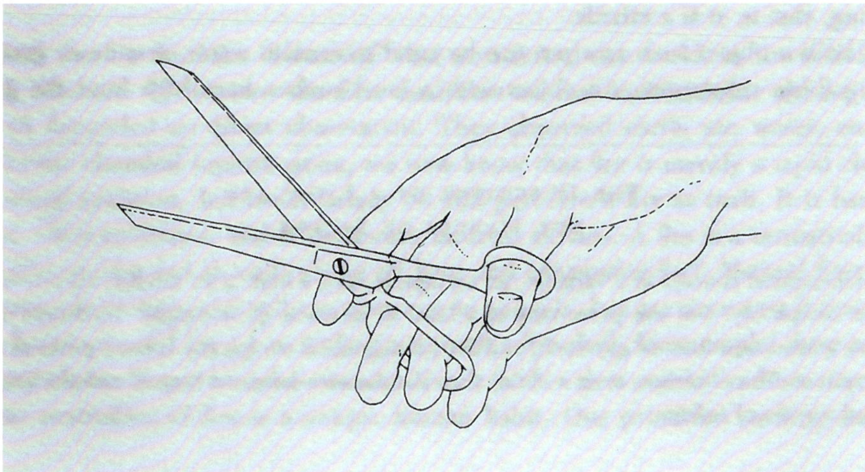

Figure 1.6. Diagram of a hand holding a pair of scissors. James J. Gibson, *The Ecological Approach to Visual Perception* (Boston: Houghton Mifflin, 1979).

the nurturing to the predatory to the hierarchical and so on. At this level, the affordance denoted a complex and mutual *responsive* set of relations between subject and environment.

The affordance, in short, was not a localizable quality that inhered in either the object of perception or its subject. It was an environmental bridge. "I prefer to say," wrote Gibson, "that the real postbox (the only one) affords letter-mailing to a letter-writing human in a community with a postal system. . . . To feel a special attraction to it when one has a letter to mail is not surprising, but the main fact is that it is perceived as part of the environment—as an item of the neighborhood in which we live."[54] The affordance, and its strangely contingent-yet-real status was, for Gibson, a kind of deus ex machina for philosophy, psychology, and perceptual science:

> There has been endless debate among philosophers and psychologists as to whether values are physical or phenomenal, in the world of matter or only in the world of mind. For affordances as distinguished from values, the debate does not apply. Affordances are neither in the one world or the other inasmuch as the theory of two worlds is rejected. There is only one environment, although it contains many observers with limited opportunities for them to live in it.[55]

Affordances bound organism and environment, and while Gibson never went this far, it is almost as though they became mutually generative in their "reciprocity," "complementarity," or "mutuality," as he frequently said. Moreover, the two entities were constantly engaged in a patterned interaction, something like an energetic meshing that made a consistent understanding of reality possible. With this meshing, interestingly, both sides were empowered: "Acts are *not* responses to stimuli, and percepts are not responses to stimuli. An observer is not 'bombarded' by stimuli. He extracts invariants from a flux of stimulation. Affordances, and the stimulus information to specify affordances, are neither subjective nor objective but transcend this dichotomy. The actor/perceiver and the environment are *complementary*."[56] Gibson's revelations called for a fuller phenomenological model, one grounded not in the figure of a detached observer gazing into an abstract space (pictorial or real) but in the concept of a dynamic and immersive field where the senses were constantly active and interactive among themselves and with the patterned environment.

It would be easy, and not entirely inaccurate, to discuss Gibson's work as being linked to that great, nebulous, and rebellious tendency within twentieth-century philosophy, phenomenology. His emphasis on the "physical frames" of the sense organs harked back to the work of Jakob von Uexküll but also resonated with contemporaneous accounts of perceptual "embodiment." Like Martin Heidegger, Gibson understood perception in relation to a "world," a material and situated reality coproduced by subject and raw nature ("earth" for Heidegger). Like Maurice Merleau-Ponty, Gibson situated the sense organs in their physical setting of the body—fleshly, directional, stereoscopic, and usually in motion. And, like phenomenologists more generally, Gibson saw his approach as a kind of demystification of Cartesian metaphysics, the most salient feature of which was the isolation of the thinking subject from the world of spatial extension. But if *embodiment* (an almost exhausted word at our present stage of critical and aesthetic theory) was an integral part of Gibson's theories, for him it was not so much the reinstantiation of human faculties into a material and corpulent structure, but rather the ontological restoration of the world itself within the structures of human perception. The subject was not a contained synthesis of eye and mind (and body), but rather an entity ecologically opened up to the "invariants" of the world of space and things.[57]

Erwin Straus: Environmentalizing Embodiment

One self-identified phenomenologist, however, is quite relevant to this discussion of the way in which perception engendered certain models of environmental interaction: the neurologist and philosopher Erwin Straus. Like many of the other researchers featured here, Straus was a humanist among empiricists. His work constituted not only one of the most remarkable corpuses of thought on the human sensorium but also one of the most sustained critiques of scientific specialism and research methods in the twentieth century. Straus was a clinical researcher and a pedagogue who, interestingly in regard to the present study, taught at Black Mountain College in the late 1930s and early 1940s. This institutional setting indicates that he would have been exposed and amenable to the kinds of avant-garde postures elaborated here. Accordingly, his books would enter the environmental research manifold as a critique of vulgar behaviorism and a new modeling of the subject as an emergent process at the intersection of perception and environment.

Among Straus's writings, it was perhaps 1963's quite accessible *The Primary World of Senses* that would have the greatest impact in design culture and environmental theory (although, admittedly, this impact was modest). The book effectively reads like a philosophical echo of Gibson's emerging theories, albeit without the concern to establish the invariant reality of the world. Nonetheless, Straus's model of the perceiving subject was shaped by the theories of emergence of Henri Bergson and Heidegger, but it was likewise formed against the backdrop of Straus's antipathy toward modern scientific method, especially as the latter addressed itself to the problems of sensing and knowing. Since the time such experiments became common in the nineteenth century, Straus held, the isolation of the human (or otherwise) subject in a laboratory setting subjected to a series of perceptual events, isolates, or images was always already a fallacious and misguided affair. Those conducting these experiments overestimated their ability to distinguish cause and effect and sought to relegate complex interactions to specific locations and "organs" (like the optic nerve). Perhaps their most serious failure, however, was that they did not admit to the consequences of the presence of the scientific observer in a setting devoted to the observation of observation.

Straus's common themes included, accordingly, frequent attacks on Cartesian dualism, but also on the epistemological fallacies of Ivan Pavlov's conclusions regarding his famous studies on conditioned learning in dogs (and, by extension, the conclusions of generations of behaviorists that followed). In fact, such scientific activity, especially as it related to exploring the living organism's sensory relations with the world, was, for Straus, a "belated fulfillment of Cartesianism."[58] Straus's critique of Pavlov was essentially a thoroughgoing deconstruction of scientific metanarratives. Not only was Pavlov's mechanistic reductionism misguided, but it was inspired by the hidden metaphysical aspiration of illuminating the veiled truth of human life by explaining all phenomena in terms of physiology (thus eliminating the need for any "subjective" language).

This fallacious dynamic played out in Pavlov's laboratories precisely because of their *environments*. According to Straus, even as Pavlov so assiduously eliminated stimulating variables by isolating his dogs in the white, nullified space of his labs—"in an atmosphere of uniform, immutable silence"[59]—he was effectively only projecting his own atomizing epistemology and metaphysics onto the *Umwelten* of his subjects. This reduced his dogs to "isolated apparatuses" whose mechanisms were wholly internalized; functions of their glands, retinas, and ganglions that had in one way or another (it did not really matter how) been "stimulated" were erroneously recognized as the only locales in need of understanding. "It is the spatial order of the central nervous system on which everything depends," Straus wrote of Pavlov's model, "the manifoldness of the phenomenal spatial order is thus reinterpreted as a temporal series of stimulated spots in the central nervous system."[60] It was as though the lived reality of the external world was mapped onto—and constrained to—the *internal* structures of the organism.

Straus's nuanced critique of Pavlov was one way of restoring to scientific consciousness a new (or old) model of the subject. The subject was not a bounded mechanism or apparatus, she was an entity produced out of the contact between a real world of potential perception and action and the moving, living, sensing body that interacted with it. Later in the text, Straus applied these principles to the epistemological categories of "within" and "without." What does it mean, he asked, to speak of the inside or outside of any space? Do these words signify spatial relations at all? Are they attributes *of* a given place or structure, or merely the subjective projections of the organism? Neither, of course, for "within" and "without," "inside" and "outside," are not physical or spatial properties any more than they are merely subjective abstractions. They emerge from the sensing subject's relation to the environment and the resulting establishment of what Straus called—not unlike Uexküll and Gibson—a "scope" or "field of action."[61] Straus applied this line of thinking to the architectural figure of the room:

> The space enclosed by the walls of a room becomes an inner space only for a being which in its totality relates itself to the totality of the world and who encounters the limits of the possibilities of its action; the boundaries of the room are that which cuts a man off from the totality of his world. Because he has the possibility of stepping beyond these boundaries, the walls and the door become limits. Because he has the power of relating himself, as an individual, to the totality of the world, then the limits themselves must be pervasive and many sided.[62]

As this passage demonstrates, Straus's delineation of these ideas became significant for theories of environmental interaction precisely insofar as it deviated from a more typical phenomenological account. Like many phenomenologies, Straus's project reads as a humanization, as an affirmation of the sensate being as a lived *whole,* and not the atomized set of mechanics described by the sciences. At the same time, though, Straus's restoration of the sensing being reads less like a full resurrection of the romantic self than like an apportioning of reality between two entities. The "field of actions" that determines what might be considered inside and outside is an emergent property of these two things: subject and environment. I quote here at length from this key section of Straus's book, because only in the flow of his prose does it become evident the degree to which he was utilizing an ontology of environment to critique the metaphysical assumptions of objective scientific considerations of the senses and their apprehension of the world:

> Just as there is no such thing as a "within" or "without" in and for itself, so there can be no self as such or world as such with fixed borderlines between them delimiting the within and the without. The borderline does not hue *[sic]* precisely to the surface of the organism's body as that which separates that body from its environment. (Neither does it separate the givens of the inner from those of the outer senses.) . . .
>
> The body is the mediator between the self and the world. It belongs fully neither to the "inner" nor to the "outer." . . .
>
> Therefore, to speak of within and without in reference to the self's relation to its world is not to speak of spatial relations. The relation of inner and outer, self and world, is not the relation of two spaces known as the bodily interior and exterior. . . .
>
> . . . The [infant's] cry renders a momentary relation of a self to the world explicit; it does not shift something from the inside to the outside. Nor is sensing to be understood as such a shifting. Like crying, sensing renders explicit the particular and momentarily defined relation of self and world. But sensing brings neither something from inside to the outside, nor something that is outside to the inside. Sensory nerves are in a place, neural processes occur in a place, but sensing is not subject to such topography. . . .
>
> The knowledge that belongs to sensing must occur where sensing itself takes place. But the theory of sensation never attempted to know sensing as it is in itself. It skipped its own proper subject matter and immediately proceeded by a detour toward a physiology of sensation. . . . Directed by the principle of deficiency, it recognized that sensing was a function of the sensory nerves. Excluded from the "within" of the alien organism and its experience, it took the relation of *within*, which has meaning only relative to an observer, and interpreted it as something objective and universal. It interpreted the field of action as a purely geometrical phenomenon. It finally convinced itself that the individual originally experiences himself within the boundaries of the surface of his body.[63]

Straus further elaborated this late reference to the reduction of the emergent "field of action" to a "purely geometrical phenomenon" in another essay, where he blamed this reduction not only on the specific topographical errors of experimental methods but also on the visual bias of Western science and philosophy in general, on its propensity to graft scientific models onto more primary "lived experiences."[64] In language that would resonate very strongly with Marshall McLuhan's historical and theoretical pursuit of "acoustic space" (see below), Straus asked, in his usual sophisticated synthesis of the phenomenal and ontic: "Does the spatial present itself in different modes in the various spheres of sensory experience—

for example, the optical and acoustical—and are there different forms of motor activity and perception that correspond to them?"[65] Once again, for Straus, the "Euclidean" model of empty, homogeneous space was a purely optical phenomenon extrapolated as the general laws of spatiality itself. To counter this fallacy, Straus constructed a textured model of the space appropriate to hearing (or of the modality of hearing appropriate to a certain experience of space).

Unlike optical space, Straus argued, acoustic space had its own distinct structure. Specifically, it implied a kind of directionality that was totally foreign to the evenness of optical space. For every sound we hear, we ask the question "Whence?" "Such a question," Straus observed, "does not originate in reflection about the sound, its source, and the existence of things in space; it coincides with hearing itself. . . . In this instance, as in all instances, we attempt to determine the direction or location of the sound source from the sound alone; the sound itself must be endowed with an original spatial character."[66] Again, here, neumenon and phenomenon are sutured together into a more tightly knit unit than phenomenology traditionally allowed. There is a mode of perception that is immanent to a certain type of spatial experience. Sound, tonality, and, eventually, the art form of music are privileged for Straus, precisely because of the spatiality immanent in them. It is, much like the models of environment I wish to evoke here, a space altogether more dynamic, palpable, and immersive than traditional optical/mathematical descriptions. For, even if we are led automatically to inquire as to the directional source of a sound, "the tone itself," for Straus, "does not extend in a single direction; rather, it approaches us, penetrating, filling, and homogenizing space. . . . Tones . . . approach us, come to us, and, surrounding us, drift on; they fill space, shaping themselves in temporal sequences."[67] When willfully shaped into music, Straus argued, tones attain a level of aesthetic "autonomy" unmatched by any other art form. Detached from any object or meaning, musical sound, more than any other perceptual modality, demonstrates the way in which perception and space interact to literally "take hold" of the subject: "It presses in on us, surrounds, seizes, and embraces us. . . . The acoustical pursues us; we are at its mercy, unable to get away."[68]

Little wonder, then, that modern Western science had privileged the visual modality of spatial perception. It provided the solace of segregation and control, of a bounded field with defined objects, of a clear distinction between foreground and background. In Straus's and Gibson's work, these distinctions were fundamentally disrupted, not by new models of the perception of the environment but by new environmental models of perception itself. Both Straus and Gibson suggested that environment gives rise to particular modalities of sensing, as much as the other way around. These were not simply questions of method, nor did they merely offer up a new *object* for scientific or philosophical speculation. They redefined the very *subject* of method and speculation in general—a subject no longer deemed capable of standing outside a system and observing it, a subject radically open to and determined by the very systems they sought to comprehend.

Gregory Bateson: Form and Context

If Gibson and Straus had utilized interactional models of environmental perception to critique the scientific description of the perceptual apparatus, Gregory Bateson would conduct a similar analysis of scientific (and aesthetic) epistemology writ large. Bateson was an anthropologist by training, but through an introduction to Warren McCulloch in 1942 he was inducted into the Macy Conferences, which would soon produce a coherent theory of cybernetics. His work then phased through various other disciplines as he was invited to conduct research in different institutional settings—a veterans' mental hospital, a dolphin research laboratory, and the social science departments at various universities.

In 1972 Bateson published his collected writings under the title *Steps to an Ecology of Mind*.[69] The timing of this publication was a bit late to inform much of the intellectual transformation characteristic of the environmental research manifold as elaborated here. (It is partly for this reason, I think, that Bateson's work is often condemned by its association with the New Age movement.) Nonetheless, many of the premises of the environmental research manifold are to be found in Bateson's elaboration of ecological thinking and perception, which stretches back to the 1940s. In particular, Bateson helps us understand the formal and aesthetic bases of environment, as well as its radical contextualism. I will return to some specific instances of these in later chapters, but here I wish to offer a brief exegesis of Bateson's understanding of these two categories: form and context.

Like those of many of the theorists included here, Bateson's project constituted something of a cybernetic critique of modern scientific method itself. The latter, Bateson held, had been steered off course by an ancient and long-forgotten choice in favor of an ontology of "substance" over "form."[70] Since that time, science had become caught in a vicious circle of attempting to induce the intrinsic attributes of stable entities through the continual analysis of data that were already mediated by the presupposition that there were stable entities with intrinsic attributes. This epistemological error was magnified in the nineteenth century by a singular act of "reification," when "energy" was taken as the key to understanding the connection between "behavioral data and the fundamentals of physical and chemical science."[71] By attempting to locate evidence of natural laws *within* things, in other words, science elided the significance of the *context* that orders the relations *among* things (and, indeed, the illusion that there are things). It was the ordering principles of context that, for Bateson, were first and foremost a matter of form. "The conservative laws of energy and matter," he wrote, "concern substance rather than form. But mental process, ideas, communication, organization, differentiation, pattern, and so on, are matters of form rather than substance."[72]

Or, as Bateson wrote in a 1969 elaboration of his seminal formulation of the "double bind": "The explanatory world of *substance* can invoke no differences and no ideas but only forces and impacts. And, per contra, the world of *form* and communication invokes no things, forces, or impacts, but only differences and ideas."[73] Reification occurs here for Bateson because an object is attributed with the properties of an idea, something that exists only "in the mind" of a particular observer or actor. "In any case," he argued in a deceptively complex formulation, "it is nonsense to say that a man was frightened by a lion, because the lion is not an idea. The man makes an *idea* of the lion." This act of reification happened for modern science just as certainly, if not as intensely, as it happens for schizophrenics. But it would be a mistake to describe Bateson as a solipsist or idealist based on this snippet of text, for even the phrase "in the mind" for him would be determined by certain types of organization occurring between an outside reality and an inside reality of mental activity. Only the interaction of the two can properly be said to be observable. "A *context* is set for a certain class of response."[74]

In these and many other passages in Bateson's writings—whether he is referring to psychological syndromes or the morphology of octopi—form and context are inextricably linked: "Goethe pointed out 150 years ago that there is a sort of syntax or grammar in the anatomy of flowering plants. A 'stem' is that which bears 'leaves'; a 'leaf' is that which has a bud in its axil; a bud is a stem which originates in the axil of a leaf; etc. The formal (*i.e.* the communicational) nature of each organ is determined by its contextual status—the context in which it occurs and the context which it sets for other parts."[75] A double bind occurs precisely because there is a "tangle" in the habitual or normative pattern of communication of a given set of messages. "Experienced breaches in the weave of contextual structure are in fact 'double binds.'"[76] Taking the original formulation of the double bind as an example, the seeds of schizophrenia are sown in the proverbial mother–child relationship when two or more injunctions that are subject to punishment (or reward) are in conflict.[77] "Do not do so and so, or I will punish you" is a primary prohibition that is negated by a secondary prohibition such as "Do not submit to my prohibitions."[78] In this context, the child is unable to formulate a satisfactory response that avoids punishment; he or she "cannot win." In this instance, "winning" would not be avoiding punishment per se, but rather recognizing the nature or context of the double bind itself. Winning would lie in the ability to make "metacommunicative" observations, or to communicate about the very nature of communication. Therefore, instead of attempting to meet the contradictory requirements of the mother's paradoxical injunctions, the child could step outside that communicational circuit to ask, "What do you mean by that?" or "What are you really trying to say?"

In other words, a satisfactory resolution of the double bind would rely on an awareness of context and, by extension, the context of context, and so on. This would indicate a mechanism of "learning about learning" that Bateson most often described in cybernetic parlance as negative feedback, or the ability to change behavior in response to environmental circumstances. The schizophrenic avoids (but does not escape) the double bind either by not accepting the literal meaning of other people's statements and other environmental signals or by taking these too literally. These two options result in acting out—challenging the truthfulness of every input—on the one hand, or, on the other hand, accepting the literal truthfulness of all statements, the agitation of which leads to withdrawal into an internal world in which the subject caught in the double bind "would find it necessary to see and hear less and less of what went on around him, and do his utmost to avoid provoking a response in his environment."[79]

I use this last (happily coincidental) turn of phrase as a way to tie the concept of the double bind back into the current discussion of environmental response. Bateson used the term *environment* in all of the vague ways that I use it in this text, to refer to any context in which anything at all is being transferred, transacted, or communicated. Significantly, however, he—and most others discussed here—did not consider environment to be the source of these communications. It was not the source of stimuli. It was not the source of order. Environment was the process of interaction that brought two realities together. Context was the ordering of these interactions. In these formulations, form is neither intrinsic to a stable entity nor purely a projection of subjective activity. It is context as a material entity with its own laws of communication with other entities. Context is form. Environment is pure context. With a few more metonymic shifts, we could arrive at the formulation that environment is form, which I do not offer as a categorical truth, but rather as a way to access the mind-set of this period in which environment, which now signals little more than a vacuum in which various entities transact, came to be figured as physical medium.

Bateson's understanding of context and its intimate relation to form came from diverse sources in philosophy, mathematics, biology, psychology, and aesthetics. The mathematical bases of form, for instance, were signaled for him by the young prodigy and student of both Bertrand Russell and R. D. Laing, George Spencer-Brown, whose 1969 *Laws of Form* would become a touchstone for many theorists interested in somehow reconciling ontology and epistemology, the world of perception and that of the ideal, unchanging reality of mathematical proofs. What Spencer-Brown understood as form was very much in tune with Bateson's emerging conception. Form was not an attribute of things. Rather, it was the result of the conscious activity of making a division, of marking out an inside and an outside. Brown wrote:

> A universe comes into being when a space is severed or taken apart. The skin of a living organism cuts off an outside from an inside. So does the circumference of a circle in a plane. By tracing the way we represent such a severance, we can begin to reconstruct, with an accuracy and coverage that appear almost uncanny, the basic forms underlying linguistic, mathematical, physical, and biological science, and can begin to see how the familiar laws of our own experience follow inexorably from the original act of severance.[80]

Form emerges here as the governing pattern deriving from this primal, "original act of severance," which, one gets the sense from Spencer-Brown's text, has as much to do with psychic individuation as it does with geometrical division.

Bateson was also inspired by the work of the British philosopher of science and history R. G. Collingwood, whom he described as "the first man to recognize—and to analyze in crystalline prose—the nature of context."[81] Collingwood's texts on nature and art took on something of a talismanic importance for Bateson.[82] But, for as much as he ascribed to Collingwood the articulation of "the nature of context" (an interestingly problematic phraseology), the latter never explicitly addressed the term or category. Nonetheless, he was a master of what I would call the "third term," or a category that disrupts the exclusivity of a prior dichotomous pair (of concepts, for instance). In art, Collingwood famously elaborated the theory of "expression." In it, he proposed that art cannot be understood in terms of the traditional dichotomy of "means" (the technical making of the work) and "ends" (the arousing of emotion in the receiver). Instead, a third term becomes necessary to avoid the fallacy that the thing conveyed—emotion—is a stable and complete entity known to an artist who crafts a support for it and then delivers it whole to an audience. (This is, I would offer, our current, and quite rightly debased, understanding of "expressionism," where art becomes little more than a vehicle for preconceived ideations.) Emotion, for Collingwood, is not some *thing* that can simply be aroused *in* a viewer. It must be more like a process that manifests only in the embodying act of expression, which requires a material support in the form of language, sound, or paint. In other words, there is no such entity as a defined emotion that can simply be transferred in the means–ends circuit. Only through expression is the emotion *formed* and made available to both artist and viewer.[83]

"Expression," here, is context. It is the third (always processual) category that, in positioning the two other terms, actually produces them. There is no such thing as emotion in the exterior reality of the world. Nor is emotion relegated purely to the interior of the subject's unconscious, where it can be at best only a formless "perturbation or excitement."[84] Likewise, it resides in neither the "means" nor the "ends" of art. Emotion is a manifestation of the act, process, and material support of expression.

In this same sense, Collingwood revised the history of Western conceptions of nature. If these had coalesced, by the seventeenth century, around the Cartesian distinction between mind and matter, this dichotomy was called into question in the nineteenth century with the rise of biology and evolutionary theory. These introduced a third term—again, not a thing or immutable principle, but a process—"life."[85] Life could not be described wholly by the movements and impacts of matter as described by physics or as the internal structures of purpose and logic described by Cartesian/Kantian epistemology. "The new biology thought of life as resembling matter and unlike mind in being wholly devoid of conscious purpose."[86]

If life had arrived to aggravate the stultifying segregation of mind and matter in the nineteenth century, for Collingwood in the twentieth century that function would fall to the new physics. Modern physics falsified the dichotomy in classical physics between matter and space. No longer was matter to be a solid "particle" occupying only one space and no other, moving in a totally homogeneous medium or "ether." The new physics erased this fallacious distinction and introduced instead the idea of a dynamic "pattern" (a term that would prove galvanizing for Bateson and many others involved in environmental culture during the period in question).

> Thus we get back to a single physical unit, the electron; but we also get a very important new conception of chemical quality, as depending not upon the merely quantitative aspect of the atom, its weight, but upon the pattern formed by the electrons that compose it. This pattern is not a static pattern but a dynamic pattern, a pattern constantly changing in a definite rhythmical way, like the rhythmical patterns discovered by the Pythagoreans in the field of acoustics. . . .
>
> This new theory of the atom as a moving pattern of electrons . . . assimilated the chemical properties of matter to the moral qualities of a mind or the vital qualities of an organism in making them a function of time.[87]

For Collingwood, "pattern" was shorthand for what would be described in Alfred North Whitehead's philosophy as "process," and in Samuel Alexander's work as "emergence" (I mention these two terms because they, like "pattern," would be significant for the theorization of environment as discussed here).[88] Likewise, the concept of pattern would become more and more significant for Bateson. It allowed him finally to bring together those two broad yet separate fields of inquiry with which he was always concerned: philosophy and science. Pattern, like context, was his third term—the third term between mind and body, between mother and child, or between organism and environment. This became most explicit in a talk Bateson gave in 1970 titled "Form, Substance, and Difference." Here, he invoked Collingwood's notion of pattern to argue for a reconceptualization of life itself. No longer could our understanding of life be limited to considerations of individual sacks of genetic material, or the homogeneous family lines created by their interbreeding. The organism, first of all, had to be recognized as genetically variegated, and furthermore, "the flexible environment must also be included along with the flexible organism because . . . the organism which destroys its environment destroys itself. The unit of survival is a flexible organism-in-its-environment."[89] Here, then, we have one formulation of the organism–environment "unit" or "system" that would become fundamental in the environmental research manifold.

Form, pattern, and context enter this formula as its conscious and immanent organization. Not just any combination of organism plus environment will result in a "unit of survival." The two must be connected according to certain morphological laws, which, in their turn, will make sense only in certain situations. These organizations change as difference or information travels through their "circuits." But, just as certainly, these differences in organizational pattern are, for Bateson, "abstractions." They are mental and do not necessarily follow the laws of energy conservation, but they are not therefore false or merely subjective. With the expanded notion of the patterned unit or circuit between interior and exterior, Bateson was able to describe a world in which "mind" is immanent in physical structures just as certainly as physical structures produce mind. Bateson transformed the notion of mind with cybernetics and ecology. It was no longer trapped in a bipolar relationship with body, but became the third term between interior and exterior. The mind is a circuit with pathways inside and outside what is known as the body. Bateson offered the very concrete example of the responsive system of a man chopping down a tree:

> Consider a tree and a man and an axe. We observe that the axe flies through the air and makes certain sorts of gashes in a preexisting cut in the side of the tree. If now we want to explain this set of phenomena, we shall be concerned with differences in the cut face of the tree, differences in the retina of the man, differences in his central nervous system, differences in his efferent neural messages, differences in the behavior of his muscles, differences in how the axe flies, to the differences which the axe then makes on the face of the tree.[90]

Furthermore, none of the series of causes and effects in this particular system make any sense except as they are patterned for and in a consciousness. They are meaningless out of context. But here, again, context denotes the very nature and forms of their interconnection.

As is likely obvious by this point in my exposition, Bateson was skeptical that science, as it was (and is) being practiced, could assimilate the epistemological shift from substance to form or pattern. He was much more optimistic about art. He had nurtured a keen aesthetic sensibility for his entire career, which only intensified in later years.[91] As one of his students wrote, he maintained that "form is secreted by process; art is secreted by living beings."[92] The issue of aesthetics would also solidify the schism that was developing between Bateson and the scientific world. In 1969 he organized a Wenner-Gren Foundation symposium titled The Moral and Aesthetic Structure of Human Adaptation. In the call for papers, he (amazingly) invoked Kant by quoting Blake:

> At heart, I believe that action, if it be planned at all, must always be planned upon an aesthetic base:
>
> He who would do good to another must do it
> in minute particulars.
> General Good is the plea of the scoundrel,
> Hypocrite, and flatterer;
> For Art and Science cannot exist but in minutely organized
> particulars.[93]

According to responses archived with Bateson's papers, many of his colleagues in the sciences took umbrage at the topic of the symposium, arguing that it failed to provide an empirical base.[94]

The same might have been said of Bateson's fleeting engagement with architecture. For another Wenner-Gren conference, in 1970, he proposed the theme of The Ecology of a Great City. Bateson developed this topic after he had been contacted by the office of New York mayor John Lindsay, for whom the relationship between the city and its inhabitants was in a state of constant crisis, much of it deriving from racial segregation and economic inequality. Bateson was not the most qualified person to organize such a conference.[95] Nonetheless, he assembled a small group of participants who might best be described as coming from the artsy side of his wide network of colleagues. The intermedia artist Frank Gillette was in attendance, as was the cybernetician and designer Warren M. Brodey (see chapter 4). While providing very little in the way of concrete design ideas, Bateson's position paper sought to "contribute something to the thinking of planners in general and so ameliorate what is becoming a major tangle of ecological pathology in the twentieth century."[96] In other words, he hoped to escape the double bind of the human–environment system.

Bateson's paper for the 1970 conference was first published in the vanguard journal *Radical Software* before being included, under a different title, in *Steps to an Ecology of Mind*.[97] In it, he managed to do two things that are material to the present thesis: first, he transposed the model of extended interior–exterior units or circuits—what Ronald Kline has described as "a new epistemology of ecological, mindlike systems (those composed of humans, machines, and the environment)"[98]—to the figure of the built environment and its inhabitants; second, he described this unit as a responsive environment. "I suggest that a healthy ecology of human civilization," he wrote, "would be defined somewhat as follows: A single system of *environment combined with high human civilization* in which the flexibility of the civilization shall match that of the environment to create an ongoing complex system, open-ended for slow change of even basic (hard-programmed) characteristics."[99] Here, programmatic flexibility (which I regard as synonymous with response) is part of the entire system—the humans in the system must change just as their environment is invested with the same learning potential. Therefore, instead of presenting data about the generalized attitudes of city dwellers, for instance, Bateson focused on the paradigms of social subject formation—"education and character formation"—and those of planners. It was, to use the phrase that Bateson borrowed from Geoffrey Vickers, "the ecology of ideas" that needed to change in the worlds of planning and everyday existence in an urban environment. Those aspects of each that seemed to be "hard-programmed" needed to be instilled with the possibility of flexibility, the ability to change their patterns. Here we have the basic double promise of responsive environments: the environment conditions us, but now that we can perceive the dynamics of that conditioning—our ecology—we can change them to be more malleable, softer, and responsive.

The difficulties of translating such paradigmatic shifts into architecture would soon be demonstrated by Sim Van der Ryn, state architect of California, who was intimately associated with the New Age culture in which Bateson found himself after his move to Santa Cruz from Hawaii in 1972. As Simon Sadler has recently observed, the holistic cybernetic ethos of this moment was being channeled into the administration of Governor Jerry Brown, who set "environmental" priorities very high.[100] Through consultations among Van der Ryn, Stewart Brand (founder of the *Whole Earth Catalog*), Ivan Illich, and Bateson, patterned relations became a part of the description of California ecology and its expressions in built form. In 1981, the Bateson Building, a project of the California Office of the State Architect, opened in Sacramento. It was Van der Ryn's attempt to produce (quoting Bateson) a "building [that] itself becomes 'the pattern which connects' us to the change and flow of climate, season, sun and shadow, constantly tuning our awareness of the natural cycles which support all life."[101]

Bateson was elaborating the aesthetics of this "pattern which connects" in his book *Mind and Nature: A Necessary Unity* at the precise moment Van der Ryn's building was being constructed.[102] Here, in prose clearly edited for a general readership (but still unable to free itself from the topological complexity of the author's thought), Bateson described his scientific search for an ultimately aesthetic sensibility that could identify and relate to what he called "the pattern which connects" all things in the world.[103] For Bateson, after all, everything was form; everything was pattern. Bateson himself often ended up speaking of complex symmetries, Fibonacci series, spirals, and so on (clearly thinking of D'Arcy Wentworth Thompson) in describing these relationships. But these were merely indices of the fact that there were no isolated objects in Bateson's system. Static entities did not exist except insofar as they entered into a relational feedback loop with one another and, perhaps most important, a perceiving, thinking subject. These relationships, as we have seen, Bateson termed "pattern," and the relationships among these relationships he described as "the pattern which connects."[104] In *Mind and Nature,* Bateson seemed freed from addressing specific researchers in specific disciplines and was able to speak of a "sacred" unity of humanity and cosmos, formally ordered by patterns, whose specific interactions happened in *context,* which he defined as "*pattern through time.*"[105] The world he described was made of nothing but pure relation. "What pattern," he wrote famously, "connects the crab to the lobster and the orchid to the primrose and all the four of them to me? And me to you? And all the six of us to the amoeba in one direction and to the backward schizophrenic in another?"[106]

In preparing his text, Bateson experienced this patterned connection quite explicitly:

> I was transcending that line which is sometimes supposed to enclose the human being. In other words, as I was writing, mind became, for me, a reflection of large parts and many parts of the natural world outside the thinker.
>
> On the whole, it was not the crudest, the simplest, the most animalistic and primitive aspects of the human species that were reflected in the natural phenomena. It was, rather, the more complex, the aesthetic, the intricate, and the elegant aspects of people that reflected nature.[107]

Here, allowing himself to spill out of his adiabatic confines, Bateson realized that the language proper to describing the human–environment system is aesthetic. It involves seeing and comparing formal patterns (patterns that also produce the subject) rather than describing unchanging quantities and substances. But this very activity removes the traditional romantic subject from the center of these perceptual and cognitive acts. "Mind is empty," Bateson stated very explicitly.[108] "It is as if the stuff of which we are made were totally transparent and therefore imperceptible and as if the only appearances of which we can be aware are cracks and planes of fracture in that transparent matrix."[109]

McLuhan's Environment

In 1965, Marshall McLuhan gave an address at Vision 65, a conference organized by graphic designer Will Burtin at Southern Illinois University in

Carbondale. Speaking just after the publication of his epoch-defining book *Understanding Media,* he turned his attention explicitly to the problem of environment:

> There is a book by Erwin Straus recently that throws new light on Pavlov's operations (the Russian psychologist). He didn't get his conditioning effects by means of stimuli or signals to his experimental subjects. Rather he did it by environmental controls. He put them in environments in which there was no sound, in which the heat and other sensory controls were very carefully adjusted and maintained steadily. Pavlov discovered that if you tried to condition animals in an ordinary environment, it did not work. The environment is the real conditioner, not the stimulus or the content.[110]

The coincidence here of McLuhan's reference to Straus might allow me to tie together some of the loose ends of this chapter. For, just like his friend Serge Boutourline, McLuhan spent the last half of the 1960s trying to perceive environment. While this aspect of his work has been largely forgotten, it was explicit in the few years following the publication of *Understanding Media,* during which it was taken up in the environmental research manifold.[111] In a book review published in the journal *Man–Environment Systems,* the architect and environmental designer Alton de Long wrote the following: "McLuhan, after all, is an environmental thinker: the environment is a cultural artifact badly in need of analysis and understanding if we are to achieve any degree of control over it. . . . McLuhan embodies the sharp polarities present in the current attempted merger between design on the one hand and social and behavioral sciences on the other."[112]

But McLuhan seemed little aware of or concerned with environmental design (architecture would interest him more). Despite his rather desperate search for studies and data on environment, he seemed incapable of stepping back to see the forest of environmental research for all of the discipline-specific trees. This lent his work the feeling of the entire manifold I am attempting to characterize here. He kept finding compelling bits and pieces of insight from various scientific and literary sources, and he was seeking, like a paranoiac pattern recognizer, to stitch them together into a comprehensive theory. Likewise, he believed deeply that such a comprehensive theory had not yet emerged precisely because of the perceptual shortcomings or blind spots of modern Western conceptions of space, not because of disciplinary miscommunication.

McLuhan's theorizing of environment was not simply a diversion from his "main" body of thinking about media; rather, it was completely coincident with and integral to that thinking. For several years, it would appear that he saw the terms *environment* and *medium* as synonymous. As early as 1962, in *The Gutenberg Galaxy,* McLuhan said that he could have used the term *environment* in place of *galaxy.*[113] As he wrote to

Edward T. Hall in 1964: "To say that any new technology or extension of man creates a new environment is a much better way of saying the medium is the message."[114] He reiterated this idea in several articles: "New media are new environments. That is why the media are the message."[115] "Medium," for McLuhan, designated not just a particular vehicle for a particular "message" or content, but rather the almost viscous, yet invisible, substance that made such transmissions possible. Like fish in water (a favorite McLuhan metaphor), humanity was constantly and unconsciously immersed in the medium of its own technological contrivances. It is no exaggeration to say that McLuhan's entire intellectual project at this time involved raising awareness of this peculiar spatiotemporal condition. As Richard Cavell writes in one of the few contemporary acknowledgments of this aspect of McLuhan's work: "Environment, in McLuhan's lexicon, has the force of 'episteme' in Foucauldian theory."[116]

McLuhan's conception of environment would even infiltrate one of his key concepts: extension (more on which in chapter 5). If older media had functioned primarily by extending or augmenting the functioning of a single sense organ (type, the eye; the wheel, the foot; television, both the eye and, more important, the ear), the new electronic environment of networks and computation extended humanity in an entirely new way: "With circuitry we have, instead of extensions of hand or foot, or back, or arm, a kind of involvement of the whole nervous system, an extension of the nervous system itself, a most profoundly involving operation."[117]

But the fact that environment was the "extension of the nervous system itself" presented certain methodological difficulties. Observation of this environment became a central issue, in the sense that the object to be observed and the observing apparatus were essentially identical. McLuhan rhetorically fetishized this paradox with the phrase "invisible environment." He argued that "the really total and saturating environments are invisible."[118] Developing ways to perceive the environmental dynamics of the new electronic or information environment would become central to his critical project at this moment. This search led him to a particular focus on pattern recognition, but it also allowed him to make certain incisive observations about the current built environment, or architecture. In another letter to Hall, McLuhan wrote: "When the environment itself is constituted by electric circuitry and information, architecture becomes the content of the new information environment. Architecture is the old technology which is automatically elevated into an art form."[119] Here, McLuhan accommodated environment and architecture to one of his most familiar conceptual dynamics: that media are invisible until they are overtaken or subsumed by new media. Only when they are assimilated into a new environment can the older modalities become visible as content or message. They are perceivable—just like Walter Benjamin's industrial dream images—only because of their outmodedness (e.g., as McLuhan famously observed, movies did not really come into focus as such until they became the "content" of television through rebroadcasts, a fact that obscured the real import of television). By the time McLuhan started theorizing environment as such, this pattern would change in significant ways. First, he integrated it with the language of environment. No longer would the outmoded medium become "content"; instead, it would become an "anti-environment," precisely that entity that resisted the self-effacing mechanisms of the dominant medium or environment.[120] Thus, with the rise of the totalizing environment, architecture was rendered as an anti-environment, as content or "art form." It resisted dematerialization and could yet be grasped through direct observation.

Anti-environment or not, architecture was a constant source of inspiration for McLuhan as his thinking about space and environment developed from early on. He had been friends with the architectural historian Sigfried Giedion for many years, for instance, before he issued his statements on the invisibility of environment. "Giedion influenced me profoundly," he said in 1967, noting that Giedion's 1941 *Space, Time and Architecture* "was one of the great events of my lifetime." He went on:

> Giedion gave us a language for tackling the structural world of architecture and artifacts of many kinds in the ordinary environment. . . . He approached them not descriptively—not by classification—but structurally. Giedion began to study the environment as a structural, artistic work—he saw language in streets, buildings, the very texture of form.[121]

Giedion's approach to "anonymous history," McLuhan felt, "accepts the entire world as an organized happening that is charged with luminous and exciting messages."[122] Indeed, Giedion's ideas would have been with McLuhan for nearly two decades at this point. The two met in the early 1950s thanks to the intercession of Jaqueline Tyrwhitt, whom Giedion had recommended for McLuhan's interdisciplinary research group at the University of Toronto.[123]

Giedion's exact influence would not be in the realm of environmental theory, but in McLuhan's earlier attempts to describe other types of radical perceptual spatialities. These initially took the form of a description of what McLuhan called "acoustic space." For McLuhan, acoustic space comprised a theory of spatial experience that ran counter to what he believed was the *visual* bias of modern Western culture, a bias he criticized in both *The Gutenberg Galaxy* and *Understanding Media.* Much of his obsession with the human sensorium had to do with overturning this particular bias, which he felt alienated the modern subject into a world that was artificially linear, solipsistic, quantitative, logical, and specialized. Just as the written alphabet had subjected language to a singular, diachronic regimentation (a development intensified exponentially by the advent of the printing press), perspectival, visual space was the result of a particular form of spatial ordering that privileged clarity, clear distinctions among various objects (and the accompanying distinction between object and "empty" space), stable orientation, and the linear processing of spatial phenomena:

> We suppress or ignore much of the world as visually given in order to locate and identify *objects* in three dimensions. It is the objects which compel our attention and orient our behavior; space becomes merely that which must be traversed in getting to or from them. . . .
>
> Auditory space has no point of favored focus. It's a sphere without fixed boundaries, space made by the thing itself, not space containing the thing. It is not pictorial space, boxed in, but dynamic, always in flux, creating its own dimensions moment by moment. It has no fixed boundaries; it is indifferent to background. The eye focuses, pinpoints, abstracts, locating each object in physical space, against a background; the ear, however, favors sound from any direction.[124]

Thus, for McLuhan (like Straus) acoustic space was replete, multidimensional, omnidirectional, and synchronous—and, perhaps most important, it was close. It embraced the subject from all sides at all times and had no use for the visual illusion of objective distance. Acoustic space was tactile space, somatic space. It was involving, interactive, and responsive.

Giedion's space conceptions were present from the very genesis of the idea of acoustic space.[125] Tyrwhitt, McLuhan, and psychology student Carl Williams generated the term during a heated seminar discussion at the University of Toronto in 1954, the exact details of which have been obscured by time and conflicting recollections. In any case, Williams's descriptions of psychological experiments dealing with the spatial perceptions of the blind ("auditory space") resonated with Tyrwhitt's descriptions of Giedion's research into the darkened environments of caves first marked by the artistic activity of prehistoric humans (where echoes and touch were just as reliable as flickering and fleeting light sources) and the burial chambers of Egyptian pyramids. The possibility of a haptic spatiality that could exist outside or in addition to sight immediately struck McLuhan, who spontaneously changed Williams's "auditory space" into "acoustic space," a reformulation that forcibly (and characteristically, for McLuhan) conflated insights from the fields of perceptual psychology, anthropology, philosophy of science, and architectural history.

Fittingly, Giedion published some of his first findings on primeval or prearchitectonic space in *Explorations,* the journal founded by McLuhan's group at Toronto. There, his descriptions of the caves and their art seemed entirely compatible with McLuhan's acoustic space conception:

> Primeval art never places objects in an immediate surrounding. Primeval art has no background. This is apparent in such large murals as the ceiling of Altamira as well as in the small ritual objects of *art*

> *mobilier.* This is inherent in the prehistoric conception of space: all linear directions have equal right and likewise all surfaces, whether they be regular or irregular.[126]

For Giedion, exploring historical space conceptions was part of a postwar research agenda that sought to ground modernist aesthetics in the most primal sources. If this was beginning to become apparent in the seminal *Space, Time and Architecture,* the conflation of the ancient and the modern would fully manifest in *Mechanization Takes Command*; *Architecture, You, and Me*; and most especially the two volumes of *The Eternal Present.*[127] In these two volumes, McLuhan found particular inspiration in Giedion's descriptions of prehistory and primeval conceptions of space and cosmos. This mythologized prehistory was a period, according to Giedion, of energetic and formal cosmic unity, in which magical animistic forces pervaded the surrounding world and, according to Spyros Papapetros, constituted "an uninterrupted continuity between human, animal, vegetal, and mineral substances: Men and women turned into bulls and deer, just as their genitals and other body parts could transform into crystalline stalagmites and merge with the rock surface."[128]

It was this fluidity of cosmic forces, natural forms, and their interpenetration with humanity that appealed to McLuhan. This fed his hope that prehistoric man, or "tribal man" (a phrase that sutured any disparities between the ancient civilizations described by archaeology and those contemporary "indigenous" societies studied by anthropologists), as he would describe him in his most popular books, existed in a sensorium that was completely different from that of modern Elizabethan and industrial man. McLuhan also shared with Giedion a profound belief in a model of spiraling historical recurrence (what Papapetros describes as a "pre/post/erous history in which the indistinct layers of prehistoric origins merge with the apocalyptic endings of *post-histoire*") that would see "electronic man" "re-tribalized," as he was fond of saying, involved once more in intimate social groupings, and ever more intimately connected with his environmental extensions.[129] "The electronic age," McLuhan wrote, "will drift quite naturally into Oriental modes of cosmic humanism and total involvement of everybody in everybody and of all spaces and all cultures converged into a kind of mosaic without walls."[130] For Giedion, history's circular movement was returning contemporary culture to an "emanating" space conception. Just as the boundless space of primeval art had connected individual and cosmos—and rejected the linear hierarchies of vertical, perspectival space—contemporary art and architecture were rediscovering this dynamic unity. "Buildings, like sculptures, radiate their own spatial atmosphere, and we have again become sensitive to the emanating powers of volumes in space," Giedion wrote.[131]

McLuhan embraced this return to primeval spatial emanation wholeheartedly, but by the time he was reading *The Beginnings of Architecture* (volume 2 of *The Eternal Present*) in the early sixties, his understanding of the phenomenon had morphed from acoustic space to all-encompassing environment—environment as ethereal but nonetheless graspable material, and totalizing extension of the entire perceiving apparatus of the human subject.[132] In this sense, he went far beyond Giedion's contemporary space conception, which, as Henri Lefebvre would charge, implicitly relied on "a pre-existing space—Euclidean space—in which all human emotions and expectations proceed to invest themselves and make themselves tangible."[133] Even emanation, in other words, had to play out *in* some space. Environment was, by contrast, space itself as emanation. If, in the past, cosmic forces had filled the vacuum of space, weaving disparate entities together into a sacred fabric of subject, object, and interval, McLuhan believed that electronics were making such unities possible once more.

To be more precise, such unities were immanent. They were forming and reorganizing social life whether or not the affected (or effected) subjects were aware of it. The capacity of electronics to register these systemic changes provided, for McLuhan, an opportunity for—not a guarantee of—phenomenological access and a degree of technical manipulability. In this sense, we can discern the peculiar ambivalence of McLuhan's environment. The new electronic and information environment both intensified and offered a way to perceive (and therefore resist) its "brainwashing" effects. This environment—the environment of the "circuit"—allowed change to accelerate so rapidly that it could finally be perceived, albeit in very particular ways. "As data can be processed very rapidly we move literally into the world of pattern recognition, out of the world of mere data classification," McLuhan wrote. He went on to observe that "if the environment or process of change gets going at a clip consistent with electronic information movement, it becomes very easy to perceive social patterns for the first time in human history."[134]

Pattern recognition was literally the ability to model different environments based on new sensory modalities or organizations. The electronic age had brought with it the possibility of configuring and reconfiguring the sensory world of individuals and cultural groups. As the architect, artist, or executive manipulated these perceptual variables, people in differently programmed environments could experience different space conceptions—different constructions of reality. These experiences produced a kind of comparative overlay in which distinctions and similarities between these environments would produce perceptible forms. This was pattern, for McLuhan.

Ultimately, this patterned environment was a particular intensification of space as ecstatic perception—a phenomenological mode of "embodied," reintegrated sensation. By the same token, it was an apparatus, a biopolitical suite of conditioning technologies.[135] The Cartesian and Euclidean voids that had once surrounded the subject were being sutured into tightly knit assemblages capable of resolving artificial modern hierarchies of inside and out, foreground and background, mind and matter. "For twenty-five hundred years of artistic history," McLuhan would say, "the arts have been engaged in separating man from his environment. Now, suddenly, the western world plunges with this new technology into a state in which man is once more engaged in merging with his environment."[136] Electronics would render space itself as a kind of proprioceptive substance, malleable and "programmable."

This implied a more visceral relationship with space itself, as a saturating, involving field, replete with the stuff of human perception and interaction. McLuhan's was a rigorous explication of the "saturated latencies" of postindustrialism as "environment itself," as the bringing forward of backgrounds and intervals that had previously remained moored in an invisible ether.[137] In the end, he seemed to care little whether the environment comprised "the geometry of the room," its "sensory components," or the particular content of a linguistic, mathematical, or aesthetic situation. What mattered were its newfound visibility and viscosity, qualities that rendered it designable and architectonic. "This new multisensuous world is one of making in which space is not a cavity to be filled but a possibility to be shaped," he wrote.[138] Rendered thus, the environment could then perform its ultimate task of receding once again, making way for some kind of Dionysian-Joycean-postindustrial programmer.

McLuhan himself was quick to call this new actor forth, for it was a very short leap from perceiving the outlines of environment—or feeling its visceral effects—to conceiving the means of its design. Indeed, the two were virtually the same. Once the patterns of this immersive, proprioceptive environment were discerned, according to McLuhan, a new conception of aesthetics and design became not only possible but imperative. His discourse at this moment therefore took on a distinctly operative tone and was addressed not just to the inhabitants of the new electronic world but also specifically to that world's architects and artists. "It has been said," McLuhan wrote in a 1968 essay titled "Environment as Programmed Happening," "that the present time offers us such immediate access to the entire range of cultures of other times that the architect can orchestrate different spaces, with their differing sensuous involvements, with the same freedom as the composer and conductor." "This situation," he would conclude, "puts artists and architects in a totally new role of making and generating values, where previously we had been spectators."[139] McLuhan began to see the conditioning aspects of environment not simply as a negative form of brainwashing but as an opportunity to take control of the environment and turn it toward more productive, human ends. He maintained that humanity, instead of merely undergoing passive environmental conditioning, was now in a position to "modulate" space and time in such a way that their mechanisms could be designed.

In many statements during these years, McLuhan described this potential in terms of the creation of responsive environments that would literally (re)create various sensory worlds for therapeutic, pedagogical, or productive purposes. Indeed, subject formation would become the main focus of his theorization of environment, and he would insist that humankind should use its newfound control of environment to turn it into a "teaching machine."[140] Taking the example of childhood development, McLuhan described the child's entry into the linguistic world as synesthetic and "totally involving." Children do not learn language by reading grammatical lessons, but by constantly interacting with their surroundings. This is a level of experiential immersion that McLuhan hoped to bring to everyone: "It will be possible in this generation, I hope, to *program the environment* in such a way that we can learn a second language as we learned our mother tongue, rapidly and totally, as a means of perception and of discovery."[141]

In a letter to Hall, he elaborated a bit more on the specific functionality such an environment might entail:

> It is possible to design a computer-controlled space in which the geometry of the room, as well as all its other sensory components, could be precisely varied. Groups of students could be taught various types of problems under these controlled conditions. Depending on their cultural and perceptual bias, one could discover exactly the focus for the various senses which would enable them to learn any given problem in math or biology or language at maximal speed. These levels would in turn reveal the sensory parameters of the culture. A Chinese could be provided with an environment which would enable him to see the West as if it were the East.[142]

Here we see the programmed environment as a cross-cultural teaching tool, made possible by the designer's access to the sensory worlds of subjects from varying cultures. But an experimental classroom was only the most immediate, realizable application. McLuhan soon extended propositions about this total environment to all levels of design activity. In a letter to Jaqueline Tyrwhitt, he wrote: "My own phrase for city planning is that the city has become a teaching machine. The planner's job is to program the entire environment by an artistic modulation of sensory usage. Art is a CARE package dispatched to undernourished areas of the human sensorium."[143] Architecture, planning, and art find a new and strange form of synthesis here, meeting each other in a resonant space in which the specificity of each is sublated into generalized aesthetic interaction. "The art object is replaced by participation in the art process. This is the essential meaning of electric circuitry and responsive environments. The artist leaves the Ivory Tower for the Control Tower, and abandons the shaping of art objects in order to program the environment itself as a work of art."[144]

2

Pattern Watchers

> How can we talk about what's going on? Search for rhythms and patterns. In this stage of evolution following the death of man, the analysis moves from the study of fixed entities that are capable of ownership to the invisible transaction of the phylo/ontogenetic organism with environmental forces.
>
> —John Brockman, *By the Late John Brockman,* 1969

> I think, however, that when we talk this way, and that while those things that we talk about are quite simple and obvious, they are nevertheless somewhat mystifying and sound possibly even a little crazy to those who are not used to dealing in patterns.
>
> —Edward T. Hall, letter to Marshall McLuhan, 1962

> The shapes of mathematics are abstract, of course, and the shapes of architecture concrete and human. But that difference is inessential.
>
> —Christopher Alexander, *Notes on the Synthesis of Form,* 1966

If one term might enact or embody the peculiar paradoxes of both environment and response, it is *pattern.* It is tempting to say that patterns constituted the medium of environment as it was being elaborated during the moment under consideration in this study, but this formulation proves problematic in a number of ways, not the least of which is that pattern is also form. To be more precise, patterns proliferated at this moment as meaningful forms—perceptible sets of phenomena made not from tangible substances but from mathematical qualities such as symmetry and repetition. They were shapes pulsing in time and truncating in space, phasing in and out of material reality. They were often the only entities linking the invisible yet undeniable presence of environment with the substantiating powers of human perception. Patterns were understood as simultaneously "out there" to be recognized and potential structures to be realized. In this regard, they emerged as socio-organic-aesthetic links between the subject's internal and external worlds. Patterns could not exist in isolation. They had meaning only insofar as they were relations, translations, overlays, or filters. They existed only insofar as they modified one another. Pattern became something like the material trace of metonymic slippage, the movement from one frame of reference to another, the feeling that all of this has happened before or is happening according to plan. Patterns offered the desideratum of absolute synchronization while constantly mapping and tracing the movements of human–environment desynchronization.

The difficulty in perceiving and recording the patterns of existence lent them a peculiar polyvalence in the arts and sciences in the 1960s and 1970s.[1] They offered social scientists a potentially verifiable set of phenomena (even if these were most appropriately described in the language of aesthetics), just as they ensured a certain mathematical rigor in the work of artists and designers seeking a structural basis for spatial arrangements of all types. But the closer patterns came to being explicated as observable objects, the more they embedded themselves as attributes of the observing subject. These methodological and ontological vagaries would prove anathema to certain segments of the scientific community, but they fell directly in line with the ecological and holistic approaches of this moment and became the veritable raw material for systems-based anthropologies, environmental psychology, and adaptive models of design. Pattern functioned in the 1970s as a metadisciplinary shifter whose indeterminacy was instrumentalized within the discursive and design fields—a kind of grammatical figure that could seamlessly alter frames of reference, shift the applicability of "data" from specific cases to general principles, or effect imperceptible reversals of figure and ground. But this mobility came at a cost. Even as they quite literally held together the precarious components of environment, patterns nonetheless threatened to reveal its fundamentally aesthetic conditions.

These generalities can be demonstrated only by a retracing of the movements of patterned objects and ideas through various institutional and disciplinary *topoi*. Some of these were realized as published documents or designed objects, but much of this activity took place in fleeting and urgent conversations, only bits of which are preserved in the archive. Let's begin there, in the midst of the formal and discursive tangle of environmental patterning. I quote in full a letter from the architect Christopher Alexander to the anthropologist Edward T. Hall, dated April 30, 1970:

> Dear Ed,
>
> Mayer Spivack wrote to me recently, and said you and he had had some discussions about patterns and he asked me to send you a draft of a chapter he had read, which might interest you, and perhaps help clarify some of the discussion. The chapter discusses the problem of writing a pattern.
>
> The pattern language itself is functioning now—and within a month or two we shall be starting to publish it, as a kind of contin-

> ually up-datable journal. I hope you like it when you see it, and that you will contribute some patterns of your own to it.[2]

An architect writing to an anthropologist at the behest of a psychiatrist, and that term, *pattern*, pinning their parallel discourses to an ostensibly common project—but what, exactly, was this project? And what did patterns allow these specialists to articulate about the human–environment system?

In order to begin to answer these daunting questions, I focus in this chapter on the work and networks of Edward T. Hall, whose research formed an important point of overlap among the diverse fields sharing a stake in the environmental research manifold. Hall was both a translator of disparate (and seemingly incompatible) data from these various fields and the author of his own unique insights into patterns. He pioneered a scientific notation system he called proxemics and was one of several postwar writers to theorize the notion of human "extensions" discussed in chapter 5. Ultimately, Hall worked in the efflorescence of that lingering modernist utopianism that aspired to reorganize the patterns structuring the subject's interior and exterior worlds.

It will quickly become apparent how Hall's work functioned in the professional milieus of architecture and planning in the late 1960s and early 1970s. He served as expert witness and consultant, an individual uncannily well placed to offer observations on the human shortcomings of the contemporary built environment and the basic tenets that might be followed in order to reform it. The latter would prove difficult, however, and architecture's attempted assimilation of immaterial human patterning would end only when the limits of the architecture–environment interface were demonstrated.

Hall devised proxemics initially as an informal and poetic descriptor of human–environment patterning but would eventually systematize it into a rigorous notational system that could be processed with the aid of computers. Hall would position proxemics as a kind of disciplinary panacea—a method that could empirically verify the existential material of life itself, that could quantify human interactions with others as well as the surrounding world. Proxemics was thus an early model for social constructionism, with the significant proviso that Hall refused to relinquish the belief that such systems of construction could be observed and analyzed as if from a distance.

Pattern Recognition

The strange mixture of quantitative and qualitative properties that constituted both environment and pattern was recognized by one very unlikely observer: the famous literary agent, intermedia pioneer, and promoter of "intermedia kinetic environments" John Brockman, whose words I have borrowed for one of this chapter's epigraphs. In 1969 Brockman published something of an unacknowledged masterpiece in the history of what would come to be known as posthumanism. It was titled *By the Late John Brockman* and was inspired by a conversation that Brockman had with Hall in which the latter speculated about a moment in human history when "cave men" arrived at a self-conscious realization they were using language—that "we're talking."[3] This observation was revelatory for Brockman because it unmasked what he felt was a natural, innate phenomenon as an invention, as an artificial construct or extension that profoundly altered the course of human evolution. Brockman then identified virtually all other human systems or extensions as equally artificial and, accordingly, the human subject as little more than an agglomeration of artificial systems, an "abstraction." His prose poem began with his own epitaph "John Brockman, 1941–1969" (Brockman is still very much alive at this writing) and, on the next page, the single sentence "Man is dead." Instead of the classical subject viewed as the seat of reason and will, the *res cogitans,* Brockman described all of life as a series of transactional events among equally transient systems. The subject became just one more porous element in a patterned network of other such elements.[4]

In a sense, Brockman took patterning much further than Hall, who remained, like his friend Marshall McLuhan, a modernist who felt that patterns might yet be optimized toward an ameliorative goal. Nonetheless, Hall's acquaintance with Brockman, and with many other figures in the design and art vanguard in the postwar period, speaks to the broad scope of his research program and his desire for his anthropology to improve everyday life for as many people as possible. Patterns, and the subject's place within them, had been an integral component in Hall's work since he began writing for an academic audience.[5] He also understood these as indelibly tied to lived space and time. Hall was an expert in what would come to be called nonverbal communication—body language and other types of unspoken, even unconscious movements, gestures, and postures that, if understood, could be decoded like any other language. In 1970, Ray Birdwhistell described such communication as the "patterned interdependence of human beings."[6]

Trained as an anthropologist in the 1930s, Hall moved among government, private, and academic positions for the rest of his career. In several positions, beginning in 1950 at the Foreign Service Institute (a federal training institution founded under President Harry S. Truman), he worked with businesspeople, technicians, and diplomats who traveled overseas and dealt with foreign cultures, seeking to acclimate them to the behavioral atmospheres they were about to encounter. Even when communicants were fluent in a given verbal language, different cultural contexts produced different behavioral patterns and different conceptions of time and space, which, if misunderstood, could lead to disrupted communication, resulting in the loss of vast amounts of money, wasted energy, and even risk to human lives. During his travels, Hall made careful observations of myriad unconscious activities undertaken in different countries. He postulated, for instance, that Arabs needed to be close to the person they were talking to and preferred frequent physical contact; they were flummoxed when dealing with Anglos who required at least eighteen inches of space between themselves and their conversants, and who kept their arms folded in front of their chests, or at their sides.

Such episodes of "culture shock" seem unsurprising (and reductionist) to us now, but at the time Hall's observations had the force of revelation. His work seemed to hint at an entire world of experience resting just below the threshold of human perception. Culture, which was always a pattern, was for him an "ether" that flowed between all things, a medium for every act of human perception, creation, and communication.[7] The problem with culture, however, was that it was nigh impossible to see and feel, and therefore the average person was totally unaware of the ways in which culture determined his or her worldview. This lack of awareness in turn led to interpersonal as well as cross-cultural pattern interference, the tensions of the Cold War, and the failures of negotiations between different groups, whether in business mergers or hostage crises. For Hall, culture was indelibly linked to environment, and patterns were the structures that ordered both.

This became Hall's stock-in-trade: being able to see and describe this invisible cultural environment. It was an environment made up of tangible entities and invisible patterns governing the subject's relation to them. Hall could somehow evoke these, render them in everyday language, bring them forward to perception in a compelling way. There was always a sense that he could see a world that others could not. His only recourse was the comparative study of patterns: to observe the behaviors of members of one culture and superimpose them onto the members of another—to observe that Arabs deal with personal space differently than Americans; that Mexicans understand money in fundamentally different ways than the Japanese; that children communicate in a "high-context" format, while scientists rely on a "low-context" symbolic language; and so on. It was a project fixed uncomfortably between existential speculation and the basest types of essentialism.

Hall's first effort at a comprehensive study of communicational patterns was his 1959 *The Silent Language*. As the title suggested, it described how there were worlds of meaning in the ways people carried themselves and interacted, but these worlds were hidden to all but the most perceptive. The book drew largely on Hall's experiences as a consultant and appeared just before he took a teaching and research position at the Illinois Institute of Technology. Returning to the world of institutional anthropology proved difficult for Hall. He was a holistic thinker, his system a total one. He had trouble readjusting to the mandates of academic research requirements, strict specialization, verifiability, and "laboratory" conditions. Most of his work fell outside these narrow confines; indeed, it was about the formation of such confines in the first instance.

Which is not to say that Hall did not believe in scientific observation or quantifiable methods. He did; it was simply that the phenomena he intended to observe could not be quantified with any existing system. Thus, in the wake of the incredible success of *The Silent Language,* he began to craft his own notation system that could record the universe of intersubjective nuance laid before him. He christened the system *proxemics,* a name that indicated that space was the main organizing feature of the patterns he wished to describe. Both roots of the neologism were spatial: the *proximal* was a measure of relative, subjective distance, while the *emic* was an indication that the observations made were from an interior position. (In anthropology, the complementary *etic* suffix is used to denote an observer foreign to, or outside, the phenomena being recorded in the field; it also indicates a greater degree of objectivity.)

Hall's fascination with space and environment was already apparent in *The Silent Language,* where he described "the elaborate patterning of behavior which prescribes our handling of time, our spatial relationships, our attitudes toward work, play and learning."[8] Indeed, Hall published his book as a way of bringing "culture" to the consciousness of the reader and sharing his understanding that "behind the apparent mystery, confusion, and disorganization of life there is order." He described this order further as a kind of musical score: "Man was able to exploit the potential of music only when he started writing musical scores. This is what must be done for culture."[9] In another context, writing about method, he made the connections between pattern and culture explicit:

> Cultural systems grow informally by a process that is as yet undescribed and . . . out of awareness. . . . It is at this point that it is possible to begin to abstract from informants' responses the sets, isolates, *and* patterns that constitute the system. The current fashion of emphasizing content has stressed the sets at the expense of pattern analysis. Only by analyzing all three organizational levels is it possible to provide adequate descriptions of a cultural system. . . . The paradox is that only in translation or contrast do patterns become apparent.[10]

"Patterns," Hall wrote in *The Silent Language,* "are those implicit cultural rules by means of which sets are arranged so that they take on meaning. . . . Too little has been known about patterns and how they operate. True, the rules which hold for many aspects of culture could be quoted, but there was no theory of patterning, no account of how one analyzes and describes patterns."[11]

Hall was therefore an early (and adamant) proponent of what would soon be known as social constructionism.[12] "*Experience,*" he insisted, "*is something man projects upon the outside world as he gains it in its culturally determined form.*" He continued: "There is a growing accumulation of evidence to indicate that man has no direct contact with experience per se but that there is an intervening set of patterns which channel his senses and his thoughts."[13] In this sense, patterns determined what could be perceived. But in another instance, Hall indicated that patterns were also the objects of perception: "A pattern is a meaningful arrangement of sets" observed by groups in similar pattern families.

> A tastefully decorated room is a meaningful arrangement of sets to women who belong to the same group and who are aware of the art of decorating a room. Men are likely to look at the room as a set, to see it as one thing, and to respond to the over-all effect. What they don't see, which many women do, is the detail. It is the detail in a pattern that tells one woman so many things about another.[14]

Patterns shifted in this architectural figure, metonymically, from one scale to another, from one subject position to another, at times projected outward by the observer and at others forming a context or predetermination for what they were able to observe.

Patterns were also prone to other movements. They could exist in any medium—language, space, time, art, science. They could be retrospective or prospective, personal or social. All of this shifting might make the category seem meaningless, or at least not fit for scientific observation. For Hall, however, it was just a matter of time and methodological refinement. He had already identified three laws of patterning: order, selection, and congruence. Order indicated acceptable sequences (typically diachronic) for patterns, selection determined how patterns could be combined with one another, and congruence represented a kind of metalaw of pattern, "a pattern of patterns."[15] Congruence, Hall wrote, "is what all writers are trying to achieve in terms of their own style, and what everyone wants to find as he moves through life. On the highest level the human reaction to congruence is one of awe or ecstasy. Complete congruence is rare. One might say that it exists when an individual makes use of all the potentials of a pattern."[16] At this level, pattern appears as something sublime, as a full recognition of the hidden webs connecting the worlds of perception and experience. Indeed, Hall indicated, the scientific study of congruence was in its infancy, and only in the world of art was congruence to be found.

That patterns (at a certain level) were fundamentally spatial was also something Hall indicated in *The Silent Language.* One of the last chapters, titled "Space Speaks," was perhaps the one that most captured the attention of the public, especially that of architects and designers struggling with the questions of the moment: the human scale, hierarchies of needs, the urban crisis, design methods, and so on. Hall's observations emerged alongside those of Jane Jacobs and Kevin Lynch, for instance, who were also contributing to a multidimensional understanding of the built environment, one based not on the strict dictates of modernist functionalism but on the habitus created by ingrained patterns of human use and perception.[17]

Encouraged by the response to his observations, and still vexed by the methodological shortcomings of pattern analysis in the realm of human behavior, Hall set about a more focused study of how people use space and the ways in which those uses could be notated for data analysis—creating a musical score of human environmental existence, if you will. This would be proxemics, and its enumeration would occupy him for more than a decade.[18] During that time, proxemics never really attained the status of scientific method, existing instead in a tantalizing nether region of sociocultural potentiality, promising to unlock the secrets of "how man unconsciously structures microspace" (as proxemics was defined at one point).[19] Hall chose the term itself for its suggestiveness, rejecting other neologisms such as: "human topology, *chaology* (the study of boundaries), [and] *choriology* (the study of organized space)."[20]

It almost goes without saying that such a science failed to find a ready-made research method. No singular body of "laws" could account for the complexity of phenomena Hall observed, and no laboratory could reproduce the conditions of the "natural" environment in which proxemic events took place. As a result, proxemics became a synthetic method, a kind of dynamic repository of observations, data, and procedures taken from virtually every realm of inquiry, from the hard sciences to the social sciences and the humanities. Hall relied on Heini Hediger's studies of spatial distance in animals, Erving Goffman's concept of the "facade," James J. Gibson's perceptual psychology, Humphry Osmond's notions of sociopetal and sociofugal spaces, Ray Birdwhistell's kinesics, Charles Hockett's structuralist linguistics, and Benjamin Lee Whorf's models of linguistically constructed realities. Hall also made special mention of several nonscientific sources that had guided his research: Maurice Grosser's *The Painter's Eye,* Alexander Dorner's *The Way beyond "Art,"* R. Buckminster Fuller's theories of technology, Sigfried Giedion's work, Marshall McLuhan's theories of communication and environment, and Ernö Goldfinger's 1940s essays on spatial experience.[21]

Hall's capacious interests derived at least in part from his self-described pragmatism, and from his willingness to work beyond the confines of strict scientific method. He sought out anyone who might be able to help him observe and articulate the patterns he felt intuitively around him. He made some of his key contacts in the late 1940s during a teaching stint at Bennington College, where he became friends with Erich Fromm, through whom he met many of the key figures in transactional psychology. Hall taught about cultural perception in Alexander Dorner's classes, was the professor of Allegra Fuller (who introduced him to her father, Buckminster

Fuller), and had regular counseling sessions (Bennington required weekly meetings between professors and students) with many of the dancers in Martha Hill's studios, who, he claimed, taught him a great deal about nonverbal communication through their discussions about choreography.[22]

In all of these disparate sources, Hall recognized patterns of spatial experience as yet unidentified by any single science. In their own respective ways, these sources (and the many others on which Hall drew) were all about the new environment, expressed as a dynamized conception of space, context, interval, or structure. Many of these quasi-utopian pronouncements also presented examples of the "congruence" Hall was seeking—a new synthesis of humanistic and scientific disciplines that was both descriptive and critical, diagnostic and operative. But this synthesis was elusive. Any path to it was caught up in the very cultural patterns it sought to analyze. Such a project amounted to observing the mechanisms of observation itself.

Perhaps this complexity accounts for some of the appeal of the spatial/environmental component in Hall's work, which provided a kind of visual model, or metaphor, of immersion that illustrated the difficulties involved in tracking proxemic phenomena. Hall's most complete and influential account of proxemic patterning was addressed to this spatial aspect of his interests. The 1966 publication of *The Hidden Dimension* would secure Hall's fame among the design professions and send his research, and that of his wife, Mildred Reed Hall, into a distinctly architectural direction for the next decade.

The Hidden Dimension, like Hall's earlier book, posited culture as a subconscious arrangement of patterns determining human behavior. But the task of revealing these patterns had only grown more urgent in the five years since *The Silent Language* appeared. Urban crises were intensifying and technological change was speeding up, and, as Hall viewed it, all this was taking place without the benefit of an understanding of the most basic premises of how humans interact and use space. The built environment seemed an immediately accessible subject in this regard, and Hall sought to reach administrators, as well as architects, with his observations. He began with some very basic premises, noting that "while buildings and towns cannot make up for social injustice, and much more than good city planning is needed to make a democracy work, there is still a close link between mankind and its extensions. No matter what happens in the world of human beings, it happens in a spatial setting, and the design of that setting has a deep and persisting influence on the people in that setting."[23] (This, of course, was a recapitulation of the entire ethos of responsive environments at the time.)

In this sense, *The Hidden Dimension* brought the built environment into the orbit of Hall's concerns with cultural patterning. And once again, this patterning was indelibly bound to the ability (or inability) to perceive the ways in which space both constrained and was constrained by socially or subjectively constructed realities. Hall again referenced the difficulties of grappling with the cultural mediation of experience, writing:

> People from different cultures not only speak different languages but, what is possibly more important, *inhabit different sensory worlds.* Selective screening of sensory data admits some things while filtering out others, so that *experience as it is perceived* through one set of culturally patterned sensory screens is quite different from experience perceived through another. The architectural and urban environments that people create are expressions of this filtering-screening process. In fact, from these man-altered environments, it is possible to learn how different people use their senses.[24]

Here, just as patterns had before, the architectural figure moves from object of perception to perceptual frame. This oscillation was not uncharacteristic of the nature of the responsive environment as I have been elaborating it here. In addressing the ways in which humankind was transcending its biological fate, Hall formulated a very nice definition: "The relationship between man and the cultural dimension is one in which both *man and his environment participate in molding each other.* Man is now in the position of actually creating the total world in which he lives, what the ethologists refer to as his biotope. In creating this world he is actually determining *what kind of organism* he will be."[25]

Indeed, this biological foundation would be apparent throughout *The Hidden Dimension.* The chapters moved from discussions of territoriality and implications of overcrowding in animal populations to the topic of sensory perception before ending with several cross-cultural proxemic analyses. Hall included two lengthy analyses of biological experiments: a study of deer populations on James Island in Maryland by John Christian and his colleagues, and, more famously, a controlled study of rats conducted by John B. Calhoun in a barn in the town of Rockland in the same state.[26] Both studies revealed that overcrowding had implications beyond simply affecting the availability of food (the Malthusian doctrine). In both instances, as populations swelled, biochemical and behavioral changes occurred in the animals. Endocrine levels (and, presumably, stress) rose measurably, which led to erratic behavior and death.

In Calhoun's pens, crowding induced the rats to deviate from most normal patterns associated with mating, social hierarchies, and feeding. At a certain point, when the population density got high enough, Calhoun observed a "behavioral sink": "the outcome of any behavioral process that collects animals together in unusually great numbers. The unhealthy connotations of the term are not accidental: a behavioral sink does act to aggravate all forms of pathology that can be found within a group."[27] Here, it seemed, was an ethological proof for the problems of the inner city and the failures of modern housing projects, to name only the most obvious examples.

These were the connections made by Tom Wolfe, for instance, when he spent time with Hall for a *New York* magazine article in 1966:

> I just spent two days with Edward T. Hall, an anthropologist, watching thousands of my fellow New Yorkers short-circuiting themselves into hot little twitching death balls with jolts of their own adrenalin. Dr. Hall says it is overcrowding that does it. Overcrowding gets the adrenalin going, and the adrenalin gets them hyped up. And here they are, hyped up, turning bilious, nephritic, queer, autistic, sadistic, barren, batty, sloppy, hot-in-the-pants, chancred-on-the-flankers, leering, puling, numb—the usual New York, in other words, and God knows what else.[28]

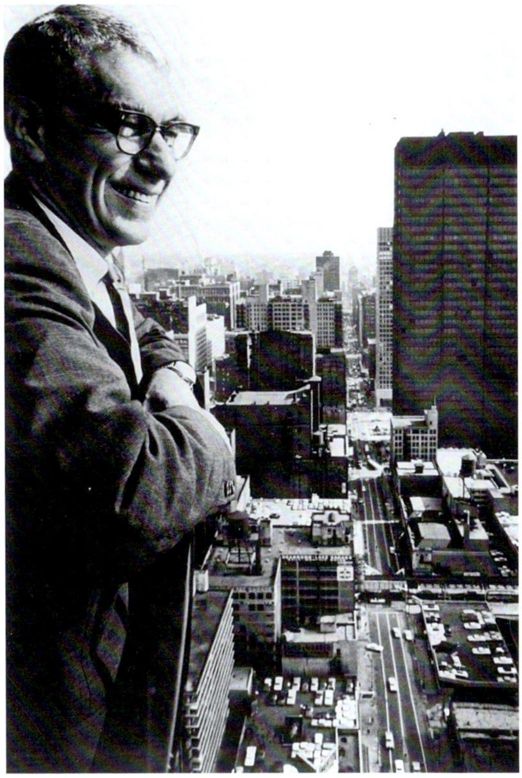

Figure 2.1. Edward T. Hall around the time of his interview with Tom Wolfe. The two visited Grand Central Station, ascended to the Pan Am Building, and then took a car up to Harlem to observe human behavior in different social settings. University of Arizona Libraries, Special Collections: Edward T. Hall Papers. Courtesy of Karin Bergh Hall.

In Wolfe's report, his description of standing with Hall and looking down into Grand Central Station was very much like Calhoun's description of looking into his rat pens in Rockland:

> The floor was filled with poor white humans, running around, dodging, blinking their eyes, making a sound like a pen full of starving rats or something.
>
> "Listen to them skid," says Dr. Hall.
>
> He was right. The poor old etiolate animals were out there skidding on their rubber soles. You could hear it once he pointed it out. They stop short to keep from hitting somebody or because they are disoriented and they suddenly stop and look around, and they skid on their rubber-sole shoes, and a screech goes up. They pour out onto the floor down the escalators from the Pan-Am building, from 42nd Street, from Lexington Avenue, up out of subways, down into subways, railroad trains, up into helicopters. . . .
>
> They screech! And the adrenal glands in all those poor white animals enlarge, micrometer by micrometer, to the size of cantaloupes. Dr. Hall pulls a Minox camera out of a holster he has on his belt and starts shooting away at the human scurry. The Sink![29]

"You could hear it once he pointed it out." This was Hall's role, in a sense, to perceive the invisible structures and patterns filling cultural space, structures that few others could perceive.

He set about this task methodically, defining the anthropological study of space according to three proxemic attributes of the environment: "fixed-feature space," "semifixed-feature space," and "informal space." In Hall's formulations, "features" were not necessarily physical—they were combinations of obdurate things and equally obdurate (or modifiable) patterns. Fixed features, then, included not only walls and buildings that could not be moved but also the cultural conventions that had dictated their positions in the first place—the streets themselves as well as the tradition of the Roman grid. Accordingly, semifixed features included furniture along with the interpersonal patterns seen in the use of furniture in different types of spaces—the proverbial park bench and its users, positioning themselves relative to each other. The last proxemic category described by Hall was perhaps the most significant, primarily because of its insidious nature: "I have called this category *informal space* because it is unstated, not because it lacks form or has no importance. Indeed . . . informal spatial patterns have distinct bounds, and such deep, if unvoiced, significance that they form an essential part of the culture. To misunderstand this significance may invite disaster."[30]

Proxemics was meant to enable the precise measurement of this synthesis of natural and cultural history and the intersubjective patterns it both comprised and produced. It was a quantification of what Goffman had described as "the stuff of encounters," which arose for Hall whenever two subjects met and "there was interference between two patterns, or a perceived absence of patterning, during an encounter."[31] If proxemic observation was to attain the status of scientific verifiability that Hall intended (he bristled at the many characterizations of his work as anecdotal or qualitative), researchers had to be trained in its basic premises, and a consistent notational system had to be implemented. Hall began to formalize the latter in 1963. On this occasion he outlined a minimal program for quickly notating what he believed to be the eight basic components of human interactions in environments:

1. postural–sex identifiers
2. sociofugal–sociopetal orientation (SFP axis)
3. kinesthetic factors
4. touch code
5. retinal combinations
6. thermal code
7. olfaction code
8. voice loudness scale[32]

The notation system was meant to quantify the meaningful variations of the behavioral "proxemes" listed above: the irreducible units of bodily

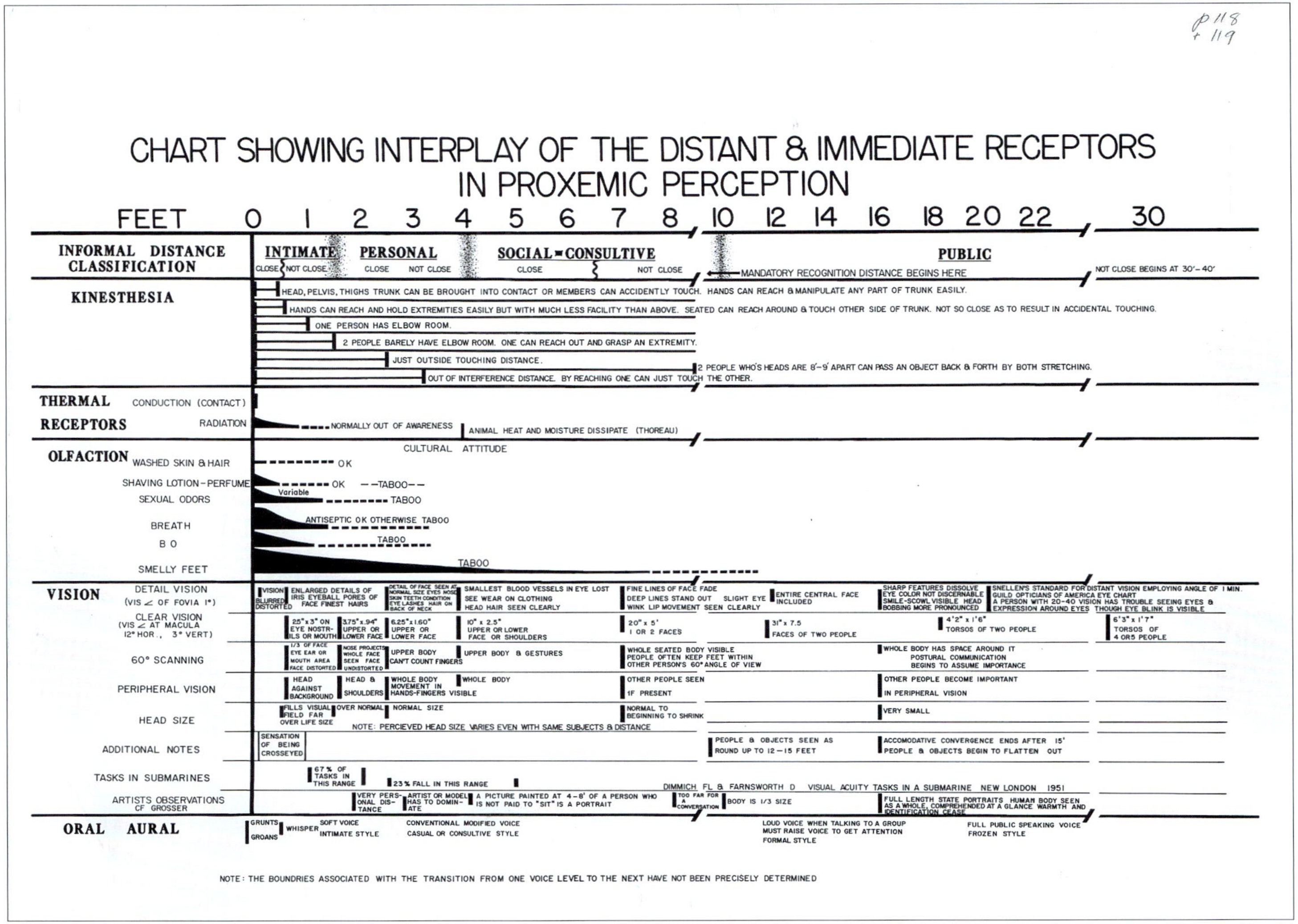

Figure 2.2. "Interplay of the Distant and Immediate Receptors in Proxemic Perception." The human sensory apparatus is subjected to a spatial and cultural graphing, and spheres or bubbles of personal space are registered by different sense organs. University of Arizona Libraries, Special Collections: Edward T. Hall Papers. Courtesy of Karin Bergh Hall.

and perceptual interactions of subjects among themselves and with their surroundings. Did people face one another, and at what distance? Could physical contact occur if desired? Was regular eye contact maintained? Could the heat of the other's body be felt, or that person's smell be registered? Further, what consistencies could be observed when these phenomena were recorded for large numbers of people? Did patterns emerge that could be linked to specific social groups, genders, and so on? All of these variables were assigned pictographic and numerical values; Hall thought that the pictographs would be used initially, but that the number values, once memorized, would be favored for efficiency and eventual computer input.

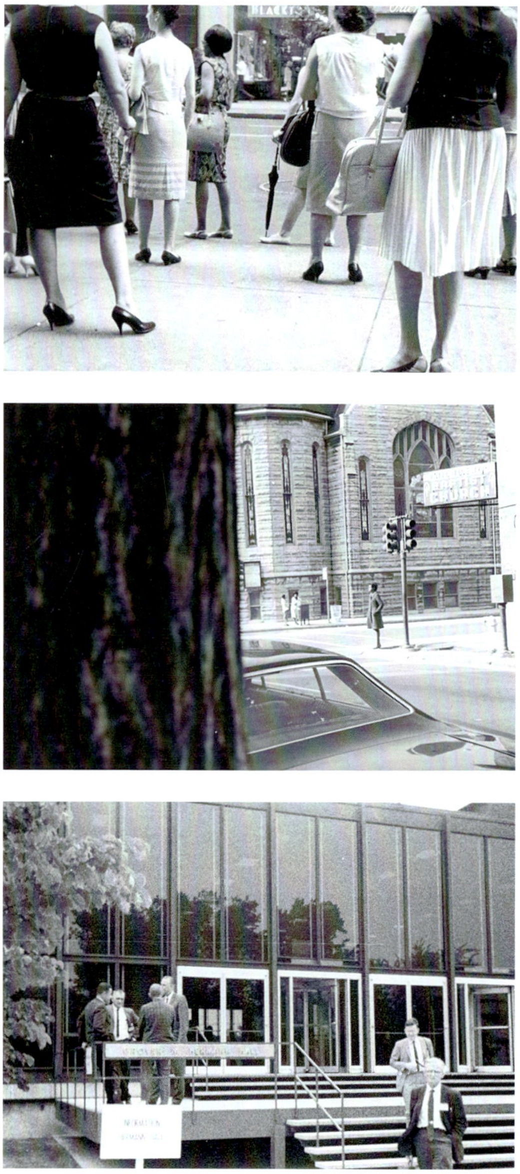

Figure 2.3. A selection of photographs of unidentified subjects in public spaces for proxemic analysis. These were most likely taken in Chicago circa 1965. University of Arizona Libraries, Special Collections: Edward T. Hall Papers. Courtesy of Karin Bergh Hall.

At both this earlier stage and later, Hall's data collection and analysis methods were themselves patterned in interesting ways. They were also significantly mediated by specific regimes of visuality, public versus private space, and various levels of cultural enfranchisement. Perhaps the most interesting permutation of the method involved working from photographs. These could be taken of different groups of people at various scales or distances. The photographs would then be traced, so that racial and social markers were removed from the figures. The resulting outlined groupings would, in turn, be notated for their proxemic structures—how close people stood to one another, how their bodies were oriented toward (or away from) others during conversation, physical contact, eye contact, and so on. The notations were then aggregated and attributed back to certain racial or social profiles.

Many of the photographs Hall notated were taken circa 1965, just a year or two after he took up his position at IIT (Plates 2 and 3). Chicago would prove to be a charged atmosphere in which to proxemically analyze the interactions of people in different racial groups. Much of the material that survives in Hall's archive is therefore concerned with the patterned interactions of African Americans and white Americans in their own spaces and in various spaces of encounter. Hall's specific

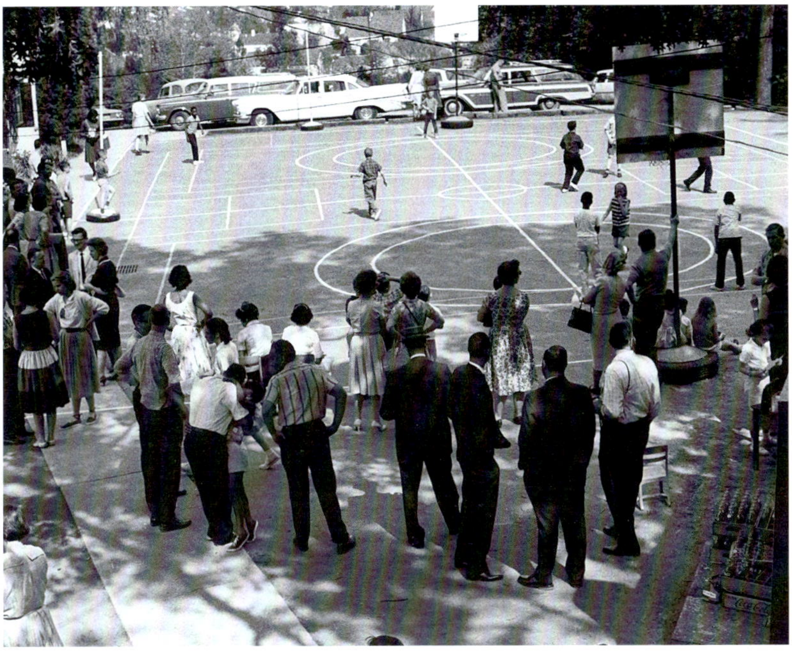

Figure 2.4. Photograph of a crowd at a school basketball court, with a tracing and complete notation of a similar image. The photographs were traced to eliminate many of the visual clues that might trigger unconscious bias on the part of the observer. University of Arizona Libraries, Special Collections: Edward T. Hall Papers. Courtesy of Karin Bergh Hall.

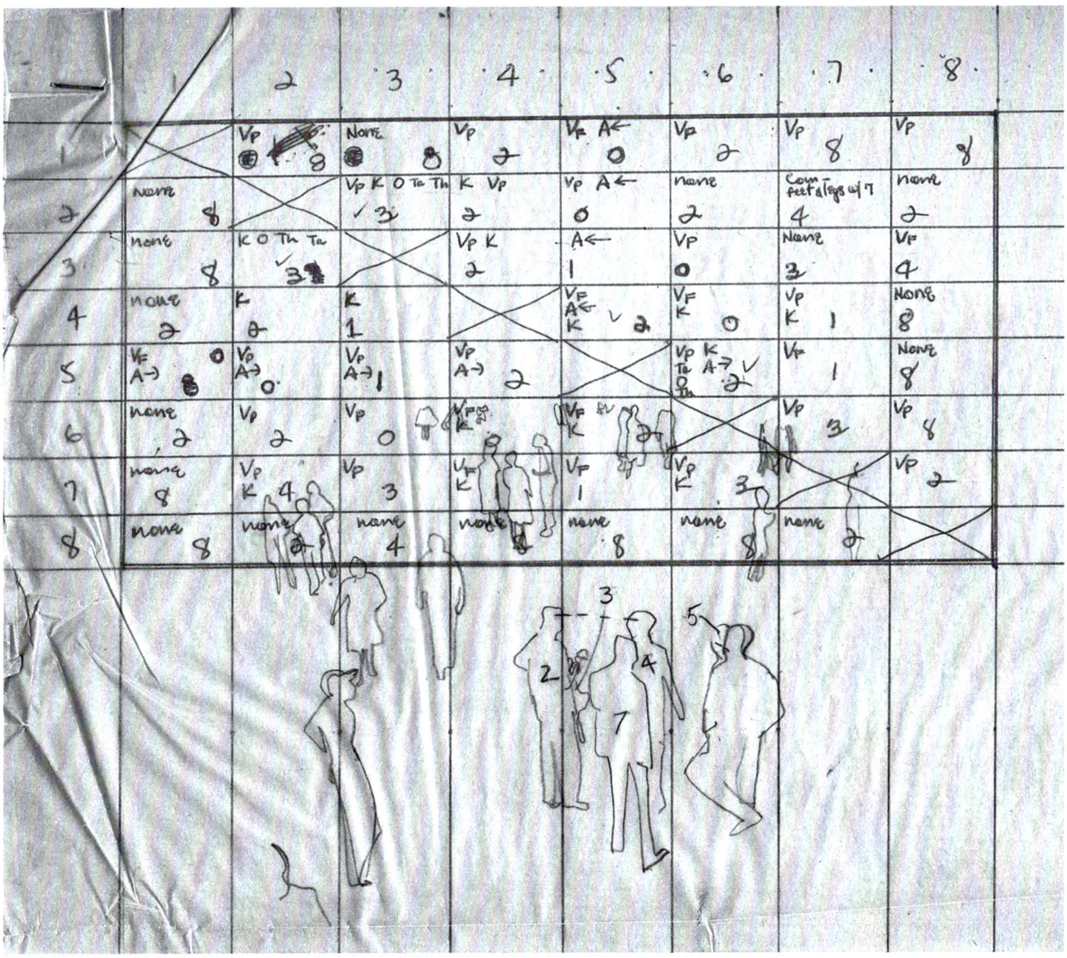

research program and the methods he developed for utilizing proxemics are detailed in the 1974 *Handbook for Proxemic Research.*[33] This is a fascinating text because, even though it presents itself as a technical manual for the implementation of proxemics as an observational science, it is actually a diaristic account of the heuristics of cross-cultural communication patterns and how to record these for analysis (by computer or otherwise). Hall's ostensible goal in producing the book was to codify proxemics as a coherent and objective system of notation—one that could describe behavioral patterns numerically for (ultimately) computer input.[34] It also became a record of extremely complex pattern interactions among several types of actors: researcher, subject, interpreter, technician, photographer, and so on. Here, Hall was inspired to test a host of solutions to the problems of bias in data collection, examining instances in which observers' own cultural patterns may have influenced their interpretation of behaviors.

"The proxemicist never judges; he only records what's happening," Hall wrote.[35] Nonetheless, his heuristic implementations of proxemic notation revealed a continually biased dynamic, one in which cultural patterns impeded direct pattern recognition. In this regard, the attempt to establish the proxemic method became a deep dive into the social construction of reality. Hall was never naive enough to believe he could transcend the cultural frame projected in any observational setting, but he did arrive at an observational and notational system that he felt could account for that frame. "The way I've set up the program," he wrote, "is that one should be able to compare—using a computer—just about any transaction at any point in time at any place on the globe and the effect of the observer on that transaction, as well as the effect of the person who is coding the data on both of them. It's an elaborate program."[36]

An elaborate program indeed—one that apparently required Hall to become more and more aware of the patterns structuring proxemics itself. He established a laboratory at IIT, and from 1964 to 1966 he conducted field research in Chicago. The initial impetus for the project was to help African American members of the Isham YMCA JOBS program hone their job interview skills (as the program originally provided technical job training alone). Hall's goal was to "learn as much as possible about how the JOBS trainees used space, the meaning of intrusions, how they read each other's behavior and emotions."[37] Hall set about this work by constructing a model office adjoined to a blinded observation space (subjects were aware they were being observed and recorded). Hall's intuition was that cultural miscommunication contributed to the poor performance of working-class African Americans in interview situations, which typically involved middle-class white interviewers. He tested this by constructing an office space that included systems of screens, walls, and cameras elaborated so that subjects could be properly insulated from the influence of the observing apparatus. He also took great pains to select for the roles associated with the research, initially using his own (white) research assistants to conduct interviews and then switching to interviewers from the same

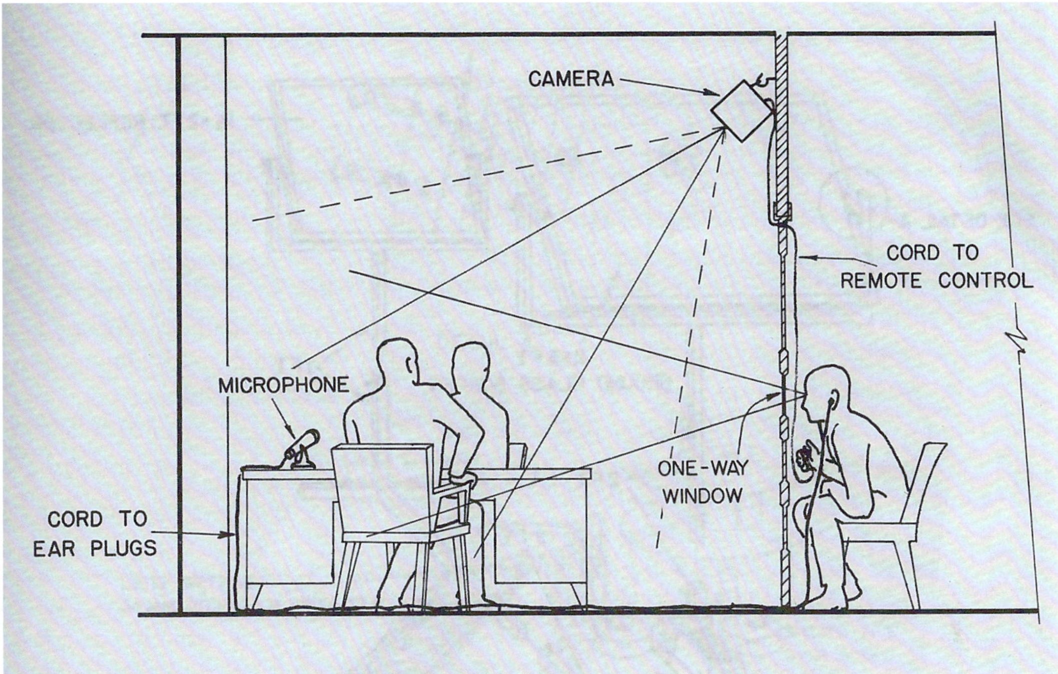

Figure 3. Interview office showing placement of camera and observer.

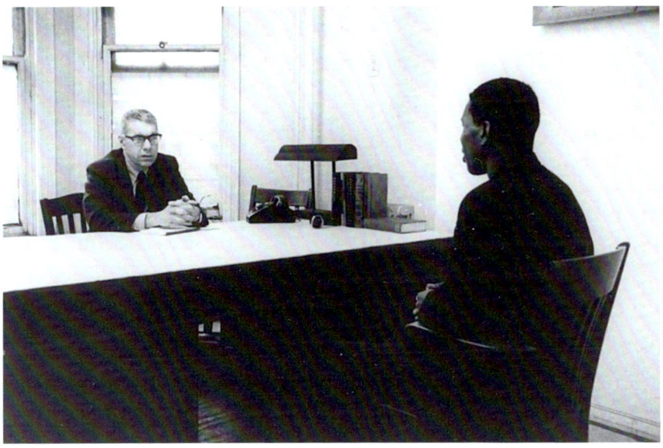

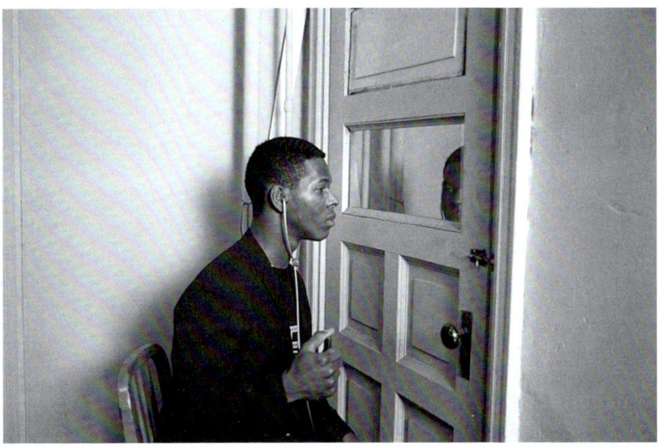

Figure 2.5. Interview office from Edward T. Hall's research on section from Edward T. Hall, *Handbook for Proxemic Research* (1974); Edward Hall interviewing subject (circa 1965); subject takes on the role of observer. University of Arizona Libraries, Special Collections: Edward T. Hall Papers. Courtesy of Karin Bergh Hall.

social/racial community as the interviewees, among other modifications to the interview scenario.

Indeed, no sooner was the laboratory setting established than it began to undergo a series of modifications. In time, these modifications would become the subject of the research as much as the individuals in the JOBS program, because Hall realized that every subject position within the interview setting was enmeshed in cultural patterns—from the interviewer to the interviewee to the person controlling the camera and microphone and finally to the person observing and coding the visual and audio records. Hall began to rotate researchers and subjects through these positions, first asking interview subjects to take on the role of the interviewer, then asking them to record the sessions on film, and then having them participate in the review of the proxemic data. In these scenarios, the JOBS trainees became much more than receivers of wisdom from cultural "gatekeepers," as Hall called them. They became proxemicists themselves, attuned to the invisible patterns involved in "*the use of micro-space in interethnic encounters*."[38]

For Hall, this work revealed that individuals truly existed in their own sensory realms, and that their very realities were determined by their cultural patterns. A gatekeeper conducting an interview in the real world could perceive only the content of the interviewee's comportment, not the patterns dictating that comportment. In cases where these patterns were not shared by the involved parties, behavioral cues were consistently misinterpreted in both directions, even when the content of verbal statements was communicated clearly. Even in this highly controlled environment, context imposed constantly shifting patterns of environmental reality that simply could not be perceived by most people. As these mechanics became more evident, Hall's research focused increasingly on the methods of recording and interpreting the proxemic data. Proxemics was used effectively to observe its own means of observation.

Each interview was recorded by camera and microphone as well as by a live observer. These live observations (during which, presumably, notations were made) were supplemented by secondary analyses of the recorded films. However, Hall found that in order for the proxemic content of a situation to be properly "released" to the person performing the secondary analysis, a very high degree of immersion in the images was necessary. For this reason Hall designed and constructed a special viewing apparatus using a projector and a rear-projection screen to magnify and place the filmic image as close to the observer as possible, allowing the person "to make full use of foveal vision," which was key in avoiding distraction and projecting oneself fully into the filmic space.[39] This device, which at first glance appeared to be a rather elementary assemblage of film equipment, ground glass, and aluminum struts, was in reality an apparatus designed to transcend perceptual patterning. It ostensibly pulled the observing subject so close to the recorded document that the subject's own culturally patterned screen was penetrated.

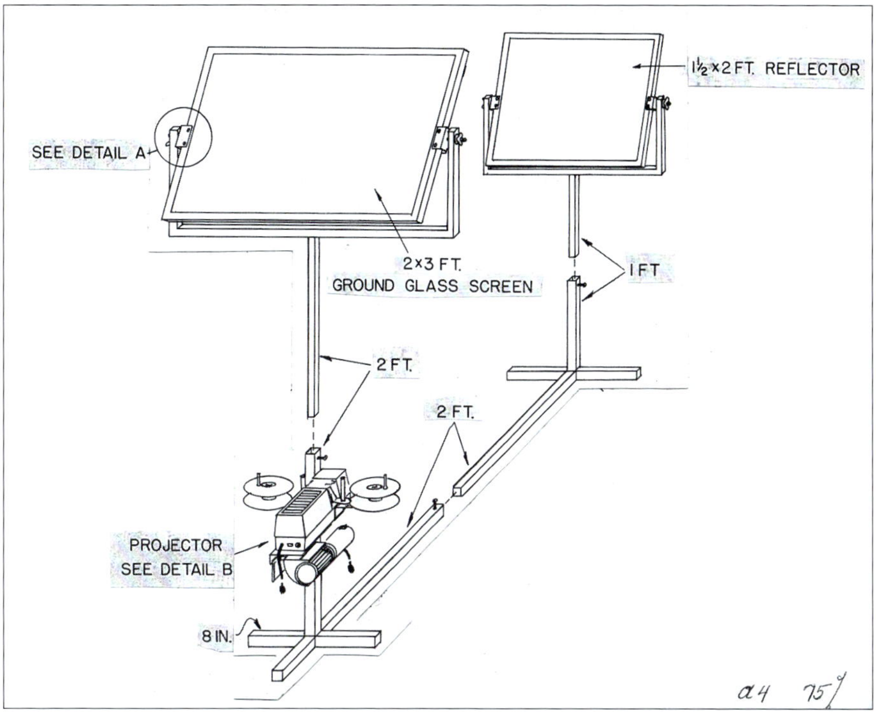

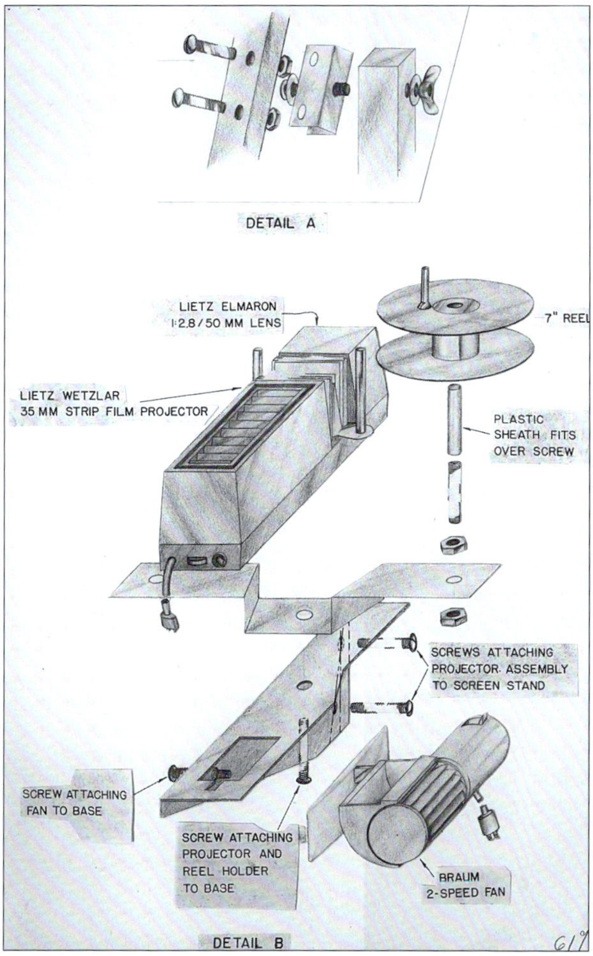

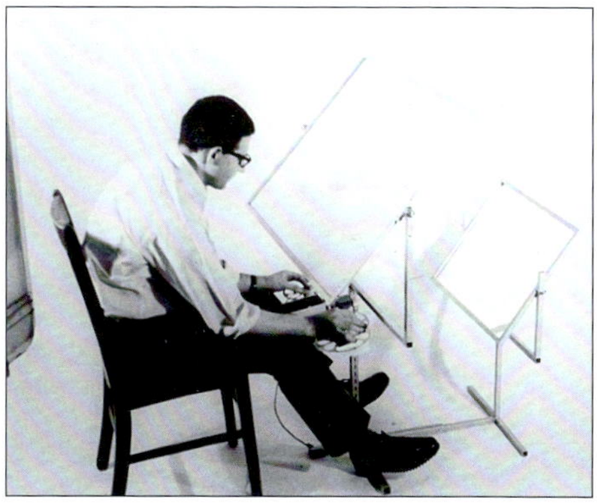

Figure 2.6. Projection apparatus for proxemic immersion/notation, circa 1966. University of Arizona Libraries, Special Collections: Edward T. Hall Papers. Courtesy of Karin Bergh Hall.

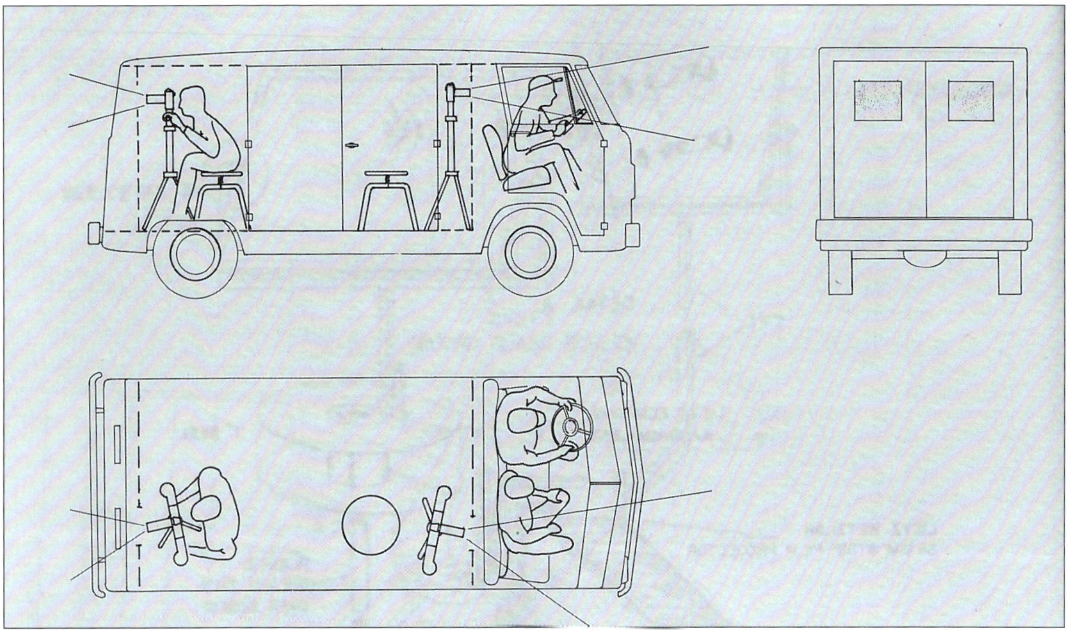

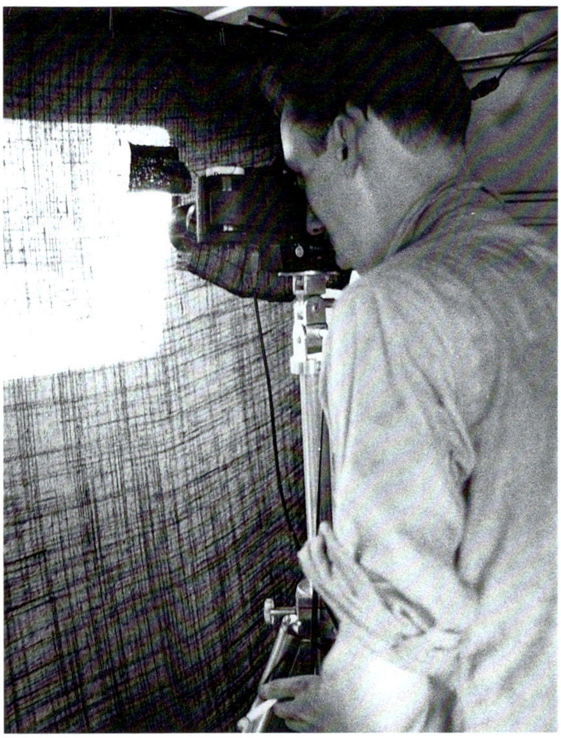

Figure 2.7. Section and plan of the camera-equipped panel truck; a researcher working from the truck. *Handbook for Proxemic Research* (1974). University of Arizona Libraries, Special Collections: Edward T. Hall Papers. Courtesy of Karin Bergh Hall.

Similar considerations also drove the design of a mobile research unit for observations made in the "field." This was a van that could be taken into the streets of Chicago to record the interpersonal activities of people in their "natural" environments. Thousands of photographs were produced from these experiments, all of which could potentially be traced and coded for their embedded proxemic data. These images are disturbing, of course, for their imposition of a surveillance condition on the subjects in question. Nonetheless, Hall was strict about their handling. In addition to protecting the anonymity of the subjects (itself troubling in the way it reduced them to fauna glimpsed in the wild), Hall's projection/immersion apparatus was used to notate the filmic evidence obtained.

But as much as Hall's notations were meant to capture the fleeting patterns of human interactions *in* space, and as much as it seems as though he was starting from scratch in these endeavors, it must be acknowledged that around the same time other notational systems dealing with space and architecture were being developed. As early as 1961, Hall wrote to Kevin Lynch to praise the "ingeneous *[sic]* system that [he] had developed for getting people to note down what they had seen as they traveled a standard route."[40] Equally, he was fascinated by Phillip Thiel's "A Sequence-Experience Notation for Architectural and Urban Spaces," which Thiel introduced with the following very telling metaphor: "Architecture may well be 'frozen music,' like a phonograph record; but man is the pickup whose movement realizes the experience."[41] Thiel shared Hall's desire to write a kind of score for human experience, and he was also inspired by some of the same sources: Lynch, Kepes, and McLuhan, for instance. But perhaps it was the choreographer and landscape designer Lawrence Halprin who had the most direct impact. Halprin's notion of scoring in urban space was essential to the development of Hall's proxemic notations, which would likewise attempt to account for the affordances in a given environment and the subject's ostensibly conscious responses to them. Hall also noted his debt to a series of essays by the architect Ernö Goldfinger that appeared twenty years prior in the *Architectural Review.*

These remarkable essays must be counted among the first documents of any environmental or architectural psychology. They also deal very directly with the perception of space and its effect on the human body and mind. Indeed, Goldfinger's stated purpose was to explicate the ways in which "enclosed space" had "biological" implications for both human "psychology" and "physiology."[42] Counterintuitively, though, Goldfinger's understanding of "enclosed space" was not strictly architectural. Indeed, he believed that the human subject was always within enclosed space, whether that space was a room, a street, or a clearing in a forest. In this sense, spatial enclosure became perceptual and territorial; it involved quantitative aspects, such as scale, as well as the qualitative responses of subjects. These Goldfinger illustrated in a series of sketches that placed human figures in a number of spatial situations, confined by distant, ethereal territorial boundaries or tightly encased in structures such as plaster

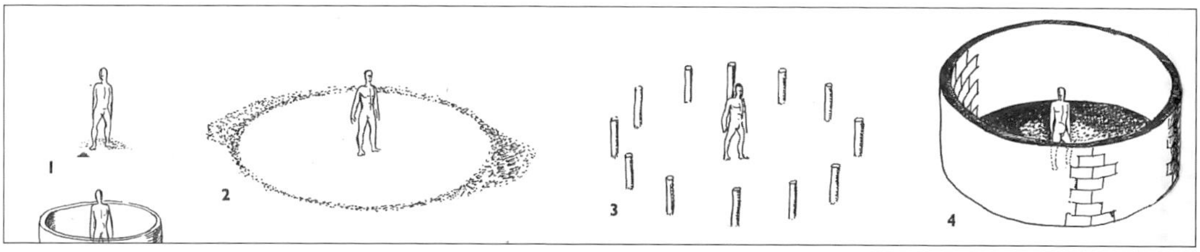

Figure 2.8. "1. A Person standing free in a limitless desert. 2. surrounded by the imaginary barriers of a pattern. 3. the barrier has become more tangible, but the sensation is still mainly suggested. 4. the barrier is real." From Ernö Goldfinger, "The Sensation of Space," *The Architectural Review* 90 (November 1941): 128–31. Courtesy of *The Architectural Review.*

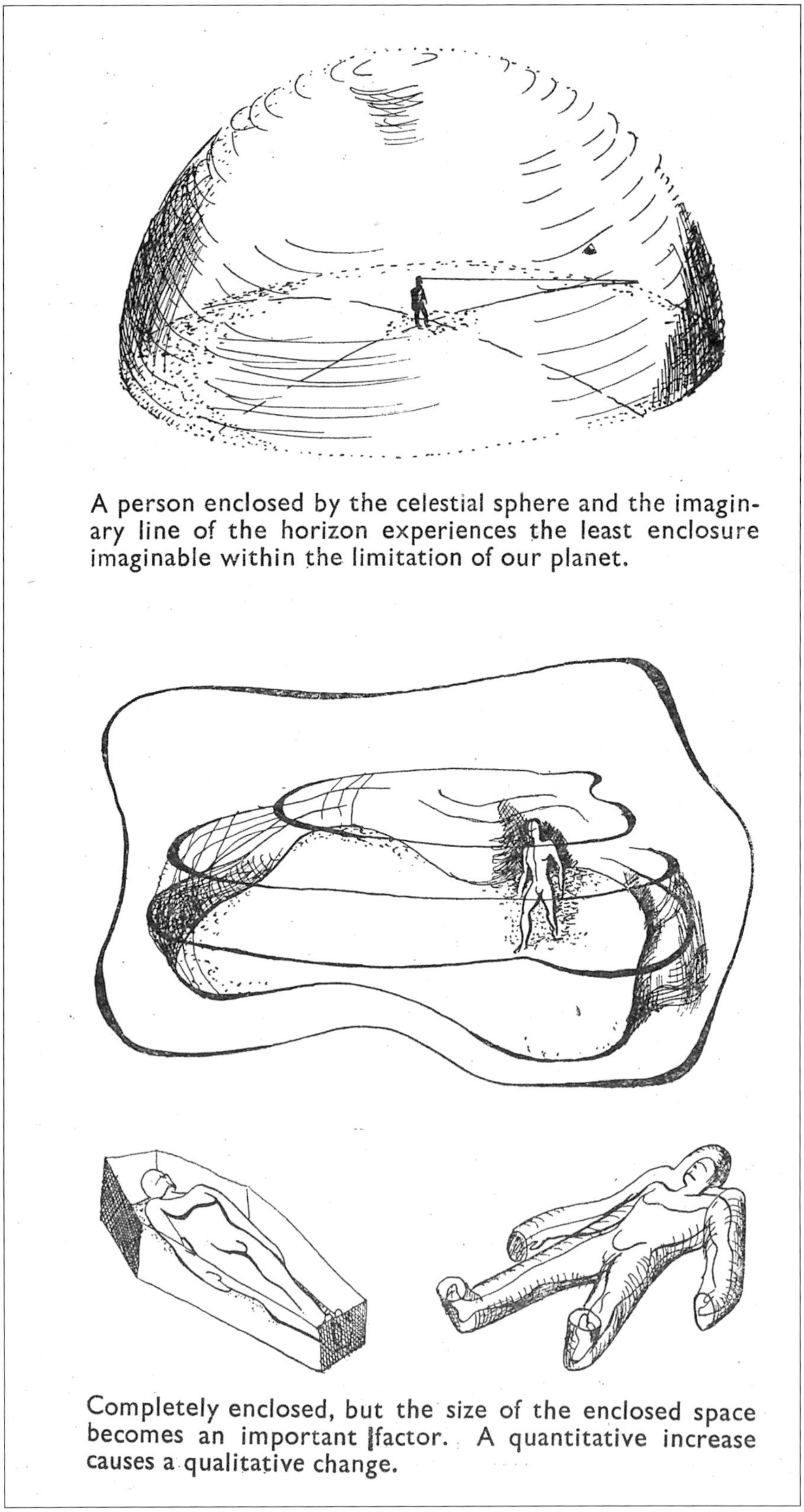

Figure 2.9. Always enclosed: these drawings demonstrate the ways in which the human experience of space can be determined by material or immaterial boundaries. From Ernö Goldfinger, "The Sensation of Space," *The Architectural Review* 90 (November 1941): 128–31. Courtesy of *The Architectural Review.*

casts or coffins. These little drawings strongly resemble Frederick Kiesler's illustrations of human environments of these same years (see chapter 3). One sequence shows the building up of the physical substantiality of enclosing structures. Initially, a figure stands alone in "a limitless desert." The next step in establishing a sense of enclosure is not a physical wall but "the imaginary barriers of a pattern."[43]

I speculate that Goldfinger's psychological nuance, and especially his radical understanding of "enclosure" (defined as much by human perceptual capacities as by physical structures), impressed Hall a great deal and encouraged him to develop one of his most enduring motifs: a conception of an attenuated humanity, a subject caught up in invisible patterns, stretched and flattened by the tensions produced by the conflicts between current fixed-feature spaces and informal space.

These dynamics played out very literally in the space around the subject. This image of an individual simultaneously at the center of a set of cultural and physical patterns and pushed by them toward some unknown margin would inform another of Hall's enduring motifs, in which the human being did not simply interact with the solid fixed features of a given space but projected a kind of immaterial "bubble" around him- or herself, the dimensions of which were determined by cultural patterning. Hall arrived at this conception by doing away with the traditional notion "that man's boundary begins and ends with his skin." Instead, he wished to replace this model with one that included "man as surrounded by a series of expanding and contracting fields."[44] For Hall these fields were generated by both biology and culture:

> Every living thing has a physical boundary that separates it from its external environment. Beginning with the bacteria and the

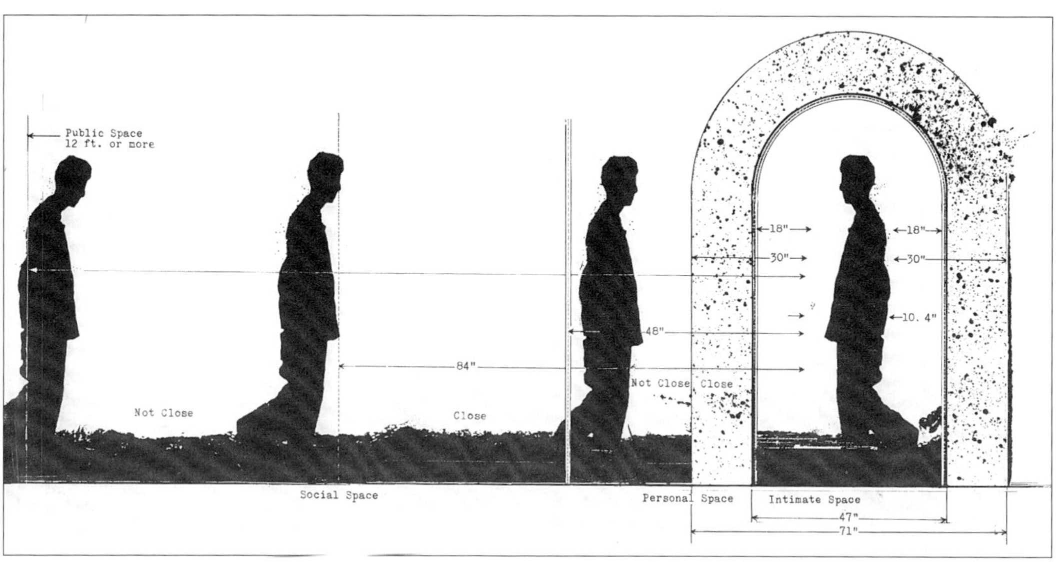

Figure 2.10. Proxemic distances or bubbles from public space to intimate space. Illustration from Edward T. Hall, "Proxemics and Design," *Design & Environment* 2, no. 4 (Winter 1971): 25.

> simple cell and ending with man, every organism has a detectable limit which marks where it begins and ends. A short distance up the phylogenetic scale, however, another non-physical boundary appears that exists outside the physical one. This new boundary is harder to delimit than the first but is just as real. We call this the "organism's territory." . . . Man has developed his territoriality to an almost unbelievable extent. Yet we treat space somewhat as we treat sex. It is there but we don't talk about it. And if we do, we certainly are not expected to get technical or serious about it.[45]

The nonphysical boundary described by Hall was not explicitly architectural, yet it implicated architecture as an "extension" of the organism, as defining the boundary of its existential bubble. Hall's bubbles were generated out of a kind of feedback loop with architecture proper, defined by it but also distorted by it. The shape of the sphere, for instance, derived very literally from domed architectural spaces. To be more precise, Hall was inspired by Sigfried Giedion's phenomenal descriptions of historic building types and tectonic principles:

> The potential of the dome and the vault in creating "superspace" was not realized until the first five centuries A.D. by the Romans. The capacity was there but the awareness of the relationship of man to large enclosed spaces was not. Western man did not see himself in space until much later. As a matter of fact, man has only gradually begun to fully experience himself in space on the level of everyday life using all his senses.[46]

Giedion's image of the domed "superspace" provides Hall with a spherical architectural figure, physically echoing the "bubble" projected by the subject. By the same token, Hall's bubbles were the "spherological" translation of pattern into actual space.[47] They were immaterial projections that nonetheless constrained the subject's behavior in the world. They were perhaps the key in moving from the more abstract realm of relational pattern into the physical world of building: "If, however, one sees man surrounded by a series of invisible bubbles which have measurable dimensions, architecture can be seen in a new light."[48]

Proxemic Architecture

Proxemics would prove tantalizing for the design professions, which had been grappling with quantifying and instrumentalizing even the most basic data regarding human needs and environmental response.[49] Hall became something of a celebrity within the architectural profession. Even before the publication of *The Hidden Dimension* he had consulted on Christopher Alexander's plans for the San Francisco transit system, BART, and had addressed the housing question for governmental organizations at city, state, and federal levels. He was often a passionate advocate for better environments for underrepresented populations. While working in Washington, D.C., toward the end of the 1950s, he spoke out against a plan to utilize only artificial lighting in new school buildings. Later, in the 1970s, he was enlisted as an expert witness in a class action suit against the D.C. prison administration; his testimony concerned the "environment" of the facility in question, which he argued was tantamount to corporal punishment, would heighten stress and aggressivity, and so on. He contracted with the National Bureau of Standards, an agency of the U.S. Department of Commerce, to consult on a "Building Systems Innovation Project," with the aim of helping the project incorporate proxemic principles. In 1971, Hall and Mildred Reed Hall conducted an elaborate study of the inhabitants and environment of the Pruitt-Igoe housing project in St. Louis. Obviously, their recommendations to humanize that particular environment went unheeded. The Halls undertook this project while also working on a lengthy study of the behavioral aspects of Eero Saarinen's John Deere Headquarters building in Moline, Illinois (more on this study below).

In addition to these more civic/scientific activities, Hall had a significant impact on vanguard architecture culture. He was invited to present guest lectures at various meetings of the American Institute of Architects as well as a plethora of architecture schools, mostly after 1966. In 1964, while at IIT, Hall collaborated with John Entenza to organize a lecture series for the Graham Foundation that treated "the general theme of recent scientific developments of interest to architects in the field of perception and the relationship of man to his environment."[50] Also, thanks to his Chicago connections, he had a productive relationship with architect Bertrand Goldberg. He contracted with Goldberg to produce a study of the social benefits of the latter's Stony Brook Health Sciences Center project (1967) and, subsequently, River City, a mixed-use residential and commercial project in Chicago (1972–86). Hall corresponded frequently with architects overseas as well, most notably Ernö Goldfinger and the Italian designer of bombastic buildings Manfredi Nicoletti, who became one of Hall's most vocal proponents in Italy. Not surprisingly, Hall was also friendly with many in the emerging environmental research manifold: Ian McHarg, Lawrence Halprin, Aristide Esser, Alton De Long, and many others.

Proxemics appeared to many of these institutions and individuals as one key to synthesizing the disparate parts of a fragmented discipline. At the very moment that architecture was starting to appear as impossibly small and circumscribed in relation to an ever-expanding conception of environment, Hall offered surprisingly realizable proposals for opening architecture up to the insights provided by psychology, anthropology, economics, and cross-cultural analysis. But if proxemics held out the promise of revealing a world of hidden patterns that might form the basis of a future design method, in practice the value of its results were more

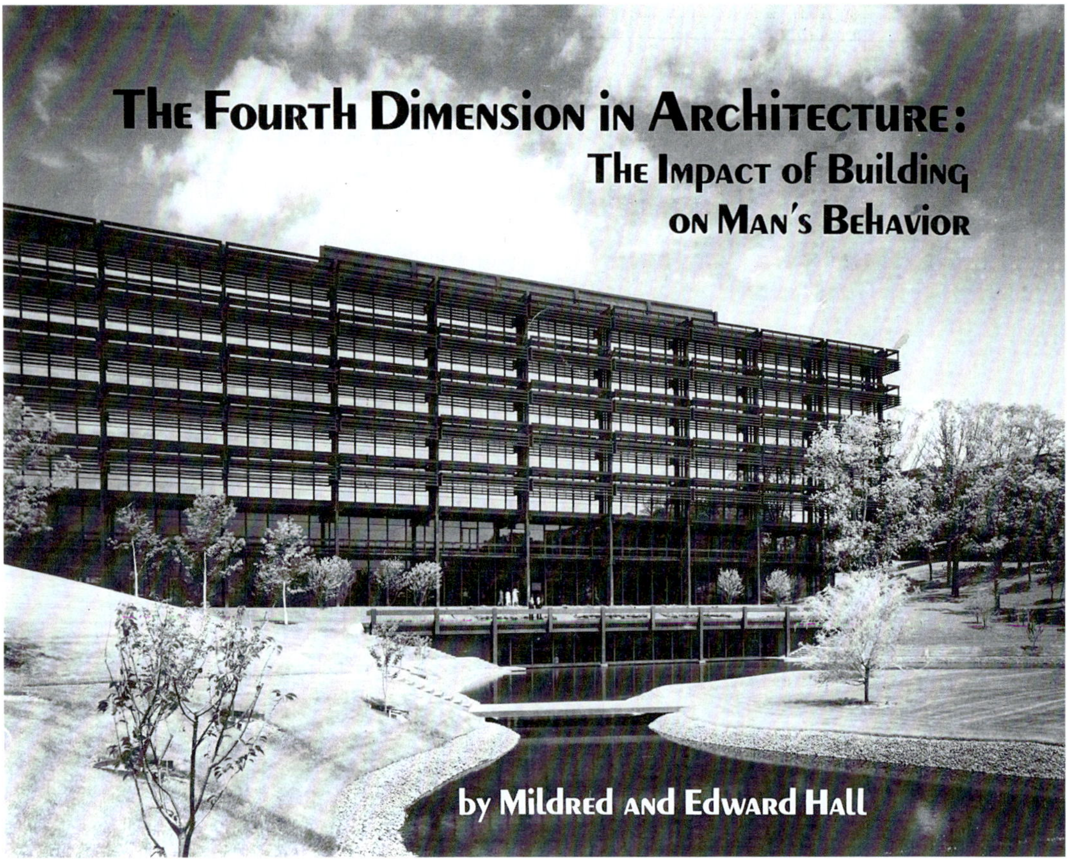

Figure 2.11. Mildred Hall and Edward Hall, *The Fourth Dimension in Architecture: The Impact of Building on Man's Behavior* (Santa Fe, N.M.: Sunstone Press, 1975). Courtesy of Sunstone Press.

ambiguous. These had a very specific instance of application when, in 1964, Hall and his wife embarked on a five-year study of the new John Deere Headquarters designed by Eero Saarinen.

Working independently, but with the full participation of company management, the Halls conducted a series of interviews with select employees, once before their move into the new structure, again just after the building opened, and then five years later. This extensive project would, in theory, provide an almost laboratory-like consistency to the usually nebulous parameters involved in usability studies and the like. Furthermore, it would provide the Halls with a concrete example for exploring their theses about the interrelatedness of environment and subject, to counter "the Western view . . . that human processes, particularly behavior, are independent of environmental controls and influence."[51] The result of their study was a book titled *The Fourth Dimension in Architecture: The Impact of Building on Man's Behavior,* a slim volume with beautiful photographs of the project by Ezra Stoller and surprisingly little insight into the book's subtitle.

The Halls' interviews revealed mixed responses to the building's organization. Its clean lines and extensive use of glass maximized its picturesque relationship to the surrounding prairies, lakes, and trees. Inside, opinions

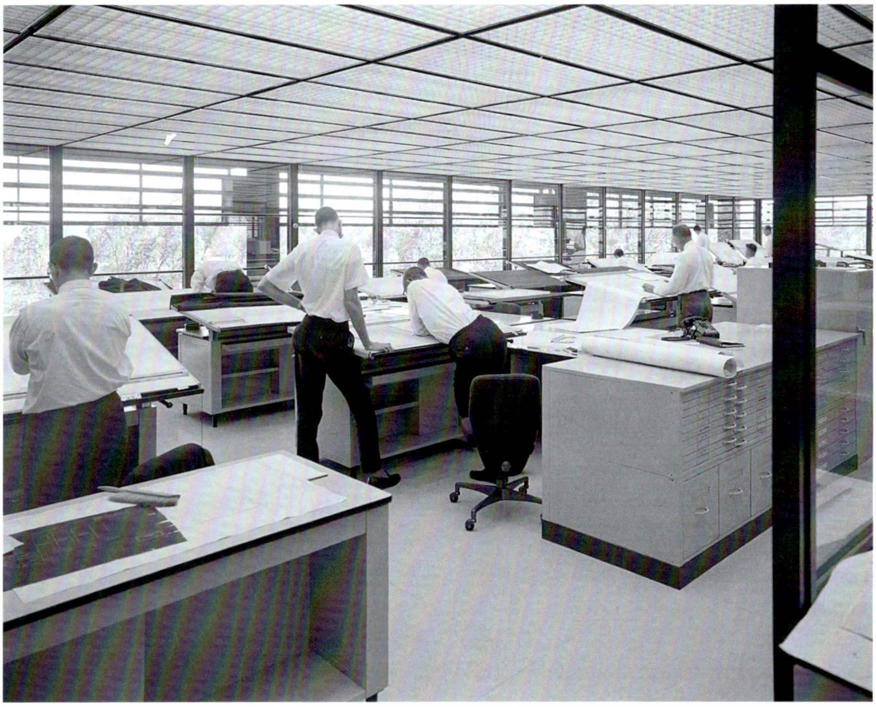

Figure 2.12. Eero Saarinen, John Deere Headquarters, Moline, Illinois (1963). Copyright Ezra Stoller/Esto.

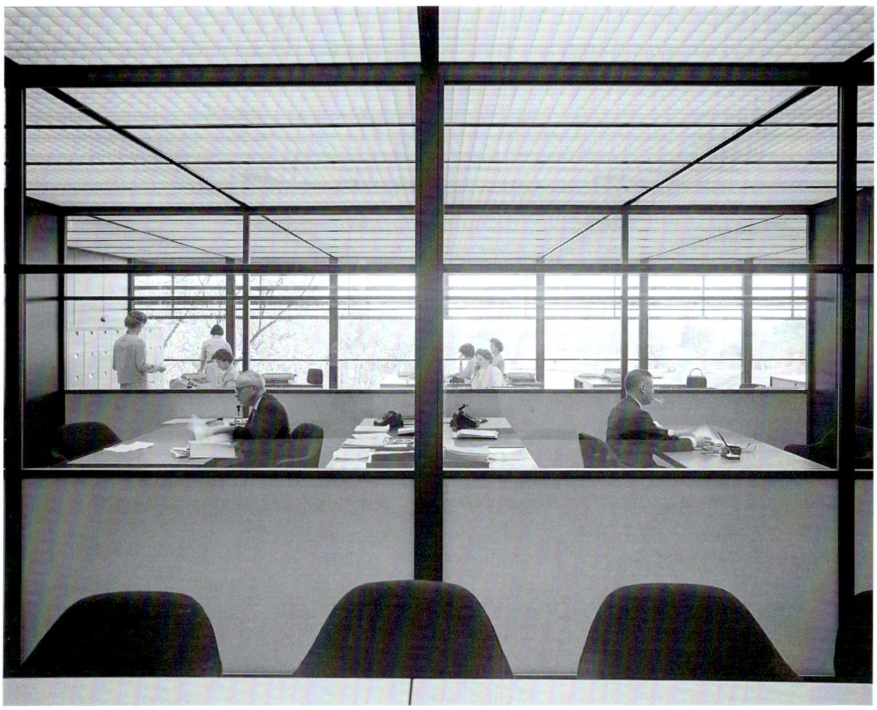

Figure 2.13. Eero Saarinen, John Deere Headquarters, Moline, Illinois (1963). Copyright Ezra Stoller/Esto.

were split on progressive gestures such as open office pens and standardized work spaces. Negative consensus was apparent regarding the lack of color in the interiors and the lack of private spaces for socializing or for women to "rest."[52] Many felt the building was "tiring." Its efficient lines and fluorescent ceiling panels apparently provided little respite for those seeking to pause in their duties. Company policy, and Saarinen's vision, dictated minimal personalization of space. Everything had to be cleaned off of desks at the end of the day. The building's remote location (most of the John Deere offices had been in downtown Moline previously) dictated that everyone utilize the company cafeteria and facilitated the shortening of lunch breaks to a half hour, a development decried by many employees.

Despite the mixed responses, the Halls were incredibly enthusiastic about Saarinen's "masterpiece." For them it embodied the proxemic proposition that environment is a behavioral determinant. Furthermore, it exemplified the related proposition that, just like people, buildings cannot be considered as isolated entities. Instead, according to the Halls, they are "'statements'—active agents in the human situation."[53] But these statements have structures. They are not bodiless mediators with no substance of their own. As the images in *The Fourth Dimension in Architecture* suggest, buildings and people enter into a relationship in which the solid frame of one entity interfaces with the other in extraphysical ways. These are neither random nor purely subjective, but are patterns that exist simultaneously in the material of a wall, in the perceptual apparatus and consciousness of the subject standing next to that wall, and in what hangs in the air between the two.

The question of how to design for such a situation—one in which every component or function is conceived relationally, within the medium of environment itself—would prove difficult to answer. Proxemics did not suggest its own design methods, much less forms appropriate to it. Implementation of Hall's and other researchers' proposals always seemed too expensive, too complex, too specific, or too abstract. But where Hall's influence was not felt deeply, it was felt broadly. Proxemics dovetailed with other types of behaviorist research programs, methods for design optimization, and various other "humanizing" initiatives.[54]

Nonetheless, there was one study that did attempt to utilize Hall's system rigorously. From October 1969 to August 1971, Sam A. Sloan, an architect working at the University of Sydney, led a small team of researchers who interviewed and observed ninety-seven clerks at the Australia Mutual Provident Society (AMP), an insurance company.[55] While no new building was designed, the office layout was changed based on the data gathered. On the one hand, Sloan's study was a modest one, affecting a small number of administrators in a much larger organization. On the other hand, the stakes could not have been higher. "The fact is," Sloan wrote, "that we have no effective way to measure the results of human criteria programming upon design. Short term economic success in terms of first cost or sale on one hand is compared to total failure in terms of riots at the other extreme."[56]

For Sloan (and many others), economic and cultural considerations prevented the adoption of new design methods. In this sense, the very modesty of this experiment—which, according to Sloan, "was little more taxing than a good rousing game of 'solitaire'"[57]—proved the architectural profession's inflexibility with regard to assimilating new types of program determinants, especially those based on the requirements and desires of end users. For Sloan, it was "doubtful that the architect who has been trained in the Beaux Arts School of design [would] ever be able to fully support a method that usurps his opportunity to exercise the mystic powers of 'the designer.'"[58] As a riposte to this attitude, Sloan emphasized personal preferences and unconscious tendencies in environmental interactions on the part of test subjects. The language he used in his report ranged from a kind of holistic, almost metaphysical prose to the most banal quantifications of the smallest behaviors. "The AMP clerk," he noted, as though describing an exotic species, "has specific sensory requirements in his everyday environment." Then:

> The body orientation preferred by most AMP clerks during conversation is quite

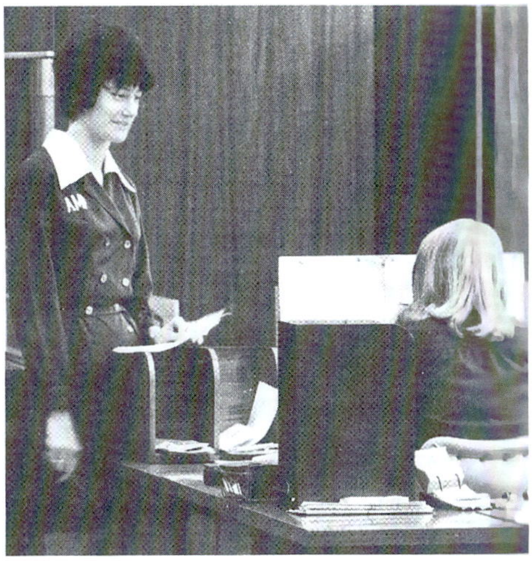

A girlfriend enters into conversation through carefully prepared slot in the fence defining the territory (it took 8 years to build)......

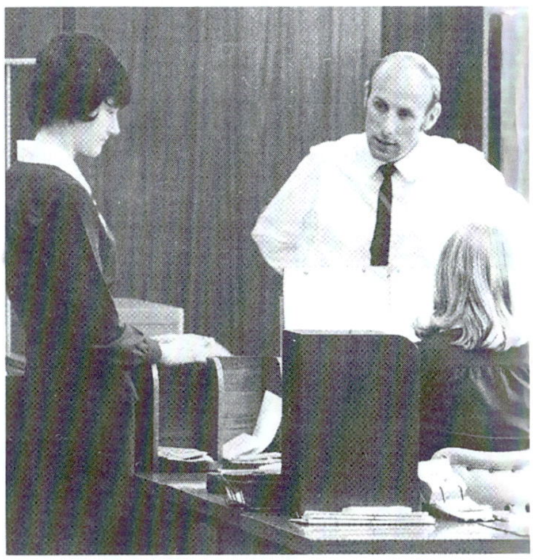

A third party enters by greeting the initial visitor and then positions himself to control the territory of the seated--owner of the space

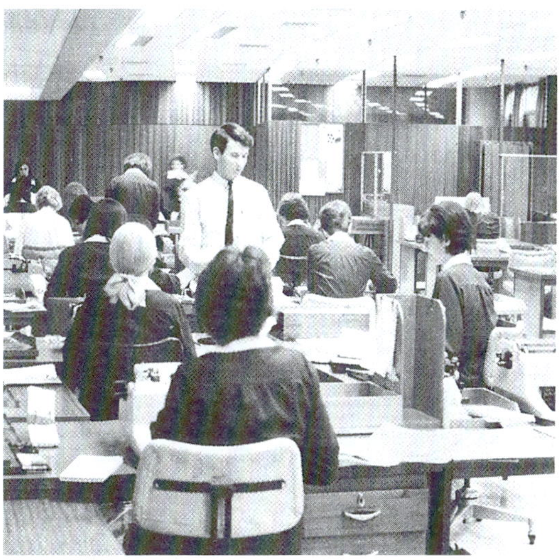

Figure 2.14. Images of clerks' interaction before layout and micro-spatial design changes were implemented in the AMP office pen. From Sam A. Sloan, "Translating Psycho-Social Criteria into Design Determinants," in *Environmental Design: Research and Practice,* proceedings of EDRA 3/AR8 conference, ed. William J. Mitchell (1972), 14.5.1–14.5.10.

> close and directly facing his conversant. 67 percent of the interactions took place with only 18 inches separating the conversants and 83 percent of the time the two were facing straight on (0°–90°). Yet in 88 percent of the interactions, there was not any body contact or other tactile contact made between the conversants.[59]

Sloan arrived at this level of detail by emulating ethological methods. Noting that "human ecological reports extrapolated from animal studies [use] their data to hypothesize human tendencies," Sloan identified three broad categories of (human) behavior: aggression, sociability, and territo-

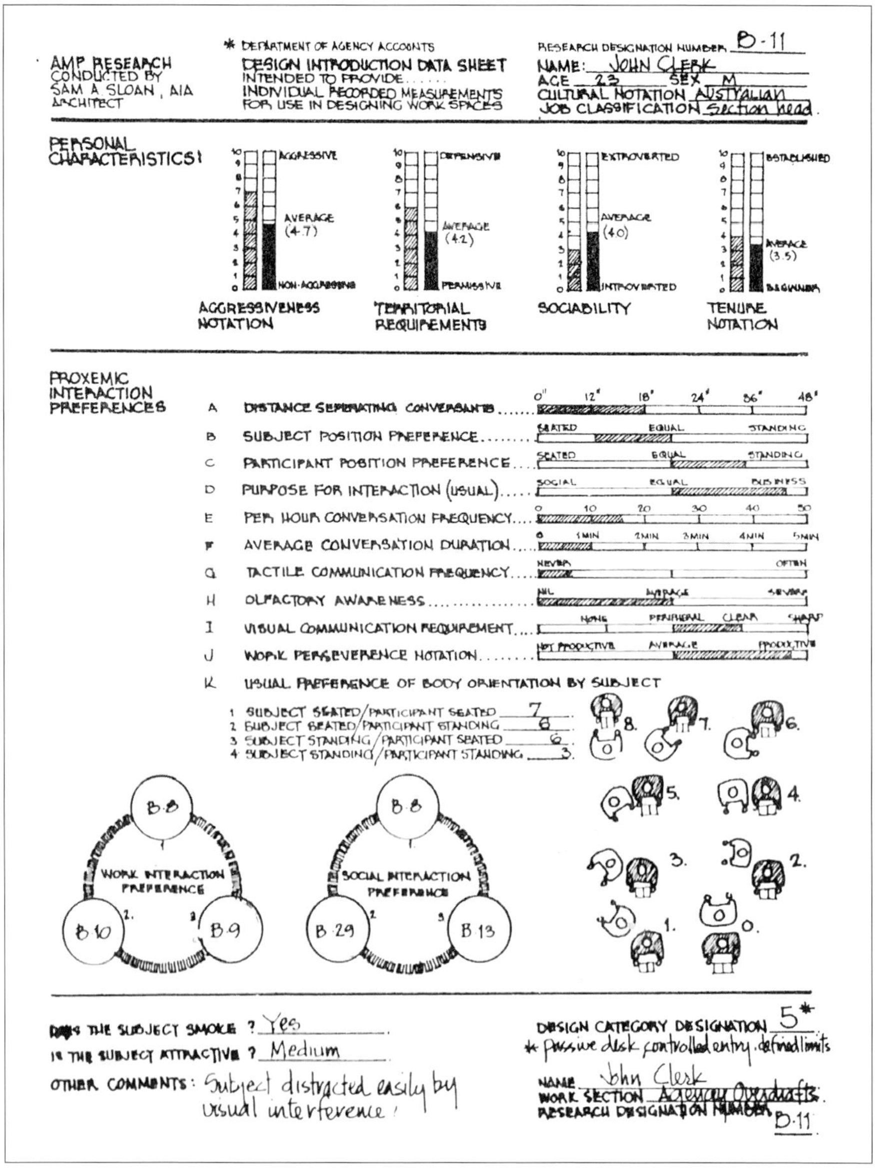

Figure 2.15. Examples of proxemic data charts completed for each employee. From Sloan, "Translating Psycho-Social Criteria into Design Determinants," in Mitchell, ed., *Environmental Design: Research and Practice,* 14.5.1–14.5.10.

riality.[60] Interview questions were drafted to solicit responses regarding these categories, and observations and notations were used to provide a schema for each clerk. The observations were quantified using Hall's notational system. They measured sociofugal and sociopetal orientations, proximity of conversants, frequency and duration of eye contact during conversations, "tactile communication frequency," "olfactory awareness," and so on. These proxemic data were then distilled into eight possible combinations of these attributes, or categories: "C1 = sociable, aggressive, territorial; C2 = sociable, unaggressive, territorial; C3 = sociable unaggressive, non-territorial," and so on. "Environmental requirements" were

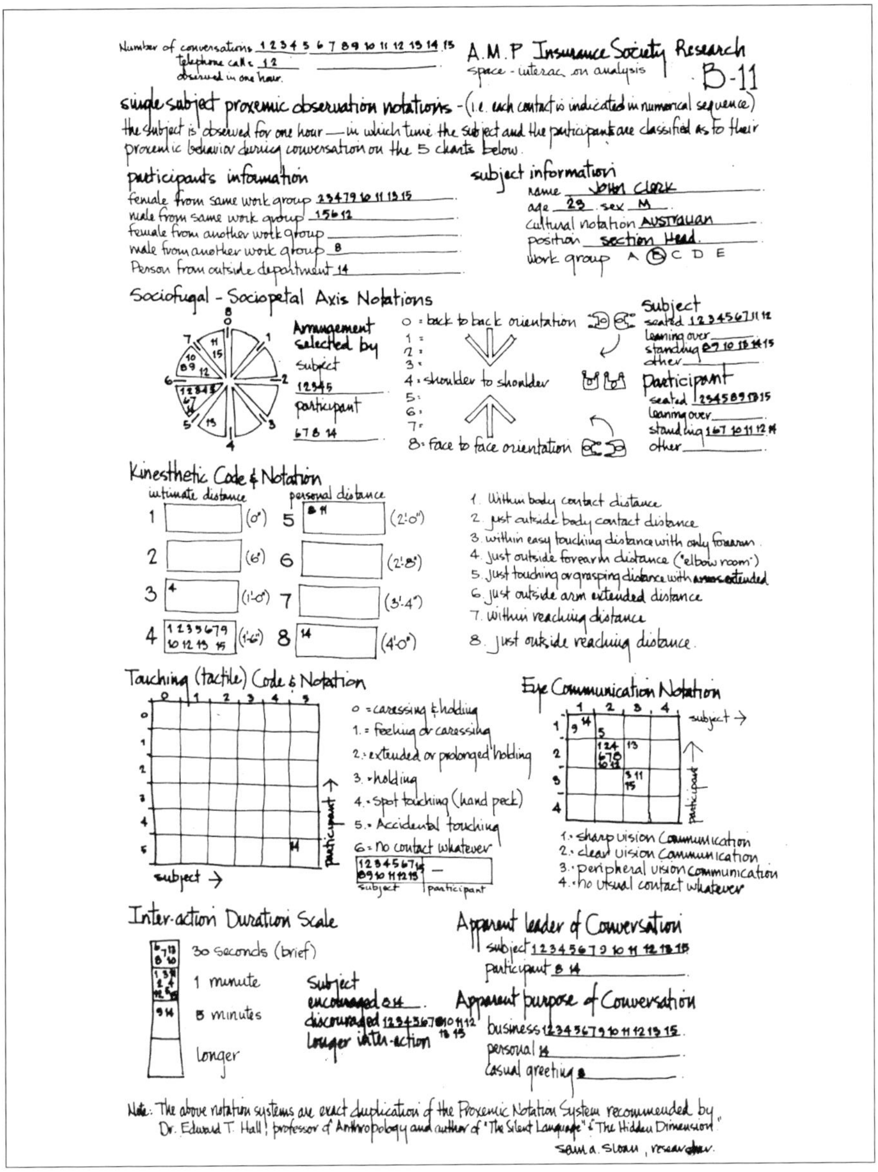

then determined that corresponded to these profiles: “C1 = active desk, controlled entry, defined limits; C2 = active desk, secluded entry, defined limits; C3 = active desk, secluded entry, undefined limits,” and so on.[61]

Desks were then rearranged and desk assignments made accordingly. Carpeting was used to define circulation areas and abate noise, and, in perhaps the most dramatic change, fabric was hung at irregular intervals to demarcate more communal and more private spaces. No walls were erected; the footprint was unchanged. The open plan remained open, but the desk arrangement took on something of a clustered feeling, with moments of sociofugal concentration and release. The bull pen atmosphere of the old arrangement had been subtly subverted, not through architectural form but through changes based on, to use Sloan’s term, the “sensory requirements” of the clerks. Immaterial proxemic patterns came to function as spatial ordering devices, pulling certain individuals closer together and allowing others to remain on the literal and figurative margins.

The results of these proxemic interventions were—perhaps predictably—positive. There were measurable increases in productivity, satisfaction, and “happiness” among the clerks, which dissipated when the office arrangement reverted to its former configuration.[62] This success notwithstanding, proxemics was not assimilated into design curriculum or

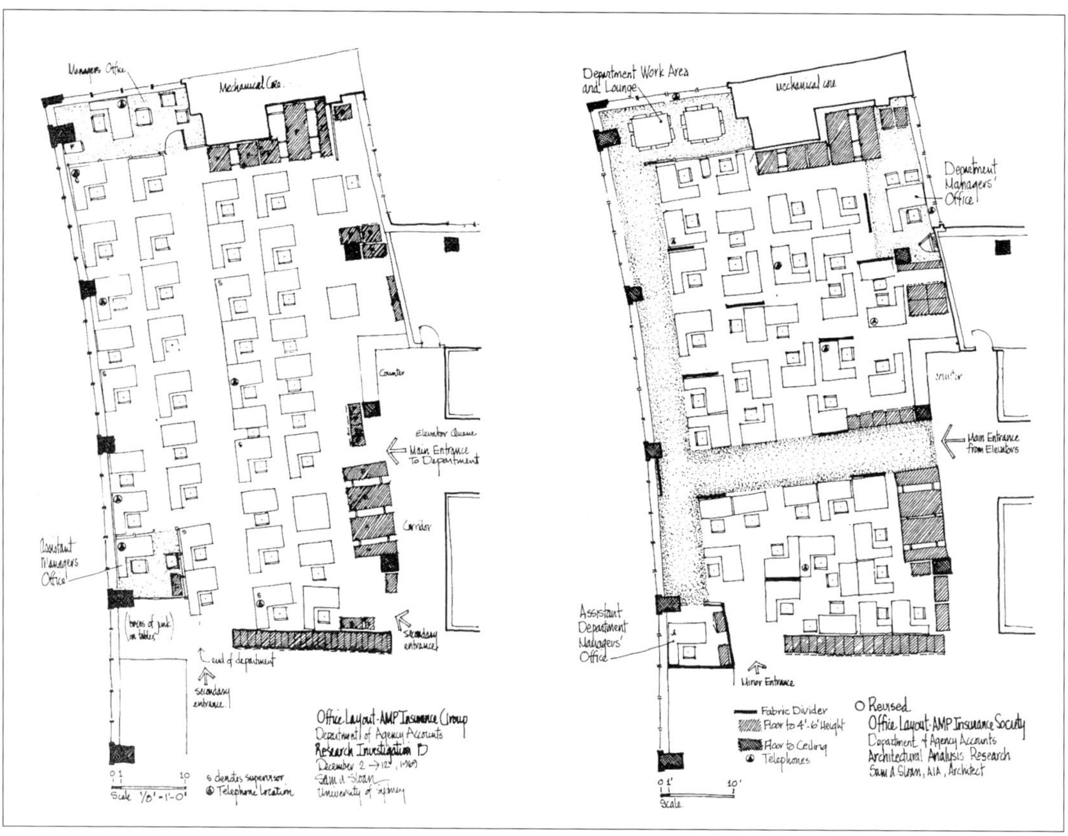

Figure 2.16. Before and after floor plans of the AMP office. From Sloan, “Translating Psycho-Social Criteria into Design Determinants,” in Mitchell, ed., *Environmental Design: Research and Practice,* 14.5.1–14.5.10.

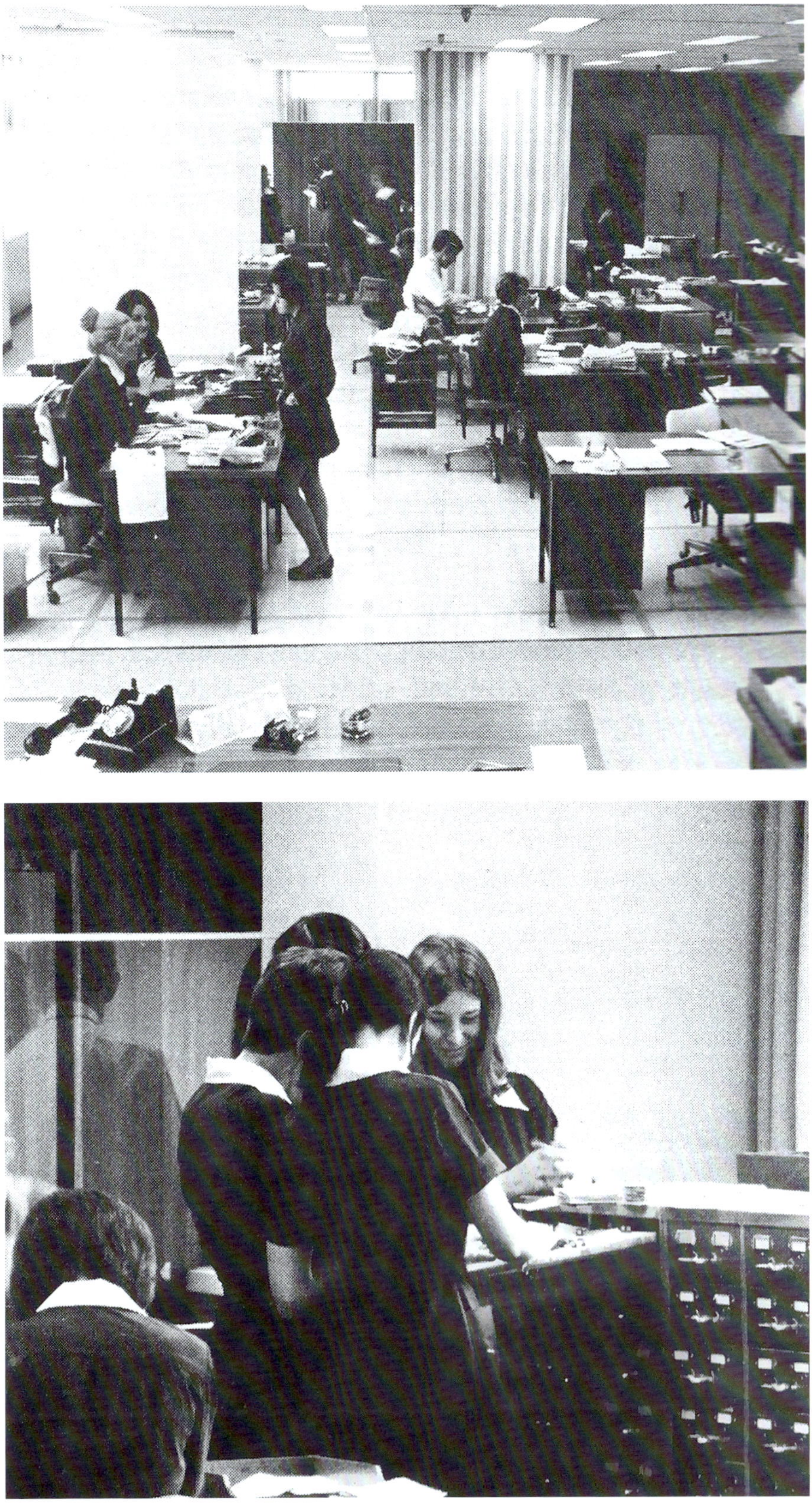

Figure 2.17. Images of clerks' interactions after proxemic data were used to reconfigure the space. From Sloan, "Translating Psycho-Social Criteria into Design Determinants," in Mitchell, ed., *Environmental Design: Research and Practice,* 14.5.1–14.5.10.

practice. Even as departments of environmental design were established at institutions on both U.S. coasts and strategic consortia were formed at other universities—for instance, between architecture programs and psychology programs—the proxemic method failed to become the great unifier of material and immaterial patterns that Hall had envisioned.

Pattern Interference

The few examples given above demonstrate the difficulties in reconciling social scientific research with architectural design. Proxemics held the promise of such a reconciliation, but in practice it either failed or produced banal statistics-based furniture rearrangements or design principles such as "Get as many people near windows as possible." The question that lingered for many was how Hall's bubbles and patterns might be translated into built form. Although the tendency of the time was to blame the data—a trap even Hall fell into as he tried to make proxemics more and more comprehensive and objective—the problem, I would argue, was actually a formal one.

Within architecture, Christopher Alexander's was the name that came to be most closely associated with pattern, and, as we have seen, his path and Hall's crossed on occasion. Indeed, Hall was one of the consultants Alexander hired when he was charged with arriving at design parameters for the BART system in San Francisco (design parameters that were quickly rejected by the engineers on the project).[63] Like Hall, Alexander was seeking a way to systematize and formalize immaterial needs, "tendencies," requirements, or patterns. But I am not suggesting here a relationship of influence. Proxemics developed independently and alongside Alexander's concept of pattern language. Comparing and contrasting the two makes for an instructive exercise in grasping how pattern functioned within design culture and environmental theory at this moment.

At certain points, distinctions and similarities between proxemics and pattern language (just to use the most definitive iteration of Alexander's ideas) are simply attributable to disciplinary distinctions, audiences, and so on. But Hall and Alexander's shared stake in environmental patterning produced enough overlap in their methods that detailed analysis is warranted. Indeed, it is startling—given the different motivations and backgrounds of the two men—how similar their ideas were. Both Hall and Alexander felt that they (more so than others) could see patterns in the environment. These patterns, for both, were neither wholly material nor immaterial, neither purely objective nor subjective. They believed that these patterns had certain structures that governed their relations, and that the right method might be applied to their definition so as to make the logic and regularity of those relations clear and communicable, to instrumentalize them. This instrumentalization would allow for a translation of patterns from objects and events observed to structures projected and realized, or—and this is where a critical difference begins to become apparent—structures to be cast off and transcended. Tracing Hall's and Alexander's evolving theories of patterns into the 1970s gives some indication of the ideological complexities thrown up by this pattern interaction.

Alexander is well known as an architectural iconoclast who has railed against the arbitrary aesthetic decisions of individual designers. Such complaints were common during these years, resulting in one of the foundational principles of the environmental design movement: that decisions about the forms of the built environment could not be capriciously made by a few, only to be imposed on the many. It is not therefore surprising that Alexander was a key figure in the institutionalization of environmental studies and design, with the formation of his Center for Environmental Structure at Berkeley, starting in 1967. Be that as it may, and despite his reputation for systematizing aesthetics out of the design process, Alexander was actually obsessed with *form*. His 1964 book *Notes on the Synthesis of Form*, based on his doctoral dissertation, and his other major publications of the mid-1960s (specifically, "The Atoms of Environmental Structure," "From a Set of Forces to a Form," and the two parts of "A City Is Not a Tree") were likewise engaged with the questions of translation that have concerned us here: how to arrive at an environmental form or structure when working from sets of observed data about human behaviors.[64]

It is not surprising, therefore, that Alexander alighted on *pattern* so many times in his work. "The atoms of environmental structure are *relations*. Relations are geometrical patterns. They are the simplest geometrical patterns in a building which can be functionally right or wrong. A list of the relations required in a building replaces the design program, and the first stages of sketch design." These are the opening lines of "The Atoms of Environmental Structure," which Alexander coauthored with Barry Poyner and which would go on to be one of the founding statements of the design methods movement.[65] Pattern, for Alexander, always referred to relations, organizations, and the interactions of different design variables. These, he held, might be mapped or diagrammed in complex ways that required new modes of thinking and visualization. The most iconic example of these modes was the "semilattice," which, as Molly Steenson observes, was a never-consummated virtual diagram of environmental interaction, including the formal and the social.[66]

In a sense, Alexander's epistemology could not assimilate pattern-cum-form. On the contrary, pattern functioned as a necessary middle step in dissociating the needs or motivations of individuals (both users and designers) from preset shapes or forms. It was a way of abstracting the former while still maintaining the suggestion of ordered relations, relations that then reacquired a pattern as they were translated into a form. This is why the word itself always appeared in Alexander's discourse at the site of a translation—when, for instance, he famously translated "need" into "tendency" in the "Atoms" paper, or, again, when he further translated "tendency" into "force" around the same time.[67] Pattern became a way of transcending the vagaries of human subjectivity (needs and so on) while maintaining an objective, behaviorally based method. It was a way of aggregating human activities or events into lines of force, which could then (in theory) be resolved as forms.

Alexander consistently invoked patterns, not just during the process of translation but at the literal sites of one entity coming into contact with another. Indeed, especially in his early work, form emerged at the site of two distinct patterns coming into contact. In *Notes on the Synthesis of Form,* Alexander described an approach to a design problem as the bifurcation of an "ensemble" into the two components of "form" and "context." A successful design is one in which the form and context achieve the proper "fit." Unsurprisingly, Alexander likened this fit to the adaptation that occurs between a "natural organism" and its "physical environment."[68] Accordingly, the form and context have a complex relationship that can be traced in any number of ways. Alexander described this tracing as the literal drawing of lines between the two pieces of the ensemble. It is the overlapping and aggregation of these lineal divisions that constitute the patterns that generate the form, or, as Alexander stated: "We ought always really to design with a number of nested, overlapped form–context boundaries in mind. Indeed, the form itself relies on its own inner organization and on the internal fitness between the pieces it is made of to control its fit as a whole to the context outside."[69]

This meshing of moments of contact (between form and context) produces the form out of a kind of friction. Furthermore, both entities in a given ensemble (form and context) are wholly dependent on one another for their very existence. A context without a form is an impossibly complex "field," whereas a form without a context would be a hopelessly useless and arbitrary thing. Indeed, the theme of friction and mutually generative properties leads Alexander to a model of design as a *subtractive* process. The designer is effectively charged with extricating form from the patterns of environment in order to produce a seamless fit between the two. "Anything in the world that makes demands of the form is context. Fitness is a relation of mutual acceptability between these two. . . . We want to put the context and the form into effortless contact or frictionless coexistence."[70]

Again, Alexander's conception of this frictionless coexistence is not dematerialized or formless. Indeed, he visualized it with an interesting analogy taken from engineering, wherein grinding an initially rough metal plate against another (already smooth) metal surface produces a perfectly smooth plate. Ink is applied to the surfaces in this procedure, and, as the two metal faces are rubbed together, any imperfections or high spots on the plate pick up the excess ink and are visible. "We grind away these high spots," Alexander wrote,

> and try to fit it against the block again. The face is level when it fits the block perfectly, so that there are no high spots which stand out any more.

> This ensemble of two metal faces is so simple that we shall not be distracted by the possibility of multiple form–context boundaries within it. There is only one such boundary worth discussion at a macroscopic level, that between the standard face (the context), and the face which we are trying to smooth (the form.) Moreover, since the context is fixed, and only the form variable, the task of smoothing a metal face serves well as a paradigm design problem.[71]

Here, the boundary between form and context is not a fixed limit with a definite shape, but an emergent point of contact between two interacting patterns.

Far from the reductive and objective design method normally attributed to Alexander, his phraseology in these passages hints at a veritable metaphysics of environmental patterning. Oddly, though—or perhaps accordingly—the *subject* is mostly absent from Alexander's examples. At a moment when designers were practically consumed with the rhetoric of human needs, end users, demographics, and environmental psychology, Alexander seemed totally uninterested in ergonomics, user satisfaction, and so on. Form and context appeared as an autonomous unit, uncomplicated by the idiosyncrasies of individuals. For Alexander's sympathizers, who so closely associate his name with environmental and humanist design, the idea that he was uninterested in people will ring very false indeed.[72] What I am suggesting, however, is that patterns allowed Alexander to bypass the fine-grained psychologizing of the environment via a kind of simultaneous reduction and accumulation of human behaviors. "Needs" or desires became abstract "tendencies." "Tendencies" could be translated to "forces." All of these terms represented a statistical and aesthetic aggregation of individual behaviors into gestures and movements that could be visualized in various ways.

This happened most pointedly in the 1966 essay "From a Set of Forces to a Form." Immediately, Alexander sought to banish the methodological fuzziness of the term "need":

> The concept of a need has several faults. It can easily be unobjective, it gives no indication of the kind of form which satisfies the need and, worst of all, it is too narrow. It leaves out many other factors which must influence the form of buildings: the force of gravity, the tendency for heat to flow across a temperature gradient, the fact that people tend to walk in straight lines, the social forces which cause a steady drift of population from rural into urban areas, the processes of production and distribution which force builders to use pre-assembled factory components, and the deeper psychological demands of human nature.

If, in the "Atoms" essay, "tendencies" functioned as a kind of statistical averaging of various behaviors, the term "forces" carried that averaging or aggregation into any type of tendency whatsoever (human or nonhuman). "All tendencies," Alexander wrote, "whether they are individual human organisms, or social systems, or mechanical systems, share the following property: when in certain states, they have inexorable tendencies to seek certain other states." Here, an implicit cybernetic model is employed so that patterns of change can be universally recognized and translated. The other benefit to the term "force" for Alexander was that it allowed him to make the observation that "forces generate form."[73]

To illustrate this principle, Alexander invoked an image of a windswept sand dune. As wind blows across the surface of the grains of sand, a certain "pattern" develops, wherein bumps and irregularities are cumulatively smoothed over by the constancy of the force (the wind). A stable rippling pattern develops and maintains its form because it conforms to its own material properties and the pressure applied by the force. This image parallels that of the metal plate from *Notes on the Synthesis of Form*. Two entities rub together until their conflicting patterns are resolved, and form emerges from this reconciliation. Alexander increased the complexity of his example by invoking a different sort of form–force interface: his own living room in a new house, where, instead of installing permanent and heavy furniture, he used lightweight pieces to turn the room into a model, or "analog," in which "the forces became temporarily active, and could push and kick the system from one state to another. After a few weeks, as people used them, the pieces fell into a stable pattern. This pattern defined the best configuration for the permanent structure."[74]

Alexander then invoked an even more complex example: his 1962 research with Marvin Manheim on the location and form of a stretch of

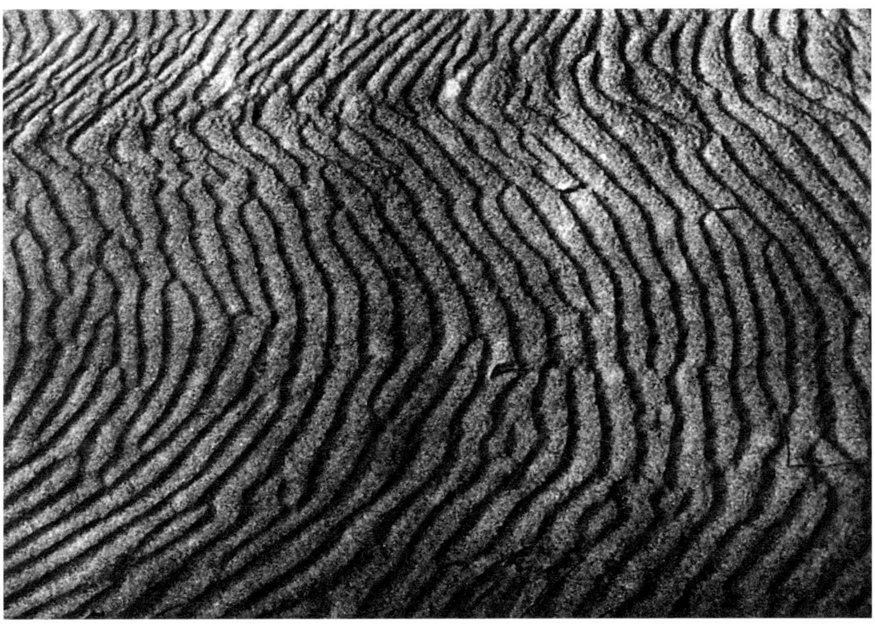

Figure 2.18. "Forces generate form. In the case of certain simple natural systems, this is literally true. In the case of complex, Man-made systems, it is a metaphor." From Christopher Alexander, "From a Set of Forces to a Form" (1966). Courtesy of Christopher Alexander.

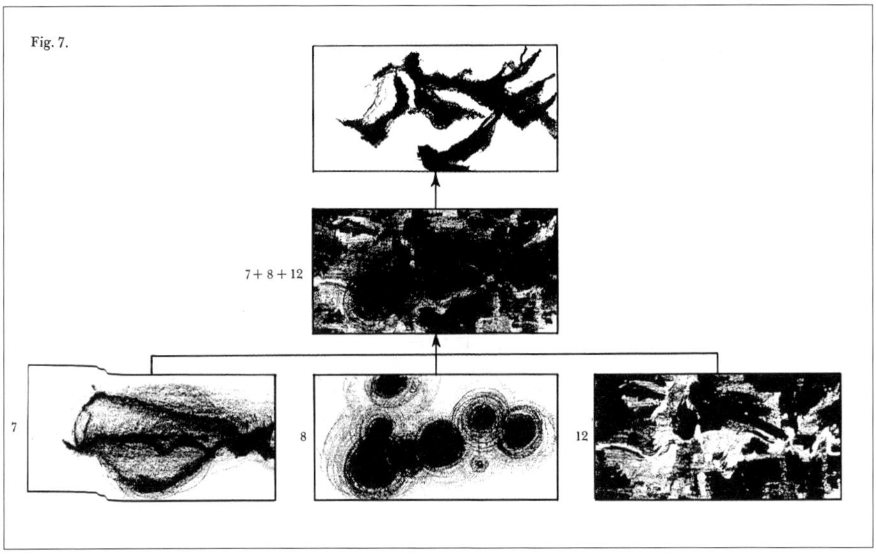

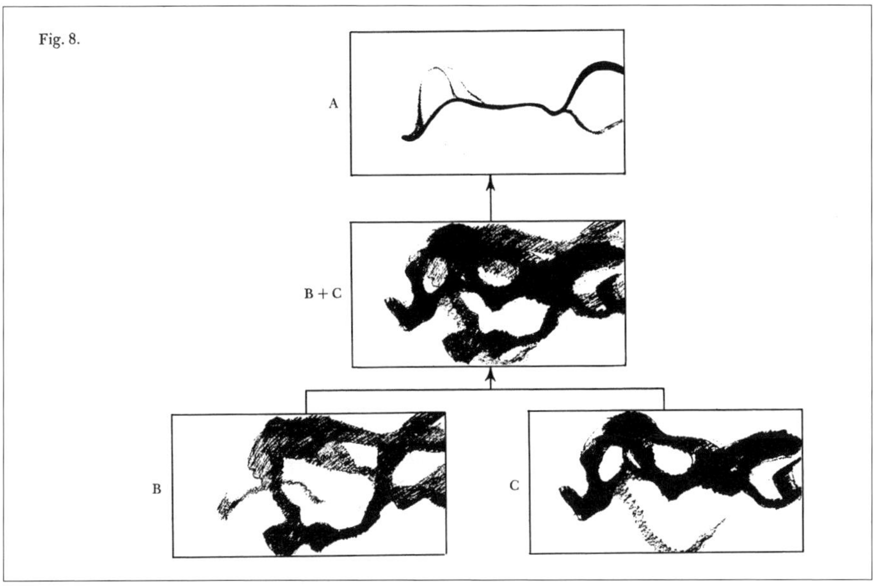

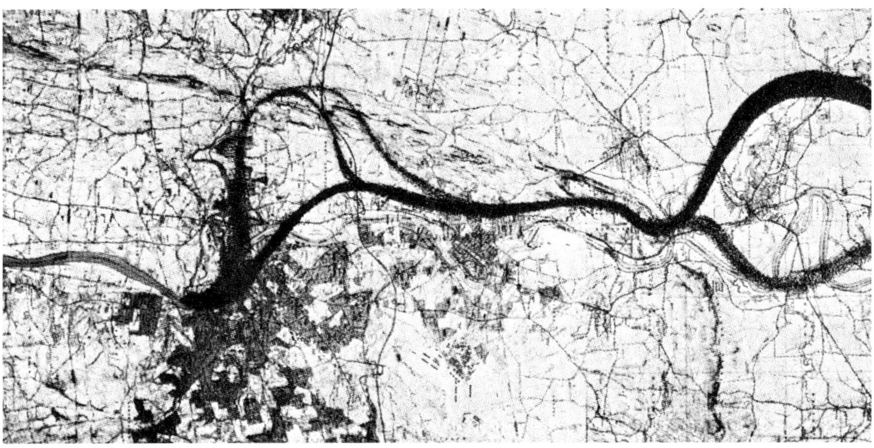

Figure 2.19. "Fusion was carried out by superimposing several patterns photographically, and then, from the darkest, most continuous areas in the composite, generating a new pattern." From Christopher Alexander and Marvin Manheim, *The Use of Diagrams in Highway Route Location* (Cambridge: School of Engineering, MIT, 1962). Courtesy of Christopher Alexander.

highway in Massachusetts.[75] Here, using a map and many sheets of transparent paper, Alexander and Manheim traced the various sociotechnical forces that they believed defined the problem of locating the highway. There were twenty-six of these in the end, including costs, technical issues, "travel time," "noise," "eyesores," and "drainage patterns." These diagrams (all of which were possessed of an aesthetic arbitrariness unacknowledged by Alexander) were then literally overlaid so that conflicts and congruencies could be identified. This cumulative visual image could then be pared down to a singular gestalt that looked something like a winding highway through the mapped landscape. Here, just like the metal plates grinding and the wind blowing across the loose sand, a number of patterned forces eroded a new form out of a complex field. The successful design had been subtracted from an environment already filled with infinitely branching patterns.

I want to take care to distinguish this notion of a subtractive design method from the more common characterization of Alexander's work as "reductive" (without disputing that it is). Alexander's reductivism most certainly derived from his desire for a methodical, rigorous, efficient, and objective approach to designing form. It was also determined by his use of the computer. Indeed, this aspect of his early techniques has been analyzed recently by several scholars, all of whom see his work as both a progenitor of and an outlier to the current digitization of architectural design.[76] Alexander needed to break design problems down into binary propositions that could be input via punch card into specific machines. I would simply add to this analysis that such a radical reduction was predicated on the assumption of environmental patterning held in common by so many designers and researchers at this moment. It was the vast universe of patterns that provided the necessary templates for selective schematization. Patterns constituted the epistemological and aesthetic conditions that allowed both the "psychological demands of human nature" and "the processes of production and distribution which force builders to use preassembled factory components" to be rendered in the same (computer or otherwise) symbolic system.

This observation is borne out as we follow Alexander's understanding of patterns in his subsequent work at Berkeley. Take, for instance, these lines from the first few pages of *A Pattern Language,* where a front porch is being added to a house using the language: "The character of the porch is given by the ten patterns in this short language. In just this way, each part of the environment is given its character by the collection of patterns which we choose to build into it. The character of what you build, will be given to it by the language of patterns you use, to generate it."[77] Here, patterns form the elements of the language, they are *-emes* that the language orders and sets into a particular relation. They are the speech acts of the environment, which can be identified, abstracted, and then recombined by the "user" of the language. But, again, the pattern is not a form. Patterns are only ever relation. Form can be arrived at only through the synthesizing of patterns and the elimination of their conflicts. This literal process of elimination generates the form of the environment. Design becomes a subtractive process; pattern delineates what can (or should) be subtracted from the morass of environment.

If *A Pattern Language* could be read as a pragmatic (if somewhat eccentric) manual for architectural design (which is how it has been received since its publication, and through its many printings), its companion volume, *The Timeless Way of Building* (1979), presented a sweeping poetic metaphysics of environmental patterns. Authored by Alexander alone, the book offered a series of observations issued as unassailable truths (it was even bound with a soft cloth covering, like a Bible). This remarkable document allows us to observe more carefully the synecdochic qualities of patterns and environments under consideration here. The tone, as I have suggested, has Alexander's characteristic rationalism, but the book gives a fuller picture of his antidualistic thinking. Of the relationship between patterns and space, he writes: "What we want to know is just how the structure of the space supports the patterns of events it does, in such a way that if we change the structure of space, we shall be able to predict what kinds of changes in patterns of events this change will generate."[78] Only by deducing these relationships can new buildings implement the (infamous) "quality without a name" shared by all successful human places and spaces.[79]

The quality without a name cannot be named precisely because it resides in the absolute specificity of relations among infinitely varying patterns. Like environment itself, it is a general principle (a law of relation, a topology) that can exist only in its radical contextualization, in which every and any element is connected to every other, and a change in one changes the entire ensemble (without, however, altering the elements' topology). Alexander navigates this *mise en abyme* in his usual stepwise fashion. He begins by isolating the "elements" of space. These could include, for example, a church nave or a cloverleaf interchange on a freeway. Churches always have naves, according to Alexander, and freeways always have cloverleaf interchanges, a state of affairs that suggests that these "elements" could be timeless. These naive observations are merely a feint, however, as Alexander quickly acknowledges that the consistency of the nave, for instance, is illusory; that "*the 'elements,' which seem like elementary building blocks, keep varying, and are different every time that they occur.*"[80] There must be some unifying property to the elements that allows us to recognize them even though they are always different. This astonishing Platonism is then fused with a thoroughgoing cybernetic process wherein what is constant is the communication or relation among those elements, such that the isolated nave is meaningless without its *relation* to an aisle or transept.

Like a physicist burrowing into the material structures of atoms, Alexander delves deeper into these elements, observing that they "themselves evaporate when we look closely at them." He continues:

> For, once we recognize that much of what we think of as an "element" in fact lies in the pattern of relationships between this thing and the things in the world around it, we then come to the second even greater realization, that the so-called element is itself nothing but a myth, and that indeed, the element itself is not just embedded in a pattern of relationships, but is *itself* entirely a pattern of relationships and nothing else.[81]

And, as the elements are progressively dissolved into their contexts, Alexander arrives at a kind of apotheosis of pattern: "and we see finally, that the world is entirely made of all these interhooking, interlocking non-material patterns."[82] In the end, it is the patterns that generate the physical environment. "They account entirely for its geometrical structure: they are the visible, coherent stuff that is repeating, and coherent there: they are the background of the variation, which makes each concrete element a little different."[83]

Of course, patterns were not visible—or coherent—to everyone. This is where we might rejoin Alexander's discourse with that of Hall. The two men shared something of a privileged perspective on the patterned environment. They could discern its symmetries, repetitions, overlaps, and complexities as if from above, tracing its invisible outlines. The problem was that they saw different things. Their patterns would have proved irreconcilable if any attempt to reconcile them had ever been made. Their patterns would have interfered with one another, producing unacceptable levels of cognitive, perceptual, and cultural dissonance. Again, I want to insist here that this irreconcilability was not simply a matter of disciplinary or methodological differences, nor was it a matter of the two individuals setting different goals. Both Hall and Alexander wandered into a realm beyond clear disciplinary distinctions; they likewise shared the goal of somehow sorting out the existing state of the world that was characterized by chaotic and counterproductive pattern clashes. Their differences were more visceral than this. They were formal. They had to do with the ontological stuff out of which they believed patterns were constructed and the phenomenal ways in which the subject related to them.

Their methods were in some instances quite similar. Both Alexander and Hall utilized the computer to aggregate their data. For Alexander, the computer was an expediency. For Hall, in contrast, the methods of observation and notation were far more important and problematic than the fairly perfunctory affair of running the numbers through a computer. Indeed, he remained very ambivalent about the latter, writing in his *Handbook for Proxemic Research*: "Using computers is like taking dope. (a) They complicate your life. (b) Once hooked, you are never free; and (c) the more you get the more you need."[84] He also noted, unlike Alexander, the way in which computer data analysis "altered" and could even "radically reduce" research options.[85] For Hall, computers reduced the resolution of patterns, whereas for Alexander, they were initially the only tools that could allow the designer to recognize patterns in the first place.

For Alexander, patterns were the (material and behavioral) stuff of lived space. The subject existed *in* this space and therefore had the potential to identify and manipulate its forms. Proxemics, on the other hand, identified a world of patterns that penetrated the subject herself, ordering her sensorium, her behaviors, and the ways in which the environment (including objects and other subjects) afforded various types of interaction. To oversimplify this contrast, we could say that for Alexander, the subject inhabited pattern, while for Hall, patterns inhabited the subject.[86] This leads us to the counterintuitive conclusion that Alexander tended to flatten the patterned environment through the processes of design, while Hall rendered a more visceral and perceptually tangible model of patterns structuring the lifeworld of the individual. Here, architecture was not an "embodiment" of information about the world and human nature (the traditional view of its metaphysical function) but rather an abstraction derived from the latter's textures, surfaces, and quasi-materiality.

Hall understood patterning as an apparatus, in other words, as a set of environing structures that preexisted the subject's ability to perceive, think, and act, and that structured those same capacities as they emerged in interaction with the surrounding world. For Hall, architecture's ability to respond to this type of patterning was limited. Architecture could accommodate but never mirror or embody ideal patterns. Like the John Deere Headquarters, it was something like a frame whose mechanisms of opening and closure could attain a level of aesthetic "congruence," a sense of equilibrium between what is permitted and what is foreclosed. These openings and blockages then had the ability to allow the subject to perceive and, possibly, transcend the patterns that were delimiting her behaviors and, ultimately, her existential possibilities. Unlike for Alexander, for Hall the idea of a "frictionless" fit between form and context was neither possible nor desirable; he saw patterns as the pulsing, phasing, evolving structures of moments of interaction between the subject and environment. In this modality, environmental interaction produced the aggregate of patterns that was recognized as the human, and not the other way around.

3

Responsive Environments

> In short, the most successful work of the near future will be kinetic in content, immaterial in nature, disposable in substance, uncommercial in attitude, and environmental in effect. Only when artists start moving toward these goals will art succeed in accomplishing its principal task, a total restructuring of our natural environment for the esthetic rejuvenation of man.
>
> —Willoughby Sharp, *Air Art,* 1969

As I begin drafting this chapter, there is a pavilion in the garden of the Victoria and Albert Museum in London made of a series of connected canopies (Plate 4). The modular canopies are based on hexagonal frames with silicon and carbon-fiber "threads" woven across them in complex patterns. Each "cell" rests horizontally on a narrow stem at a height of about four meters. The threads constitute the *mass* of the canopies, though this term is misleading. The threads' varying densities, spacing, and relative opacity serve to capture, refract, and modulate the ambient light in the open-air environment, producing a pleasant atmosphere under and around the canopy. The structure is a bit of a cross between Henri Labrouste's reading room in the Bibliothèque Nationale in Paris and an H. R. Geiger design from the 1979 film *Alien.* There is also, shielded underneath the canopy, a robotic arm. This arm can be programmed to construct, or weave, new cells for the canopy, which it does on designated occasions. This activity is actually semiautonomous. No designer directly determines the form of a cell. Rather, photo- and heat-sensitive sensors embedded in fiber-optic cable in the structure itself register the number of occupants and their patterns of use (presumably). These data are then fed through an algorithm that determines where and at what density new cells should be added.

The Elytra Filament Pavilion, as it is called, was designed by Achim Menges in collaboration with Moritz Dörstelmann, Jan Knippers, and Thomas Auer. The name is derived from the wing structures of beetles, which demonstrate nature's supreme design efficiency of "using 'less material' by having 'more form,'" an efficiency the pavilion itself seeks to instrumentalize. All of this was marshaled into this project in order to showcase

> the profound impact of emerging technologies on our conceptualization of design, engineering and making, by intensifying the visitors' architectural experience of the museum's central garden. But instead of being merely a static display, the pavilion constitutes a dynamic space and an evolving structure. The cellular canopy grows from an onsite fabrication nucleus, and it does so in response to patterns of inhabitation of the garden over time, driven by real time sensing data. The pavilion's capacity to be locally produced, to expand and to contract over time provides a vision of future inner city green areas with responsive semi-outdoor spaces that enable a broader spectrum of public activities, and thus extend the use of the scarce resource of public urban ground.[1]

The Elytra Pavilion, as technologically sophisticated as it is, is hardly a unique project. Indeed, it is a beautiful example among many projects that reflect a genuine resurgence of interest in responsive environments.[2] But to make such a statement reifies the category into specific disciplinary constellations—of architecture, of design, of installation art. But even the most cursory historical survey of the conception and implementation of such apparatuses reveals the difficulty in sketching anything resembling a complete genealogy of responsive environments as a stable class of design or aesthetic objects (indeed, the very notion of object, as we have seen, is one of the principal obstacles). In addition to developments in the fields of architecture and art, such a history would need to include the evolution of myriad mechanical and digital interfaces, technologies of simulation and virtual reality, command centers and control rooms, sealed/regulated environments such as submarines and space suits, histories of biometrics, and various forms of therapeutic environments. This list barely scratches the surface of the nearly infinite forms of apparatuses with which this study engages but cannot pretend to exhaust. Nonetheless, I will offer a narrative of the development of instances that were determinative of the ethos of responsive environments, focusing on art and architectural examples in which environment (and response) was a highly specific and central concern.[3] The list will seem especially incomplete as regards art practices in the 1960s and 1970s. I do not include, for instance, any examples of minimalism's engagement with lived space, of postminimalist land or earth art, or even those projects that engaged explicitly with ecology, such as the microenvironments devised by Newton Harrison and Helen Mayer Harrison in the late 1960s, up through our contemporary notions of sustainable design.[4] As James Nisbet has established, very particular models of environment were integral to these manifestations.[5] Equally, I avoid (inasmuch as it is possible) the by now normative lists of historical precedents for that class of architectural objects known as responsive environments, running from the work of Gordon Pask and Charles Eastman up to that of Elizabeth Diller and Ricardo Scofidio.[6] This is not a dismissal of the importance of chronicling these projects so much as it is a declaration of a slightly different set of concerns—a set of concerns that hinges on environment *itself* as a new category of aesthetic and technical concern circa 1970 and on the mutually formative actions in the human–environment system.

An indication of the complex genealogy here can be seen in the case of the first usage of the phrase *responsive environment* in reference to a design object (the term was *not* used to refer to a set of alterable architectural structures). At the end of the 1950s social psychologist Omar Khayyam Moore and engineer Richard Kobler, working at the McGraw-Edison Company in Illinois, developed what they named (and patented as) the Talking Typewriter. This device comprised a keyboard with color-coded keys married to a small computer and a speaker that could play prerecorded messages relating to the activity of the hardware. At some point, it was also given a visual monitor and/or screen that could display letters and projected images. In 1962, Moore received a Carnegie Foundation grant to test this new technology at the private Hamden Hall Country Day School in Connecticut. There, children as young as three were invited to interact with the device, which was meant to teach linguistic skills and symbolic thinking in what Moore and colleague Alan Ross Anderson described as an "autotelic" system.[7] Autotelic activities were defined as those conducted for no external incentive, stimulus, reward, or punishment—play, exploration, free communication, and so on.[8] This philosophy recommended the use of a nonhuman interlocutor, a totally neutral machine whose only apparent function was to repeat inputs from the keypad vocally and suggest further inputs. Over the next decade, the system would be tested with other "exceptional" children—those with autism, for instance, and poor African American children in Chicago.[9] By 1972, there were reportedly 150 Talking Typewriter units in use in fifty locations in the United States.[10]

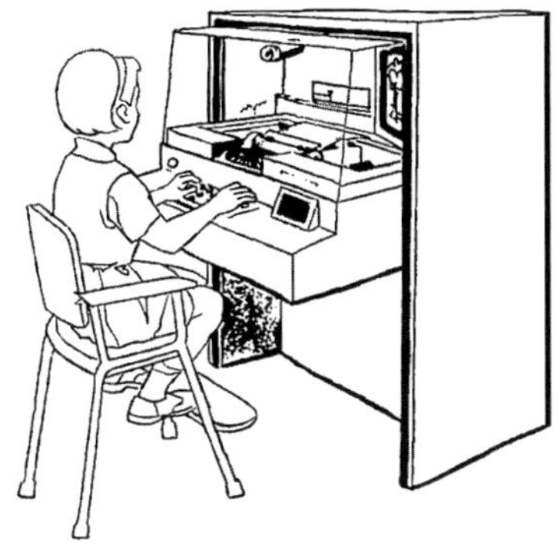

(New York City, 1968)

E | R | E
EDISON RESPONSIVE ENVIRONMENT
TALKING TYPEWRITER

Figure 3.1. "The Talking Typewriter," from *The Edison Responsive Environment Learning System; or, The Talking Typewriter,* developed by Thomas A. Edison Laboratory, a Subsidiary of McGraw-Edison Company (Palo Alto: American Institutes for Research in the Behavioral Sciences, 1972), with ERE logo.

But even from its earliest applications, the Talking Typewriter was more than just a discrete apparatus. It was an environment. Just as necessary to its functioning as its internal mechanisms and magnetic tape was the room, or "booth," in which it was housed. This was sketched in plan along with the typewriter itself in the 1962 patent filed by Moore and Kobler.[11] The booth was equipped with one-way mirrors and had a microphone built in for use by an attendant who might assist/prompt the student using the typewriter. Five such booths were grouped within

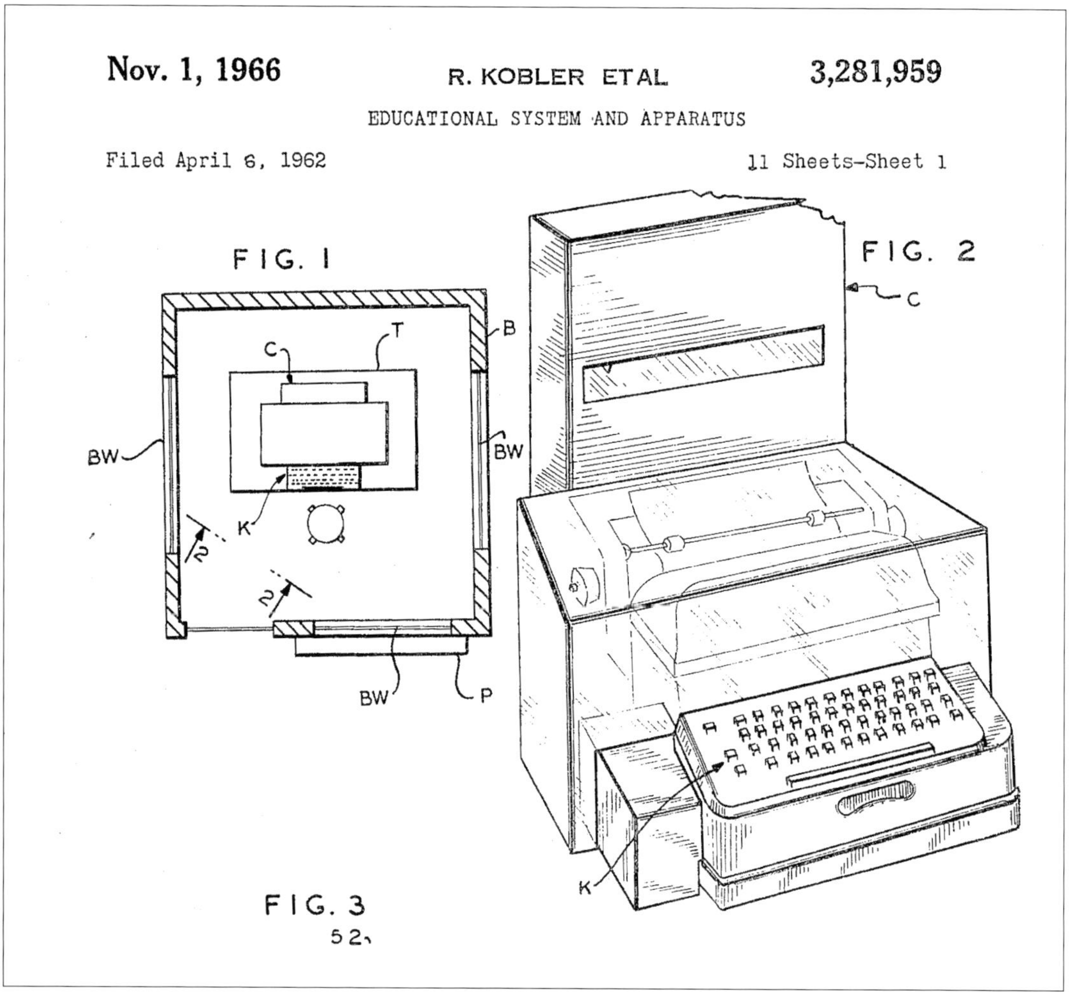

Figure 3.2. "A top down plan view of a booth with a teaching machine for an individual pupil according to the invention" and "front view of the teaching machine." Figures 1 and 2 from Richard Kobler and Omar K. Moore, Educational System and Apparatus, U.S. Patent 3,281,959, filed April 6, 1962; issued November 1, 1966.

what Moore called his Responsive Environments Laboratory, which he described thus:

> It consists of two adjoining prefabricated metal sheds, each 20' × 40', set on concrete foundations. One shed is windowless and the other has windows only in a small office area; they are centrally heated and air conditioned. The sheds are as simple as modern construction permits; they are made up of one-foot modular sections, have exposed ceiling and wall beams, and so on. In Shed 1 are five portable soundproofed booths, 7' × 7' × 7', lined along two 40' walls, leaving a middle aisle as well as small aisles between booths for observation through windows with one-way glass.[12]

This suite of interactive technology and insular architecture was ultimately dubbed the Edison Responsive Environment. The logic of the ERE's design was, according to Moore and Anderson, not panoptic (in which case a surveillance condition might have been internalized by students who could not confirm that they were being observed); rather, the design was intended to eliminate any biased conditioning from the child's environment, so that it contained no direct personifications of authority, no teachers judging, no test scores, and no classmates distracting. And while instructions could be provided via the aforementioned intercom, at least initially students received no instructions of any kind. They were introduced into the ERE and were free to explore its system. (In one iteration, the children's fingernails were painted to coordinate with the colors of the keys on the Talking Typewriter in order to facilitate matching activities.)

This type of immersive, multimodal, free-form learning was exactly what Marshall McLuhan would be describing a few years later in his own musings on responsive environments. The models espoused by both theorists—Moore and McLuhan—held that the world itself was the richest source of information, interaction, and learning. Linear, didactic, and hierarchical systems of education no longer seemed valid in the "oral" or "electronic" world. Without speculating on the pedagogical validity of the ERE, it is worth noting here that, though it seems far from the avant-garde projects that will be discussed below, its basic conception is in perfect alignment with other instances of responsive environments. Environment is understood as the source of imperceptible conditioning forces, which, when provided with the proper form or interface, can be turned from coercive or interpellative apparatuses to consciousness-expanding and evolutive ones.

The instance of the ERE is perhaps also a reminder that the field of architecture proper was seldom the locus of radical environmental speculation. There is, of course, a long history of notions of "environmental determinism" embedded in architectural discourse, but these were seldom articulated in a responsive modality.[13] And in all architectural origin stories, architecture's function as a conditioner of environment—as shelter and protection from the elements—is always recognized.[14] Largely, though, architectural design and theory have been caught up in a dichotomous (or dialectical) view of abstracted conceptions of form and space, wherein the building-object is seen as a solid figure against an environmental ground or as a phenomenological shaping of space itself as an ambiguous kind of substance.

In the postwar period (and, indeed, at exactly the moment under consideration here) the most systematic deconstruction of the fraught relationship between architecture and environment was Reyner Banham's *The Architecture of the Well-Tempered Environment.*[15] This text would constitute something of an exhumation of the repressed content of architectural form, which would turn out to be the mechanical and electronic systems embedded within it that made it habitable as an environment. These Banham termed, respectively, "structure," and "service." Like so many of his other statements, Banham's survey takes the rhetorical form of a rebuke to the discipline of architecture for its hypocritical posture relative to notions of technology and function. In other words, whether out of indignation or ignorance, structure continued to be the focus of architectural design, even when it claimed service sophistication. Banham's history, though, is not so much a history of responsive environments as it is an account of the emergence of "regenerative" architectures, or those buildings that to a greater or lesser extent relied on powered services to overcome the contextual realities of existing environments (i.e., climate).[16] In this sense, Banham's understanding of environment is highly explicated into a set of determinative attributes or substances: air, moisture, light, sound.[17] He seldom ventures into the expanding realm of environment as it was being elaborated in so many other fields even as he was drafting his book.

The exceptions to this generalization are instructive, however. Banham was undoubtedly aware of the rhetoric of the environmental research manifold and its attendant phraseology *man–environment system* and *man–environment relationship.* But the nature of this relationship struck him as perhaps too ambiguous to venture into. In the final chapter of the first edition of *The Architecture of the Well-Tempered Environment,* Banham concedes that the nature of the controls placed on environmental determinants by mechanical technologies are somewhat complicated when one considers the organisms inhabiting the structures:

> The recognition that there are no absolute environmental standards for human beings has required the environmental sciences to develop methods of assessing performance and needs that depend upon attempts to quantify subjective responses without doing injury to their human validity, to allow for the interaction of what is being assessed with other elements in the environment that are not under study, and to allow for variability in time through fatigue on the one hand, or conscious and unconscious accommodation on the other—faced with a glare of excessive light, one may reduce the amount of illumination, put on dark glasses, screw up the eyes or leave it to the contraction of the iris to compensate.[18]

Ironically, he would acknowledge those "elements in the environment that are not under study" somewhat more explicitly fifteen years later in the second edition of the book—in an added last chapter titled "A Breath of Intelligence"—once again in the figure of "dark glasses," or, more specifically, "photo-sensitive sunglasses for personal wear that change their tint and/or light absorption according to the ambient illumination."[19] In this instance, something about the embedding of responsive technologies—either chemical or digital—in the otherwise stable material of glass seems to have provoked Banham's imagination. At this point in the text he was moved to sketch in miniature the very history I hope to evoke here:

> Since the wiring for such glass might be deposited as printed circuitry on the face of the glass itself, it becomes possible to imagine an architecture that does not so much realise the glass paradise of Paul Scheerbart as go far beyond it into the realm of controllable stained glass traceried by its own circuitry in gold or silver, responding to changes in external and internal illumination, and programmed to enhance the daily routines and emotional states of the inhabitants.
>
> "Responsive" environments of this kind have been the stock in trade of futuristic science fiction for some half-century now, but as they edge their way into the realm of the applicable, we have to realise that in practise they will never be cheap.[20]

Banham's ambivalence here is remarkable; while finally admitting the possibility of a grand avant-garde synthesis of "structure" and "service," he hesitates for the most practical reason imaginable.

Perhaps it was a similar ambivalence that allowed him to overlook the explicitly environmental concerns even of those architects and projects he included in his study. While he tips his hat to the paradigm of service over structure heralded by Buckminster Fuller and his young acolytes in the Archigram group, he does not address the environmental philosophy of Richard Neutra, for instance. Though the latter's Lovell House (1927) is featured for its use of an incredible linear suspended lighting fixture in the library, Banham does not pursue Neutra's circa 1954 assertion that "physiology must direct and check the technical advance in constructed environment."[21] Even as Banham extolled Neutra's use of "thirty low-wattage colour-corrected 'daylight' bulbs," Neutra's philosophical opus *Survival through Design* had already established something of an incompatible position: that "man's own cramped-together creations, anything from underground sewage systems and subways to a badly hemmed in sky overhead, irritatingly criss-crossed by a maze of electric wires, should not prove as inescapable as fate."[22]

Neutra's understanding of environment was radically different from Banham's. The former's view was human centered and relied more on the sciences of physics, psychology, and ethology than on engineering and mechanics. In this sense, though it is easy now to dismiss Neutra's scientific dilettantism, his ideas were more in tune with the emergence of responsive environments around 1970 than were Banham's. Neutra insisted on a kind of isomorphism (and reciprocity) between the inner realm of the organism and the designed environment. He ventured: "Individual and social psychology will ultimately merge with BRAIN PHYSIOLOGY, TO GUIDE THE DESIGNER IN HIS OBSERVATION AND CREATION OF RESPONSIVE PATTERNS."[23] Sylvia Lavin has recognized in this opposition between Banham and Neutra two distinct models of the human–environment relationship as it manifested in the 1950s and 1960s. In her account, Banham is a kind of positivist, tracking and urging on the technological encroachment of systems into human space, while Neutra remains a vitalist, understanding environment as an outward projection from the subject of various affective states, which it becomes architecture's job to facilitate and ameliorate as what Lavin characterizes as "mood."[24]

We must also acknowledge here the degree to which Banham was out of step not only with the holistic ethos of responsive environments but also with their technological sophistication. For, as intent as he was on pushing traditional formalist architecture toward a new technological functionalism, Banham failed to acknowledge the radical experiments in computation that were taking place precisely in the years intervening between the first and second editions of his book.[25] In Berkeley, Salt Lake City, Austin, both Cambridges, and several other places, digital technologies were being used in new ways to compute structural requirements, systematize design, simulate architectural space, and activate environments with myriad forms of responsiveness. I describe several of these iterations of responsive environments below and in subsequent chapters.

The Avant-Garde Environment

Banham was not alone, however, in his sense that design's technological turn might well result in space-time conceptions dreamed of by the historical avant-garde but only ever hinted at in text, maquettes, and photocollages in the first decades of the twentieth century. McLuhan likewise constructed an avant-garde genealogy for his conception of environment, particularly in those movements' more or less programmatic rejection of Western "visual space." His account (gathered from a number of scattered statements) finds the modern beginnings of "acoustic space" in a number of topologically complex aesthetic gestures, starting perhaps with the Symbolist response to romanticism, as a movement away from the preoccupation with the external nature of the latter to the engagement with the *milieu intérieur* or *paysage intérieur* of the former. By delving into the dynamic complexities of the world of the senses, the Symbolists (as well as designers a century later) were able to project that interior world back out as a new type of environment.[26] Indeed, the idea that what the first wave of avant-garde artists and poets had posited as a kind of spiritual desideratum was now (circa 1970) easily achievable via technology was one of the leitmotifs of the discourse generating responsive environments.

We can evoke one of the origins of this idea, perhaps, in the avant-garde rejection of the sanctity of the art object as a solid center (of attention, of a given space, and so on) and its replacement by the subject, not as a new kind of solid center but rather as the ephemeral and emergent locus of aesthetic experience. This attitude is reflected in the foundational principles of the *Gesamtkunstwerk*, in the obsession with ambience and atmosphere, and in the subversion of figure and ground hierarchies evident in cubism, as well as in the focus on viewer involvement or participation that attended aesthetic theory and practice at the beginning of the twentieth century. In retrospect, it is apparent that these concerns constitute something like an antithesis to the modernist notion of the autonomous work or *objet*. We can see some of these dynamics play out in the history (and historiography) of modern sculpture, implicated as it was with contemporaneous models of space and environment. In an almost clairvoyant manner, the futurist Umberto Boccioni would reject the object-oriented trajectory of modern sculpture in favor of environmental interaction:

> Naturally, we will bring forth a SCULPTURE OF ENVIRONMENT [*AMBIENTE*].
>
> Traditionally a statue is carved out or delineated against the atmospheric background in which it is exhibited. Futurist painting has overcome this conception of the rhythmic continuity of the lines in a human figure and of the figure's isolation from its background and from its INVISIBLE INVOLVING SPACE [*SPAZIO AVVILUPPANTE INVISIBILE*]. . . . We therefore cast aside and proclaim the ABSOLUTE AND COMPLETE ABOLITION OF DEFINITE LINES AND CLOSED SCULPTURE. WE BREAK OPEN THE FIGURE AND ENCLOSE IT IN ENVIRONMENT. We proclaim that the environment must be part of the plastic block which is a world in itself with its own laws; that the sidewalk can jump up on your table and your head be transported across the street, while your lamp spins a web of plaster ray between one house and another.
>
> We proclaim that the whole visible world must fall in upon us, merging with us and creating harmony measurable only by the creative imagination.[27]

Of course, only a few of Boccioni's contemporaries would heed this call for an art "enclosed in environment," but the preoccupation with dynamic spatial interaction and an aesthetics of integration can be traced through the interwar period. It primarily follows the itinerary of constructivism as it migrated away from Russia in the 1930s in the work of Naum Gabo and Antoine Pevsner. It was apparent in the collective works of the De Stijl artists and designers in the Netherlands in the 1920s, which, according to Nancy Troy, produced "the painted abstract environment, in which pure color, free of all figurative associations, was merged with modern architecture to form an encompassing, total work of art."[28] And so on, from the atmospheres of German expressionist architecture to the *Merzbauen* of Kurt Schwitters to Bretonian surrealism to the performative and technical philosophy of the Bauhaus—these avant-garde precedents were constantly mined in the sixties and seventies precisely for their mobilization of a new environmentally responsive approach to both subjects and objects.

But before we address the neo-avant-garde manifestations of responsive environments, we can continue to elucidate their development before (and during) World War II. Again, using McLuhan's genealogy as guide, we can note several figures who bridge the gap between the pre- and post-war understandings of dynamic, immersive environments. Interestingly, this genealogy has been presented most succinctly by the designer Victor Papanek in an essay included in a legendary compendium by McLuhan titled *Verbi-Voco-Visual Explorations.*[29] Here, both the literary and visual production of futurism, cubism, surrealism, and Bauhaus functionalism are joined by several other figures that begin to reflect the scientistic inflection of avant-garde space that would begin to appear in the 1930s and 1940s. Among these is Alexander Dorner, whose book *The Way beyond "Art"* would become a totemic theoretical statement for many involved in the development of responsive environments. Papanek's essay quotes from this text regarding "a wholly energetic world of total changeability."[30] Dorner, without having recourse to the ubiquitous shorthand of "environment" that would pertain twenty years later, nonetheless described fundamental spatiotemporal transformations at the level of the sciences and the epistemological activity of humanity:

> Absolute infinite space . . . was now being divested of its changeless majesty by the energies of transformation. It was growing into a complicated system of variously curved spaces, which penetrated each other. . . . Nature becomes a process that changes autonomously. It includes all human energies and actions, and even man's visual observations may contribute to that inner change. Natural history and cultural history become united on a deeper level.[31]

Papanek likens Dorner's views to those of physicist Erwin Schrödinger, the implications of which he sees as profound for both art and reality: "What holds the world together is no longer the rigid framework of space represented by static material points, but the interpenetrative force of energetic waves, a force which results in self-transforming processes."[32] He then weaves these observations together with a quote by the marginal surrealist theorist and artist Wolfgang Paalen, who wrote, "The new quantum physics, Schrödinger's immaterial waves . . . have given him [the artist] a new concept of space as a sphere dynamically expanding and yet finite."[33]

In all these sources, space expands and infuses perception, thought, action, matter, energy, and cognition. It moves ineluctably away from mere space and toward what will inevitably be described as environment. To linger just a bit longer in this very important moment of the 1930s, we can point to yet another figure who seemed to anticipate both the aesthetic and the biological/ecological preconditions of responsive environments more uncannily than the others mentioned here. This was Frederick Kiesler, whose work in New York saw him move from a surrealist/*gesamtkunst* mode to that of a biotechnical engineer. Papanek (and McLuhan) acknowledged that Kiesler's iconic project for the Endless House (circa 1960) was one of several "experiments in acoustic space [that was] an attempt completely to break down linear structuring and finite limitations."[34] In retrospect, however, the Endless House appears like a more traditional *gesamtkunst* expression of Kiesler's ideas regarding environment.[35]

An altogether different model of environment would be expressed, however, in a remarkable 1939 essay in which Kiesler detailed an entire philosophy of design based on genetics, biology, and subject–environment interaction.[36] This new design method, called *biotechnique,* was based on Kiesler's philosophy of "correalism." Kiesler synthesized correalism and biotechnique in order to redefine reality itself, to reorient the basic functions of technology and architecture, and, in doing so, to reject the pseudofunctionalism of the 1920s. On the surface, this rejection entailed a shift away from thinking about design as a kind of formal manipulation of objects. Instead, Kiesler insisted, design had to address itself to the invisible forces and energies coursing through environment itself. Form, matter, a stable organism—these concepts were mere abstractions created by a literally shortsighted view of reality that focused only on the immediate illusion of static things. In fact, there was very little that was stable or static in Kiesler's universe. He developed the notion of correalism—a clear *détournement* of the label *surrealism*—as a way to describe this relational,

Figure 3.3. Frederick J. Kiesler, "On Correalism and Biotechnique: A Definition and Test of a New Approach to Building Design," *Architectural Record* 86, no. 3 (September 1939): 60–75. Courtesy of *Architectural Record.* Copyright 2018 Austrian Frederick and Lillian Kiesler Private Foundation, Vienna.

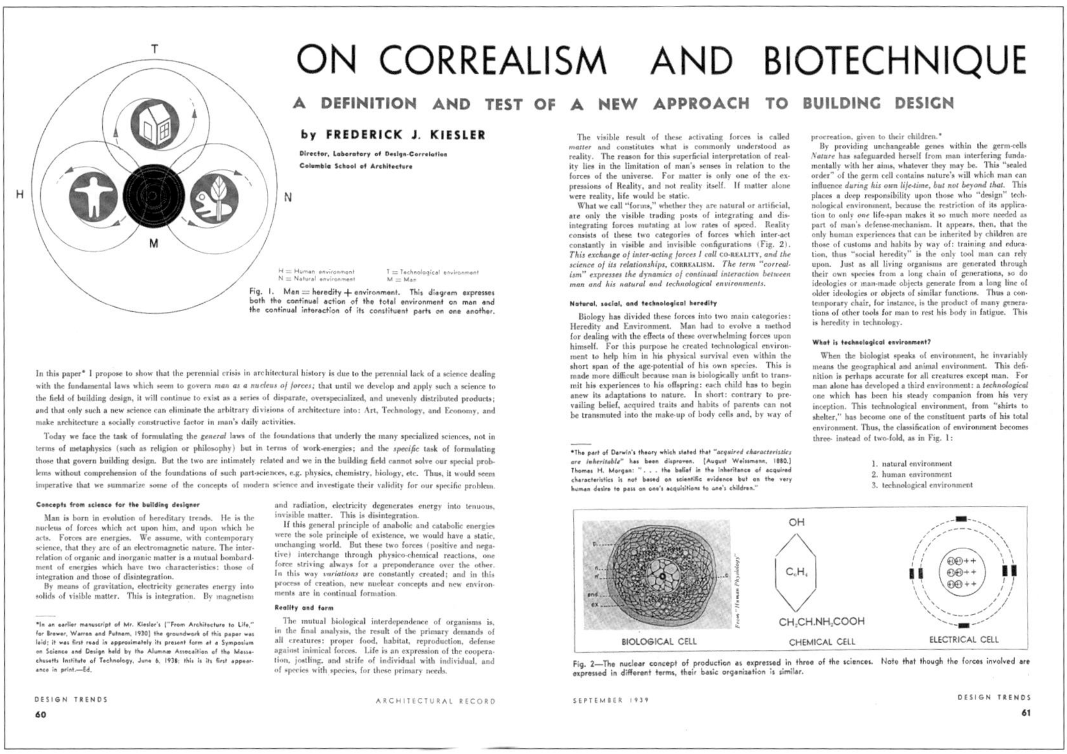

ON CORREALISM AND BIOTECHNIQUE

A DEFINITION AND TEST OF A NEW APPROACH TO BUILDING DESIGN

by FREDERICK J. KIESLER

Director, Laboratory of Design-Correlation
Columbia School of Architecture

H = Human environment
N = Natural environment
T = Technological environment
M = Man

Fig. 1. Man = heredity + environment. This diagram expresses both the continual action of the total environment on man and the continual interaction of its constituent parts on one another.

In this paper* I propose to show that the perennial crisis in architectural history is due to the perennial lack of a science dealing with the fundamental laws which seem to govern *man as a nucleus of forces;* that until we develop and apply such a science to the field of building design, it will continue to exist as a series of disparate, overspecialized, and unevenly distributed products; and that only such a new science can eliminate the arbitrary divisions of architecture into: Art, Technology, and Economy, and make architecture a socially constructive factor in man's daily activities.

Today we face the task of formulating the *general* laws of the foundations that underly the many specialized sciences, not in terms of metaphysics (such as religion or philosophy) but in terms of work-energies; and the *specific* task of formulating those that govern building design. But the two are intimately related and we in the building field cannot solve our special problems without comprehension of the foundations of such part-sciences, e.g. physics, chemistry, biology, etc. Thus, it would seem imperative that we summarize some of the concepts of modern science and investigate their validity for our specific problem.

Concepts from science for the building designer

Man is born in evolution of hereditary trends. He is the nucleus of forces which act upon him, and upon which he acts. Forces are energies. We assume, with contemporary science, that they are of an electromagnetic nature. The interrelation of organic and inorganic matter is a mutual bombardment of energies which have two characteristics: those of integration and those of disintegration.

By means of gravitation, electricity generates energy into solids of visible matter. This is integration. By magnetism and radiation, electricity degenerates energy into tenuous, invisible matter. This is disintegration.

If this general principle of anabolic and catabolic energies were the sole principle of existence, we would have a static, unchanging world. But these two forces (positive and negative) interchange through physico-chemical reactions, one force striving always for a preponderance over the other. In this way *variations* are constantly created; and in this process of creation, new nuclear concepts and new environments are in continual formation.

Reality and form

The mutual biological interdependence of organisms is, in the final analysis, the result of the primary demands of all creatures: proper food, habitat, reproduction, defense against inimical forces. Life is an expression of the cooperation, jostling, and strife of individual with individual, and of species with species, for these primary needs.

*In an earlier manuscript of Mr. Kiesler's ("From Architecture to Life," for Brewer, Warren and Putnam, 1930) the groundwork of this paper was laid; it was first read in approximately its present form at a Symposium on Science and Design held by the Alumnæ Assocaition of the Massachusetts Institute of Technology, June 6, 1938; this is its first appearance in print.—Ed.

The visible result of these activating forces is called *matter* and constitutes what is commonly understood as reality. The reason for this superficial interpretation of reality lies in the limitation of man's senses in relation to the forces of the universe. For matter is only one of the expressions of Reality, and not reality itself. If matter alone were reality, life would be static.

What we call "forms," whether they are natural or artificial, are only the visible trading posts of integrating and disintegrating forces mutating at low rates of speed. Reality consists of these two categories of forces which inter-act constantly in visible and invisible configurations (Fig. 2). *This exchange of inter-acting forces I call* CO-REALITY, *and the science of its relationships,* CORREALISM. *The term "correalism" expresses the dynamics of continual interaction between man and his natural and technological environments.*

Natural, social, and technological heredity

Biology has divided these forces into two main categories: Heredity and Environment. Man had to evolve a method for dealing with the effects of these overwhelming forces upon himself. For this purpose he created technological environment to help him in his physical survival even within the short span of the age-potential of his own species. This is made more difficult because man is biologically unfit to transmit his experiences to his offspring: each child has to begin anew its adaptations to nature. In short: contrary to prevailing belief, acquired traits and habits of parents can not be transmuted into the make-up of body cells and, by way of procreation, given to their children.*

By providing unchangeable genes within the germ-cells *Nature* has safeguarded herself from man interfering fundamentally with her aims, whatever they may be. This "sealed order" of the germ cell contains nature's will which man can influence *during his own life-time, but not beyond that.* This places a deep responsibility upon those who "design" technological environment, because the restriction of its application to only *one* life-span makes it so much more needed as part of man's defense-mechanism. It appears, then, that the only human experiences that can be inherited by children are those of customs and habits by way of: training and education, thus "social heredity" is the only tool man can rely upon. Just as all living organisms are generated through their own species from a long chain of generations, so do ideologies or man-made objects generate from a long line of older ideologies or objects of similar functions. Thus a contemporary chair, for instance, is the product of many generations of other tools for man to rest his body in fatigue. This is heredity in technology.

What is technological environment?

When the biologist speaks of environment, he invariably means the geographical and animal environment. This definition is perhaps accurate for all creatures except man. For man alone has developed a third environment: a *technological* one which has been his steady companion from his very inception. This technological environment, from "shirts to shelter," has become one of the constituent parts of his total environment. Thus, the classification of environment becomes three- instead of two-fold, as in Fig. 1:

1. natural environment
2. human environment
3. technological environment

*The part of Darwin's theory which stated that "*acquired characteristics are inheritable*" has been disproven. (August Weissmann, 1880.) Thomas H. Morgan: ". . . the belief in the inheritance of acquired characteristics is not based on scientific evidence but on the very human desire to pass on one's acquititions to one's children."

Fig. 2—The nuclear concept of production as expressed in three of the sciences. Note that though the forces involved are expressed in different terms, their basic organization is similar.

DESIGN TRENDS 60 ARCHITECTURAL RECORD SEPTEMBER 1939 DESIGN TRENDS 61 responsive, processual reality. Striking a profoundly Whiteheadian tone, Kiesler asserted:

> What we call "forms," whether they are natural or artificial, are only the visible trading posts of integrating and disintegrating forces mutating at low rates of speed. Reality consists of these two categories of forces which inter-act constantly in visible and invisible configurations. *This exchange of inter-acting forces I call* CO-REALITY, *and the science of its relationships,* CORREALISM. *The term "correalism" expresses the dynamics of continual interaction between man and his natural and technological environments.*[37]

Indeed, for Kiesler, reality was less about a bedrock of ontological entities than it was about the codependence of environmental energies. He diagrammed these in a tripartite Venn diagram, with the circulating forces of the "natural environment," the "human environment," and the "technological environment" not so much surrounding as generating "man" from the energetic overlap of their dynamic movements. These interactions Kiesler termed "total environment," and the human subject was the somewhat destabilized spiral at its center.

This subject and its well-being became for Kiesler the only true standard for conceiving a new philosophy of architecture, or the implementation of correalism as design method. Biotechnique, then, became the instrumentalization of the latter.[38] It represented a reorientation of all technical and formal activity toward the individual and social subject and its "health." Kiesler understood health in virtually thermodynamic terms, as an equilibrium between the poles of expenditure and conservation of energy, or, as he put it, "de-generation" and "re-generation."[39] According to Stephen Phillips:

> Architecture would thus function as a generator for the individual by protecting and replenishing one's energy forces; it would serve to energize both the *physis* and the *psyche* of the dweller as it coordinated the habits of everyday actions on a molar and molecular level. "If I use the chair," Kiesler maintained, "I accumulate its energy, I add it to mine"; when we use a chair we *absorb* its energy. Pseudoscientific theories of energy transfer between technology and the body situated in an ever-changing, adapting field suggested to Kiesler a state of pure automatism wherein the technological surface of elastic construction modulated in response to the body to control equilibrium and maintain good health.[40]

The "ever-changing, adapting field" referred to here is effectively the suite of environments diagrammed by Kiesler. His understanding of "technological environment" is perhaps the most germane to this discussion.[41]

For Kiesler, technological environment was both the source of human problems and the source of their solutions. "Man had to evolve a method for dealing with the effects of these overwhelming forces [of heredity and environment] upon himself. For this purpose he created technological environment to help him in his physical survival even within the short span of the age potential of his own species."[42] If other organisms had to contend only with the interactions of their genetic makeup and a relatively stable environment, humanity had complicated this formula with its technical contrivances, which together formed a new milieu. But if technological environment had alienated human beings from the natural rhythms of biological evolution, it also held the potential to enable them to reestablish control over these same processes. "What is environmental control?" asked Kiesler, defining it as "control of the human and natural environment through *technological environment*."[43]

If, over time, human production had resulted in increasing amounts of wasted energy and greater amounts of environmental disequilibrium, Kiesler maintained in a fascinating diagram, biotechnique—as the manipulation of the technological environment for the sake of human health—promised a way forward toward "reintegration" and equilibrium. But simple equilibrium or integration was not enough. (Is it ever?) Kiesler would go on to suggest (as would so many others a generation later) that human evolution itself could progress; it could become the project of a new design method.

> But man's evolution has proven that changing environment increases or decreases man's potentialities. Technological environment, being a part of the complex of environmental forces, must

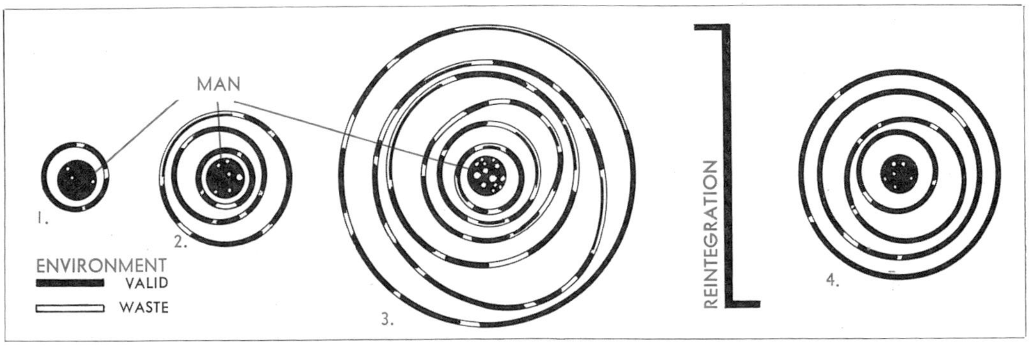

Fig. 5—Throughout his historical development man has steadily added to his technological environment. In his primitive stages this relationship was relatively well balanced (1); but through ancient and medieval times (2), this relationship became increasingly complex and unwieldy, until today (3) man's health is literally threatened by the very tools he created to protect it. Needed, therefore, is a planned re-integration of the technological environment, based upon elimination of waste (simulated) products and increased emphasis on new and higher standard types (4).

Figure 3.4. "Man's health is literally threatened by the very tools he created to protect it. Needed, therefore, is a planned re-integration of the technological environment." From Kiesler, "On Correalism and Biotechnique." Courtesy of *Architectural Record*. Copyright 2018 Austrian Frederick and Lillian Kiesler Private Foundation, Vienna.

> consciously contribute to the extraction and development of man's inherent possibilities into a higher order. What these possibilities are depends on the designer's ability to envision and realize them.[44]

Kiesler would embody these biotechnical principles in objects and buildings that relied on a psychophysical form of continuity, mobility, and response.[45] Surfaces extended topologically, components could be moved and rearranged, all in response to a newly conceived user/inhabitant.[46] The Space House of 1933 and the Endless House of circa 1960 would be the most substantial realizations of Kiesler's desire for environmental continuity. Seamless and continuous framing characterized the first, while a topological surface knotting together interior and exterior space constituted the latter.

We have in Kiesler's nascent environmental theory (forgotten by all but a few art historians) the synthetic vision of the responsive environment: an (invisible)[47] environment replete not with objects but with energies; a human subject being actively interpellated by these energies; and, finally, the possibility of *designing* the unit of subject plus environment. Kiesler would continue articulating his ideas of correalist responsiveness well into the postwar period, though his work would most often be relegated to discussions of artistic synthesis or, even more erroneously, "sculptural" architecture; this had the effect of aesthetically tamping down the dynamism of his ideas rather than setting them in motion as he desired.

Figure 3.5. Frederick Kiesler, *The Human—A Terrestrial Spectra,* undated [1937–42]. Copyright 2018 Austrian Frederick and Lillian Kiesler Private Foundation, Vienna.

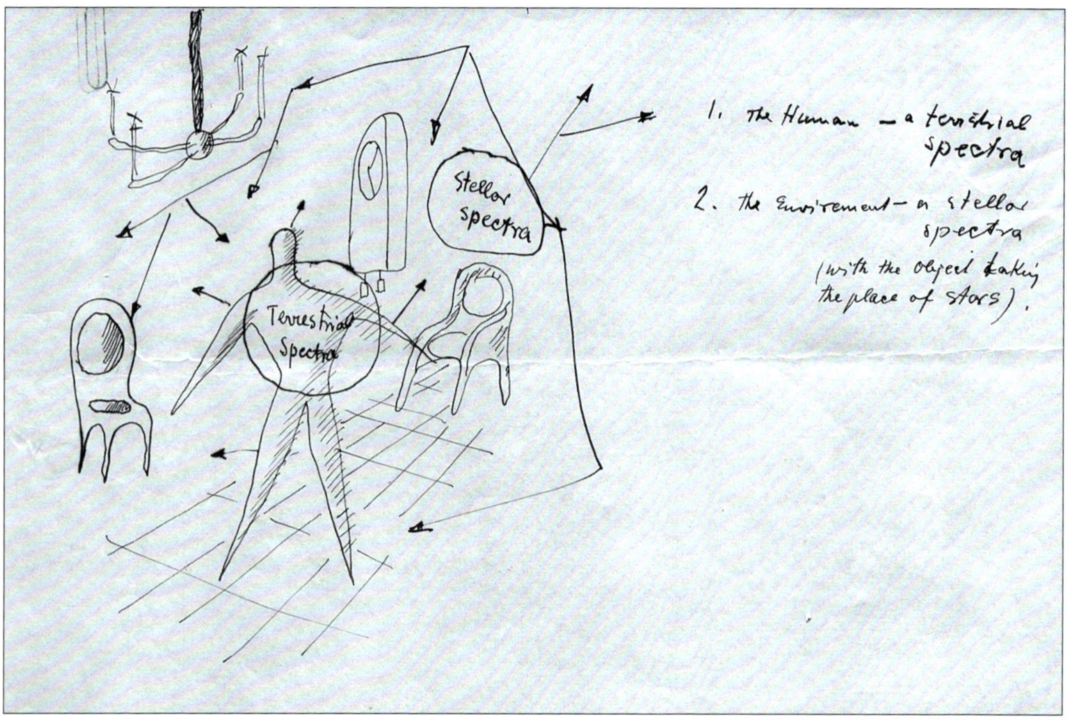

Because of this neglect, the daunting task of articulating the techno-aesthetic mechanisms of responsive environments for the postwar generation would fall to another (Austro-Hungarian) émigré: Gyorgy Kepes. While Kiesler and Kepes do not seem to have had a close relationship, they certainly followed similar directions, both navigating the neosurrealist and post-Bauhaus worlds in their respective techno-scientific-spiritual ways. Kepes's itinerary, as is well known, led him ultimately to MIT, where he became the very epitome of the promise of a "new sensibility" in postwar aesthetics with his founding of the Center for Advanced Visual Studies in 1967. For my purposes here, I can also make the observation that all of Kepes's work—from his surrealist photocollages of the 1930s to his interactive electronic environments of the 1970s—dealt with the complex interaction of subject and environment.

It must be stated at the outset as well that Kepes was not only one of the foremost conceptualizers of responsive environments but also perhaps the movement's (to use a completely hypostatory term) most energetic organizer and interdisciplinary translator. He became the node—or, as Reinhold Martin has written, a "receiver and transmitter"[48]—connecting specialists from diverse fields, including cybernetics, biology, psychology, ethology, anthropology, architecture, design, and art. Kepes desired a synthesis of these fields under the umbrella of aesthetics because of his steadfast belief in the latter as the only way to integrate and negate the vertiginous and destructive forces of what would come to be known as the military–industrial complex. The question of environment as it is understood here was absolutely central to this utopian project. We find in Kepes practically a metonymy of the development of the culture of environmental response. His earliest publications, *The Language of Vision* (1944) and *The New Landscape in Art and Science* (1956) in particular, can be seen as attempts to visualize the organizing forces of the human (technical and natural) milieu, and by the time he edited and published *Arts of the Environment* in 1972, the instrumentalization of these perceptual experiments seemed closer to realization and more relevant than ever before.[49]

Indeed, the continuity of this project can be summarized by reference to a simple gestalt diagram that Kepes used in *The Language of Vision* in which two intertwined rectilinear forms illustrated the "fluctuation of the figure and background." Like one reductive segment of a Fibonacci sequence, this composition demonstrated the give-and-take of visual dynamics just as it did the equilibrating tendencies of the human organism, whose "internal forces are acting to restore balance after each disturbance [visual stimulus] from outside."[50] The same image, now a kind of graphic or logo, was used on the dust jacket of *Arts of the Environment* in an implicitly expanded symbolic role, standing for the immanent rebalancing of natural and human environments through aesthetic integration.

As Reinhold Martin and now several others have shown, Kepes's aesthetic-biological project was deeply enmeshed with the cybernetic ethos

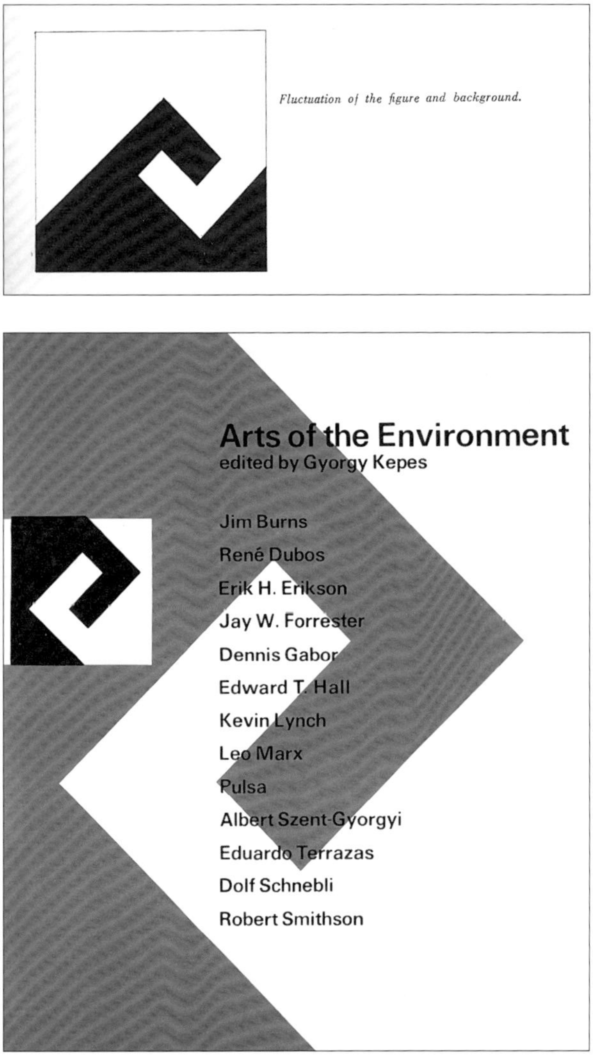

Figure 3.6. Gyorgy Kepes, gestalt diagram from *The Language of Vision* (1944) and cover of *Arts of the Environment* (1972). Copyright 1972 by George Braziller, Inc. Reprinted with the permission of George Braziller, Inc. (New York), www.georgebraziller.com.

of the 1940s and 1950s.[51] This allowed him to render virtually everything in the environment as "patterns" or "organizations"—sets of forces instead of stable and static entities. In *The New Landscape in Art and Science,* natural and human-made forms were juxtaposed in such a way as to suggest common underlying formal principles that might reveal the various hidden components of the human milieu, that might bring "into common focus visual features which were formerly too fast or too slow, too large or too small, too dense, too scattered, otherwise concealed from our eyes."[52] By somehow accessing this invisible environment, or what Kepes at this early stage preferred to render with the rather more quaint term "landscape," he hoped to "overcome the alienation between observer and object."[53] The utopian nostalgia here for a reintegration of the subject with the things around it would remain the underlying engine for Kepes's research and creative production. It would also increasingly be expressed in terms of environment and response. As with McLuhan, Kepes believed that once environmental patterning had been recognized, it would then be subject to techno-aesthetic manipulation and optimization.[54] Indeed, this was the theme of McLuhan's contribution to Kepes's 1966 volume *The Man-Made Object,* part of the famous Vision + Value Series that Kepes published with George Braziller.[55]

Not just McLuhan's but most of the contributions of the various specialists with whom Kepes interacted during the time he was publishing this series of books were, at least in Kepes's mind, working toward a common utopian goal of reintegrating humanity with an environment utterly transformed by technology. This sensibility manifested most explicitly as what we can identify as a concern for "responsive environments" in the last book in the Vision + Value Series, *Arts of the Environment.* Published in 1972, six years after its most recent predecessor in the series, it was something of an outlier both thematically and chronologically. This compendium was both broader in scope and more focused than previous volumes. Gone were the didactic image collections, and, to a certain extent, gone too was the exclusive emphasis on *vision*. This was a more visceral, urgent, polemical, political, and searching collection of texts by, admittedly, some of the usual Cambridge and East Coast fixtures (which is by no means a denigration, as these included Erik Erikson, recent Pulitzer Prize winner René Dubos, and Nobel laureate Dennis Gabor), but also by the politicized Leo Marx, the anthropologist Edward T. Hall, and contemporary artists Robert Smithson and the collective Pulsa. As Bill Arning has pointed out, the book seems something like a victory, or at least a capstone, in which Kepes realized the true scope of his decades-long project of fusing art and science for the benefit of humanity.[56]

Kepes's own contributions to *Arts of the Environment* were not his first pronouncements regarding the possibilities of a technical and aesthetic mediation of environmental interaction, but they were his most explicit. Kepes's introductory essay reads like a phenomenological and ecological explosion of his earlier interest in the fundamental structures of visual phenomena. Here, both artist and viewer (or, rather, participant) are bodily entities moving erratically through the interconnected and complex systems that constitute the earth itself. Environment in this text becomes both problem and solution: "A wildly proliferating man-made environment has shrunk living space, dimmed light, bleached color, and relentlessly expanded noise, speed, and complexity."[57] If unchecked technology had caused this disastrous state of affairs (which, frankly, Kepes acknowledges only as a pretext for his own philosophical solutions), only the new aesthetic sensibility could once again align technological interventions with the values of a new, human-centered worldview.

Kepes defined this utopian possibility by synthesizing many of the sources and insights regarding ecology, psychology, physics, and biology that have recurred so many times already in the present text. Just like Kiesler (to give one example) before him, Kepes rejected the overly objective view of Newtonian physics and Cartesian space. In their place he offered new models of processual, contingent, and transactional realities characteristic of the radical contextualism of the environmental research complex circa 1970. Moving quickly beyond observations on natural disasters, pollution, and resource management, he concerned himself with the very nature of life itself:

> Every physical form, every living form, every pattern of feeling or thought has its own unique identity, its boundaries, its extension and its wider context; it contains or is contained by another pattern; it follows or is followed by another pattern. The unique identity, discrete shape, and nature of a space-occupying substance are shaped by the boundary that separates it from and connects it

> to the space outside. An organic form lives and grows only through its intricate transactions with its environment. An optical event becomes a visually perceived figure only when seen against its ground. The quality, feeling, and meaning of a sound is cast in the matrix of the physical processes that generated it; it is not independent of its surrounding silence or the other sounds that frame it. In the same way the physical, biological, or moral individuality of man is the function of his active relationship with the physical and social environment.[58]

Perhaps most interesting in this remarkable passage is Kepes's ambivalence regarding his desire for entities to have their "own unique identity," even as he embraces the radical interconnectivity—with its dissipation of discrete objects and identities—of the environmental paradigm.

Perhaps predictably, it would be artists and designers who might be able to resolve this ambivalence, to acknowledge the physical reality of a world of porous boundaries and systemic entropy even while marshaling those forces into a higher level of subject–environment integration and control. In a sequence of propositions strongly echoing Kiesler's correalism and biotechnique (though, again, he acknowledged no particular influence), Kepes detailed the ramifications of these insights in another remarkable passage that moves from social critique to an outright utopianism of responsive environments:

> The dominant matrix of nineteenth-century attitudes was the use of Marx's term "reification"; relationships were interpreted in terms of things, objects, or commodity values. Today a reversal of this attitude has begun to appear; there is a steadily increasing movement in science and in art toward processes and systems that dematerialize the object world and discredit physical possessions. What scientists considered before as substance shaped into forms, and consequently understood as tangible objects, is now recognized as energies and their dynamic organization. In the visual arts, painters and sculptors have arrived at conclusions not unlike those of the scientists. Artists have liberated their images and forms from the inhibiting world of object. Painting has become the capture and arrangement of visual energies. Through the innovations of a number of contemporary architects and engineers, buildings are also losing their object solidity and opacity to become light and transparent, "thingless" events. . . . Architecture is making fundamental departures from its traditional position as a discrete, independent, heavy, and solid form catering mainly to the visual sense and is becoming a responding, bodiless, dynamic, interdependent structure answering to man's changing needs and growing controls. . . . Buildings and groups of buildings are no longer considered sculp-

> tural forms and their space-organizations, but rather as systems of functions, programming life patterns with the participation of those concerned.[59]

In the six years that intervened between the earlier volumes of the Vision + Value Series and this one, perhaps the signal change that Kepes's thinking underwent was from a purely visual engagement with the underlying structures of things in the world to a sublatory embrace of their real-world, immersive environmental interactions—from "pattern seeing" to "programming life patterns." These years also saw the finalization of plans for, and the inauguration of, the Center for Advanced Visual Studies (CAVS) at MIT. Certainly his years at MIT introduced Kepes to the possibility not just of an environmental *scale* for art—a concern that went back to his earliest work in Chicago, during which he flew over the city to deduce the optimum patterns for military camouflage[60]—but of incorporating technology as part of aesthetic and operative feedback loops built into the architecture of particular spaces.

Not coincidentally, Kepes spent this time refining his understanding of organism–environment interactions and the ways in which such biological and cultural principles could be integrated into a new civic art. Traces of his evolving ideas are most explicit in a series of unpublished essays with titles such as "Perception of Spatial Environment," "Perception of the Complex Dynamic Environment," and "Man-Made Environment."[61] "Contemporary man regards himself as an object within objects," Kepes wrote,

> as a separate entity isolated from everybody else. He individualizes objects and estimates them by the degree in which they differ from each other. Divorced from the field in which they exist, man and the things he creates are gradually losing their vital qualities. We must reverse this present way of thinking and acting and must extend the new scientific understanding namely, that the field and the behavior of the objects are correlative, to our social structure and to the structuring of our physical environment.[62]

Like so many other purveyors of environmental response during these years, Kepes came to see environment as both prevailing condition and deployable structure—both problem and solution. "In the rational, intellectual, objective range of our response to the surrounding world we read the multitude of electromagnetic signals coming from our environment. From these signals we impute structure, a sensed space, in meanings of substance, form, distance, and motion. Each of the environmental patterns that speak to us of sensed space has also its aspect of poetry."[63]

It would be this poetry of environmental feedback that Kepes would envision embodying at the CAVS, integrating the raw biological mechanisms of life with a new interactive art and architecture:

> Today, however, for perhaps the first time in human history the possibility of employing inner regulators on an extended body scale. *[sic]* The man-created environment is full of elements that serve as the extended body of the human organism.
>
> Our sophisticated electronic technology offers a growing range of devices, which both as physical and conceptual implements promise *that we can regain our responsiveness* and establish control over the overwhelming man-created environment.[64]

Such lofty syntheses were not easily achieved, but attempts were made. With the inspiration and collaboration of the center's fellows, for instance, Kepes realized perhaps his only true responsive environment (in the sense of a design object): a work called *Photo-Elastic Walk* (1970), installed at the Smithsonian. It comprised a darkened space with a floor embedded with screens and lights, the illumination and patterns of which would change as viewers walked across the surface (Plate 5). But this work was just a fragment of the modes of environmental response Kepes envisioned through the CAVS. Indeed, such initiatives loomed large in the center's mission statement, which called for

> the raising of the scale of work to the scale of the urban setting; media geared to all sensory modalities; incorporation of natural processes, such as cloud play, water flow, and the cyclical variations of light and weather; acceptance of the participation of "spectators" in such a way that art becomes a confluence rather than a dialogue . . . intensifying the intra-individual world and at the same time developing networks of communication between individuals and between the individual and the environment.[65]

In *Arts of the Environment* Kepes was already describing several of these projects, both impressionistically and in detail. Speaking (presumably) of the work of CAVS fellows, Kepes described "imaginative younger architects and engineers [who] have moved still further away from weight and have touched upon the possibilities of enclosing space with air currents. Like instant envelopes these currents could be turned on or off as needed by sophisticated sensing and computing devices regulated by weather conditions."[66]

In his second essay in this volume, "The Artist's Role in Environmental Self-Regulation," it was as though the early patterns revealed in *The New Landscape in Art and Science* could finally be designed as a new, interactive urban field. In an almost apocalyptic register, Kepes described the world as a "toxic carcass" whose inhabitants were "on the brink of ecological suicide."[67] In perfect continuity with his earlier formulations, he then asserted that only (certain) artists had the requisite sensibilities to integrate the natural, social, and technological aspects of this state of affairs into works that would not only register environmental materials and energies but could also mobilize and visualize these, rendering them available to viewers and participants as aesthetic interfaces. The projects and prototypes Kepes went on to describe were an admixture of high technology and the primal human experiences of elements such as water and light. His most urgent and extensive proposal entailed "combinations of pollution-abatement technology and vital aesthetic experiences."[68] More concretely, he continued, water treatment equipment could be placed in central urban settings, its complex engineering structures of tubes and valves exposed, constituting kinetic sculptures. These facilities, in turn, could be integrated with dynamic fountains, recalling the gardens at Tivoli, perhaps. Synthesizing these monumental and energetic impressions, Kepes added that the resulting works need not simply be viewed; rather,

> the water-dynamic could be programmed by involving the visitors' participation through sensors. Some water areas can be housed in inflated plastic structures. Some performances can be modulated in temperature and create a cooling oasis in summer. Refrigeration and various forms of heating could extend the morphology of water appearances, from visible freezing to kinetic air-and-water sculpture exhibiting bubbles produced by heating.[69]

Kepes did not detail how the sensors he mentioned might work, or how the viewers' presence would generate a responsive dynamic. What seemed more important to him was the assertion of the possibility of a grand synthesis of environmental materials and their techno-aesthetic potentials for responsiveness.

The other key aspect of Kepes's proposals—and those of CAVS fellows that he also described and illustrated in this essay—is that they went beyond the aestheticization of technology to the aestheticization of environmental data, "utilizing focal urban data."

> There are potent technical ways of using sophisticated instrumentation to bring into a single spatial focus the widest range of data relevant to common urban life. Distant sensors coupled to transmitters and monitoring data to a central display device may report conditions of air, noise, water, heat pollution, and traffic congestion. An intricate synergistic system can serve as an all-around feedback mechanism, reporting on the total urban environment.[70]

Illustrating what such a device might look like was a proposal by Ecuadorian artist/architect and CAVS fellow Mauricio Bueno for a Pollution Monitoring Tower, a monolith presumably embedded with precisely the types of sensors and displays described by Kepes. But while the function of such a sculpture-instrument would aid in the fight against ecological catastrophe, it would

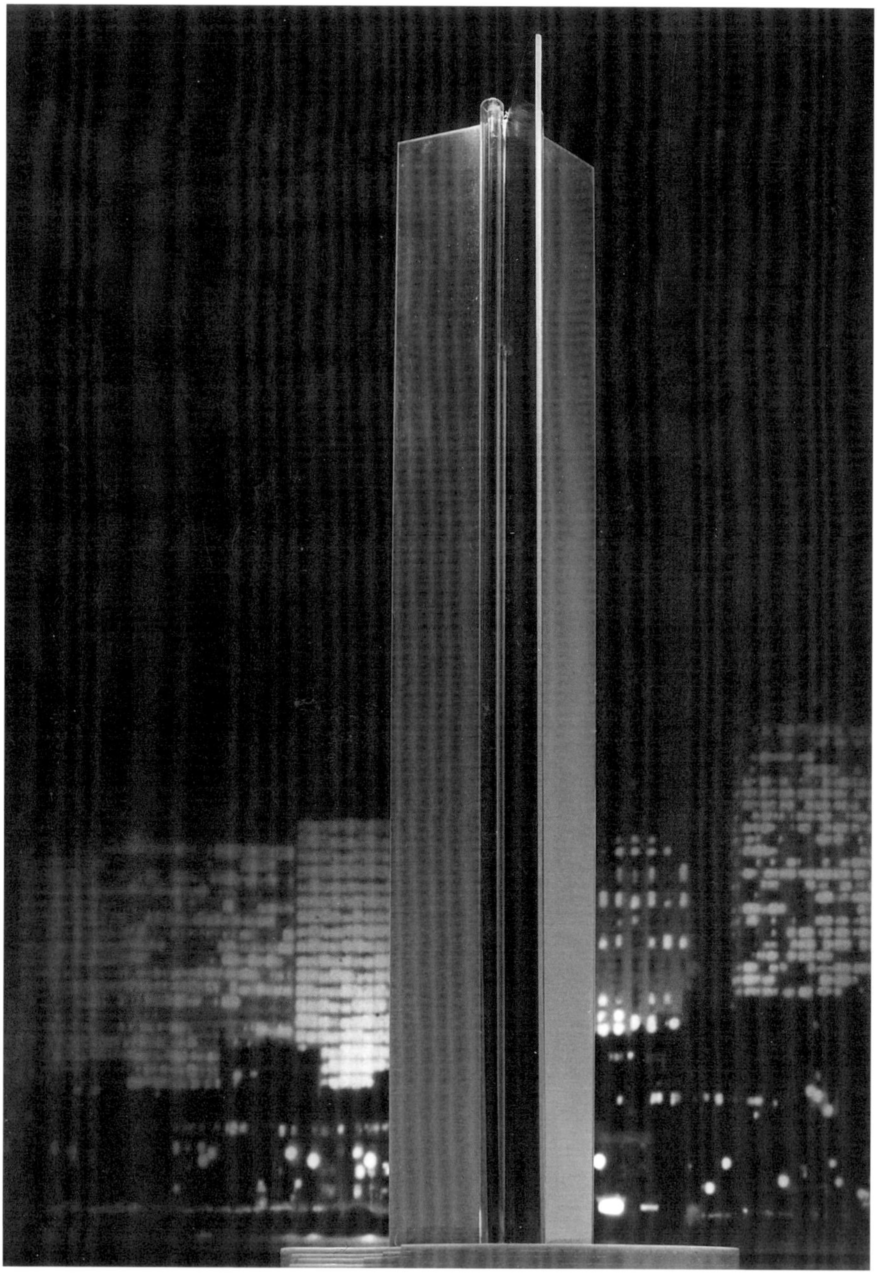

Figure 3.7. Mauricio Bueno, proposal for a Pollution Monitoring Tower (1969). Courtesy of MIT Program in Arts, Culture, and Technology.

also transcend the raw urgency of such a function, additionally instigating new forms of human interaction. Kepes wrote: "The space format given in this juxtaposition of the information core and congenial surroundings could serve to release suppressed play instincts, the sense of adventure that today is forced underground and turns to violence or drugs. Above all, it offers a sense of freedom to men who can respond to a responsive environment."[71]

The Neo-Avant-Garde Environment

While it is now commonplace to remark on Kepes's marginalization vis-à-vis contemporaneous art (and, to a lesser extent, architectural) practice at this time, the fact is that this margin was growing steadily wider well into the 1970s. The CAVS had several well-known (European) fellows (and administrators), most prominently Otto Piene and Hans Haacke.[72] By the time *Arts of the Environment* appeared, Kepes acknowledged the significance of the work of Pulsa and Robert Smithson, both of whom engaged with environment, albeit in very different registers. This was perhaps Kepes's most sincere attempt to court members of the younger American generation and to align their work with the European avant-garde tradition that has concerned us here. But the fit was uneasy; the related but not necessarily compatible worlds of the European and American neo-avant-gardes seemed to have different understandings of precisely the environmental dynamics currently under consideration.

In Europe, the postwar period saw the concern for environmental interaction manifesting across a wide range of formats, all of which seemed to derive from the purist avant-gardes of De Stijl, the Bauhaus, and constructivism (or, in the case of *nouveau réalisme,* from Dada). These would take the form of concrete art, kinetic art, optical art, and other forms of simple mechanical or aesthetic interaction.[73] If these moments of aesthetic interaction were initially condensed into a singular work or *objet,* there was also a broad tendency to see them expanded into larger environments, which, on several occasions, took the form of labyrinths. These tendencies, in their turn, would dovetail with the emergence of computer art, thanks to an international network of interdisciplinary researchers.[74] Many of these concerns, though, in a particularly ironic (though hardly coincidental) twist, would converge in the single personage of Kepes's countryman Nicolas Schöffer, who had settled in Paris. Schöffer had been involved for many years in the elaboration of explicitly cybernetic-aesthetic programs of controlling environmental ambiences through myriad feedback techniques, including sensors built into the structures of his sculptural works and direct control via computer terminal. Also, in concert with Kepes, Schöffer envisioned his work broadened to an architectural and urban scale, to the extent that the entire built environment would take on the form of a self-regulating computer system.[75]

But the very completeness of Schöffer's project prevented it from being easily accessible. It was a massive, computerized *Gesamtkunstwerk* that seemed to exist only in the utopian vision of a single creator (despite its programmatic mutability by users). Such singular and unified models of responsive environments were the exception. It was as though when such a project was presented as a fait accompli, the impracticality of its conception and realization became immediately apparent. Accordingly, and as stated above, the field of architectural design proper was seldom

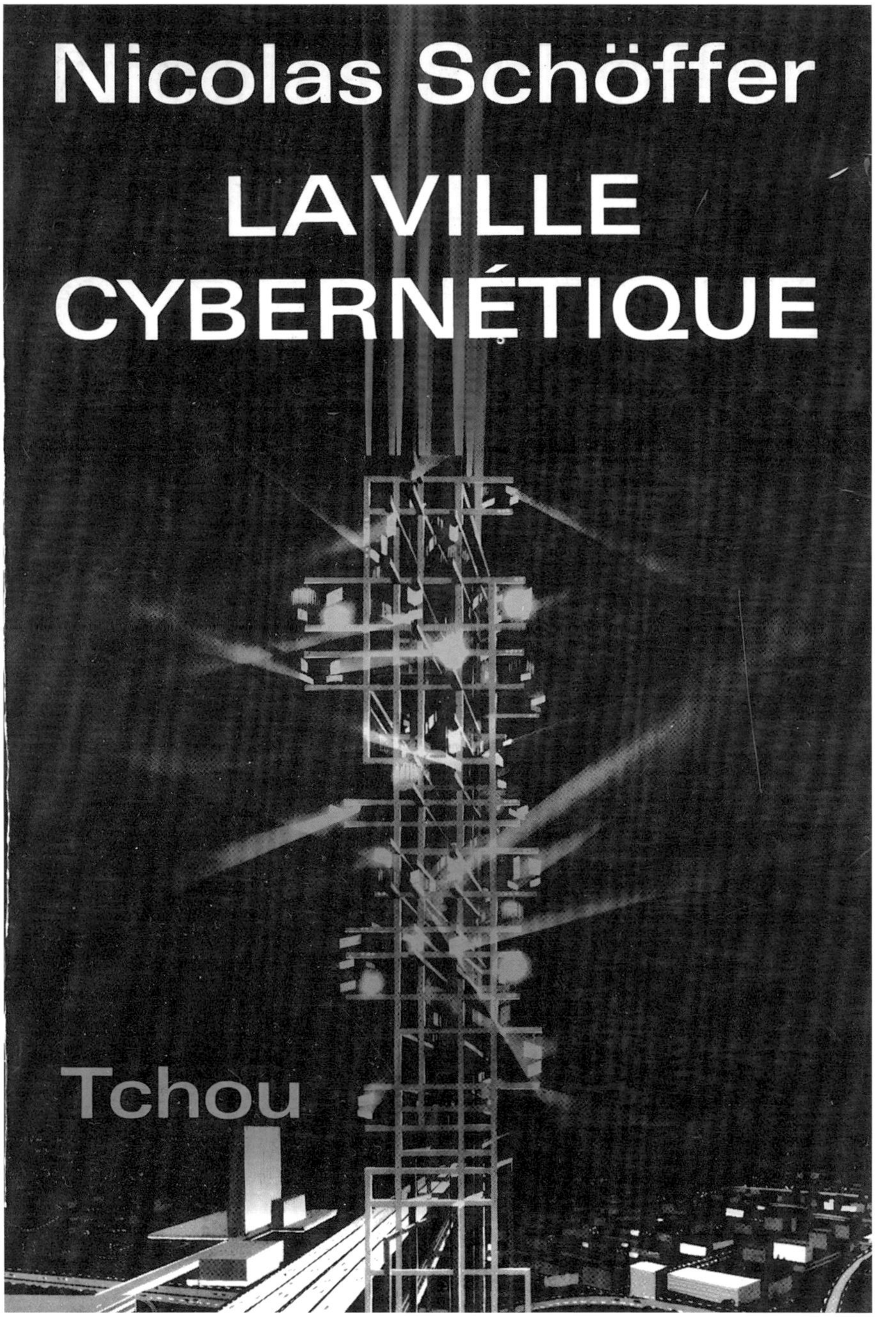

Figure 3.8. Nicolas Schöffer, Tour Lumière Cybernétique (1963). Copyright 2019 Artists Rights Society (ARS), New York/ ADAGP, Paris.

interested in such propositions. It took avant-garde theater directors, computer scientists, and technically inclined artists to make the most substantial statements about such spaces. More often, these statements emerged only in collective ways, as accumulations of tangentially related projects and concerns glimpsed in edited volumes and group exhibitions. Appropriately enough, the potential of responsive environments was (and, frankly, is) thus indicated most powerfully only indirectly, through a process of recognition of the patterns generated by the overlapping interstices between and among related works, and through disciplinary leaps of faith from technology to art, for instance, or biology to engineering. This section tracks a few of the most important such initiatives, from group exhibitions to theoretical publications that dealt primarily with art and its technological inflection.

Take, for instance, Kepes's inclusion of the work of Pulsa in *Arts of the Environment.* No doubt, in that context, the group's work appeared as one possible manifestation of the types of environmental systems Kepes was imagining. One of Pulsa's most well-known works was installed at New York's Museum of Modern Art in 1969 in a fascinating show curated by Jennifer Licht called *Spaces.* Here, five "neutral" galleries were given over to Michael Asher, Larry Bell, Dan Flavin, Robert Morris, and Franz Erhard Walther, and the museum's sculpture garden was given to Pulsa. These artists' projects, which ran the gamut of postminimalist strategies—involving sensory deprivation, found objects, participatory gestures, and so on—had clearly derived, for Licht, from the futurists, the *Gesamtkunstwerk,* and the other precedents mentioned above. Licht believed it was important to stress the ways in which the historical avant-garde had begun a project brought to fruition only by the neo-avant-garde (a term she did not use). This project involved, first of all, the explication of the invisible environment, followed by the rendering of Cartesian space as a kind of malleable plastic substance. In her introduction to the exhibition's catalog, Licht wrote:

> Actual space is, of course, immaterial. Because it cannot be perceived by any of the five senses, it must be qualified by boundary or incident, and can be comprehended through direct kinesthetic experience. In the past, space was merely an attribute of a work of art, rendered by illusionistic conventions in painting or by displacement of volume in sculpture, and the space that separated viewer and object was ignored as just distance. This invisible dimension is now being considered as an active ingredient, not simply to be represented but to be shaped and characterized by the artist, and capable of involving and merging viewer and art in a situation of greater scope and scale.[76]

Despite the diversity of these installations (as we would now reflexively describe them), Licht saw them all as partaking in the emerging environmental consciousness. She readily acknowledged the perceptual/behavioral, conditioning, manipulative—and responsive (or reactive)—properties of environment:

> Working within the almost unlimited potential of these enlarged, more spatially complex circumstances, the artist is now free to

> influence and determine, even govern, the sensations of the viewer. The human presence and perception of the spatial context have become materials of art. . . .
>
> Until social and scientific thought and parallel developments in other arts could create a context wherein art could be the conditioning of space and environment, and technological resources were available to realize theoretical concepts of space, they outstripped the artist's ability to achieve appropriate form. . . .
>
> In this "Space Age," space is no longer an abstraction. Synthesizing the greater intellectual and physical scope demanded by such times, art may be developing a new humanism in its incorporation within its context of man and his actions and reactions.[77]

(Interestingly, Licht studiously avoided using the term *environment* on all but a few occasions in the catalog. This seems to have had the practical benefit of distinguishing these works from Kaprowian happenings and the intermedia movement, where the term was used to exhaustion.) Without going into great detail regarding the installations themselves, we can note that Pulsa's multimedia and interactive environment in the sculpture garden was distinct from the others, and, accordingly, closest to the class of responsive environments we are concerned with here (Plates 6 and 7). It involved light, sound, and complex feedback mechanisms that responded to viewers' movement through the space.[78] The project was similar to an installation the group consulted on with Charles Moore and Felix Drury at the Yale Art and Architecture Building the same year.[79]

In Pulsa's contribution to *Arts of the Environment,* the group's members reflected on this and other installations in an essay titled "The City as an Artwork."[80] Here, they essentially deconstructed the entire urban milieu into conceptions of hardware and software, asserting that both of these systems needed to be restructured to be more "visible" and more participatory. In a way that seemed very much in alignment with Kepes's ideas, they imagined that interactive installations such as theirs should not be isolated to special exhibition conditions, but rather should form the basis for the city as a whole. They imagined that all urban systems would be computer monitored, and data regarding traffic, energy usage, and so on should constitute the basis of aesthetic nodes with which inhabitants could interact:

> large-scale environmental art works designed to be part of public spaces; public as well as private sensoriums; silent rooms for rest and meditation; and computer storage of facts, statistics, and the special problems and history of urban evolution. . . . Super-sensory areas should be created that would make use of the technology developed from research in bio-feedback, artificial intelligence, body navigation similar to space travel to the moon and telepathic

> experiments which demonstrate the relativistic nature of time and energy flow in travel and communication.[81]

While this logic (though not its full realization) was being played out in the MoMA sculpture garden in 1969, however, different attitudes prevailed inside. Michael Asher lined his gallery with sound-absorbent material to create an acoustically muffled space; an amplifier and speakers effected a "distribution of anonymous sound sources."[82] Here, response was figured in terms of deprivation as much as in terms of stimulation. In another room, Dan Flavin installed a gridded partition of fluorescent lights attached to a wooden frame. This work created an atmosphere to be sure, but one that hovered in tension with its Duchampian sympathies for the everyday object, signaling perhaps what Hal Foster has pointed to as Flavin's antipathy toward the ubiquity of art "environments."[83]

Such ideological and aesthetic tensions remind us that utopian and cybernetic initiatives like those of Pulsa sat somewhat uneasily with the counterculture, on the one hand, and especially the post-Greenbergian art that was developing in the 1960s, on the other. This is to say nothing of the additional tensions created by the divergent concerns of European and American practices. Art histories of this moment—for obvious logistical reasons—have tended to isolate these various phenomena in terms of both medium and geography. The differences between postminimalism, for instance, and the kinetic/interactive art appearing in Paris in the mid- to late 1960s seem far greater than the similarities. There is a very

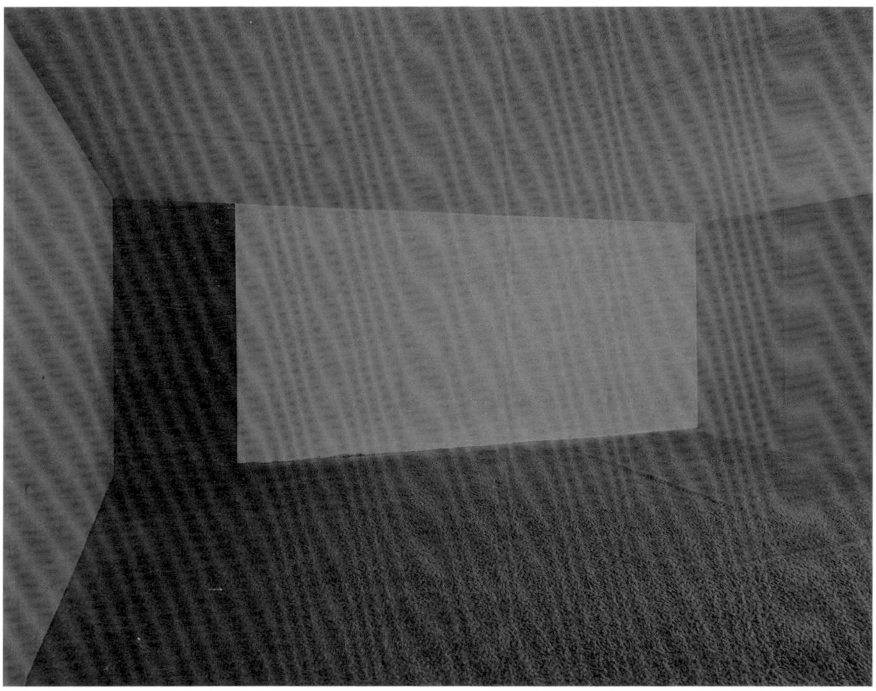

Figure 3.9. Michael Asher, Untitled (1969). "Michael Asher, in fact, employs entirely nonvisual means to organize, structure, and divide space. . . . By using sound, Asher creates, controls, and articulates sensory space" (Jennifer Licht, *Spaces* catalog). Installation view of the exhibition *Spaces* (1969–70). The Museum of Modern Art, New York, Photographic Archive. Digital image copyright The Museum of Modern Art. Licensed by SCALA / Art Resource, NY.

different historical consciousness evident in just this one instance; the Americans all but denying any relationship to the historic avant-garde, for example, while the Europeans were entangled with it in a far more complex Freudian and Marxian dynamic.[84] And what of the relationship to technology? In postminimal practice it was largely eschewed or framed in terms of culture and aesthetics, while in Europe it was seen as one among several legitimate means to new aesthetic ends. Additionally, these binary vicissitudes become infinitely more complex when intermedia, for instance, or "computer art," is factored in.[85] But despite the multiplicity of distinctions among these diverse tendencies in diverse locations, I can hazard a generalization that *environment* was one site of potential overlap (not congruence, mind you).

For instance, at virtually the same moment as the *Spaces* exhibition, Willoughby Sharp, from his base in New York, was organizing two exhibitions that would prove to be some of the most explicit evocations of the environmental impulse in the postwar period. One of these shows, titled *Kineticism: Systems Sculpture in Environmental Situations,* was mounted in Mexico City in 1968. It included a diversity of artists: works by old stalwarts like Jean Tinguely and Yaacov Agam were displayed just meters from those of Hans Haacke, Otto Piene, Julio Le Parc, Robert Morris, and Günther Uecker. The rooms presented successive experiences of immersion, disorientation, and visual ecstasy in varying degrees. The same year, Sharp was assembling work by some of the same artists (and others) for a show originating in Philadelphia. Here, the motif of air would allow him to unite such disparate artists as Morris, Andy Warhol, and David Medalla. And while the device of inflatable structures and the incorporation of vast reaches of "empty" space into the associated field of the works were common principles, it was Sharp's own radical understanding of environment that would provide the ultimate raison d'être. This is evident in the epigraph to this chapter, in which environment comes to function as a profoundly existential point of contact between the subject and the myriad systems surrounding her. Sharp would posit art as a significant mediator in this regard:

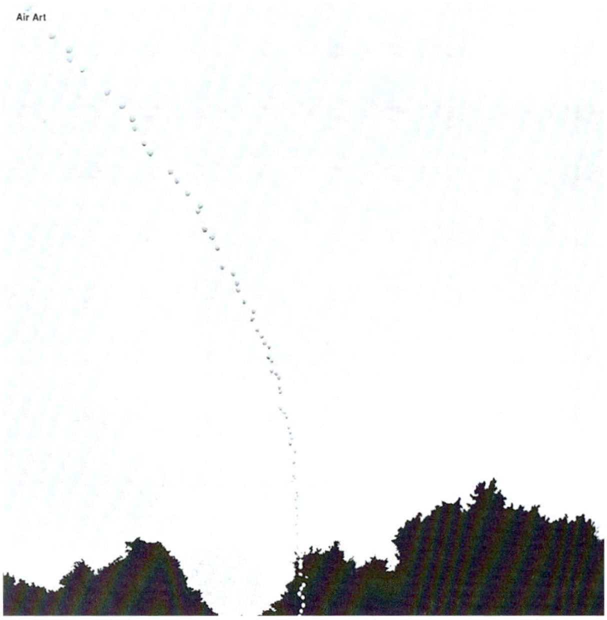

Figure 3.10. Cover of Willoughby Sharp, *Air Art* (1969), with Hans Haacke, *Skyline* (1967). Copyright Hans Haacke / Artists Rights Society, New York / VG Bild-Kunst, Bonn. Courtesy of the artist and Paula Cooper Gallery, New York.

> Our environment is an unstable activity. Any change in the environment always causes a change in man. Art is one of the elements in the matrix that creates new

> situations and sensation. . . . We have now so radically altered our environment that we must radically modify ourselves if we are going to continue to exist in this new open-ended environment. The new art facilitates this modification. It is a dynamic force which transforms life rather than transfixes it.[86]

Some of these same concerns are evident in the critical and curatorial work of Sharp's contemporary Jack Burnham, a CAVS alumnus who, despite his underestimation of kinetic art, would take up the unfinished project of reconciling science and art into an environmental situation (while recognizing the similarities and differences between responsive, interactive work and conceptual art and postminimalism, for instance). Burnham would, like Kepes, Kiesler, McLuhan, and others, set about attacking the Cartesian categories in favor of what he famously described as "systems aesthetics." As he stated in his seminal essay of that title: "A polarity is presently developing between the finite, unique work of high art, i.e., painting or sculpture, and conceptions that can loosely be termed 'unobjects,' these being either environments or artifacts that resist prevailing critical analysis."[87] Here Burnham was at pains to be inclusive in his definition of systems aesthetics (he allowed the minimalists and their European counterparts to coexist without too much tension) but also to be rigorous in his understanding of a new environmental (or unobject) approach to art as well as its linkages to the historic avant-garde. "Systems Aesthetics" would prove to be a rehearsal for the argument Burnham laid out in his book *Beyond Modern Sculpture,* where the expansive and environmental impulse became, rather than a subset of artistic activity, a teleological horizon for all art. "Systems-oriented art," Burnham wrote, "dropping the term 'sculpture'—will deal less with artifacts contrived for their formal value, and increasingly with men enmeshed *with* and *within* purposeful responsive systems."[88]

It was also Burnham who raised serious questions about not only the nature of responsive systems and environments but also the degree to which these would be technological and/or aesthetic in nature and to what extent the logic of digital systems would come to determine life within them. In his famous 1970 *Software* show at the Jewish Museum, Burnham once again curated a wide variety of practices based on the systems approach. Even the corporate sponsor of this exhibition—American Motors Corporation—recognized both the interactive and the environmental implications of the work: work that "concentrates on the interaction between people and their electronic and electromechanical surroundings. This is the same exploration, in human factors, which we use in the engineering design of our automobiles as a human environment."[89] For his part, Burnham was interested in placing interaction—as opposed to passive contemplation—at the center of the art/museum experience. The emphasis on "software" was as much a way of stressing process over object as it was of emphasizing particular technologies. These processes, in turn, would have an interventional effect on the viewer relative to the everyday environment. Burnham wanted the show to induce in the visitor a state of "introspection rather than inspection." He asked this proverbial visitor to "sense your responses when you perceive in a new way or interact with something or someone in an unusual situation."[90] This attitude was premised on the general conviction that "software" was not a particular product or technology but a way of being in a new world totally transformed by new forms of transactions between humans and their milieu. Ending his summation on a profoundly Kepesian note, Burnham insisted accordingly that the exhibition was not a collection of "technological art; rather it points to the information technologies as a pervasive environment badly in need of the sensitivity traditionally associated with art."[91]

Again, it is necessary to stress here that the word *environment* was used in the *Software* catalog (and in many of the other sources under consideration here) in ways both very broad—as a vague evocation of a general social condition—and quite literal and specific, referring to the immediate surroundings of the subject. It evoked the very manifold that so many specialists had already been attempting to "perceive" for some time, a manifold comprising energetic, informatic, and physiological systems as visceral and immersive substances. The many references to the "information environment" and "computerized environment" that characterized descriptions of the works on view had this dual meaning in common. Some of the pieces made this very explicit. Certainly, the MIT Architecture Machine Group's *Seek* project was the most significant of these, but others did this in different ways.

John Goodyear's project, for instance, measured the heat and sweat of visitors via "Thermal Experience Zones," or sheets of heat-sensitive material that changed color based on ambient conditions and the touch of viewers.[92] Goodyear went so far as to attempt to render the entire museum into such a zone by "testing" particular visitors for their various thermal responses. This test, he wrote, "points to the entire space of the Museum as a Thermal Experience Zone, and to the body of the viewer as the sensing agent."[93] Robert Barry's installation, *Ultrasonic Wave Piece,* used a room of the museum thus: "ultrasonic waves (40KHz), reflected off interior surfaces, filling selected area with invisible changing patterns and forms."[94] These projects, taken along with Asher's described above, demonstrate the degree to which environmental response was as much about invisible conditioning mechanisms as it was about technological interaction.

In this sense, the *Software* show is remarkable because it charted, in a more direct way than most other manifestations, the intersections of the environmental concerns of so many (mainly East Coast) art and technology initiatives. It brought together MIT programmers with conceptual artists and mapped the ways in which their activities could be considered alongside, for instance, the work of the intermedia artists, Gene

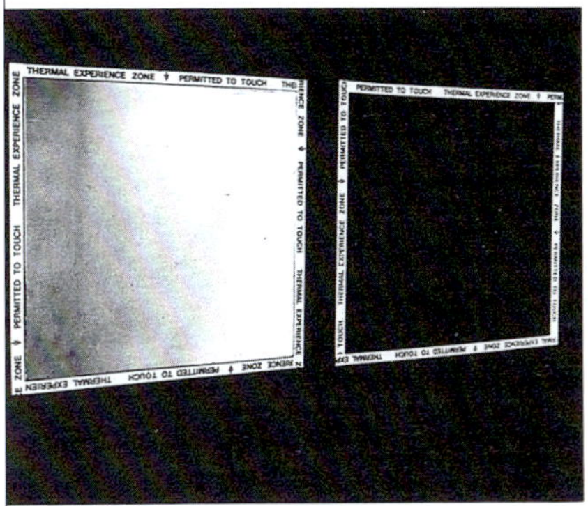

John Goodyear
Level of Heat 1970

1. Thermal Experience Zones identified by tape present the heat capacity of a variety of surfaces to the viewer's touch. Sources of heat of these surfaces include the sun, the Museum heating system (if operating) heat from the interior of the earth, heat of lighting and other electrical equipment, heat of pollutants, heat of friction, heat of the bodies of spectators.
2. Museum as Thermal Experience Zone. A test points to the entire space of the Museum as a Thermal Experience Zone, and to the body of the viewer as the sensing agent. The test will measure the perspiration of randomly chosen subjects for the duration of their visit to this exhibition. Factors involved may be the heat of the spaces, the heat of the subjects' bodies, their clothing, their physical and mental and nervous activity. Persons taking the test will be identified with a badge stating: "I am taking a thermal experience (sweat) test."

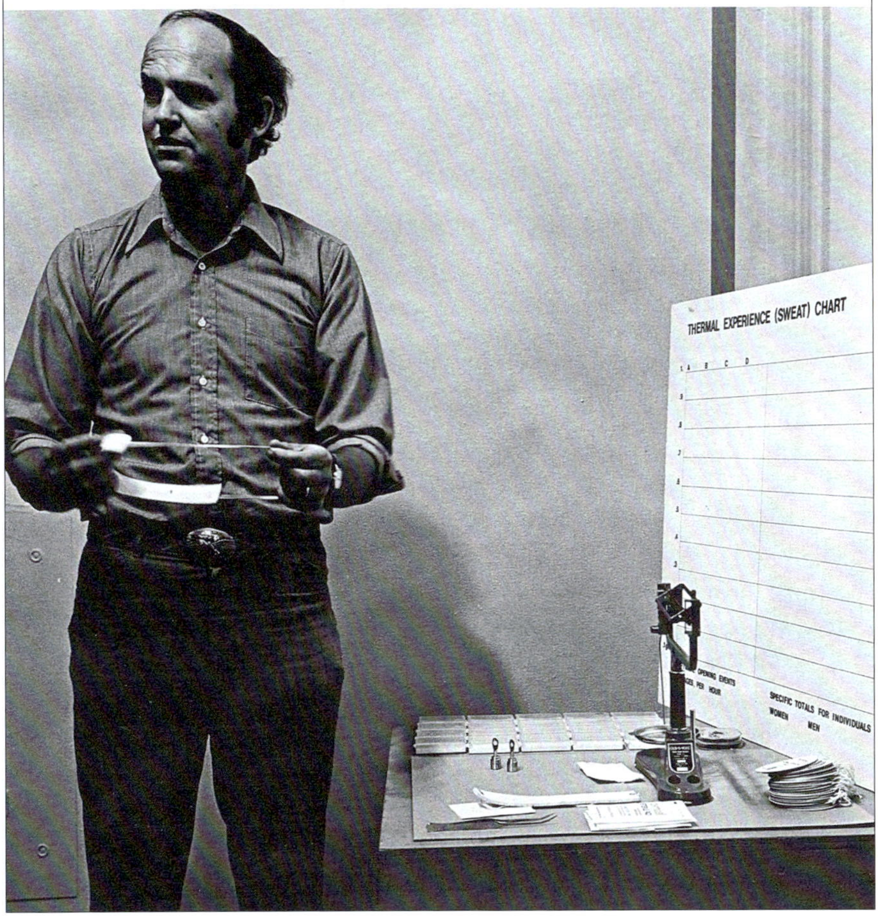

Figure 3.11. John Goodyear, *Level of Heat* (1970), as reproduced in the catalog of the exhibition *Software* at The Jewish Museum, New York, 1970. Courtesy of John Goodyear.

Youngblood's elaboration of "expanded cinema," and so on. Burnham's concept of "software" was a way to hold the tensions among these various stakeholders at bay. He saw fundamental similarities in their methods of organization, their processes (as opposed to their products), and their concern for addressing participants instead of passive viewers. This model of software accordingly precipitated a productive conflation of categories

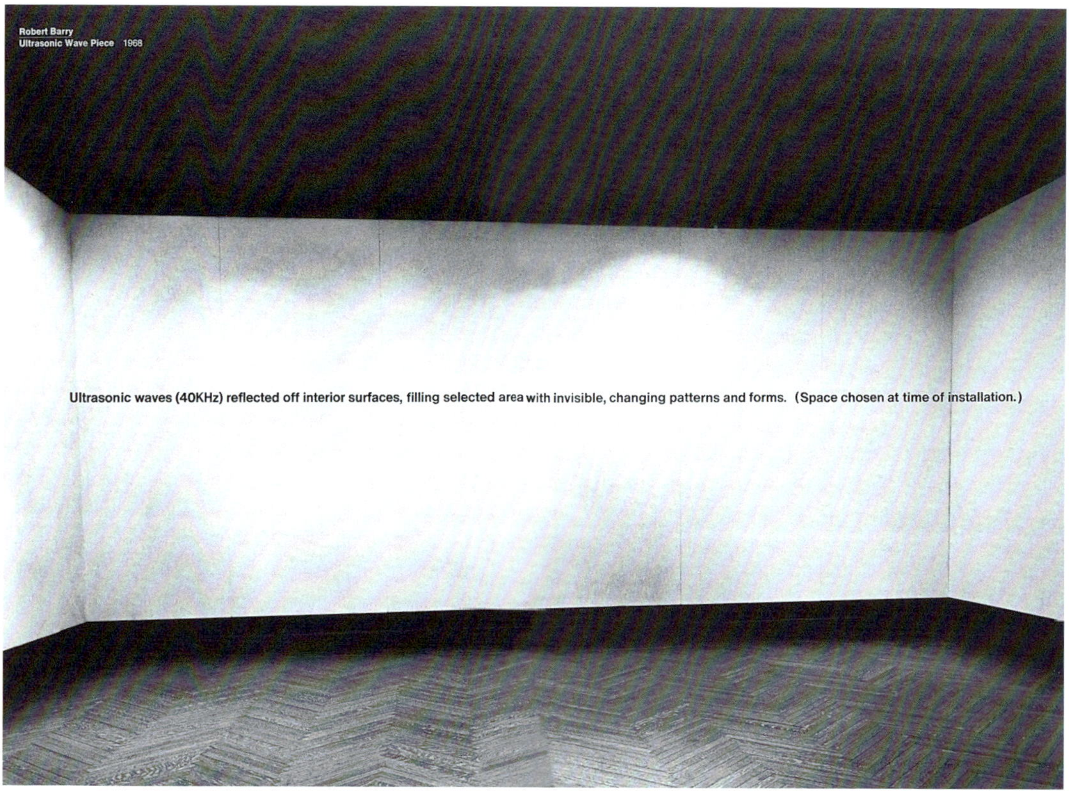

Figure 3.12. Robert Barry, *Ultrasonic Wave Piece* (1968), as reproduced in the catalog of the exhibition *Software* at The Jewish Museum, New York, 1970. Courtesy of Mary Boone Gallery, New York.

such as artistic medium, science, technology, and computation—categories that tended to be held apart by any number of apparatuses, including discipline-specific language games and institutionally specific funding structures.

But it is precisely the ways in which such conflations coagulated around the concept of environment that are pertinent here. These are also registered in two other pivotal publications from this period that attempted to reconcile contemporaneous aesthetic, technological, design, and art tendencies. Aesthetic futurologist Douglas Davis, like Burnham, also became invested in the sublatory notion of a techno-environmental art, which led him to produce a survey of recent developments. Davis's book *Art and the Future: A History/Prophecy of the Collaboration between Science, Technology and Art* followed a familiar historical narrative, wherein the avant-garde of the 1920s gave way to new types of technologically oriented abstract and kinetic work, which, predictably, would blur the boundaries between art and everyday life. Here, however, following Kepes no doubt, the language of environment infused the entire story, from retrospect to prospect. Davis titled his section on the historic material "Technology as Landscape," gave several sections over to discussing "environmental" art, and included figures such as Buckminster Fuller in his genealogy. And, even more so than Burnham, Davis recognized the existential stakes of

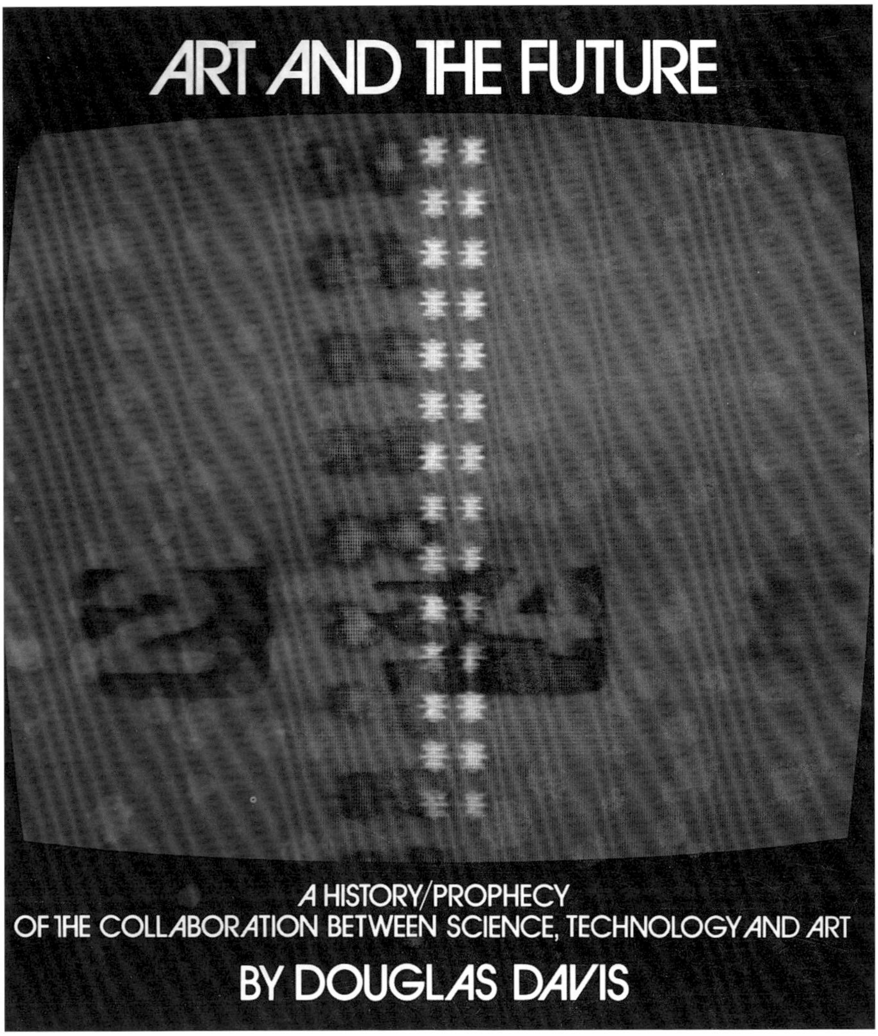

Figure 3.13. Cover of Douglas Davis, *Art and the Future: A History/Prophecy of the Collaboration between Science, Technology and Art* (1973). Courtesy of Thames and Hudson.

what he termed "the environmental-systems" movement. "We expect art to do much more than stand before us," Davis wrote. "We want it to engage in a dialogue with the environmental life process."[95]

Jim Burns is also an interesting organizer in this regard. Having worked with Anna and Lawrence Halprin in San Francisco, Burns was intimately familiar with the environmental manifold, in both its aesthetic and its technological aspects. His 1972 book *Arthropods* is one of the most symptomatic artifacts of this period. In retrospect, it seems like an ambitious attempt to bring together the counterdesign principles of many European initiatives with the countercultural aspirations in North America. Ant Farm is published here alongside Superstudio, Cedric Price, the experimental graphic design firm Onyx, the environmental/dance workshops of the Halprins, and the community-oriented work of the "young" architectural firm of Hardy, Holzman & Pfeiffer. Burns's text also forms something

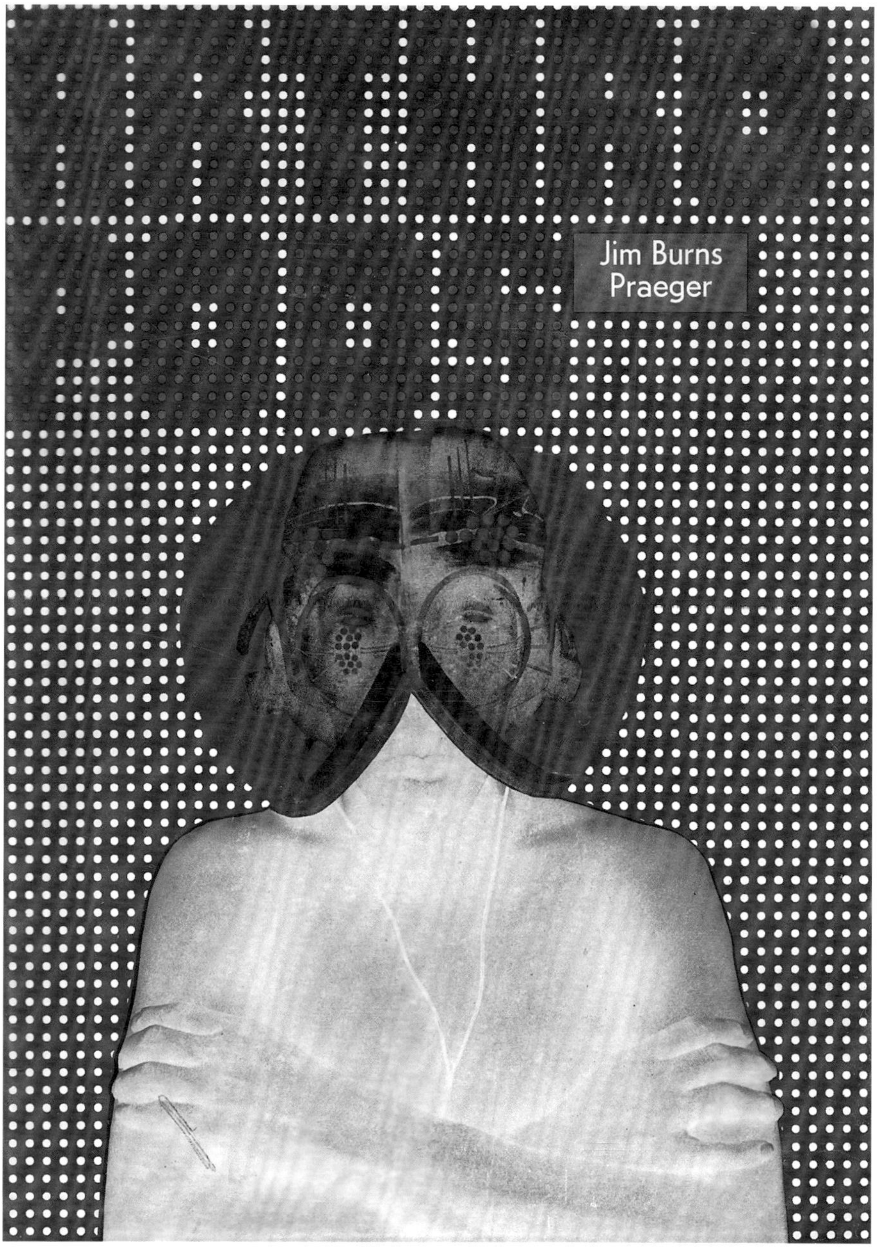

Figure 3.14. Cover of Jim Burns, *Arthropods* (1972). Reprinted with permission of Academy Editions.

of a bridge between the social radicalism of the 1960s and the more personal, therapeutic, and consciousness-oriented ethos of the 1970s. Having said that, we find in Burns's narrative the familiar arc of the work featured in this chapter: "I believe," he wrote, "that the trend is away from an elitist practice of closed-system design and planning and toward the design of things that can change, buildings that can be altered, environments that will be responsive to the needs of the people who live in them and the people—professional or 'amateur'—who will continually be responsible for what happens around them."[96] Of special note here, also, is Burns's strange usage of the word *arthropods,* which refers to a class of nonvertebrate insects with jointed bodies. Burns felt this was an apt metaphor for the groups included in the book, "since their members are articulated or interconnected for singular purposes of environmental creation."[97] (We might also note here the serendipitous connection to the similar entomological metaphor mobilized to justify the Elytra Filament Pavilion, discussed above.) Burns's book is also exemplary in that it demonstrates very clearly virtually every component of the environmental manifold—the participatory, the biological, and the technological—through its artistic, architectural, and design-oriented approaches. It is therefore not surprising that Kepes enlisted Burns to contribute to *Arts of the Environment,* where his analysis of the social implications of "megastructures" was joined to the MIT and CAVS ethos.[98]

Besides these attempts at synthesis, special attention needs to be paid to the phenomenon of intermedia. While for the concept's originator, Dick Higgins, intermedia was a way to describe the spaces "in between" virtually any media—poetry and painting, for instance—by 1970 it was becoming synonymous with a particular genre of multimedia, participatory, and performative spectacle, the kind that the Pulsa group had mounted at MoMA in 1969, for instance, or Susan Buirge and Serge Boutourline's *Televanilla,* performed at the Martinique Theater in 1968 (see chapter 1). Intermedia also represents a kind of ambivalent synthesis of the Dada strain of neo-avant-garde activity with the more constructivist or purist strains we have been preoccupied with here. Allan Kaprow, for instance, was one of the first American artists to employ the term *environment* systematically in in the postwar period.[99] Likewise, as Fred Turner has recently observed, the creators of such work believed that it "should be used to create environments, that such spaces could produce individual psychological changes, and that altered audiences could ultimately change the world."[100]

I would add to these observations that, by the early 1970s, intermedia had become one of the major bridges between the arts and an emerging *corporate* culture that sought to harness new modes of creativity for new types of enterprises. Indeed, intermedia itself became a kind of business, marketing itself to public and private institutions for training, educational, or inspirational purposes. The work of Serge Boutourline Jr. is a case in point, as is that of John Brockman and Gerd Stern. For some, the corporatized intermedia environmental experience was replacing what Kaprow had termed the "happening" a decade earlier. Brockman, for instance, a leading intermedia entrepreneur, was encouraging audiences (as early as 1966) to "hate happenings. Love Intermedia Kinetic Environments." The function of these IKEs, Brockman stated (echoing McLuhan), was "to make visible the perceptions of science. They use the environment as an art form."[101] This sentiment also drove the famous program Experiments in Art and Technology, which facilitated collaborative projects between artists and corporations. A significant number of these collaborations resulted in work that was distinctly environmental.[102]

Likewise, Stern, after founding and working with the psychedelic intermedia collective USCO, was named creative director of Intermedia Systems, Inc., which "was set up to program environmental simulations for educational, business, and research purposes."[103] George Litwin, president of the company, described its activities using the precise language of responsive environments:

> We are trying to use mixed media—multimedia technology—to create environments that have particular kinds of psychological effects. The educational applications are really manifold, for organizations, for management education, for adult learning, and for improved curriculum approaches in our colleges and high schools. We are talking about man's environment. It's been here all along. It's been influencing us all along. What we are saying is: we can begin to have some control over the environmental influences on our behavior, attitudes, and motivation. We don't have to live with whatever happens to have been created. We can program environmental influence, using media technology, and this opens up major new possibilities for learning, and for the improvement of living and working environments.[104]

Computer-Aided Environments

Environmental programming, media technologies, software, systems—where, exactly, is the *computer* in all this? As with so many other components of responsive environments, the answer is: everywhere and nowhere. As we have already seen, the computer was fundamentally important in collating and representing the massively complex data of environmental response (allowing for new modes of pattern recognition). It was the de facto object in studies of human–machine interfaces.[105] It made possible new virtual and simulated models of spatial interaction. It was indispensable in the design and control of dynamic, flexible structures. The computer was central to the ethos of responsive environments. But this is an elusive set of coordinates. For, just as surely as the computer was an invaluable tool in the creation of responsive objects (buildings, educational apparatuses, experience zones), it was also an environment in its own right. It was dispersed as a new interfacial property of the surrounding world. To put this another way: there was a very real sense in which programming and computing were not just methods of generating an environment but also activities conducted *by* a given environment. As digital pioneer Nicholas Negroponte put it in one of the definitive statements of the period, the new environment would not simply be designed with the "aid" of computers, it would be "computer-aided architecture." Computers "won't help us design," he wrote, "instead, we will live in them."[106]

Here, we can begin a discussion in earnest of the types of responsive environments described at the beginning of the chapter: technologically mediated spaces that alter their physical or ambient properties based on various inputs or status changes. And, while I have taken pains to foreground the avant-garde aesthetic foundations of these projects, it must also be acknowledged that, to a great extent, they were technologically determined. From the general trend toward miniaturization in electronics to the development of certain kinds of ambient sensors (heat, light, sound) and new or newly deployed materials (plastics, foams, gases, liquids), more and more it seemed desirable and possible to start to embed certain technologies in certain types of structures. But it was the growing power and ubiquity of computers that made it seem possible to bring all of these together into a situation that would be subject to dynamic control. Computers were perhaps the only way to coordinate the various bits of hardware that might sense environmental inputs and effect changes in a given responsive structure. They were also seen as necessary in visualizing and designing those ensembles of responsive technologies. But perhaps most important, they were the intelligence that might give something like an autonomous character to the environments in question, an ability to react spontaneously and holistically to the needs and desires of users. This would involve, in the words of Georges Teyssot, "a dialogue between the environment and its inhabitants. The dialogue can be refined and extended with the aid of modern techniques which allow us to weave the same patterns in terms of reactive environment."[107]

These attributes were evident in the first postwar "cybernetic" architectures. I have already invoked the work of Nicolas Schöffer above, but the other obligatory citation here is that seminal work the Fun Palace (1963–67), designed by Cedric Price with theater director and theorist Joan Littlewood. This work was explicitly cybernetic, being inspired directly by the work of Gordon Pask (himself a journeyman artist of interactive systems). The Fun Palace was more a media and performance platform than a building.[108] It was (in its projected iterations) replete with information/entertainment terminals and configurable physical structures. Although, in this case, computers were not effecting the structural changes, an increasing emphasis on computerization as an integral part of the architecture would continue to concern Price. He worked toward responsive environments throughout the entire period covered by this study. This work would include the Potteries Thinkbelt, a "responsive, anticipatory architecture" for an adult educational complex in England's industrial north (another attempt to incorporate mobile, responsive elements directly into processes of subject formation).[109] Price's efforts would culminate with a project planned in Florida called Generator (1976–79) (Plate 8). Here a computer interface would allow users to create different

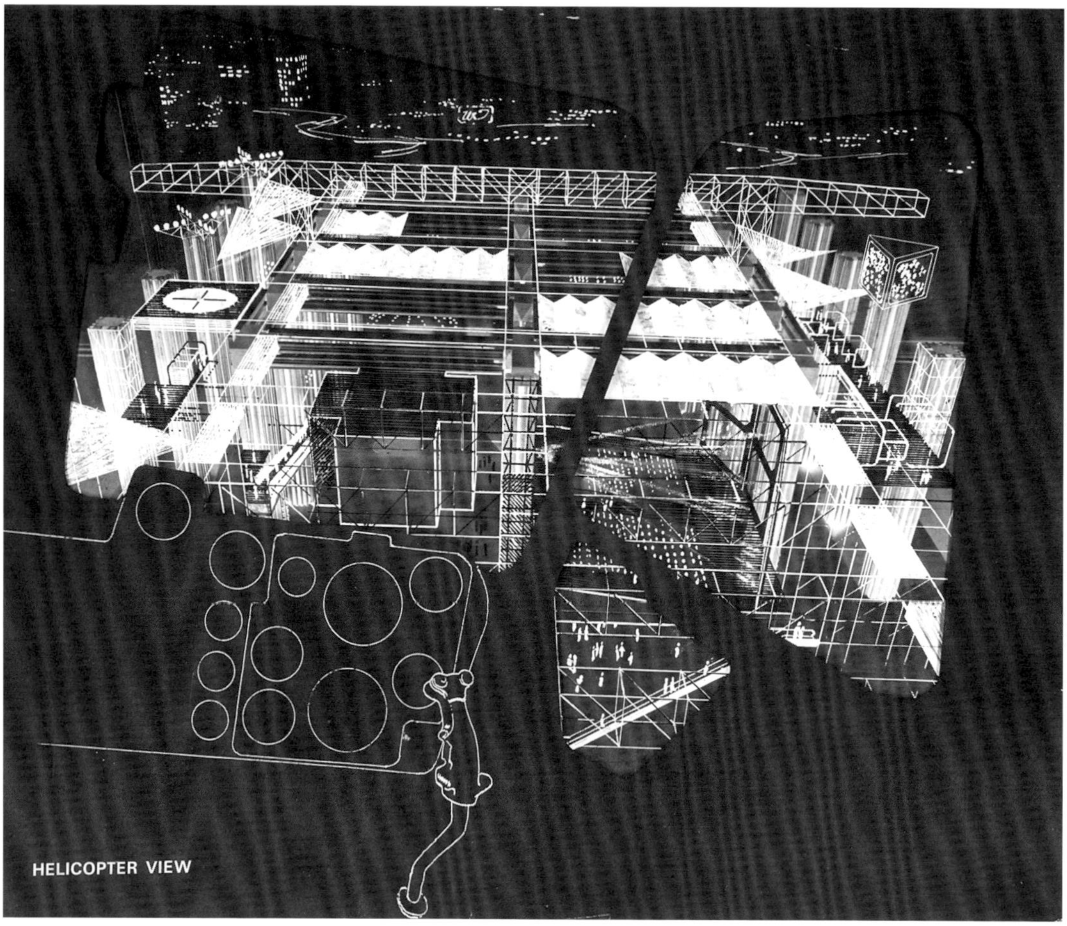

Figure 3.15. Cedric Price, Fun Palace, helicopter view (circa 1964). Cedric Price fonds Canadian Centre for Architecture.

combinations of cubic architectural units. The system also would incorporate an artificial intelligence capable of making its own configurational decisions if it got "bored" with its human users' lack of activity.[110]

In these instances, cybernetic principles were built into structures that could actively change physical or ambient conditions in the very fabric of a given architecture. But in other instances, computers were seen as giving rise to new types of spaces, spaces that we would now reflexively call virtual and that seemed to occupy a middle ground between actual and projected or simulated space. The key figure in this regard is Myron Krueger, a computer scientist and self-described computer artist. Like other commentators discussed above, Krueger saw his interactive work as a kind of evolution away from the autonomous and static object and toward a heuristic, simulative, and performative engagement with digital technology. Indeed, all of his work revolved around the notion of an expanded field of computer interfaces, one that would ineluctably become an immersive environment. Accordingly, he was responsible for articulating one of the most comprehensive theories of responsive environments from this moment. Though

Krueger's work in technological response began in the late 1960s and early 1970s, his major statement on it would not be published until 1983.[111] Here, he postulated a continuum from ecological to technological concerns that, as we have seen, was not uncommon at this moment:

> For centuries the goal of human effort was to tame nature's terrible power. Our success has been so complete, that a new world has emerged. Created by human ingenuity, it is an artificial reality.
>
> Our daily experiences are overwhelmingly formed by this reality. It is the automobile, the written word, television, and the temperature-modulated building, not the natural environment, that influence our lives.[112]

The contemporary world, Krueger argued, was one that was witnessing "the integration of all aspects of society by interconnected information, communication, and control systems. These networks and the computational power they bring will permeate our lives much as electricity does today. Cybernetic systems will sense our needs and enter our offices, homes, and cars. We will live in *Responsive Environments.*"[113]

For Krueger, the responsive environment was a cultural inevitability, but one that was subject to aesthetic refinement. In this sense, his projects became laboratories where laypersons could gain a better understanding of technology, but also where technologists could learn about the qualitative aspects of human–machine interaction. Krueger attempted to go beyond the default interfaces of keyboard, light pen, and mouse to systems that used video and movement detection to map bodily postures and produce graphic responses to those inputs.[114] In this sense his projects were somewhere between art installations and tech demos. In 1969, Krueger collaborated with physicist Dan Sandlin in the installation of a work called *GLOWFLOW* at the University of Wisconsin–Madison. Here, a room was turned into a support for various visual and audio phenomena that were triggered by pressure-sensitive plates in the floor. Based on participants' movement through the space, phosphorescent particles suspended in water would illuminate and electronic music would play. While Krueger was excited by the immersive qualities of this project, he was underwhelmed by its actual responsiveness.

The next year he created his own work, *METAPLAY,* at the same university gallery. *METAPLAY* comprised a far more complex network of digital and analog input and output systems that essentially attempted to turn the user's body into a computer interface. To achieve this, Krueger transferred the graphics from a computer monitor into a live video feed so that the latter could be experienced at a room-size (environmental) scale. Simultaneously, a video camera was also recording the space, while a computer effected rudimentary mapping of the participants' positions and movements. Graphic representations of these were then projected onto the screen via the video feed in real time. In another iteration, a human "facilitator" sat in another room and, using Sketchpad software, drew images with which participants could interact via the projection. In this instance, the two graphic sources were sutured in the video images: the Sketchpad drawings and the renderings of the participants' bodies. A participant could, for instance, open a cartoon door, take a virtual shower, or navigate a labyrinth.

The culmination of these earlier works was—instead of a specific installation—an interactive platform called *VIDEOPLACE,* which Krueger initiated in 1972 and continued to elaborate for the next two decades. This project again used video cameras tracking the movements of human bodies and their mediation via a graphical user interface. Krueger posited that two users in two separate spaces could interact with one another in a "third"

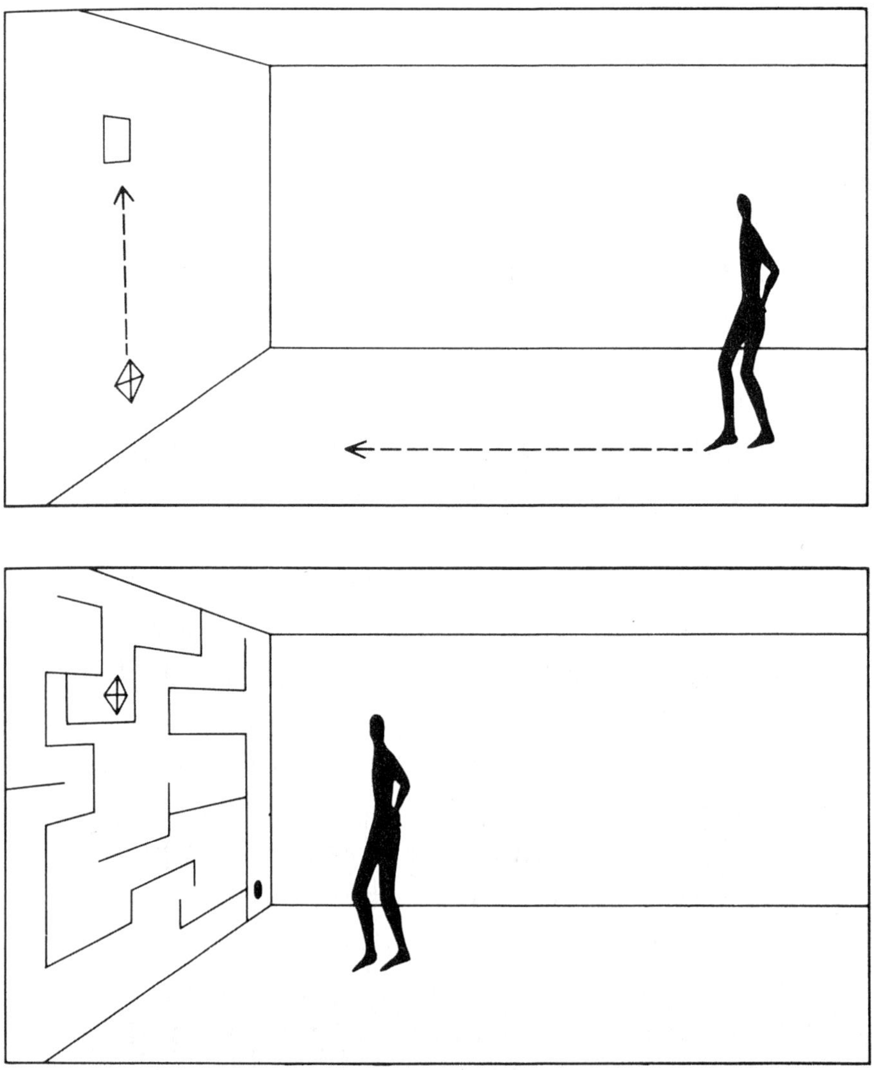

Figure 3.16. Myron Krueger, *METAPLAY* (1970).

virtual space created by the visual overlapping of the video recordings of the computer displays. The users' images could be integrated into illusory situations that existed only in this virtual realm. The graphical representations of the users could be mapped *into* simulated spaces, rooms, underwater environments, and so on. The users could in turn "touch" and manipulate these simulated environments. They could "throw" balls, open and close doors, and traverse landscapes. Interestingly, while Krueger understood his evolving thinking on responsive environments to be a continual expansion of interaction in general, his turn to virtual reality redirected his aesthetic project to a more discipline-specific focus on the computer interface. Chris Salter has observed that in *VIDEOPLACE* the bodily and performative aspects of Krueger's earlier works "were downplayed in favor of clearly establishing the loop of action and response between the participant, the computational apparatus, and the screen."[115]

It is also easy to relegate Krueger's work to a place—both ahead of and out of step with its time—in the history of video game design. Be that as it may, Krueger's environmental concerns and his attempt to humanize technology in order to facilitate the interactive nature of his work align his ideas with the others discussed here. For him, the computer interface became a tool for consciousness-raising, for revealing an environment that might otherwise remain hidden. "During the balance of this century," he wrote,

> responsive technology will move ever closer to us, becoming the standard interface through which we gain most of our experience. It will intercede in our personal relationships and between us and our tools. The appearance in our homes of isolated devices, such as calculators, video games, microprocessors, and two-way cable TV, augurs the knitting together of a single interactive network that we will encounter through every effective device in our environment.[116]

It was precisely this sense of an imminent sea change in human existence—and the sense that we had better get ahead of it—that would motivate many proposals for responsive environments. Likewise, the computer came to function ideologically in these statements as both problem and solution. If Schöffer and Price had suggested an atmospheric architecture animated by user feedback, and Krueger had offered a phantasmatic space of hybrid interaction, others would use computers in a humbler and more direct register. They would seek to hand the reins of design directly over to the user, to make environments more responsive by making the design process itself accessible to nonspecialists.[117] An example of this was the Israeli French architect Yona Friedman's project for the Flatwriter, an interface that was connected to his famous visionary systems for prefabricated building components. The Flatwriter would take user data—such as number of children or desired function of spaces—and translate it into an architectural plan that would be incorporated into one of Friedman's space grids. Here, the computer would act as interlocutor between user and building system, a relationship that would eliminate the need for architects.

This was the same impetus behind much of the work being done by Negroponte and others under the auspices of the MIT Architecture Machine Group and, later, Media Lab. For them, the computer's role was not simply to assist the designer in mechanical or menial tasks but to rise to the level of true interlocutor, partner, and intellectual equal. This relationship, in turn, would alter the structures constituting the built environment, making them more nuanced, flexible, and transformable. In retrospect, Negroponte's insistence on continuing to use the word *architecture* in his widely read publications of the period seems (intentionally) ironic, given that he was one of the key protagonists in the conception and realization of various methods of displacing both architectural objects in the traditional sense and the traditional role of the architect. Negroponte and colleagues accomplished this by deploying the computer in all the ways listed above: as design tool, space simulator, and intelligent coordinator.

By the same token, it would be disingenuous (even if not entirely wrong) to claim that Negroponte was a designer of responsive environments. He and his associates did as much to question and disrupt that field of inquiry as they did in the case of architecture proper. They had little use for the vanguard rhetoric of the intermedia entrepreneurs. They seemed little interested in their colleague Kepes's utopian programs and grand syntheses; they had no professed faith in the architect or artist as a particularly sensitive individual who might reintegrate the systemic imbalances of the world in the late twentieth century. By eschewing these staples of the progressive (environmental) design world, the MIT group appeared as radical pragmatists. They intended to approach the problems in the soberest of terms, using the technological resources of the world's premiere technical university and the sponsorship of the U.S. Department of Defense.[118] In this sense, Negroponte's preferred use of the word *architecture* in his major publications was not simply an ironic gesture aimed at a discipline on the verge of dissipation but also a rigorous attempt to avoid abstraction, to embed the processes of response in specific materials, structures, and definable interfaces that would avoid the nebulous saturation of the concept of environment. "The whole issue of responsive environments is a very, very suspect one," he said in 1972, "because we don't know *how* they should respond. We all feel they *ought* to respond, but the only examples are the most banal, second-rate light shows."[119]

It would be easy to counter Negroponte's skepticism on this occasion by mentioning any number of responsive environments he oversaw during these years at MIT—the *Seek* installation (1970), which was the biggest hit at the *Software* exhibition at the Jewish Museum; the Urban5 design computer (1973); and the Aspen Movie Map (1978). All of these were computer-aided environments in the various modalities I have invoked, but for Negroponte these were partial and heuristic experiments that failed insofar as they placed the computer (and architecture) at the *center* of a given environmental interaction. They were not meant to generate environments from computational procedures (even if that is what they ended up doing). Rather, they were so many attempts to get the computer out of the way—out of the way of a human subject attempting to interface with the fullness of an environment that was always already highly responsive. For Negroponte, the design of responsive environments was not unconsummated. It was redundant.

Environment therefore functioned in Negroponte's discourse not as the object of design but as its existential fabric. But the MIT group, seeking to avoid such metaphysical sentiments, still had need of some language that could accommodate the field of design activity and the objects and procedures it would generate. An ether was necessary. For Negroponte (as for several of the other researchers in this account), this was "context." Context was the invisible, relational, epistemological substance that bound together the components of design problems as well as their understanding by sensitive and intelligent agents (human or machine). A comprehension of context was what artificial intelligence lacked and what eluded the machinic recognition of patterns; it was the missing ingredient of a truly productive human–computer "symbiosis" that might be able to engender a true "environmental humanism."[120] The machine's lack of contextual perception or comprehension was why machines could not "get" jokes or "appreciate" other nonlinear events.[121] (I would argue that this includes all aesthetic phenomena, as well.) But, as we saw with the example of Gregory Bateson, context was far more than just a set of references for a shifting signifier. It was environment manifested as meaningful pattern among elements, systems, and actors.

Discussions of the role of context in communications theory were part and parcel of cybernetics and, within the MIT milieu, were promoted most enthusiastically by Avery R. Johnson, a student of Warren S. McCulloch and an aspiring designer of responsive environments (whom I will discuss in chapter 4). While context would be fundamental to Negroponte's conception of the designer–machine partnership in his 1970 book *The Architecture Machine,* it would feature even more prominently in the follow-up, *Soft Architecture Machines,* where it became more than just an issue of communication between two nodes and more of an immersive experience. In *Soft Architecture Machines,* Negroponte turned to his colleague Johnson, but also other communications theorists and linguists, to ponder the role of context and the nature of how an architectural "language" might function. The problem of machine understanding (and translation, for instance) of language was, for Negroponte, yet another indication of why machines could not yet handle complex design problems. Language was not simply a set of semantic entities ordered by a syntactic system; it existed in "a highly self-referent context," replete with shifters and other indicators of action and affordance within a particular situation.[122]

Negroponte turned to Johnson to expand the notion of context into actual spatial relations, or the "distance," and other intervening mediations between sender and receiver. At one end of Johnson's scale (illustrated in quaint stick-figure form, reminiscent of the drawings Yona Friedman had doubtless produced for students at MIT during these years) is the low-context and highly symbolic dialogue between two scientists; the scale then passes through several types of interface, including "environ-

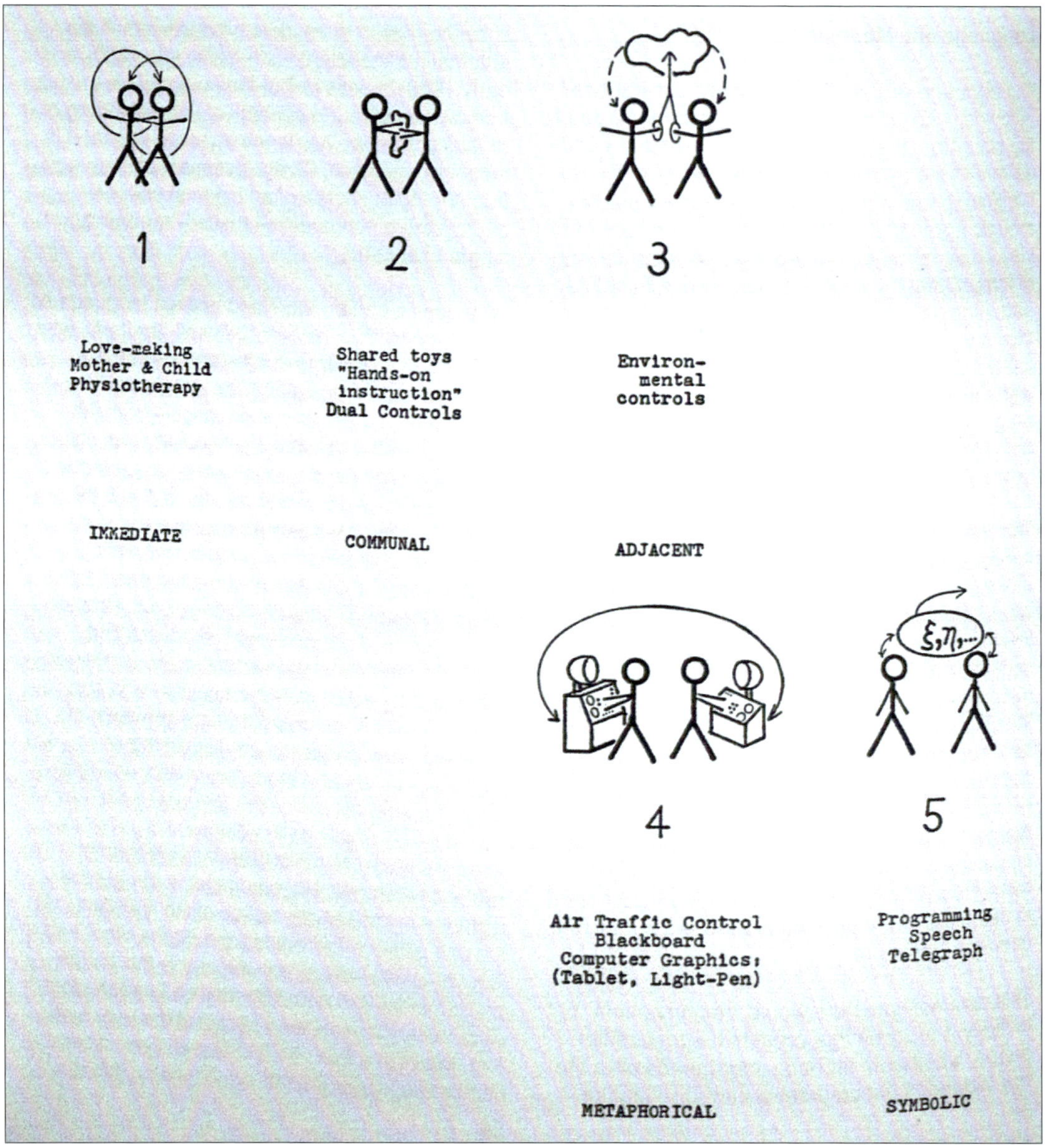

Figure 3.17. Avery Johnson, schematic of communicational distances, from "immediate" to "symbolic" (circa 1971).

mental controls," before arriving at the other end, with the incredibly high-context and immediate communication between two lovers. This was clearly the end of the scale that interested Negroponte, which he aspired to impute to machines so that they might become the friendly conversational design partners he imagined. But he also extended the proposition of context a step further, to ponder the way in which architecture itself is like a language, with both its semantic/syntactic aspect and its contextual/communicational one:

> Can architecture be viewed as a three-dimensional language? If so, does it not follow that it too might be subject to contextual variations? Rather than viewing the built environment as an efficient corpus of concrete, steel, and wood, let us consider it to be a language somewhere in the middle of Avery Johnson's scale. This would imply that my behavior within the built environment and the meaning I attach to that environment are as important as (I really believe more important than) the physical thing itself.[123]

Here, despite the objectivity and specificity of the MIT ethos, context intervenes as that principle that rends solid, static objects apart in favor of an immaterial biopsychosocial medium (environment).

In accordance with this implicit and reluctant acknowledgment of environment, Negroponte devoted a section of *Soft Architecture Machines* to "intelligent environments." As in the rest of the book, he invited a guest author to introduce the section and then followed the introduction with a kind of expansion/rebuttal of his own. In this instance Sean Wellesley-Miller was the author. (Wellesley-Miller is an interesting character in the context of this chapter, as his work really bridges that of the intermedia/happenings scene, inflatable design, and the types of programming architectures that were emerging at MIT.)[124] In his essay, while admitting the "science fiction" prospect and economic infeasibility (echoing Banham) of responsive and intelligent environments, Wellesley-Miller dared to speculate on their implementation even amid the "energy crisis, environmental pollution, political bugging, and all the other sad facts of the sober seventies."[125] He invoked the degree to which many responsive systems had already been implemented, as if out of a sense of absolute necessity: traffic control systems, thermostats, and elevators (the nonlinear behavior of which is "purposeful if not intelligent").[126]

Wellesley-Miller then speculated that buildings could become intelligent environments with far-reaching capabilities. Such a building "would not only be able to monitor and regulate environmental conditions but also to mediate activity patterns through the allocation of functional spaces. In short, it would know what was going on inside itself and could manage things so as to, say, maximize personal contact, minimize long distances, conserve space, handle lighting or what have you on a day-to-day or hour-to-hour basis to provide a more efficient and gracious environment."[127] "The concept of a physically responsive environment," he concluded, "is being turned from dream to reality by the force, appropriately enough, of environmental circumstances themselves. We are making buildings more context responsive, and in doing so we should not forget that a building's final context of response is the needs and senses of its inhabitants."[128]

It was precisely the "needs and senses" of inhabitants that Negroponte addressed in his essay on responsive architecture. How might these subjects be "sensed" by the "machine"? How would the intangibles of human needs and desires be registered and remembered in the hardware and software of this new kind of environment? At what point would the machine gain enough of its own agency to anticipate these needs and desires? When might such a sensing, thinking environment be able to engage in even a noninstrumental dialogue with its inhabitants? When would it be able—and here Negroponte reprised the theme from *The Architecture Machine*—to comprehend a highly contextualized gesture? "Maybe a house is a home," Negroponte wrote, "only once it can appreciate your jokes."[129] In this way (as ever), Negroponte was insistent on distancing himself from simple, linear input/output models of environmental intelligence. The thermostat was the negative example here. An air conditioner programmed to maintain "72 degrees and 50 percent humidity" uses a simple algorithm and establishes an overriding, authoritative form of control. For Negroponte, it was necessary to consider both a simpler imperative and a more complex one. How might such a system be programmed to "maintain a comfortable temperature and humidity"?[130] This subtle shift in the conceptual parameters of response raised fundamentally existential questions regarding the interactions of human subjects, technologies, and environments writ large.

But Negroponte's arguments were not directed only at old-fashioned thermostats. They were directed at what, by the early 1970s, was the growing body of proposals for more and less sophisticated responsive environments. These included published accounts (theoretical statements and experiments) by Avery Johnson, Warren Brodey, Edward Allen, Mark Lavin, and Charles Eastman.[131] Among these were many proposals for systems with expansive and nuanced sensors that would provoke physical alterations in environmental conditions: windows that would open or close based on time of day or sleeping patterns, furniture that would inflate to a desired level of comfort and support, room partitions that would change size and/or shape based on occupancy and functional requirements. These, for Negroponte, were little better than thermostats. This type of response was misguided because the system is "ignorant of context, because it is generative of a complacency hitherto unseen."[132]

This notion of complacency also hints at the ethical and political is-

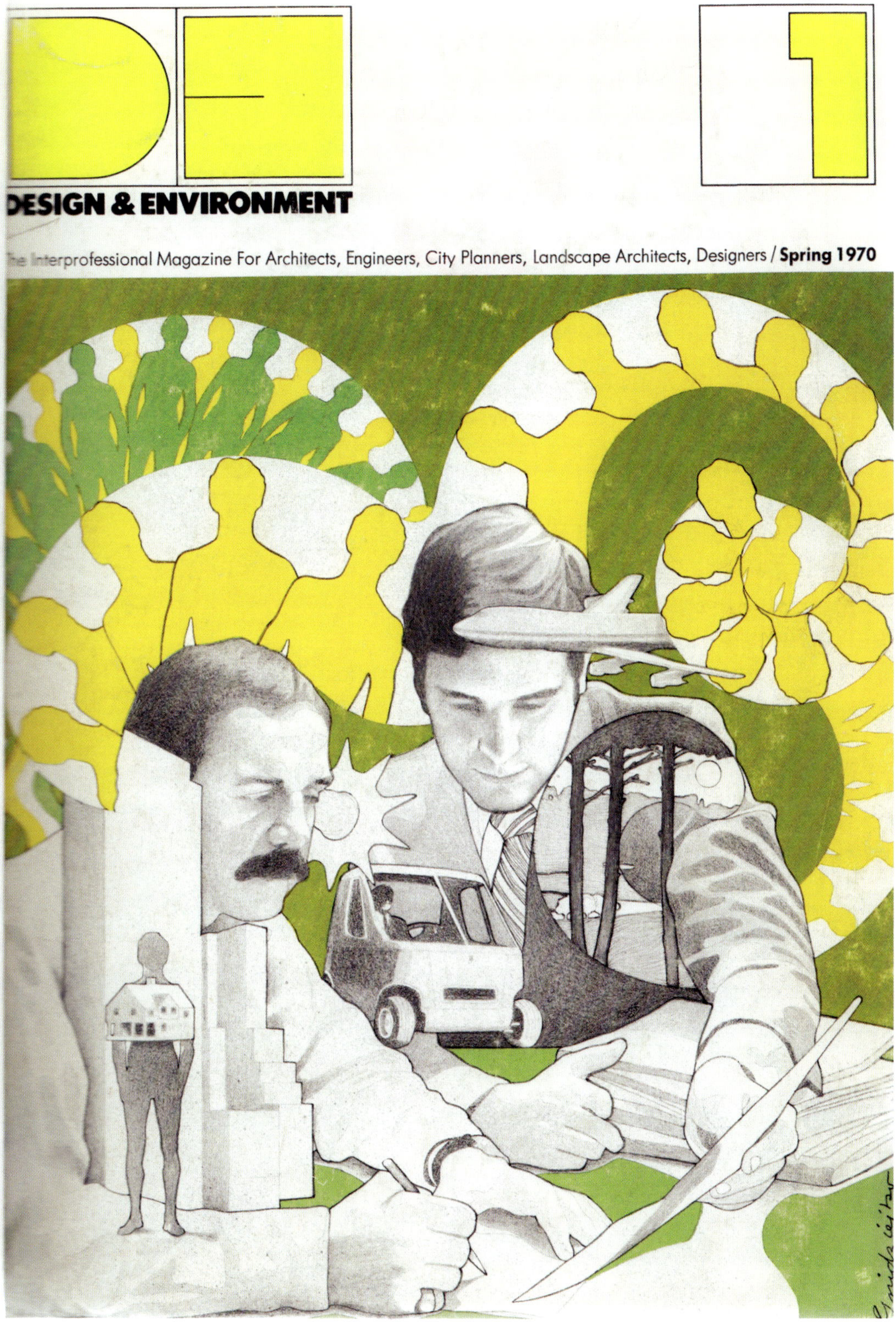

Plate 1. Cover of *Design & Environment* 1 (Spring 1970).

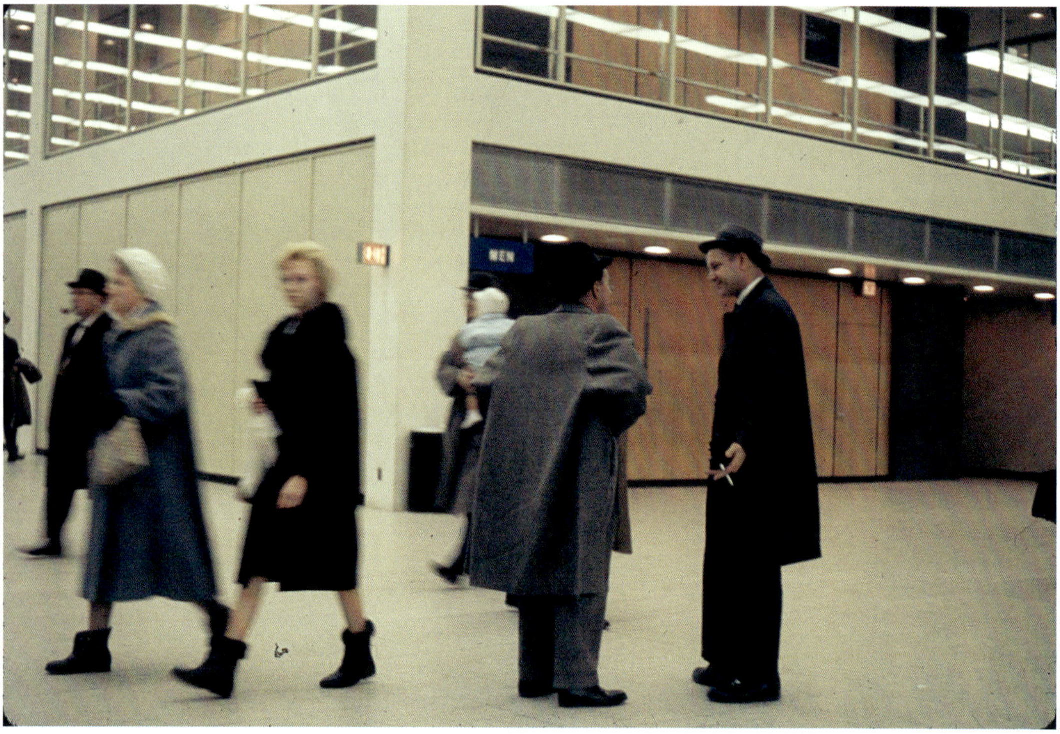

Plate 2. Proxemic research photograph taken in the "field" (most likely taken in Chicago circa 1965). University of Arizona Libraries, Special Collections: Edward T. Hall Papers. Courtesy of Karin Bergh Hall.

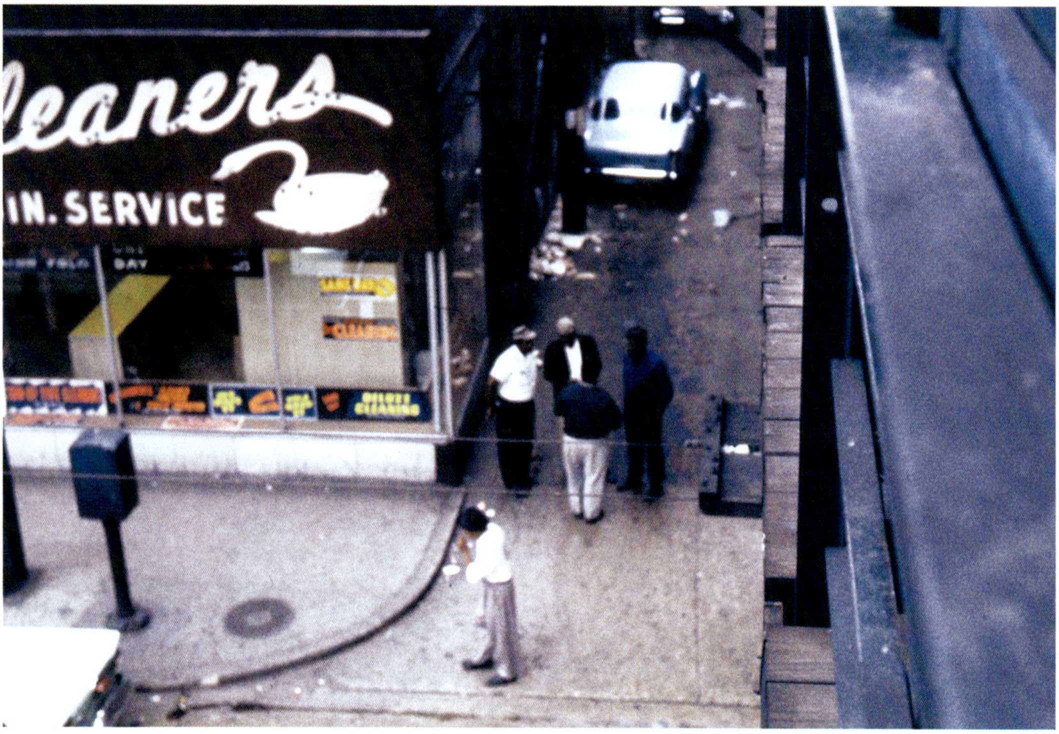

Plate 3. Proxemic research photograph taken in the "field" (most likely taken in Chicago circa 1965). University of Arizona Libraries, Special Collections: Edward T. Hall Papers. Courtesy of Karin Bergh Hall.

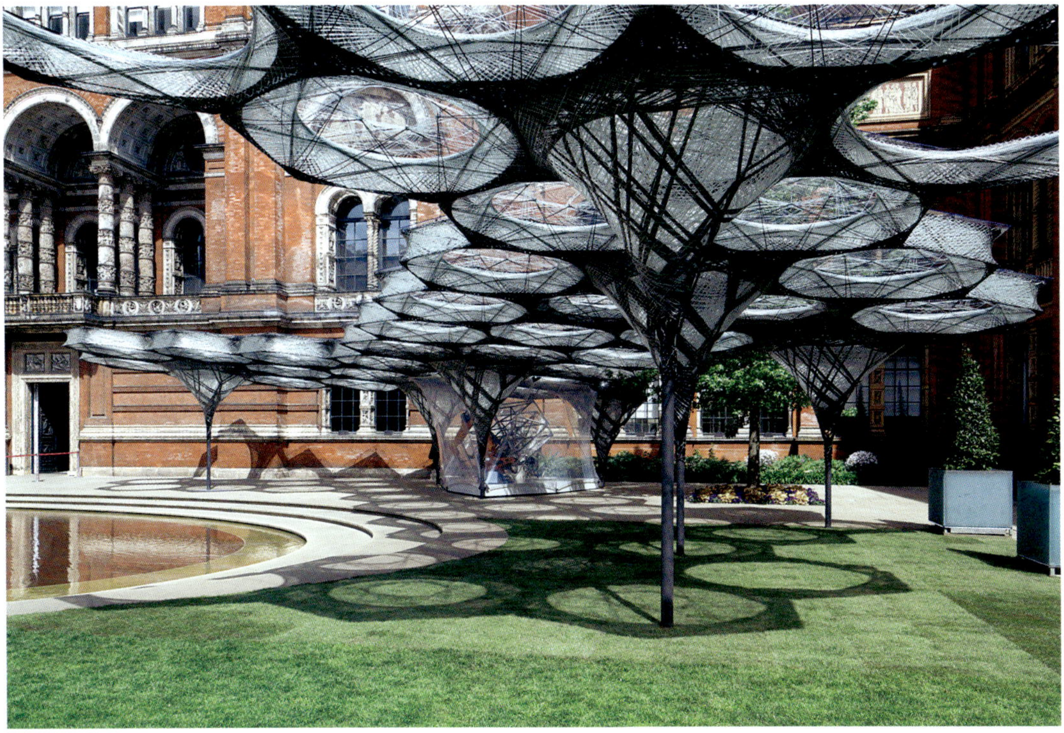

Plate 4. Achim Menges and Jan Knippers, Elytra Filament Pavilion, Victoria and Albert Museum (2016). Photograph by ♥ NAARO. Courtesy of Achim Menges.

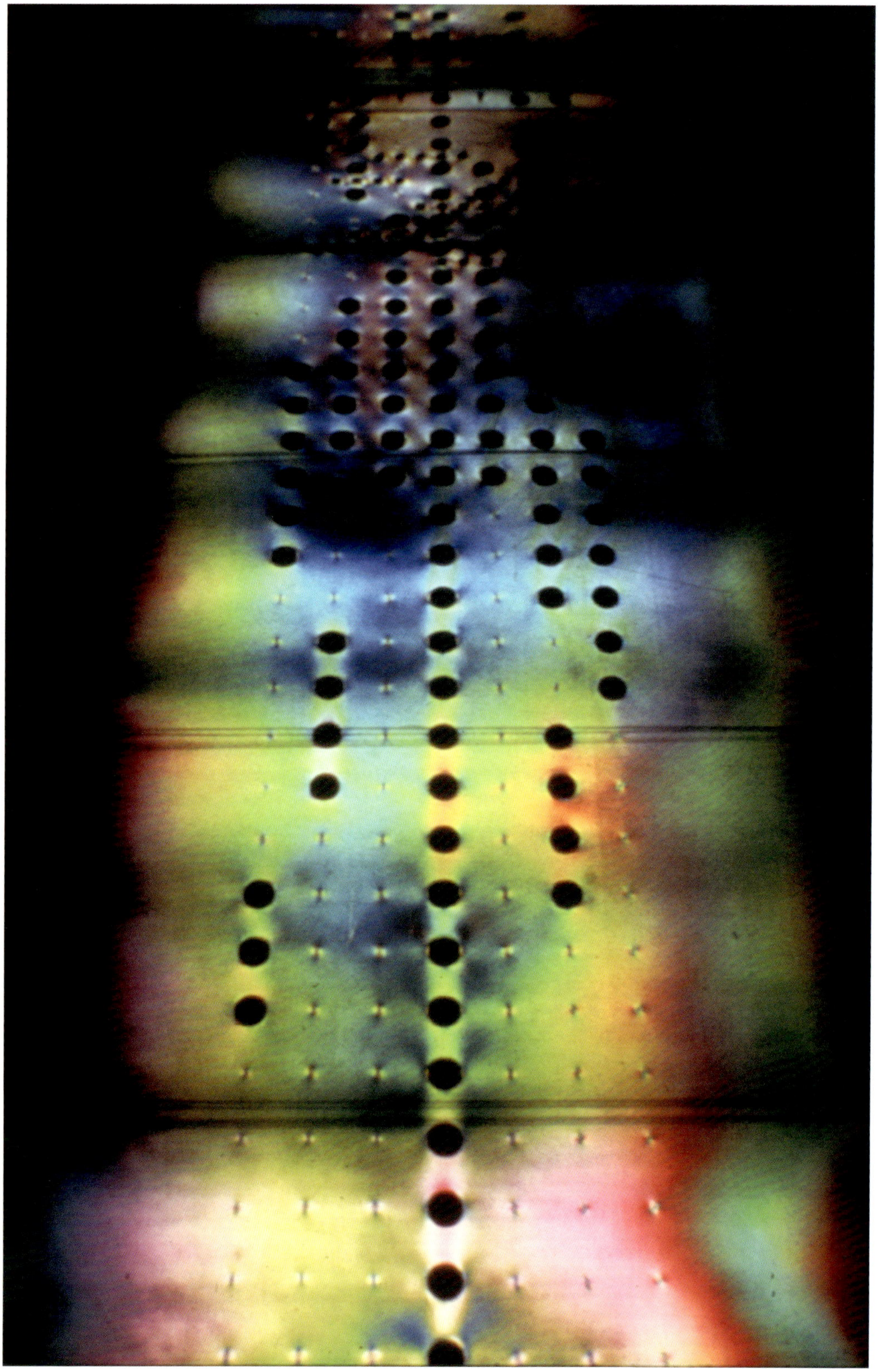

Plate 5. Gyorgy Kepes, *Photo-Elastic Walk* (1970). Massachusetts Institute of Technology. Courtesy of MIT Program in Arts, Culture, and Technology.

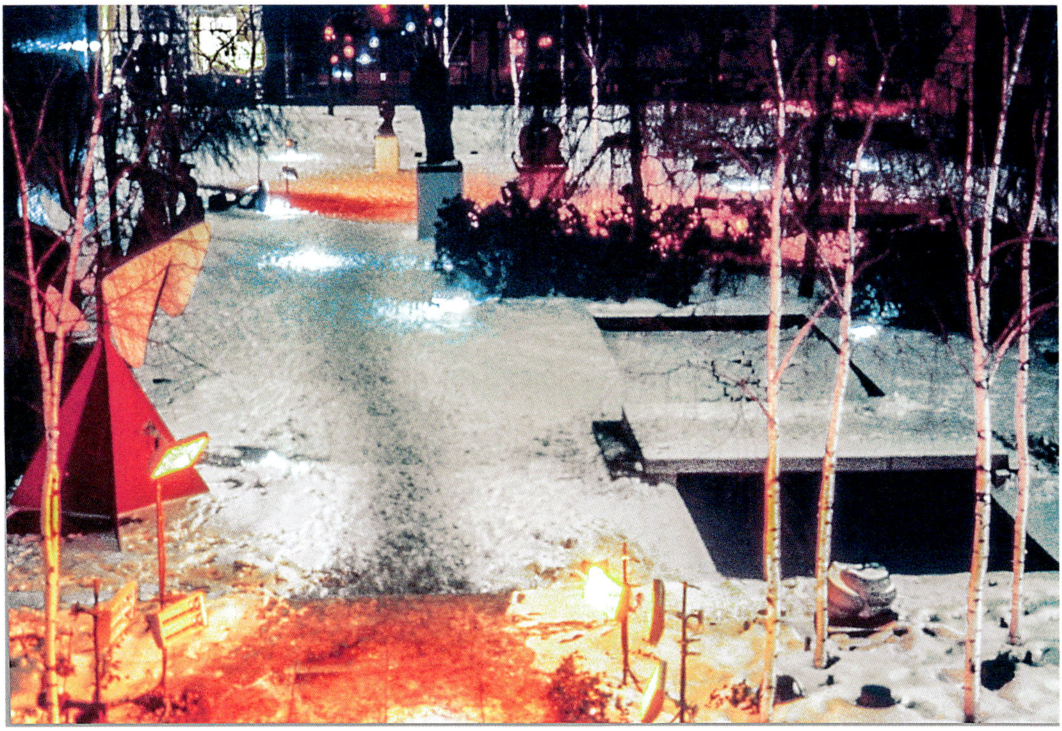

Plate 6. Pulsa installation for *Spaces,* Sculpture Garden, Museum of Modern Art, New York (1970). Installation of twenty strobe lights, twenty loudspeakers, banks of infrared heaters.

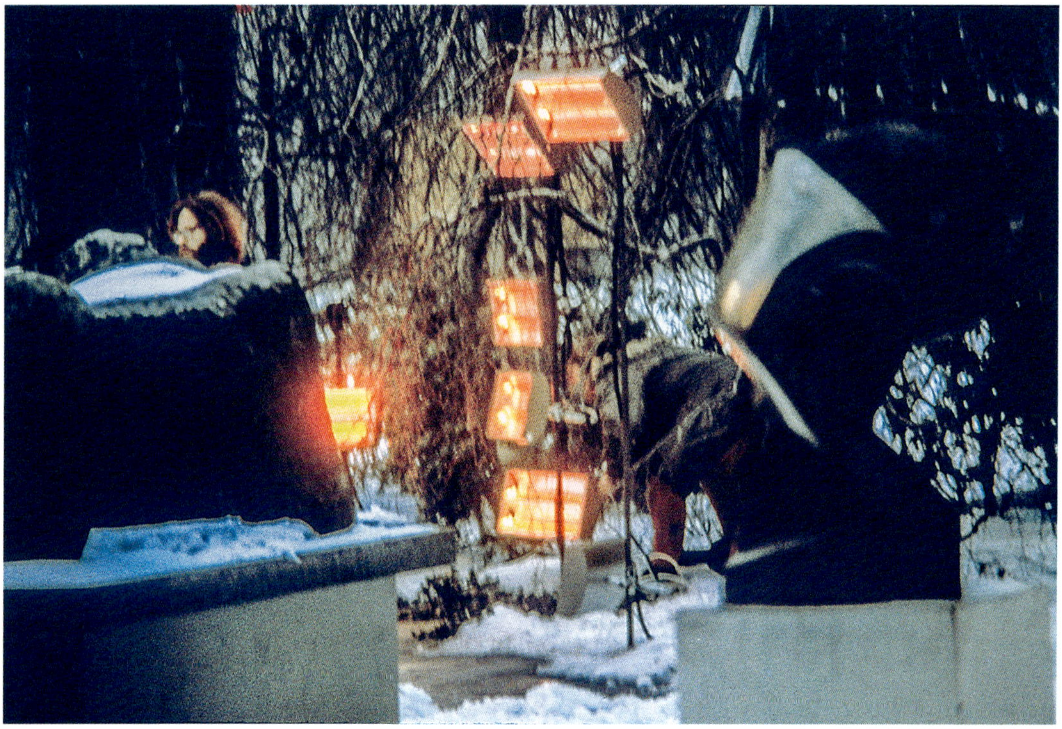

Plate 7. Pulsa Installation for *Spaces,* Sculpture Garden, Museum of Modern Art, New York (1970). Photoelectric feedback loop controlling bank of infrared heaters. http://creativecommons.org/licenses/by/4.0.

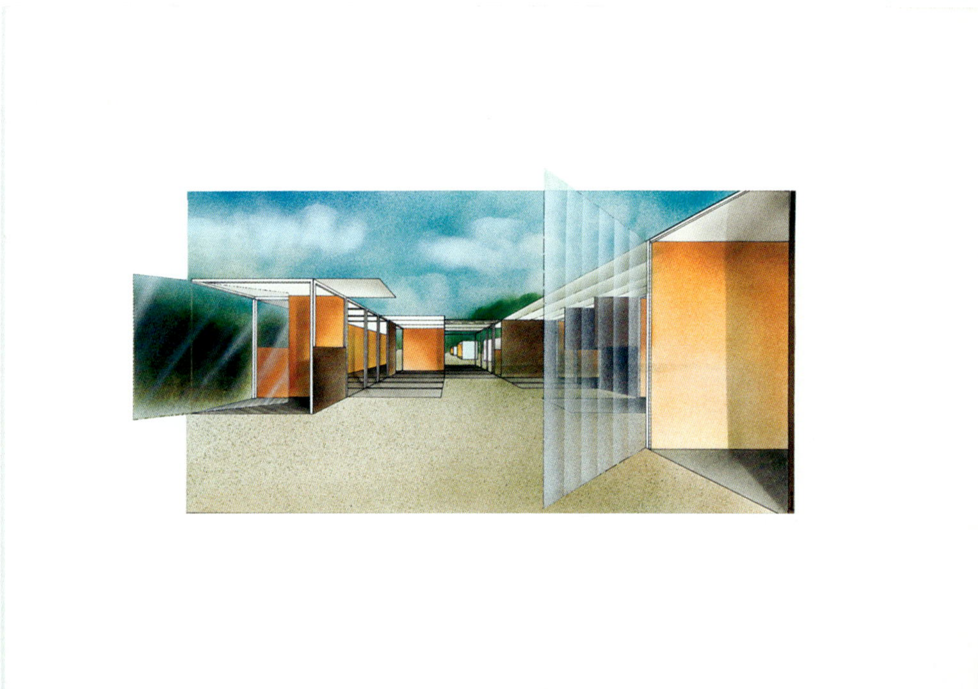

Plate 8. Cedric Price, architect, and Jeremie, draftsman, rendered perspective view of cubes for Generator, Yulee, Florida (1979). Cedric Price fonds, Canadian Centre for Architecture.

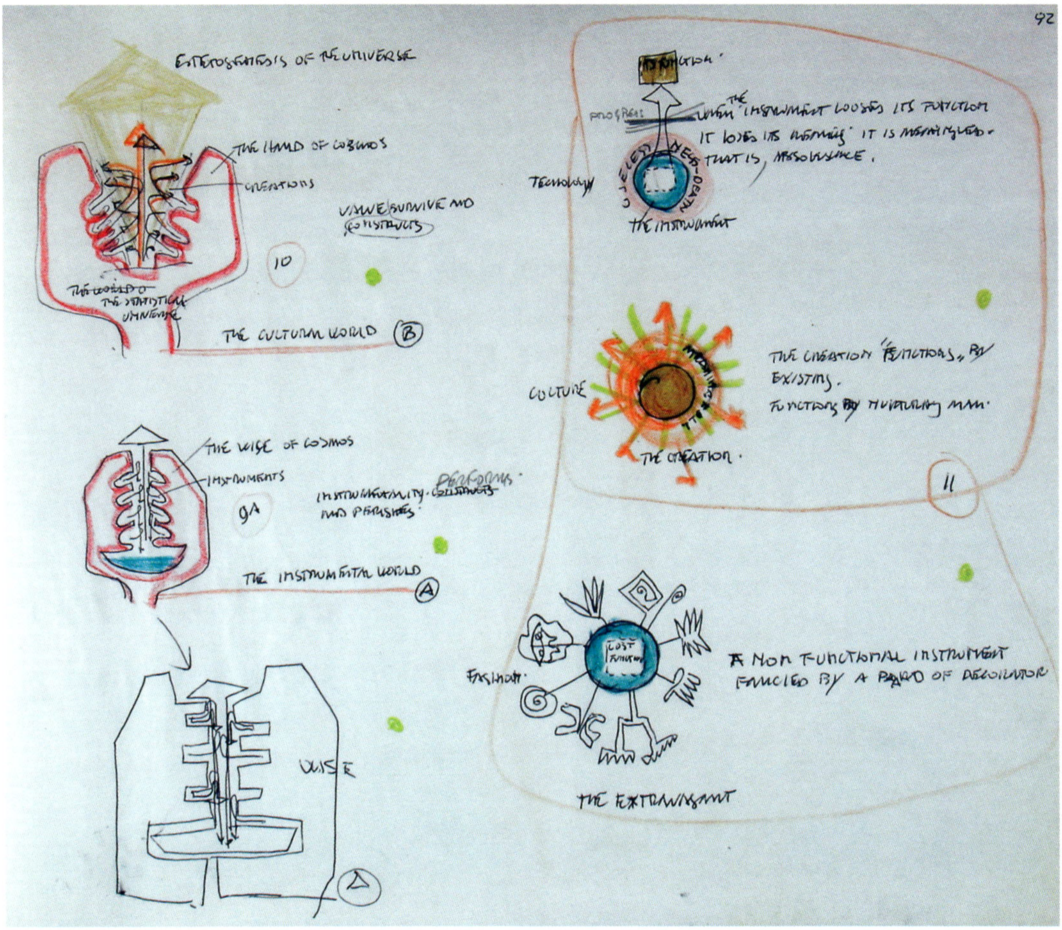

Plate 9. Matter and technology form a physical structure that compresses and constrains human and cosmic energy, pressing it into ever more specific and miniaturized formal configurations. "Esthetogenesis of the Universe: The Hand of Cosmos and the Vise of Cosmos." Paolo Soleri, sketches for esthetogenesis concept, circa December 1965, from Sketchbook 5, Arcologies and *The City in the Image of Man*. Courtesy of Cosanti Foundation.

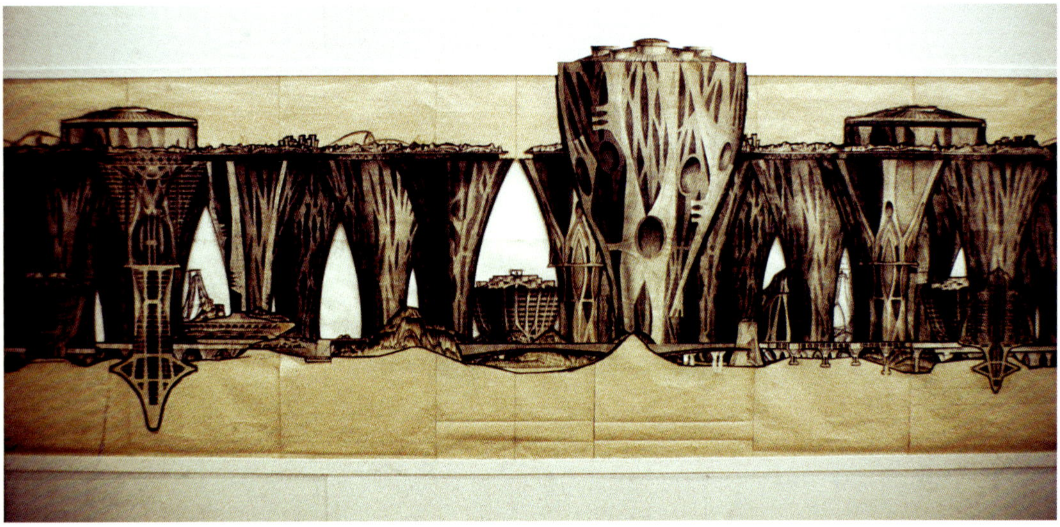

Plate 10. Paolo Soleri, Mesa City—Higher Learning Complex. Scroll of composite images from Higher Learning Center print series, early 1960s. From *The Sketchbooks of Paolo Soleri* (Cambridge: MIT Press, 1971). Photograph by Ivan Pintar.

sues raised by such environments. In terms very familiar to us today, the idea that the environment was collecting vast amounts of user data was disturbing. In such a situation, Negroponte argued, "Big Brother is not only watching, he is measuring your pulse, metering your galvanic skin resistance, smelling your breath."[133] The solution to this state of affairs, for Negroponte, was not the removal of such technologies from environments but the enhancement of their intelligence and autonomy. Instead of poking and prodding your exact physiological and psychological states, a responsive architecture would "know" you in a much more intimate (but less intrusive) way. It would anticipate responses based not on huge amounts of gathered or sensed data but on context. It would not require what Negroponte characterized as "high-resolution" data; rather, it would use "low-resolution" data that could then be synthesized with environmental awareness. The best example available to him at the time was a thesis project incorporated into the Architecture Machine itself by Mark Lavin in 1973. Called GREET, this system comprised a photosensitive doorjamb, weight sensors in a floor plate, and a computer networked with the rest of the systems in the lab. When an individual walked into the room, the sensors would create a "profile" based on weight and a very vague visual mapping. The system could then recognize this profile whenever the individual in question reentered the room. The doorway "knew" the user as soon as he or she came in; no fingerprints were taken, no retinas scanned, and no dongle was required. But what should the room *do* given what it now knows?

The Responsive House

Negroponte's and others' misgivings were on full display at a 1972 workshop at MIT titled The Responsive House. Organized by Edward Allen, the symposium was devoted to the role of the user of architecture and the various ways in which the user could be empowered to effect changes in the environment. This was perhaps the most incisive attempt to survey the emerging landscape of responsive technologies and participatory social strategies of the era. Among the participants were Christopher Alexander, Steve Baer, N. J. Habraken, Negroponte, Sim Van der Ryn, and Wellesley-Miller (Avery R. Johnson also made a presentation, discussed in detail in chapter 4; Wolf Hilbertz, who is the subject of chapter 5, was in attendance as well). Most participants addressed how user needs could be accounted for in the design process; post hoc modifications to buildings; the general methodology of gathering and interpreting data suggested by fields such as biology, psychology, and anthropology; and how these data might be synthesized with architectural and urban design. The case studies presented also ran the gamut of the classes of machine intelligence and environmental response, from the Chomskyan "deep structures" of

Figure 3.18. Cover of Edward Allen, editor, *The Responsive House* (Cambridge: MIT Press, 1974).

Alexander's pattern language to the do-it-yourself constructions of Steve Baer's zomes to computer simulations and the "courteous" environments imagined by Avery Johnson.[134]

The symposium, recorded in the complete published proceedings (in a beautiful volume designed by Muriel Cooper), appears now like an ambivalent time capsule. It captures a moment of transition between the social aspirations of the sixties and the more specific, personal, economic, community, and technological concerns of the seventies. In this instance, these broader issues were attached directly to the notion of response. For while the symposium was attended almost exclusively by designers, it was nonetheless a showcase of how designers had assimilated the findings of the environmental research manifold. Ecology, evolution, biology, anthropology, and psychology were all marshaled to justify various design approaches. After the symposium, the organizer, Edward Allen, questioned the very basis of such approaches, as he expressed in his introduction to the published proceedings:

> The question is, simply, to *what* should a responsive dwelling respond? What areas of human need are best answered by a change in the architecture of the immediate environment? And what sorts of responses might a building make to such needs? We found ourselves as a group incapable of defining responsiveness in housing, and, paradoxically, those who had the most difficulty in furnishing plausible examples of responsiveness were not those participants describing relatively ponderous, hard-to-change, traditional construction systems, but those who proposed technologies [that] are capable of instant response through pneumatic or electronic means.[135]

It was this charged sense of both the ethics and the aesthetics of responsive environments that animated the workshop, and that, as I will remark below, seems absent from current discourse.

Could "machines" really make architecture that was more human, or was the answer for everyone to directly build their own dwellings using time-tested techniques? How could digital technologies not only aid in the design and decision-making process but be integrated with the architecture itself and programmed to make changes in real time? What would be the best materials to make such real-time transformations possible—simple prefab frames, more topologically complex space structures, pneumatics, extruded foams and plastics? Finally, could machine intelligence be leveraged in real-time environmental situations, and, if so, what should such an actor be able to know and how should it be able to behave?

Perhaps the symposium's most remarkable presentation, in its breadth and rhetorical power, was that of Wellesley-Miller, who managed to frame the work of the MIT milieu in the most comprehensive ways. Wellesley-Miller fully understood the historical ramifications of the timing of the discussion, weaving into his account the environmental crisis, global demographics (population increase and generational turnover), economic projections, and technological advances (consideration of geopolitics was limited to a comparison of European planned economies and the American free market).[136] He framed the necessity for responsive building systems primarily in terms of ecology and the economies of current industrialized building. Given the urgent needs met by the latter, how could a system be implemented that would be more responsive to the former? How could that system be more responsive to inhabitants and communities in a specific built milieu? Prefabrication and mass production, Wellesley-Miller indicated, were suitable to the regimented economies and dire postwar need for housing in Western and Eastern Europe, but they quickly met their limitations. The resulting buildings were massive, obtrusive, immutable, inhumanly homogeneous, and environmentally harmful.

This situation called not only for different economies of scale, production methods, and so on, but also for a complete paradigm shift:

> 1. Abandon "housing." After all, "houses" are a solution to the problem, and not the problem itself, which is the provision of living facilities. (But this runs into the "social acceptance" problem.)
> 2. Try to change the technological basis of "industrialization" and develop a new building technology more truly suited to our needs. (This runs into a host of problems ranging from research funding to vested interest groups and building codes.)
> 3. Some combination of 1 and 2. This seems attractive, since it would allow a more evolutionary approach to the problem of retotalization.[137]

A shift in typological definition added to new, responsive technologies—this formed the basis for Wellesley-Miller's delineation of not only new building techniques but new design and habitation programs as well. This was perhaps one of the signal effects of the discourse on responsive environments: the way in which this traditional hierarchy of activities would be changed as a result of the assimilation of a design "intelligence," mobile components, and constant user-initiated feedback. Formerly clear distinctions between design, construction, and living itself would be blurred. Wellesley-Miller continued:

> Environmental protection, energy conservation, ecological integration, recycling, structural efficiency, ease and malleability of construction and user control, are starting points. The articulation of space comes later, perhaps too much so. The concern is to develop a building technology that is both humanly and environmentally responsive; the beginnings, if you like, of a humanistic biotechnology.
>
> A distinctive feature of responsive building technology is that it is "function" rather than "product" oriented; it is concerned with fabricating living facilities rather than houses *per se*. In this respect it is closer to the communications industry, which is not devoted to a particular product, but rather concerned with developing means of communication.[138]

Here we can clearly see the programming ethos of MIT dovetailing with the other models of environment I have been elaborating. Environment is not merely something to be preserved; rather, it is something to be instrumentalized into a responsive conditioning system that ultimately shapes the subject as much as the other way around. Inhabitants become users, manipulating an apparatus that seems to disappear into ubiquitous data flows. But Wellesley-Miller's was not purely a narrative of cybernetic dematerialization: "Yet there is an aesthetic, applied and implicit," he wrote, "a respect for place; a feel for simplicity; a striving for organismic integration; out of which issues a new space, at once pure and funky, charged with the sharp pleasure of a tensed cable, the crystalline logic of a space frame, the fat, carveable squishiness of foam, the billowing responsive mass of an inflatable; softened by growth and the exigencies of time, place, people, and funds."[139] This is truly a hybrid situation, in which virtually all environmental conditions are granted equal footing in the design conception; metal, people, and money all rendered as flows and variables that eradicate any clear distinctions between the material and immaterial, inside and outside, product and process, body and mind.

Wellesley-Miller not only provided a possible model for what responsive buildings might be like in the near future, but he also speculated about these buildings' subjects. Who, he asked, would be the inhabitant who would see the benefit of engaging in an ongoing dialogue with the environment, and how might that dialogue be facilitated? Would the response built into that environment be the meeting of needs or requests? Would it be the provision of entertainment? Would it be the simulation of different environments within the architectural frame? Or would it simply take the form of the provision of tools for people to make their own decisions, design and build their own environments, and subsequently alter them as needed? Would response reside in the subject or the object?

> Design becomes a continuous activity that merges with user control; production and assembly shade off into adaptation, extension, and upgrading. The system is in a constant state of adaptation and evolution in response to changing needs and visions of the occupant, an articulation in time. In fact it becomes difficult to speak of a building's age or lifetime. Like the human body, it is constantly changing its tissue while maintaining a more slowly changing functional pattern. . . .
>
> We have a long way to go and but little time. But the vision is there: evolutionary domestic eco-systems, responsive environments, a new peace and joy. The people are there: you and I.[140]

Are these not the same people (you and I) who might have sheltered under the canopies of nanocarbon filaments of the Elytra Pavilion at the Victoria and Albert Museum in the summer of 2016? These individuals formed a community of users whose movements and behavioral patterns were not so much input into the adaptive building system as picked up by it. Their interactions with the space then evolved as new canopies were fabricated by the robotic arm and lifted into place, further altering the physical and perceptual attributes of the environment. The structures themselves seem to fade behind the dynamic processes of data modeling, new fabrication techniques, and community interaction—the same stew that was simmering forty-five years ago.

Strangely, though, the same sense of immanence—of that which is just about to arrive—still characterizes the rhetoric of responsive environments. I do not make this observation out of skepticism. It is no longer a matter of whether we think these types of technologies possible. In many ways, such environments arrived some time ago (indeed, they were already pervasive when Wellesley-Miller, Negroponte, Kepes, et al. made their observations), they just were not delivered by artists or architects. Conditioning atmospheres made of vague combinations of material and immaterial substances, natural and synthetic structures, and the constant flux of information and energy constitute our world. In this sense, contemporary projects do not seem belated; they seem redundant. Building surfaces turned into "screens," permutations of spatial structures or ambiences based on "crowdsourced" data gathering, "smart" materials, biomimesis, and so on represent not expansions of our technological environments but condensations of them into cognizable and pseudomanipulable interfaces.

The idea is the same among the earlier formulations and the current proposals for immersive technological interaction—that, somehow, our inconceivably complex environment might be perceived, directly or virtually, and thereby become subject to strategic manipulation. The "user" becomes a designer who does not just respond to various environmental conditions but also programs or solicits responses in/from the same. These gestures and concepts are not the delayed realization of past aspirations. They are new sublimations of environmental conditions that must first be forgotten or obscured before they can be re-created in miniature.

4

Soft Control Material

In October 1973, Gregory Bateson received a letter from Avery R. Johnson requesting to join the former's research team at the University of California, Santa Cruz. The young cybernetician, having finished his work at MIT's Media Lab, felt that Bateson was one of the few comprehensive theorists of environmental interaction. In describing his own interests, Johnson wrote:

> I am strongly of the opinion that the role of the efferent side of behavior is more important to the processes of perception than is the entelechy of the sensory system(s) involved. It has led me to a position of strong interest in the communication of touch-and-movement because, unlike vision and hearing, it is usually impossible to isolate input and output from each other.
>
> Along that line I have a pet project that I am always seeking somehow and somewhere to get off the ground and that is to develop a tactile-kinesthetic interface with a dedicated minicomputer sufficient to give one a way to participate in a complex wallow of interactions. No other "display" scheme could possibly convey the world of ecological relationships as one in which you, the observer, can play an effective role with your efferent side and therefore your full range of perceptual apparatus in gear.[1]

Johnson invoked the languages of biology and computer science equally. In his letter, he attached himself to ascendant ideas of ecology and interfaces, and displayed his familiarity with current perceptual psychology (likely the work of J. J. Gibson). He also demonstrated a certain ambiguity, moving very quickly from theoretical abstraction to a specific point of application, the "tactile-kinesthetic interface."

Johnson did not go into further detail about this pet project, although he had indeed spent the past few years of his life working on it quite intensively, first in Cambridge and then at a private facility where he entered into a business partnership to develop the device commercially. This chapter is devoted to this interface, and to the particular environmental models it implied. But what was it? The object in question is a liminal one, so I want to make a provisional attempt to describe, exactly, what it is I am talking about (though, soon enough, the futility of this attempt will become not only evident but material to the present investigation).

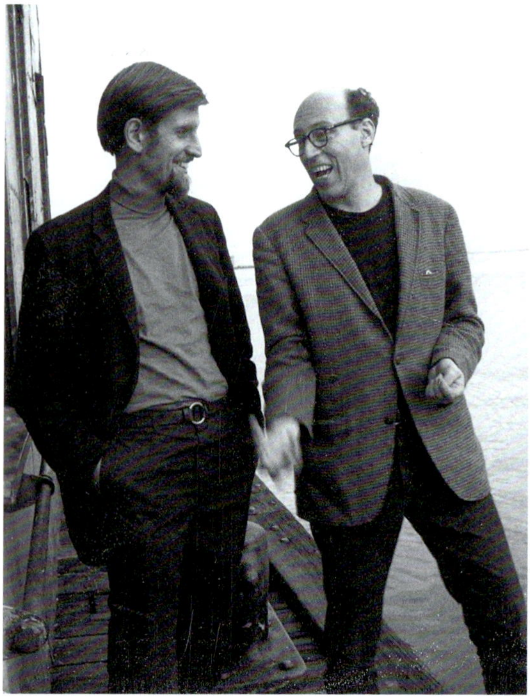

Figure 4.1. Avery R. Johnson and Warren M. Brodey, circa 1970, from Smithsonian Institution Archives. The Ecology, Tool, & Toy logo traces a topological loop, its terms folding into one another in mutually generative fashion. Courtesy of Warren Brodey.

The object has a name: Soft Control Material, or SCM. Technical specifications and drawings of SCM can be found in the patent filing for the device: U.S. Patent 3,818,487. Further evidence as to its physical properties and behaviors can be found in multiple, scattered descriptions issued by its inventors: Johnson and the psychiatrist Warren M. Brodey. SCM can be located in time and space, at least to a degree. It was incubated beginning at a private laboratory in Cambridge funded by a wealthy friend of Brodey.[2] Founded in 1967, this undertaking was initially called the Environmental Ecology Laboratory. Brodey also had ties with the Massachusetts Institute of Technology, where Warren S. McCulloch was a close friend and very much aware of his work. This led McCulloch to introduce Brodey to Johnson (one of his students) because of their shared concerns with environmental interaction.[3] Later, in 1970, they would found the company Ecology, Tool, & Toy (the logo of which resembles the beginning of a Klein bottle—a significant topological form, as we will see below). This facility was relocated to a noninstitutional setting in New Hampshire on a piece of property with a house and a few outbuildings, all next to an old quarry. Indeed, the place became known simply as "the quarry" to the many cyberneticians, scientists, designers, and artists who would visit there to camp out, party, and experiment. It was from here that in 1972 Brodey and Johnson filed their patent for Soft Control Material.

That patent (the only real outcome of the company) described not a singular object but rather a suite of interdependent technologies—high and low, digital and analog—comprising a sponge-like material made from foam and/or Freon-filled plastic bladders, special types of valves, and various articulated cladding surfaces. The Freon in the bladders would react to ambient temperature changes (from the sun or contact with an organic body) and expand or contract accordingly, causing the surface of the structure to change, or "breathe," or "respond" to various inputs. These qualities would make SCM effective for various applications, according to Brodey and Johnson. At the most pragmatic level, they foresaw the development of actively ergonomic furniture: "a chair-like structure, that if you move so it rocks forward inflates a pad under the small of your back so that it is well supported, or oscillates several rhythmically swelling air bags so they relax your back."[4] On another occasion, the suite of inflatable and stiff components were imagined as arrayed on a flat surface, constituting a "pleasing and changing wallpaper, which changes its texture, reflectivity, color, etc., as heat or light is applied to various portions thereof."[5] And these were just two of infinite possible applications, according to the inventors, some of which might also include lounge chairs, toys, and mattresses that would be "a sophisticated improvement to the water bed."[6] (In fact, the water bed had been patented just a year before by a San Francisco–based corporation called Innerspace Environments for not dissimilar therapeutic purposes.)[7]

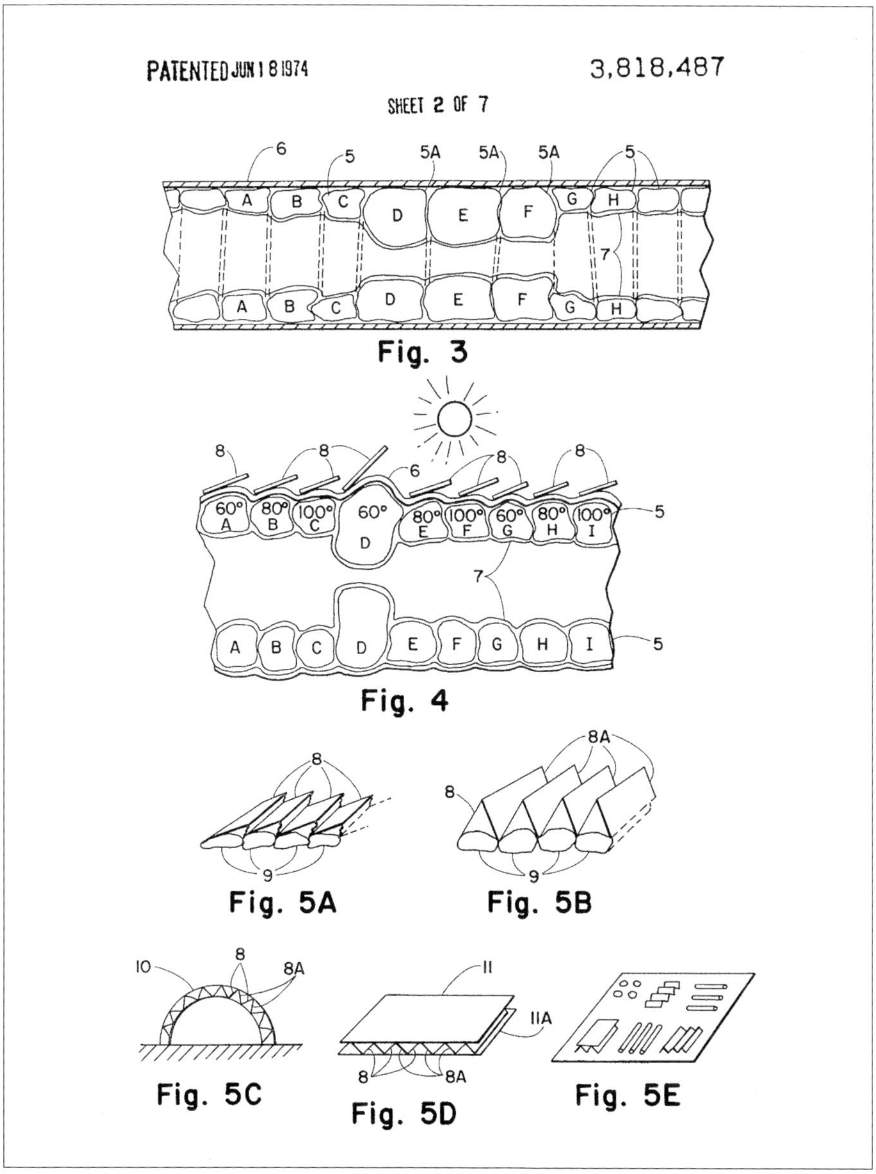

Figure 4.2. Composite image of drawings from the patent showing applications of SCM. W. Brodey and A. R. Johnson, Soft Control Material, U.S. Patent 3,818,487, filed April 24, 1972; issued June 18, 1974.

Soft Control Material was not a finite object with a distinct form, but was ultimately conceived as a self-organizing, biomimetic metastructure (both tool and toy) for facilitating new types of human–environment communication—a "medium" that might, in Brodey's words, "provide instantaneous feedback and thereby allow infolding with time, memory, energy, [and] relation."[8] This, in turn, would effect for the subject a virtuous topology of environmental discovery and new types of ecological and "interspecies" relationships, which could lead, ultimately, to a conscious evolution of humanity.

Before describing further the conception and function of Soft Control Material, I should also point out that, like the products of so many tech start-ups, SCM was a failure; no successful applications of SCM are recorded or preserved. Though no physical traces of SCM remain, the articulation of this product within a certain disciplinary and historical moment is exemplary of the way in which design became an integral part of the environmental research manifold around 1970. Here, design activity moved away from the production of discrete objects and toward the techno-aesthetic manipulation and optimization of interfaces between the subject and its milieu. In what follows I will extend this proposition further to suggest that design did not just respond to new conceptions of environment and ecology; rather, the latter were inconceivable without the emergence of a particular design modality. Another way of saying this is that SCM evokes a moment (as do other projects profiled in this study) in which designing *for* the environment and designing *an* environment were not yet clearly distinguishable.

On Softness

In 1972, Nicholas Negroponte introduced his book *Soft Architecture Machines* by stating that it arose out of a certain tension between two complementary (if not irreconcilable) models: the artificial intelligence models proposed by Marvin Minsky and Seymour Papert and the "soft robots" of Brodey and Johnson.[9] Though he saw "no evidence of progress or even potential" in Brodey and Johnson's ideas, Negroponte must have been drawn to their search for a responsive machine, which, unlike the AIs proposed by Minsky and Papert, was devoted to more than the solving of linear problems.[10] Brodey and Johnson's approach involved a holistic set of procedures that relied on an awareness of environmental conditions often described as "context," a deceptively simple-sounding name for a complex notion. This context could be discerned only in a heuristic, soft, "low-resolution" manner more akin to "squinting" than to clearly defining the irreducible parts of a problem.[11]

By the time Negroponte made these observations, there was a well-established body of "soft" structures within design culture. These included inflatable architectures and furniture as well as items made of extruded or "blown" materials like rubber and foam. Most of these foregrounded the attributes of ephemerality, spontaneity, and sensuousness against what were seen as the ossified, inhuman structures of the built and political environment.[12] There were interesting variants on these themes in both Europe and the United States, and in each context they took on countercultural connotations.[13] For Negroponte, though, most inflatables and the like presented the danger of falling into mere formalism. He often warned that without sufficient technical mediation, these structures might become "Miesian mushies" or "soft Soleris."[14] Suffice it to say that as far as Negroponte, Brodey, and Johnson were concerned, softness was not just a material or formal property; rather, it represented a new paradigm of mutual interaction.[15]

It is not difficult to speculate that Negroponte gleaned his own use of the terms *soft* and *context* from Brodey and Johnson, respectively.[16] Brodey utilized the phrase *soft architecture* as early as 1967 to characterize the types of technology he wished to develop.[17] He saw all around him a world confined by the rigid orthogonals of conventional technologies. These devices were "abstract," to borrow a term from Gilbert Simondon, a French philosopher of technology whose ideas were taking shape at the same time as those of Brodey and Johnson; that is, they were conceived for singular purposes, made from solid materials, constructed in linear assemblages, and incapable of adaptation.[18] Against this paradigm, Brodey proposed a new, soft conception of environmental technologies:

> The concept of an intelligent environment softened by a gentle control which stands in place of steel bones and stone muscles is refreshing. . . . To date we have not endowed our environment with this creative flexibility; the intelligence we have commonly achieved is uncreative, stupid and in large measure hostile to human well-being. We have allowed hard shell machines to multiply and control us. Man is a captive of his increasingly automated mechanical environment.[19]

Here, softness emerged as a structural quality of technologies and environments writ large. It was not confined to computer programming or to specific design applications. Rather, it stood for a new type of *emergence* in all interfaces.

Soft technologies were, for Brodey, nonlinear, biomimetic, somatically intelligent, complex assemblages. They inverted the insidious logic of industrial technologies, which offered themselves up as simple tools subservient to the human will, but which in fact constrained human activity into rigid and unchanging patterns—a formulation that subverted Heidegger's conception of the tool being "ready-to-hand" into Marx's reification, in which *things* dictated the logic of human interaction.[20] But it was not just the technology that was malleable. The user also had to soften, had to

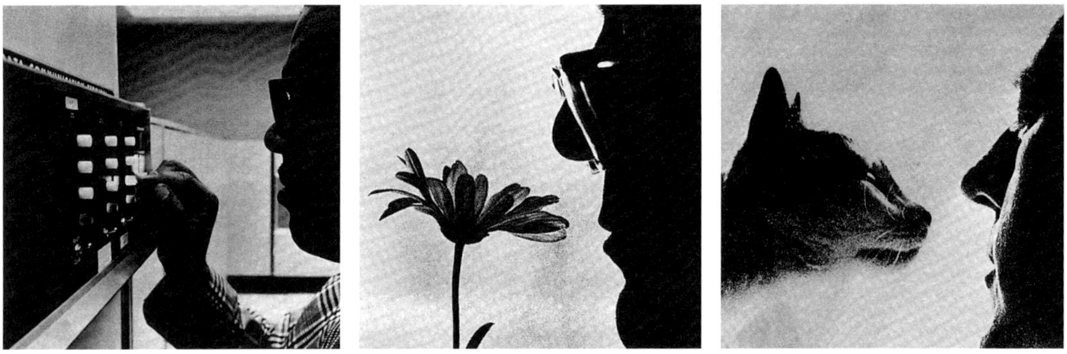

Figure 4.3. Photographs by George de Vincent, from Warren M. Brodey and Nilo Lindgren, "Human Enhancement through Evolutionary Technology," *IEEE Spectrum* 4, no. 9 (September 1967): 87–97. Courtesy of Warren Brodey.

become open to new patterns and behaviors. Herein lay the ultimate significance of softness in design: rather than mere pliability, it involved the mutual interaction of subject and object, to the point that the two would alternate positions within the system, each sometimes receiving signals from and sometimes sending signals to the other.

The most immediate goal of this mutual softening was a more effective world of interfaces, one in which machine activity would not only respond to an immediate need but could also augment and facilitate a range of other actions. "Present controls," Brodey wrote, "are like those of an adding machine that pays attention to the user only through the commands it is given. It regulates the human being by making all but his simplest, most ritualistic commands meaningless."[21] A series of photographs taken for Brodey by George de Vincent illustrated a stepwise move away from this linear conception by showing a man in three different attitudes of interaction: with a traditional machine, in a multisensory engagement with a flower, and, finally, in a mutually reactive engagement with a cat. This sequence suggested that soft interfaces and environments would go far beyond more congenial interactions to include mutual learning. "The ideal environment would replace toggles and switches by a skillful mutual man–machine sensing of the advantages and disadvantages of a particular cooperative behavior. The environment would itself grow with the user."[22]

On Control

Brodey and Johnson's understanding of machines placed in new configurations of soft technical reciprocity with their users and environments was not generated ex nihilo. It was a tangible development of the cybernetic ethos of MIT in the postwar period, where human–machine interaction was being explored from many different perspectives, and the rhetoric of data and research was quickly colonizing the architecture and design labs.[23] Indeed, it seems likely that the use of the word *control* in the name of SCM was a reflexive reference to Norbert Wiener's landmark book of 1948, *Cybernetics; or, Control and Communication in the Animal and the Machine.*[24] We can be even more specific in stating that, for Brodey and

Johnson, two landmark works in early cybernetics formed the foundation for their design activity. These were "Behavior, Purpose, Teleology," by Arturo Rosenblueth, Wiener, and Julian Bigelow, and, perhaps even more significant, Warren S. McCulloch and Walter Pitts's "A Logical Calculus of the Ideas Immanent in Nervous Activity," both published in 1943.[25] The former was a remarkably concise statement whose ramifications would be felt throughout the human and hard sciences. In it, Rosenblueth, Wiener, and Bigelow insisted on studying "behaviors" instead of "functions"—of either organisms or machines—relations between object and environment, over and above the "intrinsic organization of the entity studied."[26] So, too, they redefined the old philosophical notion of teleology, rejecting its connotations of grand, determining purpose in favor of a model of purposeful responses to feedback, a self-regulating series of moves to achieve a particular goal. Also of significance for the future development of SCM were the authors' remarks on the differences between organic and synthetic machines. From the old, "functional" perspective the two were irremediably disparate in their internal structures, but from the new, cybernetic or behavioral perspective, the differences became irrelevant, insofar as both could establish purposeful behaviors in active dialogue with their environments. As Rosenblueth et al. stated toward the end of their essay: "If an engineer were to design a robot, roughly similar in behavior to an animal organism, he would not attempt *at present* to make it out of proteins and other colloids. He would probably build it out of metallic parts, some dielectrics and many vacuum tubes."[27] Just a little over a quarter century after this description was written, Brodey and Johnson seemed to feel that the time was ripe to move away from "metallic parts" and toward a new model of a teleological machine.

No less important (indeed, more so) to their conception of SCM was the work of Warren S. McCulloch on "nervous nets" or "neural nets." This work was essentially a new cybernetic modeling system for thought itself as a series of logical equations based on the "all-or-none character of nervous activity."[28] Just as Wiener and his colleagues had transcended the metaphysical residues of "functionalism," McCulloch and Pitts sought to do away with the need for what they felt was a mystical conception of the psyche. For them, nervous activity, or thought, could be perfectly modeled using logical propositions along with the physical or topological structures of synapses. It was merely a matter of determining the possible combinations of "all-or-none" (binary) states. According to Orit Halpern, these philosophical propositions would have profound ramifications in the postwar period by fundamentally altering paradigms of consciousness and cognition in a way that "would forever impact future conceptions of minds and machines and [would] lay at the heart of models ranging from the treatment of schizophrenia to the architecture of the stored program computer."[29]

But while it is easy to see these classic texts merely as distant forerunners of our current systems, the case of Soft Control Material allows us to

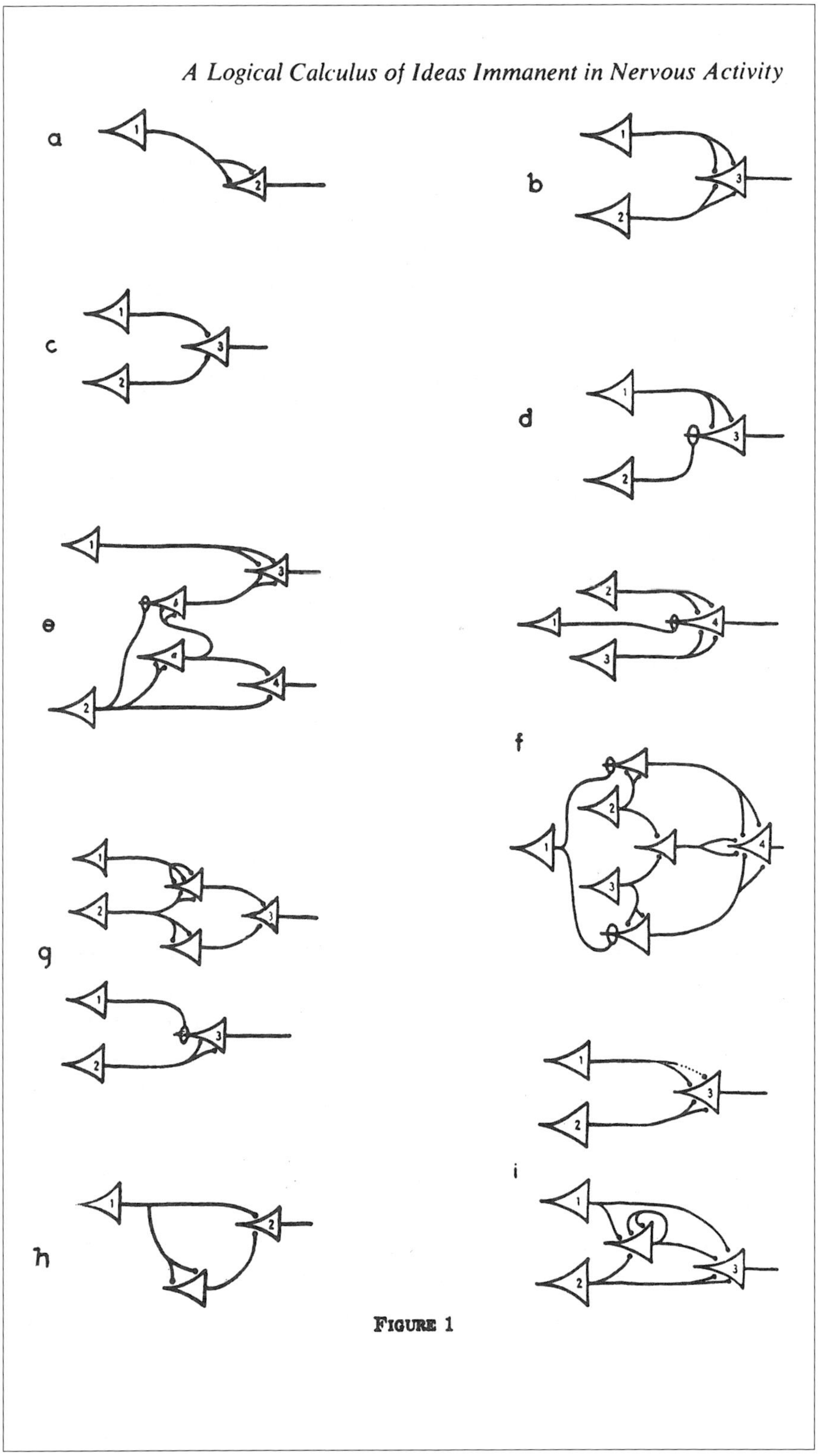

Figure 4.4. "The role of our brains in determining the epistemic relations of our theories to our observations and of these to the facts is all too clear, for it is apparent that every idea and every sensation is realized by activity within that net, and by no such activity are the actual afferents fully determined." Diagram of "Neural Nets," from Warren S. McCulloch and Walter H. Pitts, "A Logical Calculus of the Ideas Immanent in Nervous Activity," *Bulletin of Mathematical Biology* 5, no. 4 (December 1943): 130. Copyright 1943 University of Chicago Press.

examine a middle point in these developments, a moment in which design researchers were *literally* trying to construct the systems described theoretically in first-order cybernetics. Bearing this in mind, I want to linger a bit longer on the ramifications of Wiener's and McCulloch's respective ontologies. Consider for a moment the spatiotemporal models implied in each case. For Wiener et al., a given entity was defined not by its internal structure or reality but rather by its relationship to its environment. Famously, "negative feedback" from an attempt to reach a "goal" would direct the behavior of the entity, which would change over time in order to achieve the desired result. Interestingly, this model contrasts markedly with that of McCulloch and Pitts's nervous nets. The latter were conceived merely as highly redundant sequences of one or zero states, which had little to no connection to an external stimulus.[30] But this abstraction should not be taken as a form of idealism. It was intimately tied to the physiology of the net, so much so that the topology of that net and its possible pathways became fully autonomous, their form and content merging into one. McCulloch maintained that neighboring neurons had more to do with a given neuron's state than any external stimulus. Again, in Halpern's words: "From within a net (or network) the boundary between perception and cognition, the separation between interiority and exteriority, and the organization of causal time are indifferentiable."[31] For McCulloch and Pitts, then, the metaphysics inherent in the question of reconciling sense data and thought, noumenon and phenomenon, inside and outside, were moot. The real arose directly from the internal configuration of neurons. "With determination of the net," they wrote, "the unknowable object of knowledge, the 'thing in itself,' ceases to be unknowable."[32]

The models proposed by Wiener and McCulloch are intriguingly irreconcilable. In Wiener's model, behavior and teleology require external sources of information and a linear sequence of events (feedback and response). In McCulloch's, the source of the stimulus ceases to matter, and time is flattened into a merely predictive activity (the current state of the neural net can beget only certain future states, but the current state might have arisen from any circumstance). "Thus our knowledge of the world," according to McCulloch and Pitts, "is incomplete as to space and indefinite as to time."[33] But what at first seems like the primary importance of a spatial distinction (organism versus environment) may be just the opposite. In both models, cybernetics intervenes as a method of eliminating difference: between the organic and synthetic in the case of Wiener et al. and between stimulus and response in the case of McCulloch and Pitts. The result in both cases is a paradoxically abstract yet material entity whose behaviors demonstrate a tantalizing autonomy, established on the one hand by purpose and on the other by a self-organizing topology. Put another way, the ontological distinction between organism and environment becomes irrelevant in both cases; one is subsumed into the other. For Wiener, the actor overflows its boundaries, spilling into its surroundings, while for McCulloch the actor absorbs all external phenomena into its own fabric. In both cases, though, the notion of "control" is *not* equivalent to determination. The tension between environment and entity becomes the source of a kind of contingent self-determination in which the "self" in question gains in power precisely by relinquishing its classical, Cartesian insularity. The conception of Soft Control Material drew on both of these complementary perspectives—of an entity integrating its environmental inputs even while it is disintegrating into that very environment.

Brodey spent the better part of the 1960s familiarizing himself with these interactions and their applications in specific technologies. Initially, these were sensing and feedback technologies that could conceivably be attached to the human organism, whose states could be quantified and computed. These data could then be used to program specific responses in a given system. As with many of the projects littering the pages of this study, a certain tension was produced in this quest to measure personal states at too fine a grain. "Imagine," wrote Brodey, using the example of a highly skilled tennis coach,

> a machine that . . . tracks your behavior, that attempts to teach you a new control skill or a new conceptual skill and gives you cues as to what you are doing wrong. Furthermore, the machine gauges how far off your actions are from the program you are trying to learn, and "knows" the state of your perception; it is able to "drive" your perception gradually and sensitively, pushing you into unknown territory, into making you feel somewhat absurd and awkward just as you do when you are learning . . . new tennis movements. Suppose, in fact, this machine could sense factors about you that even a human instructor would miss—how your temperature was rising or falling, how the acid production of your stomach was beginning to increase, or how your eyes were actually tracking during certain tasks.[34]

But this level of knowledge was ambiguous. What would the machine responses to such inputs actually be, and would not the greater levels of information actually require more circumscribed interactions?

Already, Brodey was beginning to reconceptualize interaction in a more minimal way, even when computers were utilized. Though work at his Environmental Ecology Laboratory was never fully developed or reconciled, he was interested in utilizing computers to both algorithmically and graphically chart different models of interactions between entities in specific contexts or environments. In one published demonstration, various graphical dots were placed in proximity in virtual spaces ruled by various sets of determinants, such as "gravity" and "wind." The dots were then set in motion and tracked as they were being attracted to or repelled by the presence of the others in the changing contextual configurations.[35]

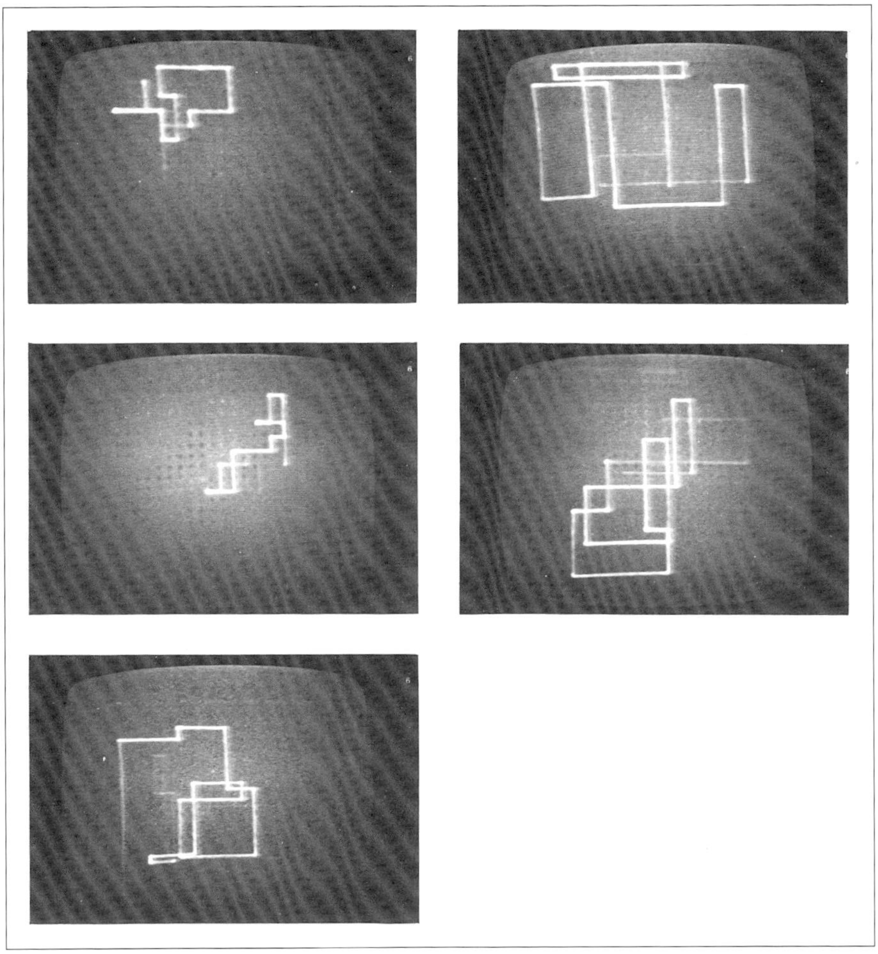

Figure 4.5. "The squares you are looking at were generated by our computer, which cost a good deal of money . . . but it makes beautiful squares. Look at the squares and you will see the architecture that lives around us. The computer made these squares. The squares move. You could build buildings from these squares." Images from computer simulation of environmental interactions of elements, from Warren Brodey, "Experiments in Evolutionary Environmental Ecology," in *Computer Graphics in Architecture and Design,* ed. Murray Milne (New Haven, Conn.: Yale School of Art and Architecture, 1969). Courtesy of Warren Brodey.

These dots could be understood as any actor—human or nonhuman—in virtually any network. The simulation became much more about the patterns of interactions than about tracking the dots themselves.

But Brodey was also keenly interested in surprisingly (from our perspective) "analog" technologies. He actually became less interested in computers, for instance, than in servomechanisms and self-organizing control circuits. Ultimately, both Brodey and Johnson were drawn to these relatively simple technologies because they felt that there lay the key to biomimesis. While some were attempting to complexify digital computers to the point that they could solve high-level problems (Minsky et al.), others were working within a completely different paradigm in which only the simplest biological functions were capable of being imitated or, better, replicated. Instead of artificial intelligence, then, these researchers wanted to build physical systems that would demonstrate the lowest levels of "behavior": response to stimuli and elementary forms of "learning."

The most famous example of such a system was provisionally realized

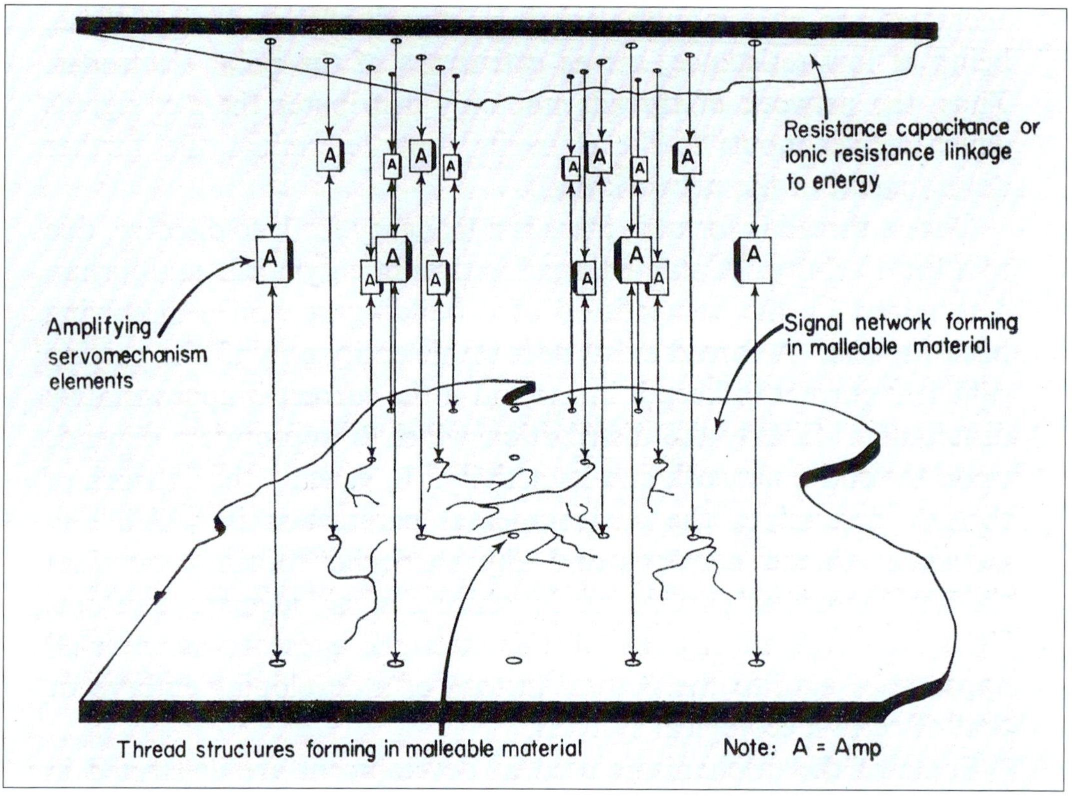

Figure 4.6. Gordon Pask, section of a physical model of a chemical computer, from Gordon Pask, "The Natural History of Networks," in *Self-Organizing Systems: Proceedings of an Interdisciplinary Conference,* ed. Marshall C. Yovits and Scott Cameron (New York: Pergamon Press, 1960), 247. Copyright Gordon Pask Archive, Department of Contemporary History, University of Vienna.

by the cyberneticians Gordon Pask and Stafford Beer. In the late 1950s they constructed a physical "model," as Pask described it, of a self-organizing "chemical" or "biological" computer. The structure comprised electrodes with conductors reaching into a ferrous sulfate solution. Electrical currents varying in intensity (based on certain inputs) would stimulate the growth of iron filaments, or "threads," within the solution. Those filaments would establish physical networks of conductivity, allowing more electricity to pass at some points than at others. Pask imagined that this computer could be inserted into any complex system and, eventually, learn to govern that system toward a state of stability or equilibrium. In historian Andrew Pickering's words:

> The present thread structure helps determine how the structure will evolve in relation to currents flowing through the electrodes, and hence the growth of the thread structure exhibits a path dependence in time: it depends in detail on both the history of the inputs through the electrodes and on the emerging responses of the system to those. The system thus has a memory, so it can learn. This was Pask's idea: the chemical computer could function as an adaptive controller, in the lineage of the homeostat.[36]

Although it was not the only experiment to pique the interest of Brodey and Johnson, this specific example is especially significant for two reasons. The first is reflected by the fact that Pask's diagram of the computer bears a striking resemblance to the sections of Brodey and Johnson's patent application illustrating Soft Control Material. Both technologies called for a number of conductive elements and circuits to affect a malleable and changeable material; changes in that material would then determine its future behaviors. The second reason is that Pask's approach, inspired by Heinz von Foerster and, indeed, McCulloch's nets, was fundamentally different from most programming theory at the time. Instead of designing ever more complex hardware and software to tackle ever more complex problems, Pask was looking for a minimal structure whose basic responses would grow in complexity, or evolve, over time.[37]

Brodey and Johnson's understanding of this intimate reciprocity between input and output, organism and environment—this soft control—went through its own evolution as the 1960s approached the 1970s. Brodey, for instance, had been busy researching all manner of interfaces and control mechanisms, including new types of electronic switches, so-called self-organizing control systems (i.e., the dynamic sensor-computation systems used in aircraft navigation), the multifaceted human–computer interfaces developed by Douglas Engelbart (including what we now call GUIs and somatic augmentation devices such as the mouse), early versions of virtual reality ocular headsets, and so on up to the notion of artificial intelligence.[38] In 1967, in his essay "Soft Architecture," Brodey imagined a kind of synthesis of all of these means of environmental control:

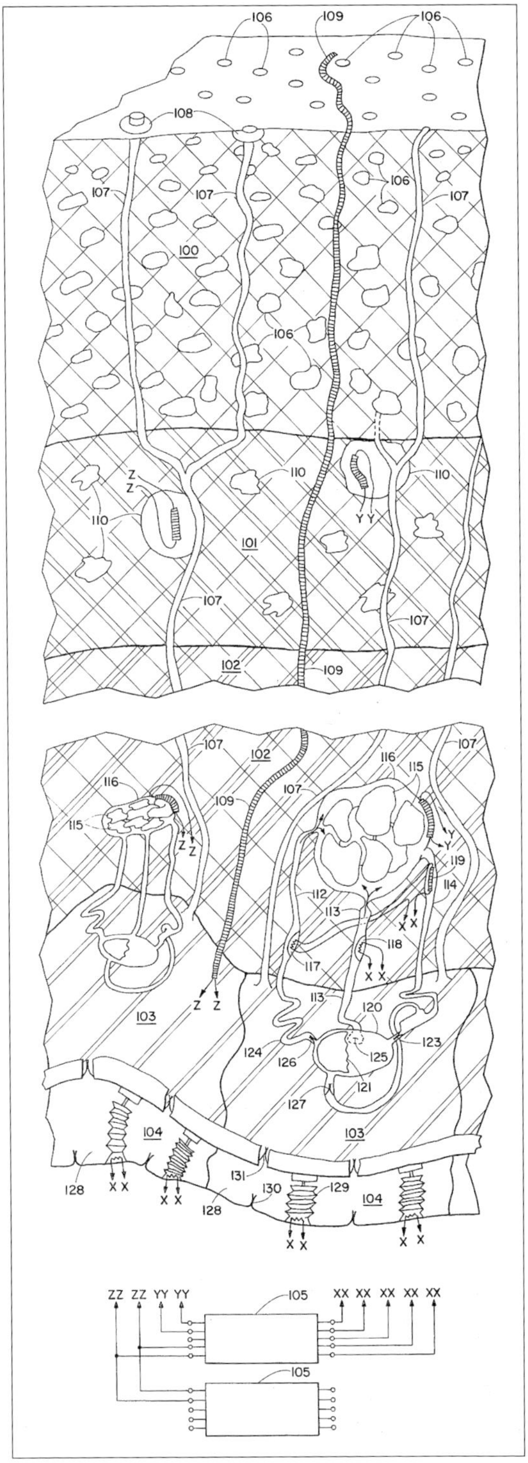

Figure 4.7. Warren Brodey and Avery Johnson, section of Soft Control Material. W. Brodey and A. R. Johnson, Soft Control Material, U.S. Patent 3,818,487, filed April 24, 1972; issued June 18, 1974.

> The man will . . . be instrumented so that his behavior can be monitored. We will use as many ways as we can of measuring the man's outputs—both physiological and behavioral: heart rate, electroencephalogram, surface heat, core heat, head movement, hand movement, etc. . . . Now, remembering that our purpose is to develop a truly interconnected network of feedbacks, let us connect the man's output behaviors—heart pulse accelerations, for example—so that they become data which the computer uses to adjust environmental parameters.[39]

However, likely because of both the technical limitations Negroponte signaled and the philosophical pathways opened by McCulloch, Pask, and others, Brodey and Johnson did not pursue such complicated technologies. Johnson, writing in 1971–72, described the current approach to what had become SCM. It was emphatically not a complex orchestration of digital technologies. It was not

> a mechanical or electronic Big Brother Robot which is hyper-attentive to you, watching your every movement and every change of heart-rate or respiration or alpha-rhythm as if to quiz you constantly and surreptitiously to find out what you want. No, that sort of behavior is not at all courteous. That way of imagining "intelligence" assumes that the data which the robot is collecting can somehow be made meaningful (decoded, interpreted, translated) so as to tell it what to do next. It's the old "decision model" which we have already laid to rest.[40]

But what was the alternative? How might a given technology process input signals without a guiding algorithm? How might a machine "perceive," or "sense," or make sense of its surroundings? How might AI be brought into the design process? As Negroponte had recognized, there were two possible responses to these questions:

> One approach is to attempt to embed knowledge directly (both facts and methods for manipulating those facts) into a computer, in some sense to capitalize upon the time we, as humans collectively, have taken to learn these "facts." The other route is to understand and impart to machines the learning process itself (which includes learning how to learn and, more important, the desire to learn) with the notion that machines could subsequently mature in a manner not dissimilar to that of humans.[41]

The first approach was a linear, mechanical/digital one that focused on defining specific problems, parsing them, atomizing them, and determining the "subdivision of tasks that lend themselves to 'skillful' solution." "The second approach tackles learning and self-reference, recognizing that any conversation or interaction between machine and man or between machine and environment is altered by context, in particular by a domain of 'relevant' previous experiences."[42]

There was no doubt that the former solution held the most potential for realization, but its confining rigidity and predetermination clashed with Brodey and Johnson's cybernetically inspired penchant for autonomy and self-organization (of themselves and of their tools and toys). Their response was stunningly counterintuitive. Instead of developing a complex, fully realized AI of some kind, they started at the opposite end of the evolutionary scale, implementing a more physical, analog, or *material* method. If a machine's emulation of the activities of a complex organism was always compromised by Cartesian biases and mechanical assumptions, perhaps the machine could instead emulate the activities of simple organisms. This led to a new way to think about complexity. In "Soft Architecture," Brodey wrote: "An environment may be simple or *complex*. If simple, it can still be made complicated, but a multiplication of simple people or of simple devices does not create intelligence, unless they are organized on the next level—a complex group."[43] Later, in a 1969 article in *Architectural Design,* he continued to develop this line of thought: "Our computers could help us [model complex interactions], but first we must have some way of structuring what we humans do and how we handle complex phenomena. *Our* pattern recognition systems are complex but we must begin with awareness that perhaps we can be simple if we can find the right way of modeling our complexity."[44]

Johnson, especially, was working toward a formal instrumentalization of these models of simple perceptual interactions in complex contexts. His most systematic statement on this topic can be found in an essay titled "Organization, Perception, and Control in Living Systems," which was ostensibly his attempt to formulate a new type of industrial management system.[45] In large part, Johnson's argument in this pivotal essay rehearsed the critique of industrial technologies we saw above: that technology was far too linear, insular, and rigid. He was especially concerned that in contemporary management systems, these qualities had become hidden by the "intelligent" behavior of computers, which, despite their speed, were still simply linear problem solvers that relied solely on predefined parameters. In other words, computers functioned nothing like *living organisms* that were in a constant state of active exchange with their environments. "Animals deal with a highly complex, ambiguous world while performing the simplest of behaviors," Johnson wrote.[46]

In articulating a way in which machines might reach a similar level of complex simplicity, Johnson shifted the traditional meanings of inputs and outputs, of stimulus and response, that had characterized previous biological and technological theories of systems. Like his mentor McCulloch, Johnson adopted a radically behaviorist position in which the importance of the "content" of the stimulus or input was negligible relative to the change in, or response of, the system itself. Accordingly, just like Wiener, Johnson opened up his definition of the system to include its environment or context. But if cybernetics had once been concerned with extracting the signal from its context (usually considered noise), Johnson was exploring a more positive understanding of the latter. "The sensory input is not the event," Johnson wrote. "I repeat. THE SENSORY INPUT IS NOT THE EVENT. It is a metaphoric statement about the event or object. It remains for the organism to discern the meaning of the metaphor through some further behavior which is more than simply a passive, sensory observation."[47] "Information is ambiguity resolved by transaction with the environment," he continued, strongly echoing Bateson, "it is not just that the active transaction delivers us the information. OUR PARTICIPATION IN THE PROCESS IS THE PERCEPTION OF THE INFORMATION. . . . It is up to the organism to change itself for the purposes of acquiring elucidation."[48]

For Johnson, the processes of perception, cognition, and response were not discrete activities that could be separated into a diachronic sequence of abstract propositions or machinic functions. They were self-referential behaviors woven into the very fabric of a given context or environment. Speaking explicitly of control systems (for most of the essay, it is ambiguous whether Johnson is referring to organic or nonorganic entities), he stated:

> There may and should be a highly flexible set of relationships possible between the sensors that detect changes and the effectors that produce them. The system itself must never be content to remain a passive observer of incoming data; it must participate in exploration. In fact, it is becoming increasingly evident that any self-organizing system must, in effect, play with itself in a manner which includes part of the environment in the loop.[49]

What followed in the essay was essentially a manifesto for a qualitatively different "interface," one that would establish new kinds of relationships with its environment. Johnson sketched a historical timeline of developments in cybernetics that pointed to this possibility. If control systems had initially relied solely on inputs from their operators, first-order cybernetics had developed an interface that functioned as a kind of mediator between the environment (or "world" in Johnson's diagrams) and the processor, using negative feedback to make corrections toward a "purpose" (to use Wiener's term). Now, Johnson maintained, the interface had arrived at a point where it could essentially receive and "metabolize" inputs from both the processor and the environment with a minimum of human maintenance: "Any system which has the responsibility for organizing itself and for discovering the meaning of things must trust, at least at first, to learn what it can from the behavior of its interface with the world."[50] This is a radical departure from the interfaces of the previous decades, in which a "user" or programmer manipulated a series of identifiable controls to achieve different functions in the processor. In Johnson's model, the interface relies only minimally on the processor, and the interface opens out to the world itself, repositioning the "user" as coactor.

> Self-organizing systems are of a devious ilk and hide their colors when you try to isolate them. Instead, present the system in some active, responsive embodiment and let the observer explore its responsiveness. Allow him the opportunity to tweak it with *his interface*—his reach, grasp, poke, stratagem, and perturbation—so that he in his turn may "know" the system as only an active participant can ever know it.[51]

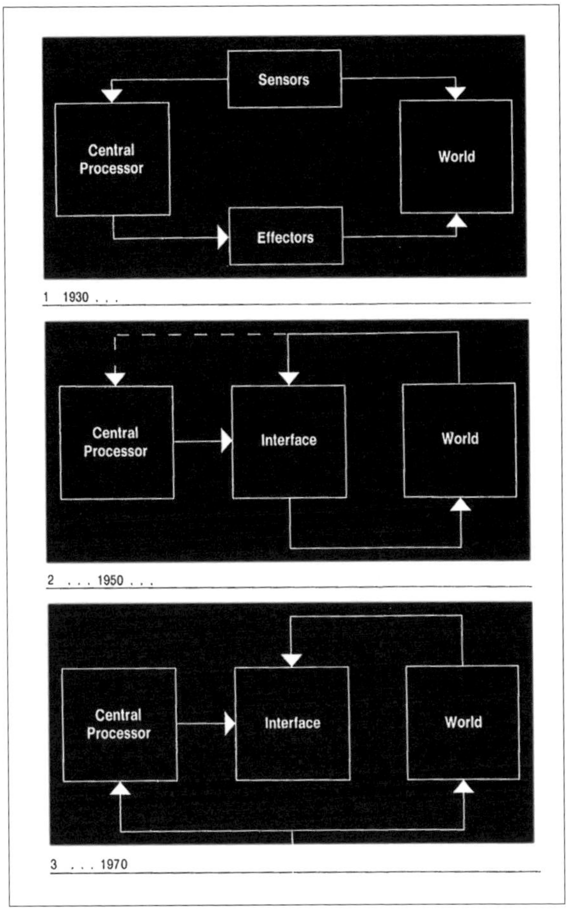

Figure 4.8. Diagrams of the evolution of interfaces over time. In each successive iteration, the environment, or "world," takes on a more active role. From Avery R. Johnson, "Organization, Perception, and Control in Living Systems," *Industrial Management Review* 10, no. 2 (Winter 1969).

Here we have a coherent statement about a radical change in the very nature of the way in which human subjects might relate to machines (and their environments). Instead of an interface as a "medium"—"a radically mediated boundary through which the complexity of the coordinated systems is simplified and managed through the use of *limits*"[52]—we have a correlation between two semiautonomous entities, both of which expand their limits and gain in complexity over time.

On Material

This model of a "soft control"—of a mutual inflection of interfaces—goes some way in explaining the characterization of the technology as "material" in the first place. Why not call it a device? Apparatus? System? I speculate that *material* connoted for Brodey and Johnson a kind of substance out of which many different behaviors and structures could evolve.[53] Material was "stuff," to use Johnson's term, that might, like some synthetic primordial ooze, give birth to lifelike technologies:

> When we start trying to imitate biology (and move into the area now called bionics), we find it strangely difficult so long as we attempt the imitation with rigid materials: so long, for example, as we describe a man's movements as if he were merely an animated skeleton. A breakthrough into the realm of soft materials, with thermodynamic energy relationships, suddenly puts you into a position to fulfill the desired biological paradigm within the frame of ordinary, non-living materials.[54]

Brodey and Johnson began referring more and more to microbes, single-celled organisms, worms, and the like. They began building objects that exhibited very basic physical responses to various stimuli. "I built a worm-like lively thing one day two years ago," Brodey wrote in 1972. "I made it about a foot long and about 3" in diameter out of polyurethane. I had valves, actually fluidic-flip-flops on-off valves, and I attached them so each of the 5 segments swelled then contracted one after the other."[55]

These passages indicate another attitudinal change vis-à-vis the mainstream programming community (at MIT and elsewhere). *Material* implied for Brodey and Johnson a physical, real-time approach to design. Herein lay another reason for employing the term: it was antiprescriptive. Johnson and Brodey were never able to describe SCM in its complete or finite form. Johnson readily acknowledged this: "I will not talk about form. That, my friend, will come about when you, the materials, the control and energy sources get together."[56] A material is something that can take many forms, find many applications, produce infinite variations and unexpected outcomes. This polyvalence notwithstanding, it would become incumbent on Brodey and Johnson to stipulate some specific uses for SCM. After all, they had founded a company and filed a patent. It is here that we find the most detailed speculations about the *forms* the material might take, as well as its technical composition, which will also concern us. By the same

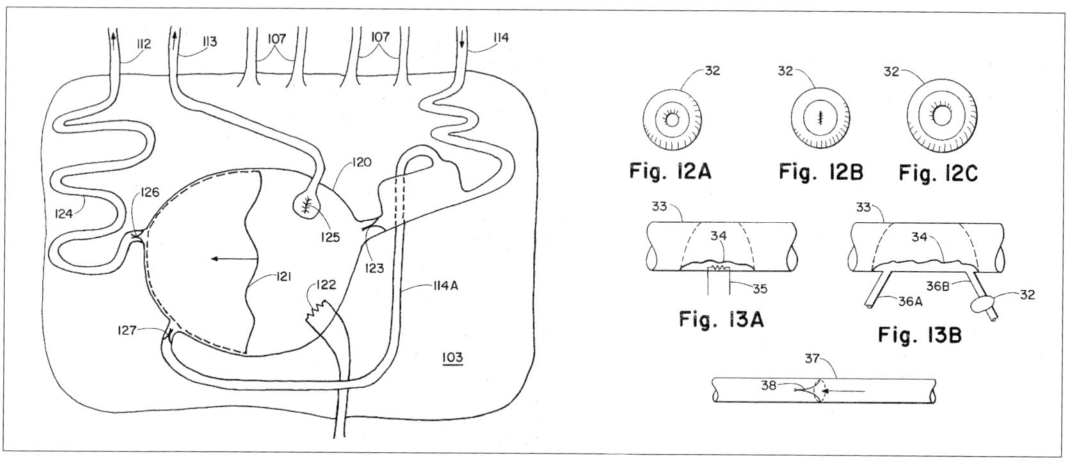

Figure 4.9. Warren Brodey and Avery Johnson, Soft Control Material, composite image of section through bladder and types of valves. W. Brodey and A. R. Johnson, Soft Control Material, U.S. Patent 3,818,487, filed April 24, 1972; issued June 18, 1974.

token, though, even these very technical descriptions can be maddeningly vague and difficult to grasp (even with the help of technical drawings). These qualities were already apparent in the description in the abstract of the patent filing:

> Soft control material usable as an interactive device with a user, or as a medium of communication between users on the tactile and least complex level. The material is self organizing; it uses distributed, self referent, and majority control of regions of the material, which allows greatly reduced amounts of information to be transmitted between units for communication therebetween.[57]

What could this possibly mean? Were these lines describing an object? An environment? Hardware? Software? Predictably, for Brodey and Johnson, the answer to all of these questions was yes.

The technical specifications for SCM might provide a better foothold. Brodey and Johnson offered many variants, and these could be combined in any imaginable configuration. The components included bags (or bubbles within a foam material) filled with liquid or gas (or, in the case of Freon, both), valves and tubes connecting these "bladders," and some sort of skin binding the ensemble of bladders together. In some instances, descriptions included "hard" components that could be affixed to the surface of the material, or even placed inside it, functioning as a kind of infrastructure. These physical components were then subject to various types of stimuli, or inputs, the most commonly referenced being temperature changes. Temperature changes could derive from various ambient conditions or from direct input from electrical circuits attached to heating elements (copper wire coils, for instance).

Using the section illustrated in Figure 4.7, we can describe a hypothetical arrangement of all these elements. Moving from top to bottom, we can discern five layers in this particular configuration: a top "cutaneous" layer (100), a "subcutaneous" layer (101), a "muscle" layer (102), a "gill" layer (103), and finally an "air storage" layer. The cutaneous layer is essentially the sensing layer. It is made of elastomeric foam embedded with tiny bubbles ("nodules") filled with Freon and stretchable tubes (107) running vertically through the layer that terminate on the surface of the material in "torus valves" (108)—essentially ring structures filled with Freon that can open or close depending on conditions. The tubes can carry liquid or air (although those with an opening on the surface of the material would likely carry air exclusively). Also lying on the surface, and then penetrating vertically through the cutaneous layer and down into other layers, are "electrically thermoresistive" strips (109). These act as sensitive thermal pickups that send signals to networked actuators in the material below. (Brodey and Johnson also indicated that photosensitive technologies were available that could render these strips light sensitive.)[58] The size, shape, and placement of these strips determines their behavior under different conditions.

The various layers underneath the skin of this SCM configuration comprise more foam, varying concentrations of tubes and nodules, and large Freon-filled sacs with tubes carrying more gas in and out. These "muscles" are designed for rapid expansion and contraction, activated by the thermoresistive strips or tubes running through the layer. Each of the muscles is connected to a "gill" in the layer below (103). This layer, with its complex network of tubes carrying different densities of Freon, acts as a kind of pressure valve for the muscles above. Moving still further down through the layers, we find near the bottom small "bellows" that expand and contract, pumping air up through the gills; this function has physical ramifications for the rest of the assemblage. Finally, all the layers rest on a "control system" (105) of electric circuits and semiconductors that can receive the signals of the thermoresistive strips and transmit them as electrical signals (Z, X, Y) back into the material. Fortunately, a self-organizing control system had recently (1969) been patented by R. L. Barron. This device was designed to regulate the performance of a given electronic system (or plant) without the use of long-term stored memory.

The other notable technical component here, of course, is the ubiquitous use of Freon. While it later came to be associated with ozone depletion and environmental damage, these characteristics would have been unknown to Brodey and Johnson. For them, Freon was one of many new resources (such as the Raysistor and the self-organizing control unit) available to be integrated into their own technologies. Manufactured by DuPont (as were many of the plastic and foam products Brodey and Johnson also used in their experiments), Freon is a stable gas that changes into liquid form at certain temperatures. Various admixtures of the gas allow for precise control of different boiling points (which determine if the chemical is gaseous or liquid). Brodey and Johnson felt that by varying the Freon mixtures in the nodules embedded in SCM, they could establish lifelike rhythms of expansion and contraction in the ensemble, with some bladders growing before others, then contracting again accordingly, depending on the boiling point.

All the layers combined in this configuration would yield a pile about 25 centimeters thick. The control unit would be an additional 7 centimeters or so, but it could likely be embedded in the bottom layer of the material. Roughly the size of a thick cushion or mattress, the assemblage would constitute something of an embodied and ergonomically inviting black box, a Turing test for life instead of for intelligence.[59] And, indeed, this was one of the primary functions of SCM: physical interaction. A hand or body pressing against the surface would alter the compression of the various nodules and bladders below and would activate a response from the thermoresistive components. These changes in the system would be communicated to the control unit, which in turn could translate the inputs into an ever-changing array of electrical signals sent back up into the system. While all of these structural changes were taking place, the user might simply feel the material rise up in those areas receiving the most pressure, or sense an undulating movement across the surface as one layer after another contracted.

But why? Though SCM was designed ergonomically, it was not meant to achieve a predefined goal of comfort, bodily correction, or therapy. SCM would act almost independently, as an organism in its own right, entering into a relationship with the user. According to the patent filing, "A certain amount of time after which a user coacts with the material, he learns the general characteristics of the material, and can communicate with it in a tactile mode."[60] This was not a device to be used, but rather a nonorganic organism with which to communicate and from which to learn. Pressed intimately against an organic body, it would embrace or resist that body in "meaningful" (nonpredetermined) patterns. These, in turn, would allow for the deprogramming of the user and pave the way for a more human, environmentally conscious "program."

On Topology

With this focus on the internal structures and mechanisms of SCM, as well as the many characterizations of it as biomimetic, it is easy to lose sight of its *environmental* functions. Is this not what self-organization is, after all, a system resisting the centripetal gravity of its surroundings, maintaining its internal integrity against the chaotic and entropic forces in the environment?[61] Perhaps, but SCM was nonetheless conceived as a radically open, porous organism, and, moreover, one that would become a kind of consciousness machine transforming the human subject's relationship to its environment. In order to understand the mechanics of these processes, it is necessary to recall the conception(s) of environment available to Brodey and Johnson at this moment, as they were much more radical, in a sense, than those we currently utilize.

While there was no single source for their understanding of what, exactly an—or the—environment was, certainly the work of Gregory Bateson loomed largest. Brodey had been with Bateson in Hawaii in the 1960s during his experiments with dolphins, and Johnson would later relocate his family to Santa Cruz to join the group coalescing around Bateson in the mid-1970s. Discussion of Bateson's implication in the development of cybernetics, his multiple interests in psychology, anthropology, and biology, and the holistic manner in which he began to package his ideas is beyond the scope of this chapter, but suffice it to say these were all consonant with Brodey and Johnson's approach. Perhaps a single formulation of Bateson's will clarify the connections between his thinking and the formulation of SCM. In *Steps to an Ecology of Mind*, Bateson used the example of the development of the horse to illustrate how his own thinking about evolution had become progressively ecological:

> But I could not then see that the evolution of the horse from *Eohippus* was not a one-sided adjustment to life on grassy plains. Surely the grassy plains themselves were evolved *pari passu* with the evolution of the teeth and hooves of the horses and other ungulates. Turf was the evolving response of the vegetation to the evolution of the horse. It is the *context* which evolves.[62]

Here, context or environment is conceived as a kind of connective tissue (or "pattern," as Bateson would describe it) weaving disparate entities together, giving them a platform for mutual inflection (see chapter 1).

In this perspective, SCM was less a design object than a machine for making environments tangible. We can begin to approach this conception from one of Brodey's later, more poetic evocations of interacting with SCM:

> If I am lying down on a floor area which is an air structure made of interwoven kleinforms that can expand or contract depending in part on their neighbors' behavior, the heat and light in the room, and on how I interface with its efforts to reduce its information to a manageable level, and the space itself is like being under the soft umbrella of an oak tree waving lively in the wind, or being inside a bubble of scum lively with creatures . . . what would it be like? Would we use verbal language as we know it, at all?[63]

This short passage contains many of the hallmarks of the ambiguity of SCM and the various models of environment in the midst of which it was located. At one moment, the material is a ground, at another a canopy. With another series of metonymic shifts, it becomes a tree, then the interior of a bubble of liquid foam teeming with organic life. It is object, environment, and organism simultaneously; it is both inside and outside, micro- and macrocosm, something to be grasped that might yet grasp and encircle the user. Finally, in an apparent non sequitur, Brodey proposes that these physical interactions might have some profound impact on language.

This shifting of scales and functions is inherent in all of the evocations of SCM issued by its inventors. These shifts are not merely metaphorical; they reflect the way in which environment was conceived by cybernetics and ecology at this time. Environment denoted "nature," orientation within various technological networks, ecological connection to other subjects, and communicational context. Environment was no longer simply that which encircled a given entity; it was that which produced that entity and was produced by it. SCM embodied virtually all of these dynamics. It was a topological engine of spatiotemporal transformation, taking in air and accepting touch and then metabolizing those as communicative responses and evolving behaviors. These behaviors, in turn, would be received by a user as low-resolution “information” that could provoke further types of interaction—two (or more) interfaces interfacing (“interfacing in depth”).[64]

The model of topology figured in virtually all of Brodey and Johnson’s statements. As it related to SCM, it referred to both the internal organization of the components relative to one another—nodule to tube to valve, and so on—and the way the material itself related to the environment. Brodey and Johnson even anticipated that some of the bladders embedded in the foam of SCM could be structured like that most fundamental topological figure, the Klein bottle (a boundless surface form made of a self-penetrating “tube”): “It is obvious that combinations of tubes and Klein Bottles may be provided to form sophisticated logical and lively structures which may be used for control purposes, sensory input and output devices, etc.”[65]

It was topology that allowed Brodey and Johnson to interface with the experimenters at the journal *Radical Software.* Apparently, sometime in 1970, the video artist Paul Ryan worked with Brodey at the property in New Hampshire on “soft control systems using plastic membranes.”[66] The

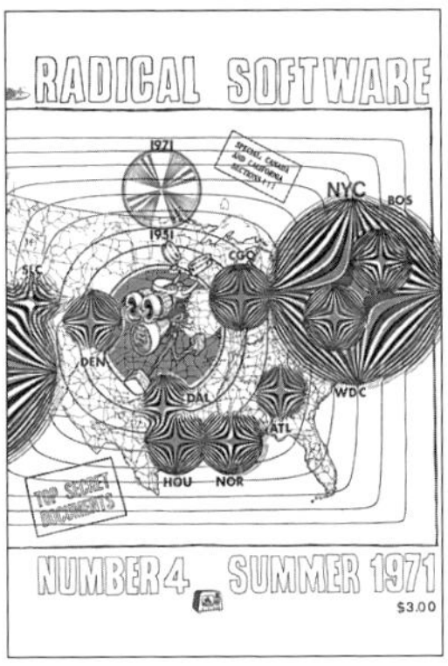

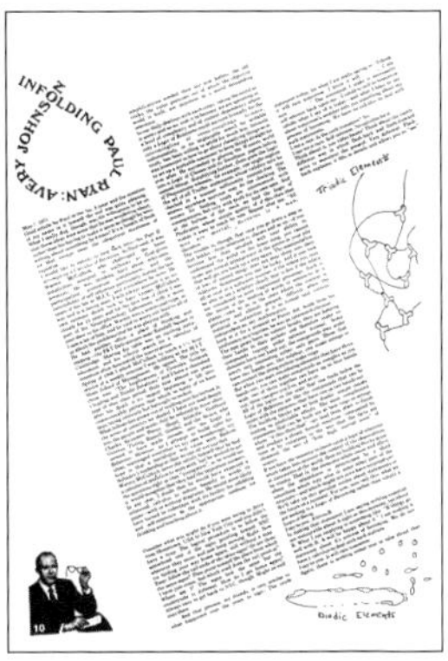

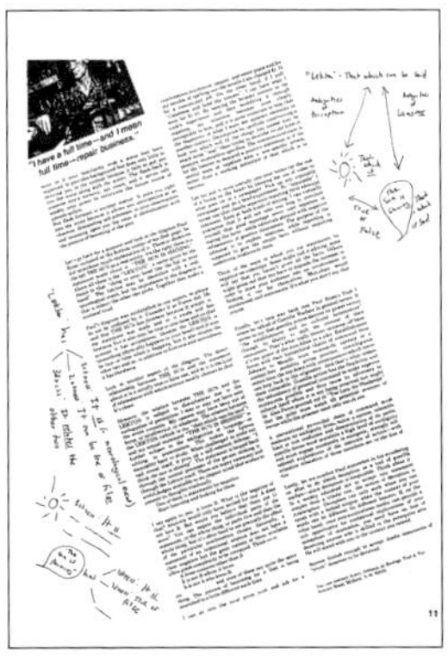

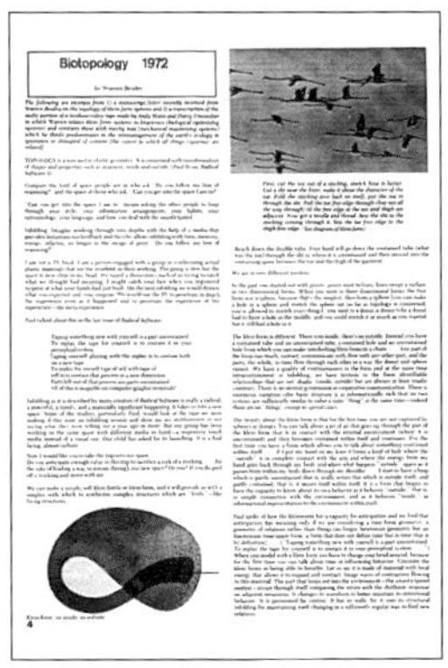

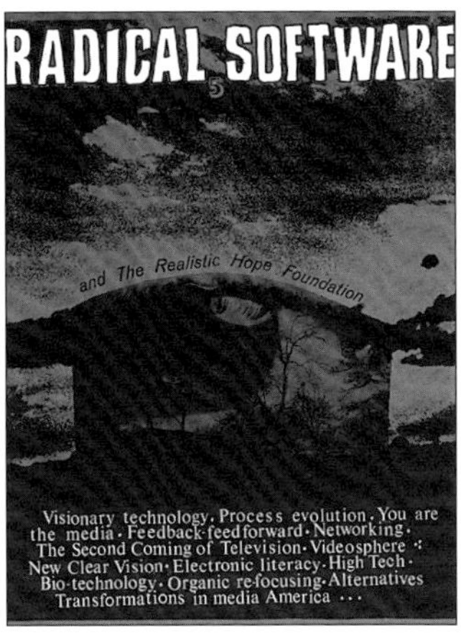

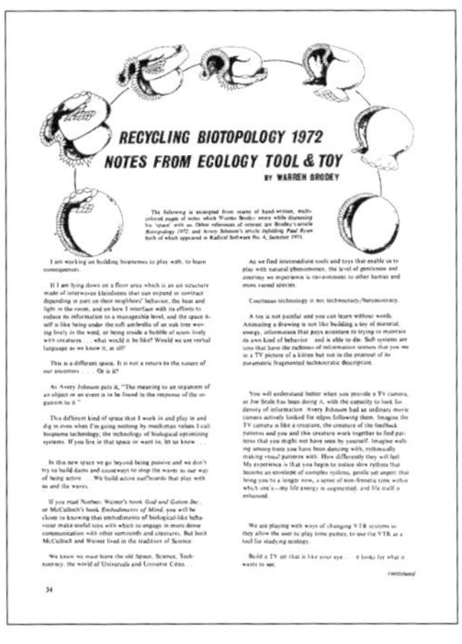

Figure 4.10. Covers and articles by Brodey and Johnson in *Radical Software.* Courtesy of Davidson Gigliotti and the Daniel Langlois Foundation (radicalsoftware.org).

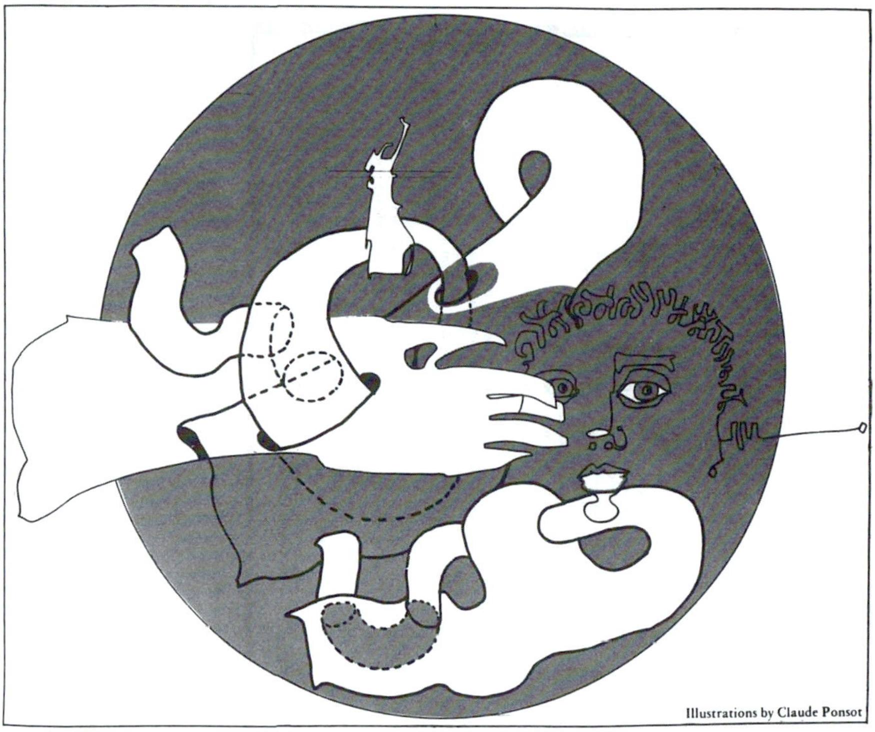

Figure 4.11. Illustrations by Claude Ponsot for an essay by Paul Ryan, "Cybernetic Guerrilla Warfare," *Radical Software* 1, no. 3 (1971): 1–2. Courtesy of Davidson Gigliotti and the Daniel Langlois Foundation (radicalsoftware.org).

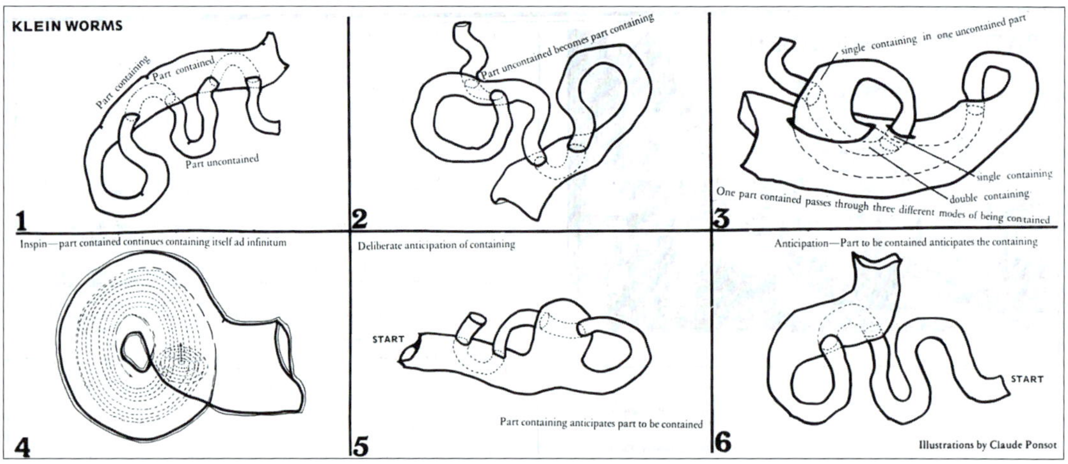

immediate result of these interactions was Ryan's seminal essay "Cybernetic Guerrilla Warfare." Ryan drew inspiration for the essay from a number of sources, including the work of Brodey, the painter Claude Ponsot (who provided illustrations), and Warren McCulloch. For Ryan, topology represented a way to construct new communicational circuits among people and their ecologies that might subvert the strict logic of inside and outside.[67] He relied on John C. Lilly's ideas about reprogramming minds and his own experiences with videotaping himself watching videotapes of himself. Writing about his contact with Brodey and Johnson, Ryan described their work as a constructive counterpoint to most of what the "inflatable subculture" had been producing, which he felt regarded inflatables as "spiritual" or "transcendent." He was enthusiastic about the idea of a self-regarding structure that could interact with users in an intelligent way.[68] Ultimately, for Ryan, these various topological models were to be used to reorganize ecological relationships into an alternative, negentropic praxis.[69]

"Cybernetic Guerrilla Warfare" also included several diagrams of different "Klein Worm" structures. In all of these, the "parts contained" and the "parts uncontained" shift into various configurations of penetrating surfaces. Insides project through outsides, and external surfaces are torqued into spirals that intersect themselves, creating temporarily internal passages. While Ryan claimed that these particular configurations were of his own devising, Brodey and Johnson had been working on producing physical models of similar structures. Indeed, their own contributions to *Radical Software* both built on Ryan's initial observations. Brodey's response was an article titled "Biotopology 1972," in which he not only expounded on topological spatial models but also provided instructions for how to make a Klein bottle from an old stocking.[70] Brodey wrote of these forms:

> The beauty about the klein form is that for the first time you are not captured by spheres or donuts. You can talk about a jet of air that goes up through the part of the klein form that is in contact with the external environment (where it is uncontained) and then becomes contained within itself and continues. For the first time you have a form which allows you to talk about something contained within itself.[71]

The topological surfaces of the Klein bottle formalized the relationship between subject and environment at this time. Environment was not an

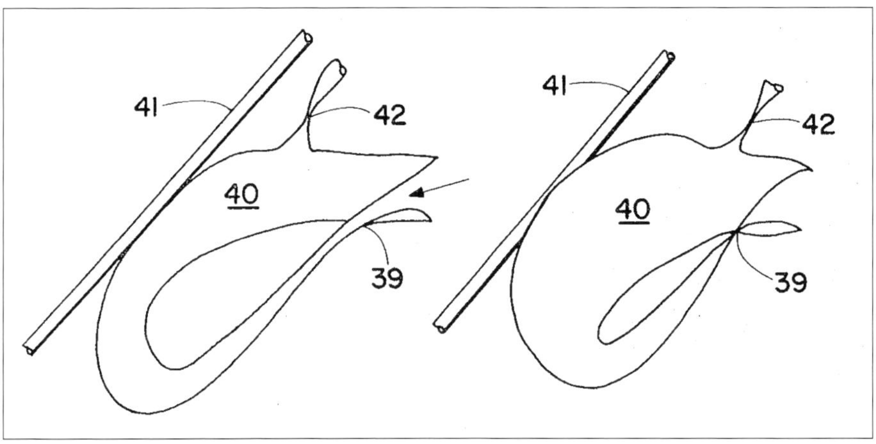

Figure 4.12. Warren Brodey and Avery Johnson, Soft Control Material, bladder in the shape of a Klein bottle. W. Brodey and A. R. Johnson, Soft Control Material, U.S. Patent 3,818,487, filed April 24, 1972; issued June 18, 1974.

external nature that could be grasped independent of human interaction. It was "context" in its ontological fullness. SCM was devised not as a tool (or toy) for discovering *the* or *an* environment but as a structure that would literally produce environment as immersive interaction among organic and nonorganic life forms. It was in the *Radical Software* article that Brodey was his most explicit about the relationship between SCM and natural ecosystems:

> We're developing systems now that operate by touch, so if you touch them you intervene in their loops. They are not paying attention to you. They're paying attention to that you've interfered with their usual mode of operation. To reestablish their mode of operations they have to behave in particular ways that allow them to continue to exist in their style which is very different from their sensing you. They don't sense you as you, as a plant doesn't sense a tree as a tree. It senses that it has more shade and it must grow in a different way to find its sun. The other plant, the tree, in a way presses upon it; it becomes environment to it just as we are environment to each other and for the first time we can now talk about humans as environments to the rest of the world, or humans as environments to animals—we don't think of ourselves as the center of the world anymore; we're just environment, and there are many environments.[72]

Here, much like Johnson's "context," environment is not a stable entity that can be pointed to definitively. It is constantly being reconfigured by the subject's interaction with it, and vice versa. It is the active registration of changing relationships among any number of actors.

Compare this with "sustainable" design today, which has largely pushed environment once again into the background, as a more or less stable set of systems or resources from among which the designer can choose what to disturb and what to leave untouched. What truly remains untouched in these circumstances is our conception of the subject, which likewise remains an untenably stable Cartesian end user. Despite their rather unrealistic goals, Brodey and Johnson understood that every technology, every extension or interface, transforms and displaces the subjects with which it comes into contact, as well as the complex systems out of which those subjects arise. For them, environment was response itself, filtered through the topological surfaces of biological or synthetic interfaces.

5

Cybertecture

Let's begin with another archival fragment: a 1975 call for papers issued by the German American architect Wolf Hilbertz for a conference to be held at the University of Texas at Austin in April of that year. The conference, Environmental Evolution and Technologies, was to address the following propositions:

> Man increasingly forms his own environment through his extensions. He is thereby becoming responsible for his own evolution and that of other life forms through design. The artifactual world including architecture will be an integral part of an emerging new conception of nature. This view reflects the fact that organism and environment, whether natural or artifactual, form a mutually interdependent system.[1]

Despite the rather simple and inviting poster design of the call for papers (with its illustration of what I take to be armadillos hatching from eggs and scrambling through a mutating landscape, and its hand-drawn lettering that somehow manages to evoke simultaneously biomorphic and digital forms), the claims put forward in the document are actually quite startling. If we take them literally, which I believe we ought to do, they suggest new models of nature, of the human organism, and of technology in the broadest sense. They also seem to suggest a quite radical notion of how design might mediate these emerging conceptions of environmental interaction, or "technologies as they relate to evolutionary processes."

Other details are also worth noting, including the conference title. The odd phrase *environmental evolution* grammatically confuses subject and object; is the environment evolving, or is it somehow the agent of evolution? Then there is the document's rather obtuse use of the word *artifactual* in reference to environment, which suggests that designed objects had come to constitute something like a second order of nature—their own environment, if you will. The other part of the equation here is that technology was an "extension" of the human organism with deep biological, evolutionary implications. As he drafted this call, Hilbertz was in the midst of conceiving a holistic building system that would synthesize these disparate insights and their profound and unsettling implications. He would call it (among other things) Cybertecture.

We can glance at a list of the conference participants and speculate a bit

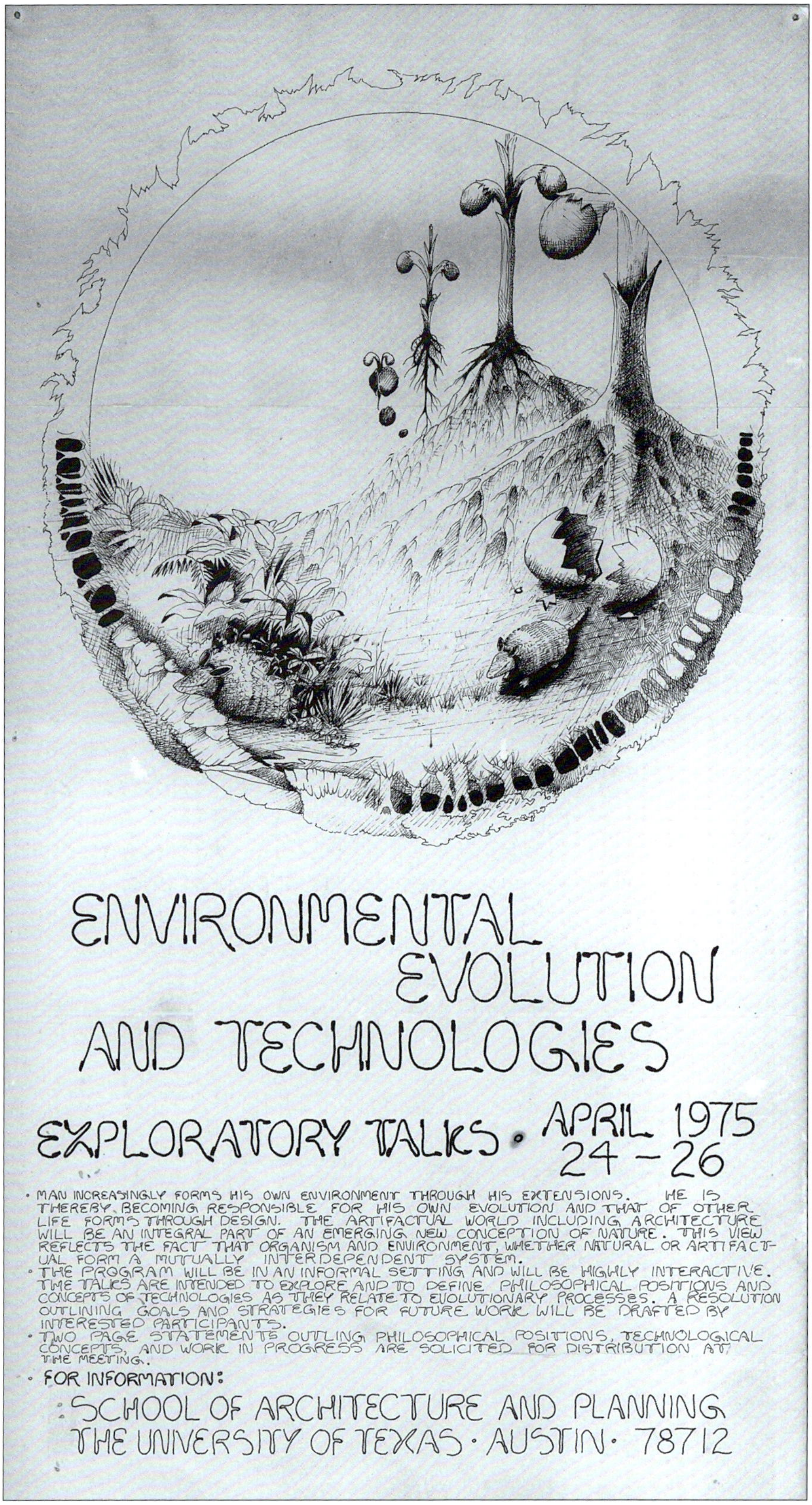

Figure 5.1. Call for papers for the conference Environmental Evolution and Technologies (1975). Illustration by Desmond Fletcher. Courtesy of Joseph Mathis.

on the proceedings. Doing so allows us to see Cybertecture situated in an emerging milieu in which architecture came to be viewed (by Hilbertz and others) not simply as a series of physical structures enclosing given spaces but as an active environmental agent that would come into spatiotemporal contact with an evolving human organism/consciousness. We can note, to indicate some familiar points of orientation, that Avery R. Johnson was in attendance (Hilbertz met Johnson at the Responsive House symposium, the unofficial reception for which apparently took place at Warren Brodey's "quarry" property, where SCM was being developed),[2] as was Paolo Soleri, who was also deeply involved in theorizing an architecture of evolving consciousness (chapter 6). Also from the architectural world was Friedrich St. Florian, who was then teaching in Austin; his presence represented a tantalizing bridge between the visionary Austrian architecture of the 1960s and this environmental moment in the United States. Emerging talents in the field of environmental design attended the conference as well: Daria Bolton Fisk, Pliny Fisk, and Ralph Knowles. There was also a contingent of systems theorists and scientists, including Ilya Prigogine and Ervin László.[3] Hilbertz's friend and UT Austin visiting professor Erich Jantsch was also there. The latter was in the midst of producing two related books: *Design for Evolution* and *Evolution and Consciousness: Human Systems in Transition*, which will concern us below.[4] This was quite a remarkable gathering for what many would have considered a provincial institution. But Hilbertz was given free rein to develop his ideas during a moment in which the dean of

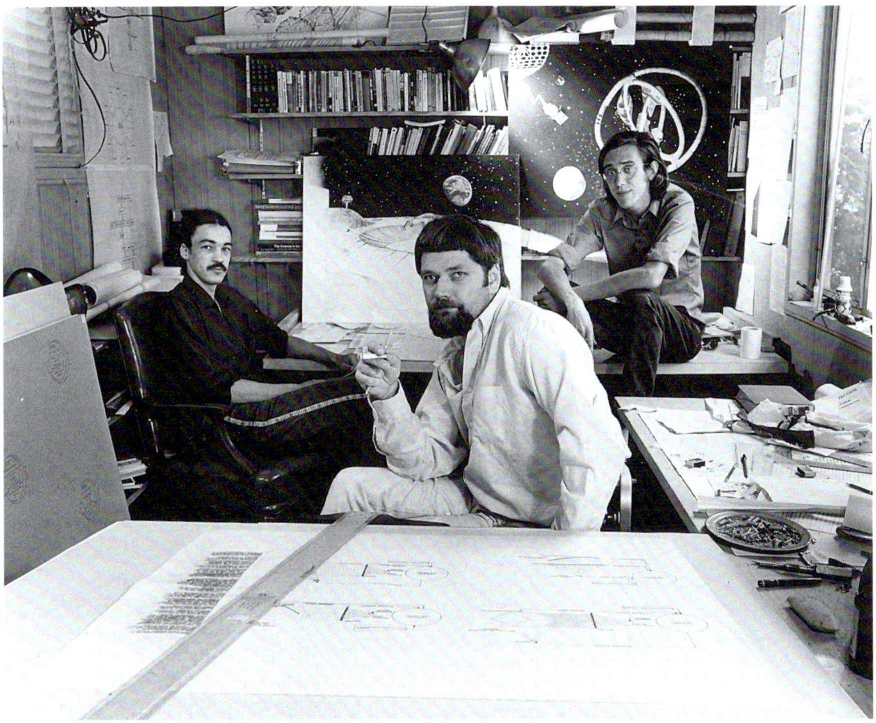

Figure 5.2. Wolf Hilbertz and students in his office at the University of Texas at Austin, circa 1971. Courtesy of Hilbertz family.

UT Austin's school of architecture, Alan Taniguchi, was reportedly attempting to turn the school into "the Berkeley of the southwest."[5]

For Hilbertz, the conference took place both at the end of a certain architectural trajectory and at the beginning of a series of career moves that would eventually see him creating a new kind of bioengineered ocean reef. His architectural path began in Germany and led him to several provincial posts in the United States. From the start, he clearly envisioned an expanded, environmentally inflected model of interactive architecture. First, at Southern University in Baton Rouge, he founded the Responsive Environment research laboratory around 1967. Shortly after, he moved to Austin, where he headed the Symbiotic Processes Laboratory (1968–78), which was part design studio and part technology lab. Here Hilbertz tested the limits of the ways in which architecture could be modified—in both function and design—by new technologies.

But even within the murky history of early experiments in digital design, Cybertecture is veiled in obscurity. At its most tangible, it was an experimental program for using computers, robots, and chemical extrusion techniques in construction. If we take a step back, however, it comes into focus as a holistic set of futurist and New Age propositions about the relationships among the human subject, technology, and the natural and cultural milieu writ large. This chapter is an attempt to reexamine these propositions, not as utopian outliers, but rather as unrefined assertions that comprise many of the ideological concerns central to historical reflections on the nature of computers and related technologies and how these might effect new approaches to design's relationship to the subject. In this instance, these assertions hinged on two key concepts that were gaining currency at this moment: that of extension and that of "conscious" evolution. In what follows, I will show how Cybertecture emerged as perhaps the single most elaborated program for describing the ways in which architecture was conceived of as the former in order to effect the latter.

Cybertecture

Considered historically and institutionally, Cybertecture occupies a liminal position. It seems to condense past technophilic discourses of functionalism and cybernetics while at the same time anticipating later models of artificial intelligence, social constructionism, and new currents in materialist and organicist thought in philosophy and design.[6] This Janus-faced quality manifested in Cybertecture both formally and programmatically. Already by 1970 it must have seemed a bit romantically *retardataire.* The few renderings we have from Hilbertz and his students belong to an earlier moment of megastructural speculation and hip gallery exhibitions of the sixties.[7] Cybertecture seemed to combine Archigram's technological enthusiasms with Frei Otto's organicism. But, one star turn in *Progressive Architecture* notwithstanding, Hilbertz presented his ideas at a series of academic conferences, the kind of institutional, "multidisciplinary" affairs that were part and parcel of the emergence of environmental and computer-aided design.[8] In these rather stodgy contexts, his work must have seemed impractical in the extreme, but, in retrospect, Cybertecture posited some of the first articulations in the design professions of what would come to be known as 3-D printing, virtual reality, mass customization, and bio- and geoengineering. Indeed, Hilbertz would later go on to develop Biorock, a technique for using electronic vibrations to stimulate coral growth on metallic structures in seawater.[9] Perhaps because of this work, his legacy has recently been bound up in histories of sustainable design.[10]

Indeed, Hilbertz was a systems thinker at heart, someone who understood the world as a series of dynamic processes instead of static objects. All of his work in design and technology would revolve around this desideratum of designing architectures that were not only capable of changing or responding but were also manifestations of systems in a dynamic state of evolution. While the Cybertecture project would attempt to leverage advanced technologies toward this goal, Hilbertz understood those technologies as merely means to an end. He demonstrated his understanding of architecture as a set of (in this case, low-tech) systems in flux with his project for Ice City, constructed in Fargo, North Dakota, in January 1973. Again, a visually appealing poster can provide some insight.

Figure 5.3. Autopia Ampere, rendering by Newton Fallis, circa 1978. Autopia was one (somewhat late) manifestation of Cybertecture. It was a floating structure "grown" from mineral accretions in seawater, constantly changing and evolving as user needs and patterns changed over time. Courtesy of Newton Fallis.

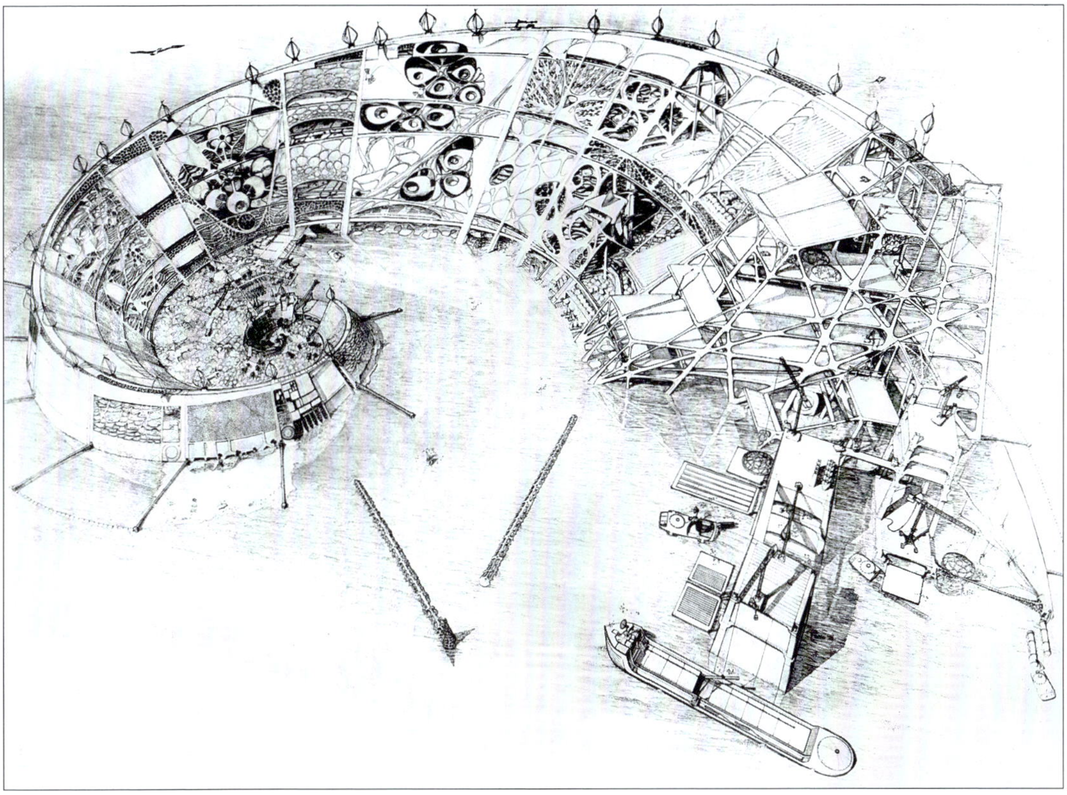

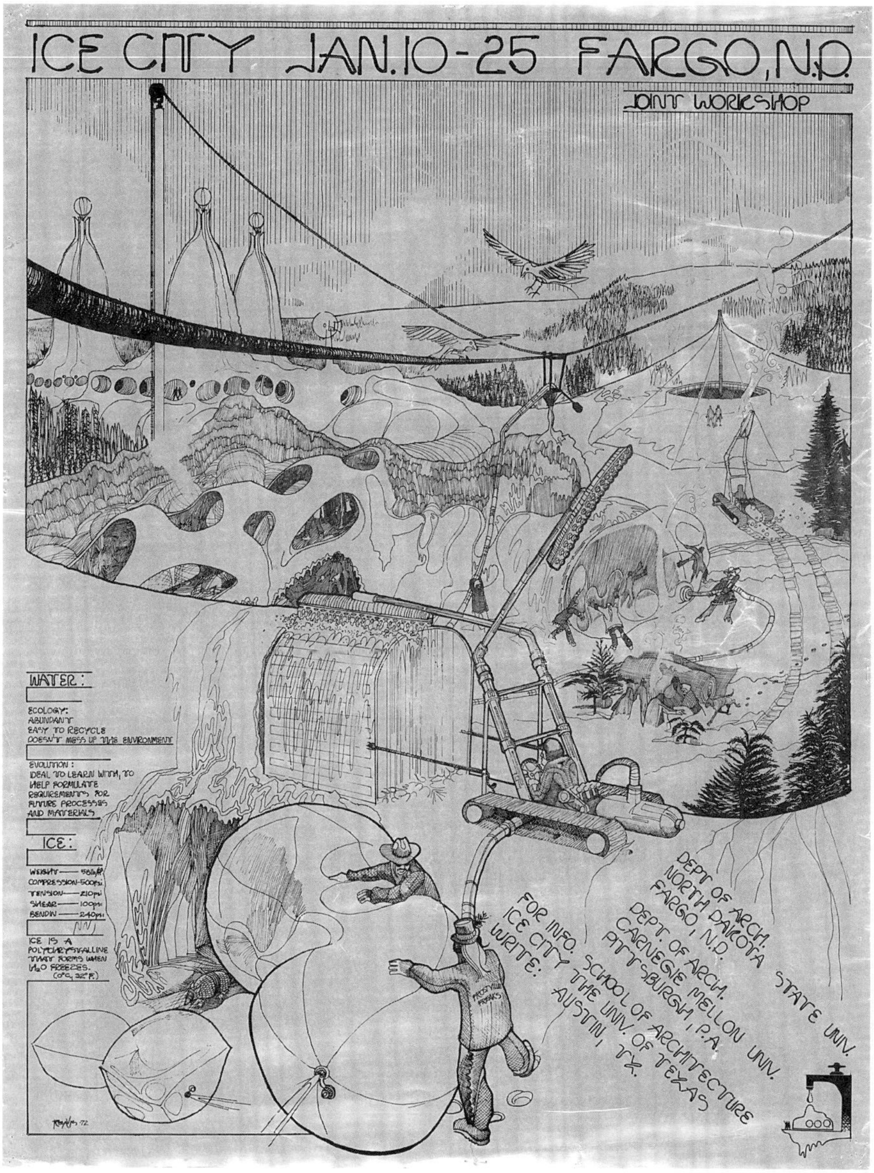

Figure 5.4. Ice City poster (1975). Courtesy of Joseph Mathis.

The Ice City poster's illustration captures a massive ensemble of biomorphic forms held up by structural wires. These apparently serve as armatures for sprayed water to cling to as it freezes, forming walls and ceilings. The water is directed by a mobile crane unit that can be positioned as desired. Water has particular qualities that interested Hilbertz—it is totally fluid but can be altered (through temperature) to become (ephemerally) a "polycrystalline" structure. The text on the poster lists the architectural and cultural attributes of this building material: "Ecology: abundant; easy to recycle; doesn't mess up the environment. Evolution: ideal to learn with, to help formulate requirements for future processes and materials."[11] Both of these qualities were inherently valuable to Hilbertz's understanding of responsive and evolutionary environments. It was as though change had to move beyond the "thermostat" model decried by Nicholas Negroponte and become almost autonomous, and part of that autonomy demanded that systemic fluidity be built into the materials, technologies, and processes of the architecture itself. Frozen water, especially in North Dakota in January, was abundant and recyclable, and the softness of water in its liquid state made it an ideal heuristic material, the evolutionary properties of which applied to its own physical transformability but also to the plasticity of the human mind utilizing it.

Hilbertz published reports on the project in both *Architectural Design* and *Man–Environment Systems* in 1973.[12] Here, the boilerplate of Cybertecture (elaborated from 1970 to 1972) was grafted onto the new dynamics of ice construction. Water, "the only inexpensive thermoplastic material available in abundance which can be easily manipulated," became the ideal heuristic/evolutionary building material.[13] Water was sprayed over inflatable structures, chicken wire, and aqueous foam forms extruded by a device operated by pulleys and winches attached to telephone poles. Because temperatures that January were unusually warm, several Ice City structures were built at night, and, despite the fact that the weather did not allow any of the resulting structures to stand for more than a few hours, Hilbertz marveled at their aesthetic properties. A group of students from Carnegie Mellon University produced a building that "enchanted us with its strange luminous interior, which, when inside, denied any sense of spatial orientation. The acoustic properties . . . were amazing in all complete structures—somewhat like standing in an anechoic chamber."[14]

Ice City, then, despite its relatively humble technologies, fueled Hilbertz's desire for an architecture of "man–animal–plant–technology–nature symbions including interpretation and effectuation of behavioral, social, and other information sources for environmental solution generation and processes" and "the environment as an evolutionary code and the interfacing of information and morphogenetic systems."[15] But by the time Ice City was being erected, Hilbertz had already imagined such systems in much more complex technological detail.

In 1971, Hilbertz described the activities of his Symbiotic Processes Laboratory, located at the University of Texas Balcones research facility (a converted industrial development some distance from the main campus). He listed the following pieces of equipment and their planned uses:

> 1. Two tapereader driven 3-D positioning devices which have generated controlled light configurations. The experimental extrusion of organic and inorganic materials for space-weaving will begin in the near future.

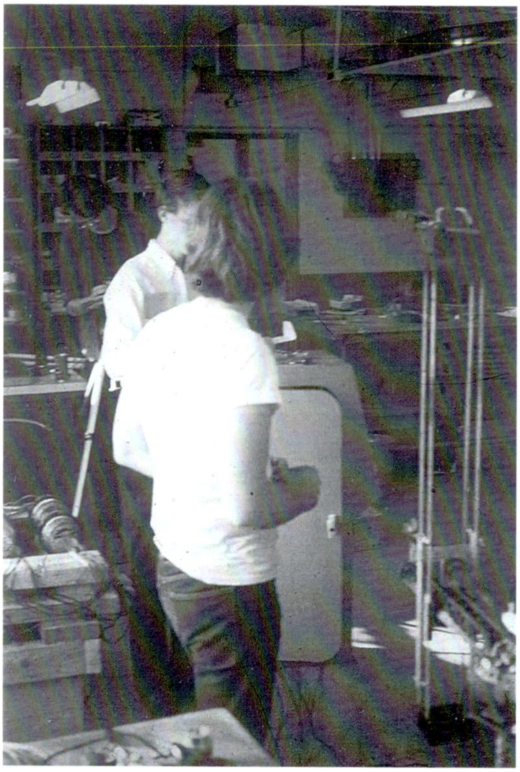

Figure 5.5. The Symbiotic Processes Laboratory at the University of Texas Balcones research facility, circa 1972. Courtesy of Newton Fallis.

2. Online interactive environment, connected to a NOVA computer with user sensory input capability and as yet an undetermined number of effector output modes.
3. Alpha wave sensor connected to 3-D plotting machinery for feedback through observation.
4. Experimental setup to use 3-D interference patterns from coherent sources to generate and manipulate physical space by photopolymerization or polymerization by other forms of energy. Suitable materials can be introduced into the static or dynamic energy field and form complex structures by accretion on the surfaces of the interference pattern which describes the contour of the desired structure.[16]

As the number of promissory clauses in this list implies, the lab's ambitious projects seldom moved beyond the most rudimentary testing phases.[17] The Balcones facility was littered with hardware left over from various research projects carried out by the mechanical and electrical engineering departments, and the nature of these materials often dictated the research program of Hilbertz's students.[18] Cybertecture is notable, however, not for the technologies it may or may not have anticipated but for the quite literal way it embodied contemporaneous models of subject–technology–environment interactions.

Just before his essay on Cybertecture was published in *Progressive Architecture,* Hilbertz presented his ideas at the Kentucky Workshop on Computer Applications to Environmental Design, which took place in April 1970 at the University of Kentucky. Here, applications of digital technology were anything but settled, and the published proceedings were overflowing with disparate paradigms, with papers on behavioral simulations of user activity, layouts of specific building types, mappings of human communicative activity, tools for graphical rendering, automated design applications, user feedback interfaces, pedagogical experiments, and more.[19] Hilbertz's presentation must have seemed both refreshingly resolved and frustratingly mystical. From his abstract:

> The proposed environmental system holds promise as an integral, interactive part of the socio-economic milieu. Structures would never be dated as they would mutate or eliminate themselves

> before becoming obsolete. Contrary to traditional architecture and planning it can create a habitat which, being the result and generator of human activities, is highly responsive to changing needs of the individual as well as society. To facilitate desired evolutionary characteristics, the proposed system must have equilibrating as well as divergence stimulating properties.[20]

From this, we can conclude that Hilbertz did not view his work as an analog process aided by computer technology; rather, he saw technology as an integral part of a much larger process of environmental change and adaptation, one that, within the fields of design, was usually characterized as responsive or evolutionary.

Amazingly, Hilbertz had already worked out the technical specifications for this evolutionary system. It was a three-part suite of technologies, or subsystems: a central processing unit, "the computer subsystem"; "robots" that processed and constructed physical structures, making up "the material distribution and reclamation subsystem"; and the built components, or "the sensing structure subsystem."[21] These subsystems worked in concert

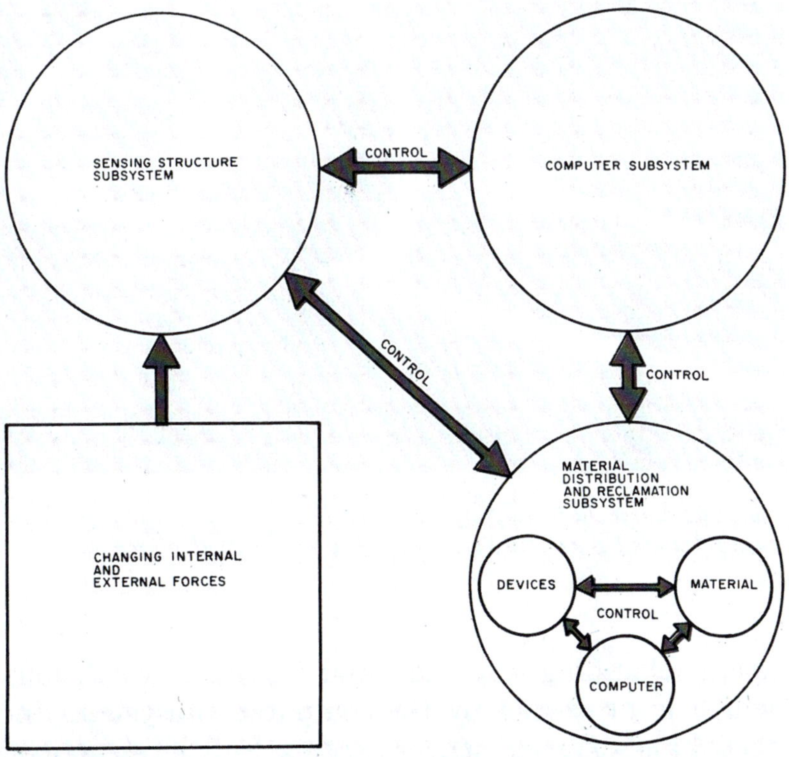

1. The Cybertecture structure and the interrelated subsystems governing form and function.

Figure 5.6. Schematic illustration of the Cybertecture system, circa 1970. Courtesy of Hilbertz family.

with "external" (natural and physical) as well as "internal" (needs and desires of users) inputs and variables. Taken as a whole, Cybertecture, or CT, would behave as a living organism, sensing environmental conditions and responding with continual physical and digital reorganization.

The exact mechanics of these processes bear review. Perhaps the least far-fetched of all the subsystems was the computer brain. Here, an artificial intelligence was embedded within the ever-changing physical configurations of CT; it was the aspect of the project that most closely resembled software, relative to the hardware it oversaw (though the distinction between these terms would break down within CT). Hilbertz described this computer: "It serves as a pattern recognizing, analyzing, synthesizing, and decision making tool. It emits impulses that cause immediate or delayed physical or organizational change of the environment in accordance with criteria designed to provide optimal environmental solutions and to determine the frequency of change."[22] For Hilbertz, this computer was a "decentralized nerve structure" that could perceive stimuli and direct command inputs, create models, and deploy construction hardware. This subsystem would also be able to determine the right moment to deconstruct CT's physical components when the latter were deemed suboptimal or when patterns changed for whatever reason.

This computer was in direct control of the material distribution and reclamation subsystem. This aspect of CT is perhaps the one that resonates most with design culture's current optimism about new materials and hardware.[23] Here, machines that Hilbertz described as "environmental robots" were capable of gathering raw materials, refining them, and then deploying them as physical structures (which appeared in various iterations as either space frames or infill, such as walls and floors). This chemical plant would transform material through any number of foreseeable processes: "gases, fluids, gravity, electromagnetic or electrostatic energy, mechanics, or any combination thereof." Materials could vary widely, according to Hilbertz, and might include "alloys, ceramic compounds, and organic as well as inorganic plastics."[24] Ideally, though, the material could be worked while in a liquid state and would congeal and harden once deployed.

In a 1970 grant application, Hilbertz and coauthor R. Mather attempted to break down the exact properties of a "materials distribution and reclamation" system.[25] The key component in this conception of the system was a distinction (apparently made by Hilbertz) between a "batch" model of recycling and a "continuous" one. In the batch system, a finite amount of raw material could be gathered, processed, and distributed. In the continuous model, the distributed material itself could subsequently be gathered and reprocessed in a never-ending cycle. As the technical system moved toward the continuous model of reclamation and distribution, it encouraged

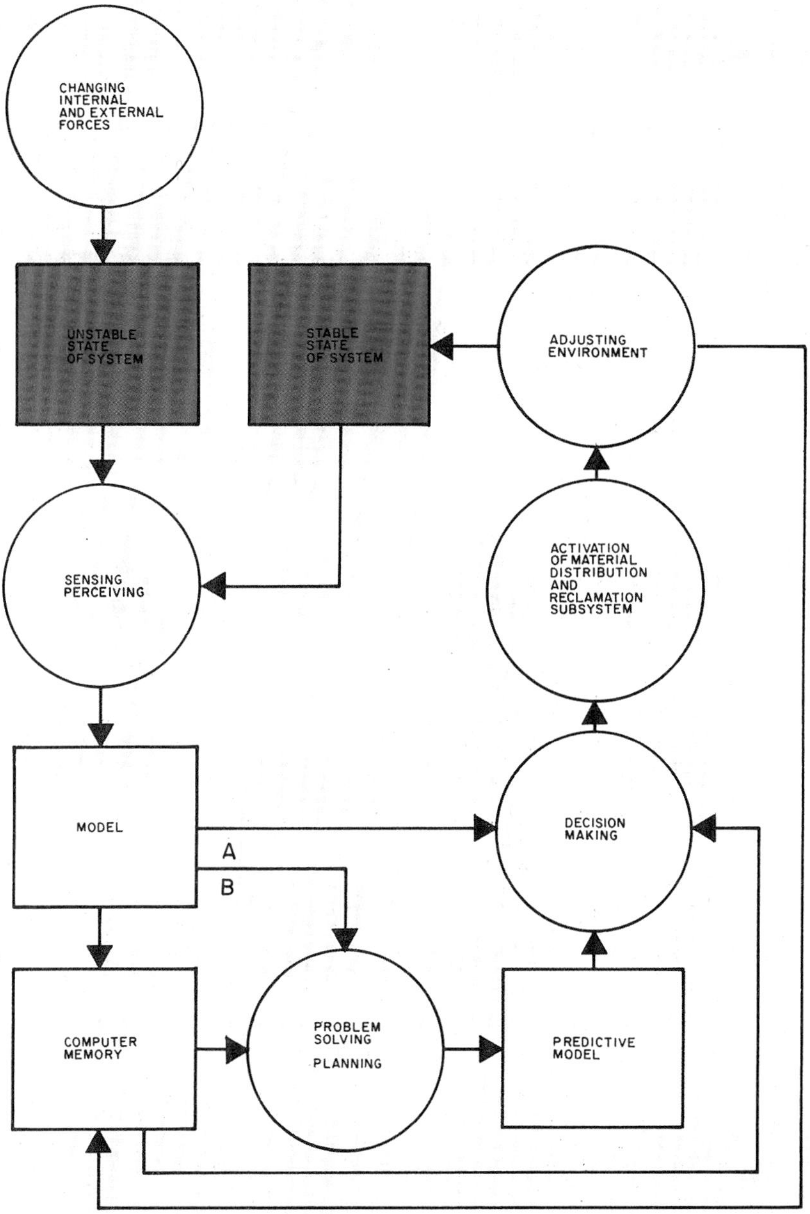

***12.** Internal and external forces render CT unstable. The change in state is perceived and forms a pattern which is the model of external and internal conditions.*

Figure 5.7. Flowchart for subsystem relationships within Cybertecture, circa 1970. Courtesy of Hilbertz family.

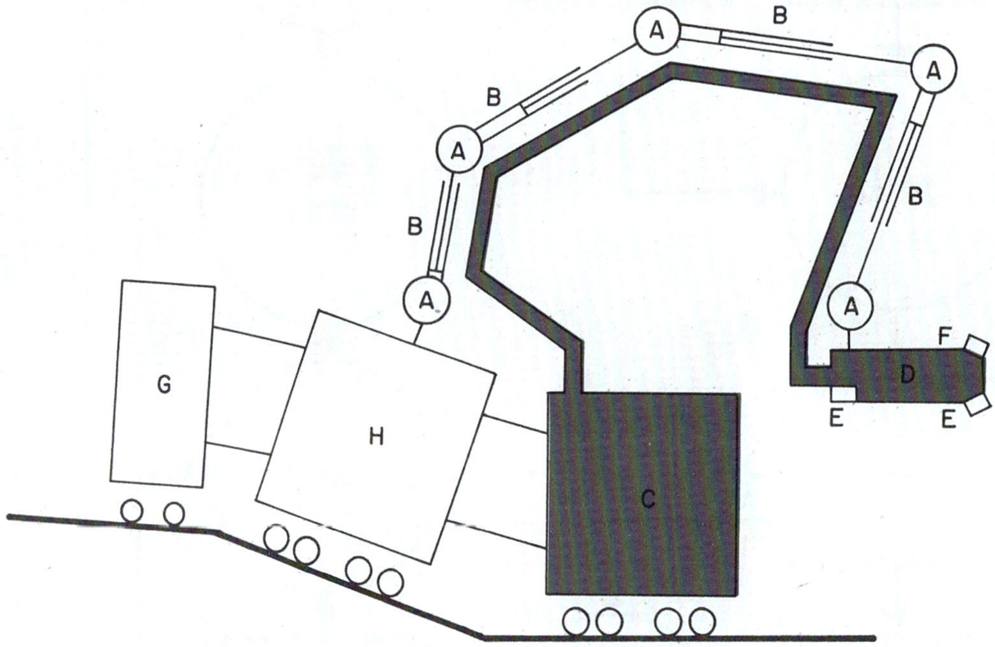

7. Several distribution and reclamation devices could be used simultaneously.

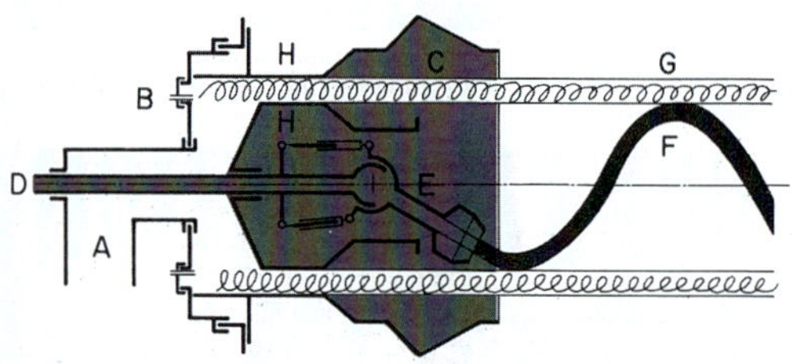

4. Longitudinal nozzle section, hypothetically moving through space and generating a structural element.

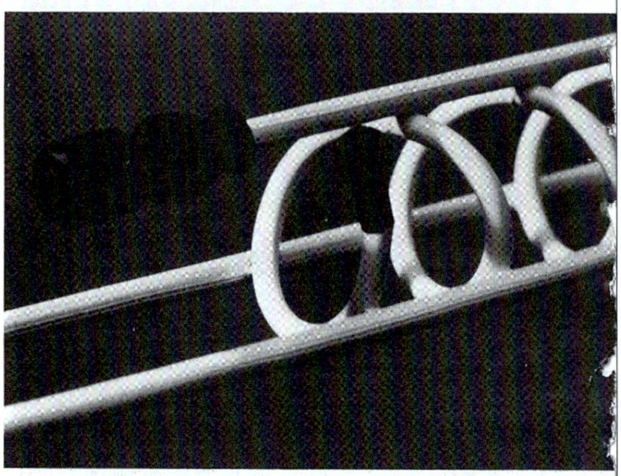

4a. The basic building system consists of three rods of filler material and a continuous coil of a structural element.

Figure 5.8. Material distribution and reclamation machines and extruded material: robotic construction in Cybertecture. Courtesy of Hilbertz family.

the tendency for the physical environment to become more responsive by both dynamic and static means:

> Dynamic: unending stream time model, automated, physical, change and movement of the environment, open ended attitude towards design and planning.
>
> Static: sliding aperture time model, change accommodated by pre-planning addition, subtraction, subdivision, within relatively static structures. Environment seeded with ambiguities which allow spontaneous change by means of the subjective input of users. Reductive attitudes toward design.[26]

Here, there is a fine slippage between matter, its technical manipulation, and the biosocial structures it engenders.

The technical description of these systems is tellingly detailed. The most direct method of getting the material into its various structural configurations out in the world was a type of extrusion. The robotic chemical plants would be outfitted with flexible arms terminating in nozzles that would extrude the semihard material in differently organized filaments. These, in turn, could be built up to form frames, for instance. But this was only one of many solutions. Hilbertz also described the use of projected "interference patterns." Here, the computer would project light through a porous grating, and the resulting light pattern would attract photopolymerized particles projected by the robot arm. These particles would

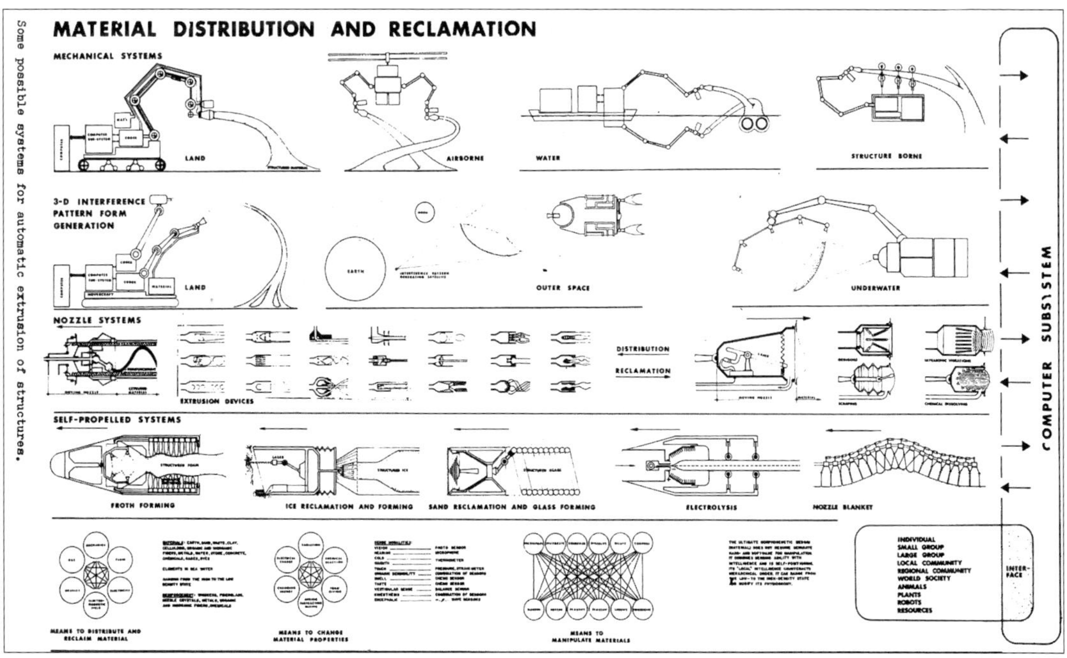

Figure 5.9. Material distribution and reclamation extrusion configuration chart. Courtesy of Hilbertz family.

accrete on the immaterial projection, thus forming a physical structure. This idea was likely fueled by Hilbertz's interest in the emerging technology of the hologram.[27] In his *Progressive Architecture* article, Hilbertz suggested that light patterns could also be produced by the rapid programmed movement of a lightbulb through space (the gestalt of which was captured in a time-lapse photograph), creating a 3-D projected image that could then literally become a physical structure.

This easy movement between the virtual projection and the actual construction was carried over into the sensing structure subsystem, or the architecture of CT. This subsystem constituted "the physical environment along with nature." Hilbertz and his students created several renderings and physical models of such structures, always with the proviso that they were contingent, subject to alteration and evolution. Nonetheless, we can discern that the computer brain and its robot servants would likely have been producing variants on space frames and other organically inspired accretions. These, of course, had their respective stylistic forerunners in the megastructural movements of the previous decade,

Figure 5.10. A robot projects interference patterns in the field. Courtesy of Newton Fallis and Hilbertz family.

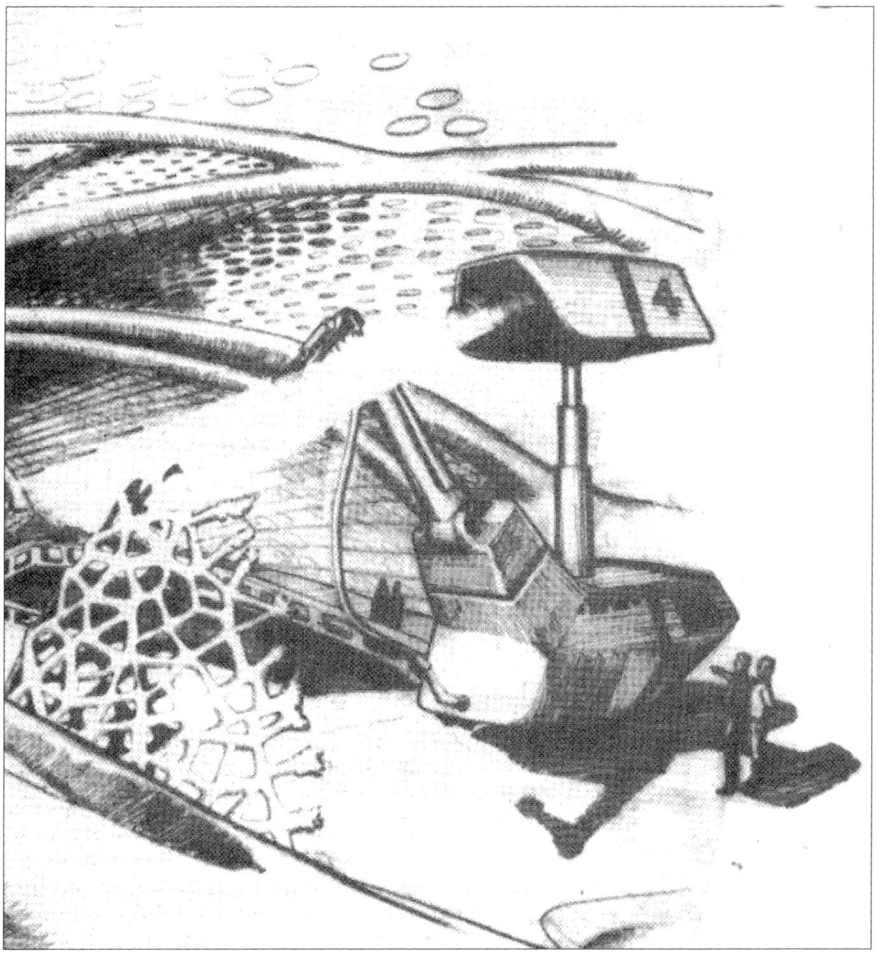

from Japanese Metabolism to the aforementioned work of Archigram and Frei Otto.[28] Of note here are the perceptual capabilities of the physical structure and its malleability. Virtually all of the material deployed by CT as constructed was to be embedded with electrodes that could "sense" what was going on around them, providing "a constant flow of information about changing internal and external conditions." According to Hilbertz,

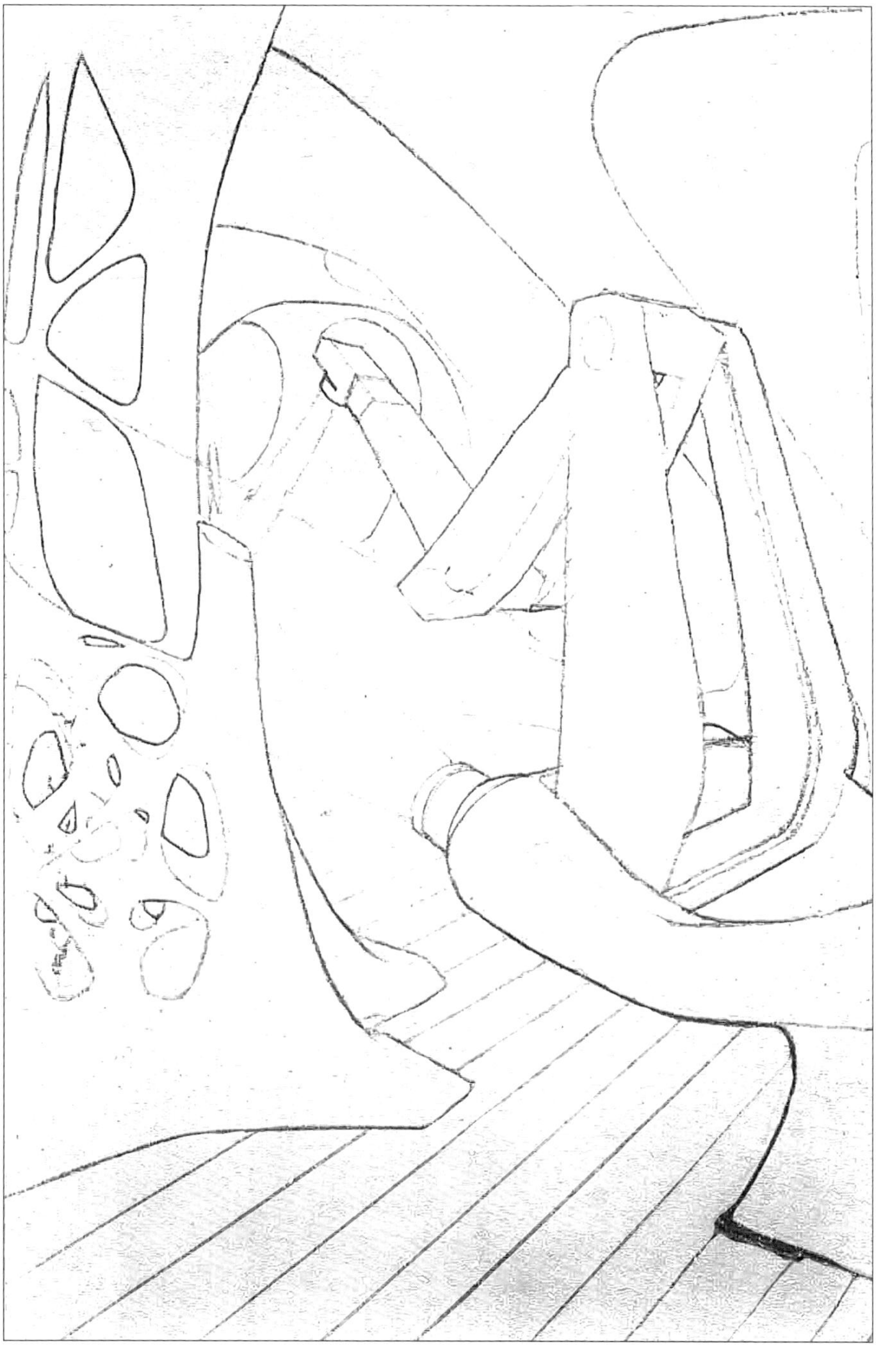

Figure 5.11. An "environmental robot" uses lasers to build a structure via subtraction. Courtesy of Newton Fallis.

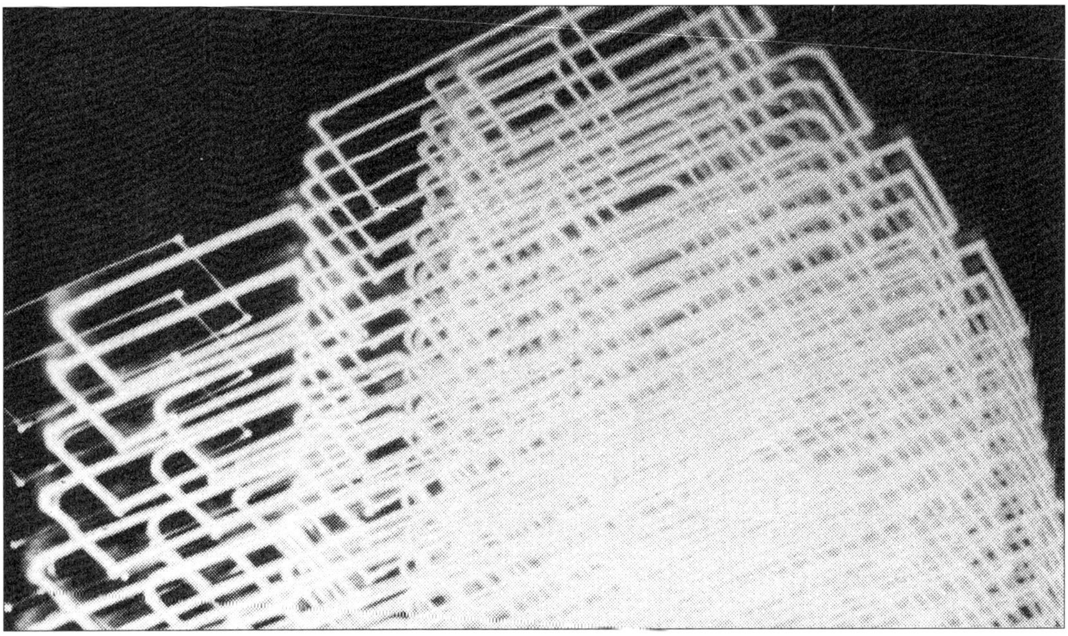

Figure 5.12. Patterned light from a rapidly moving lightbulb. Courtesy of Hilbertz family.

the "sense modalities" were "vision, hearing, taste, smell, sensibility for balance, warmth and cold, compression and tension, and kinesthesis."[29] These input devices relayed their data to the central processor, which could assess their current and future viability. If a need for change arose, the physical components could be gathered once again by the robots, "recycled," and redeployed in a different configuration. As Hilbertz explained, "Being a teleological system that employs self-improving software and hardware, it can draw 'unorganized' matter into its system like a seed which becomes a plant."[30]

If I have indulged myself with this detailed description of the technical functioning of Cybertecture, that should not be taken as an indication of my belief in CT's viability, or its lack thereof. Rather, the description serves two rhetorical purposes. The first is that it demonstrates the profound fluidity between hardware and software or material and ethereal environmental structures I hinted at above. And second, it shows how Cybertecture virtually embodies many of the intellectual and theoretical concerns characteristic of contemporaneous notions of responsive design. Indeed, Hilbertz brought these together (and forth) in such a way that his work is both exemplary and symptomatic of the peculiar vicissitudes of this moment.

Luckily, a striking documented instance of the reception of Cybertecture can allow us to gauge its status relative to other, perhaps better-known, projects of this period. In 1972, Hilbertz and a small cadre of students presented their ideas at Edward Allen's Responsive House symposium at MIT (see chapter 3). Among Hilbertz's coparticipants were the

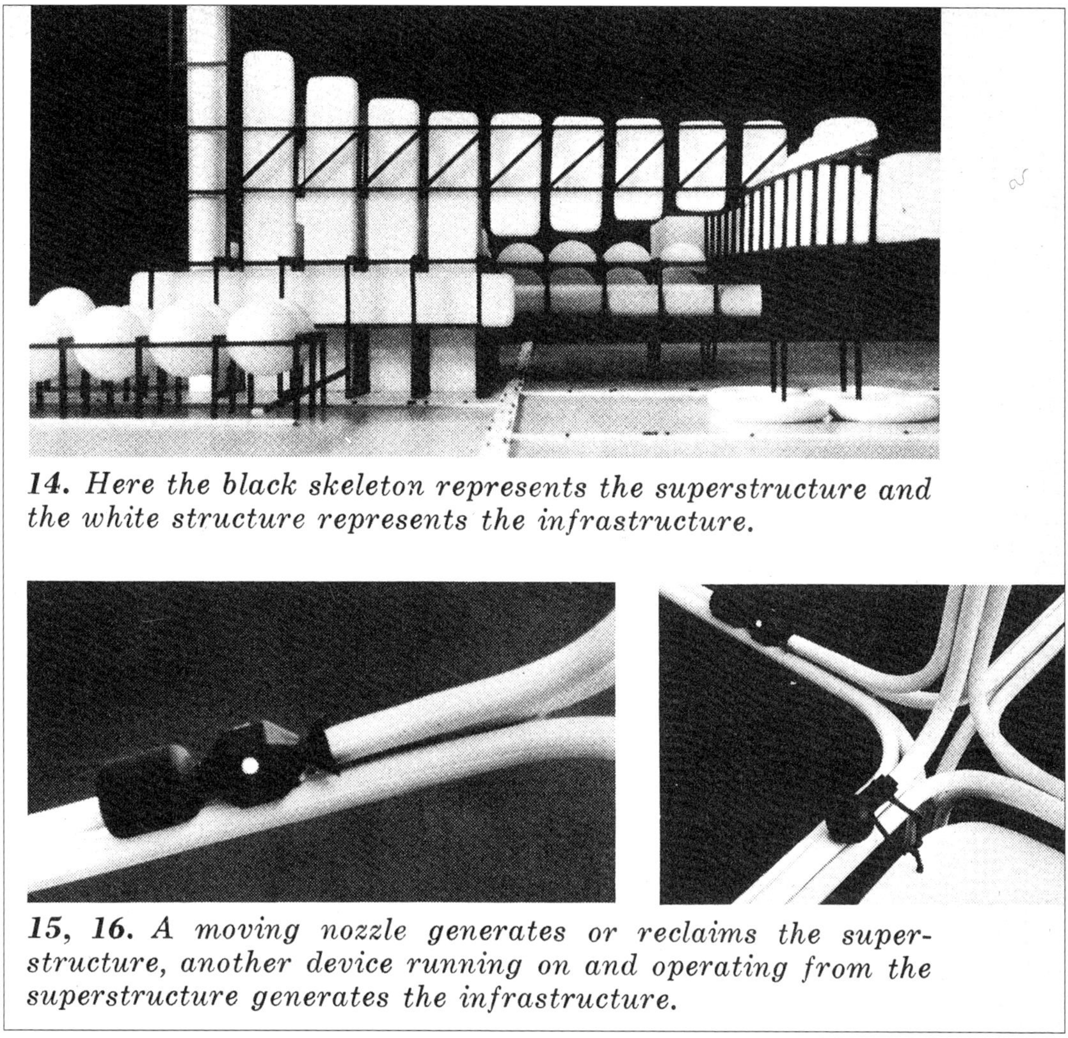

Figure 5.13. A proposed iteration of Cybertecture. Both frame and infill would be generated by the material distribution and reclamation robots. Courtesy of Hilbertz family.

luminaries of the environmental and responsive design fields: Christopher Alexander, Steve Baer, Sim Van der Ryn, Sean Wellesley-Miller, and Nicholas Negroponte. Hilbertz and his students (referred to collectively in the publication of the symposium proceedings as "the Texans") managed to stand out even in this context, with presentations titled "Strategies for Evolutionary Environments," "Evolution of Future Environments," "Structuring an Adaptive Environmental System," and "The Subtraction Method of Producing Structures with Robots."[31] The proceedings included a lengthy transcription of the debates that ensued after these particular presentations.[32] For his part, Hilbertz seems to have taken this conference as an opportunity not to elaborate the exact technical specs of CT (perhaps because his students provided that labor) but to expand on the biological, psychological, and social ramifications of such systems.

Despite Cybertecture's apparent relevance, it gained little traction at

MIT (or elsewhere, for that matter). Hilbertz's presentation was quite controversial. Among other things, the audience was taken aback by both the quality and the quantity of images Hilbertz and his students used. These included schematic drawings of the technologies of Cybertecture, detailed renderings of the structures that might be produced by the system—which had an undeniable fin de siècle vitality and visual complexity—and a plethora of photographs of organic and synthetic structures of a kind familiar to any student of modernism, including micro- and macroscopic images of bones, spiderwebs, and soap films. To make a long story short, for many of the symposium's participants, Hilbertz's organicism smacked of aestheticism.[33]

But lest Hilbertz's work be seen as simply a mystical outlier, a purely futurist invocation of the sublation of architecture into digital technologies, it should be noted that the designer of Cybertecture was very aware of his project as a historical one, linked intimately to the legacy of the avant-garde. His presentation at MIT carried an epigraph from Paul Klee, and his first sentence was as follows: "If we ever will be able to discuss what has *[sic]* been called interactive, self-organizing, adaptive, intelligent, responsive, cybernetic, or even evolutionary environments in a sense other than utopian, large scale integration of the arts, architecture, engineering, and the hard and soft sciences has to occur." Immediately, then, we find ourselves in the territory of the neo-avant-garde, with its persistent invocation of the total artwork retrofitted for the technical and ideological mandates of postindustrialism. If, for most, these mandates dictated a liquidation of formal structures in favor of a "disembodied" model of systemic information, Hilbertz attempted to keep matter as part of the equation, even if that meant hypostatizing "empty" space into a kind of malleable substance that would come to be called, simply, environment.[34] This substance had to be something with enough solidity to be formed and enough rigidity to push back against the formal patterns constituting the psyche. For Hilbertz, response lay in this interchange wherein material structures with specific formal attributes located on the inside and outside of the subject pushed against one another, forcing new organizations, new forms, to emerge.

Response and Evolution

To be fair, Hilbertz's exhaustive description of the (frankly, impossible) technical specifications of this totalizing system was a bit of a red herring. Certainly, it had the practical function of bringing his research agenda into focus for various institutional purposes (grant applications, for instance); it also provided a tangible, albeit contingent, object to present to peers, as well as an underlying program for the readings he assigned students.[35] While being cautious not to reduce the Cybertecture ensemble to mere metaphor, I would suggest that what Hilbertz really wanted was *a way to physically manipulate the ethereal components of environment in general and to render their mutual interactions with the human subject as programmable material.* This was a proposition familiar to all those attending the Responsive House symposium, and it was not altogether uncommon in the fields of architectural and environmental design by that time.

Hilbertz was a part of the growing, albeit nebulous, network of specialists involved in the environmental research manifold. In his Responsive House essay, he provided a brief list of citations that can serve as a starting point for understanding his place in this newly formed, de facto metadiscipline. Besides mentions of figures from the design avant-garde (Paul Klee and Tomás Maldonado), the majority of Hilbertz's references were to anthropologists, evolutionary biologists, psychologists, and neurologists.[36] He reached back to the obscure British doctor and philosopher David Hartley, whose book *Observations on Man, His Frame, His Duty, and His Expectations* (1749) was one of the first articulations of a modern vision of embodied perception, of a "vibratory" relationship (conducted by the Newtonian "aether") between the sense organs embedded in man's physical "frame" and the images and sensations arising in the mind.[37] But Hilbertz also demonstrated his awareness of more recent developments in the fields of biology and psychology, citing the work of biologists J. B. Calhoun and Theodosius Dobzhansky, psychologists and physiologists

Figure 5.14. Hilbertz projected that virtually all of the concepts and technological systems that characterize responsive environments would converge in our own time, by the year 2020. "Toward Evolutionary Environmental Systems Time Frame Conceptualization" (circa 1974). Courtesy of Desmond Fletcher.

. TOWARD EVOLUTIONARY ENVIRONMENTAL SYSTEMS
TIME FRAME CONCEPTUALIZATION

1970 ---> 2020

+Participatory Design +Data collecting +Responsive +Goal seeking +State maintaining systems	+Cybernetic architecture +Self organizing +Mutual causal +Adaptive experiential +Ultrastable systems +Worldwide resource planning	+Evolutionary environments +Variety producing +Synergy promoting +Worldwide ecosystems
+Anthropocentric +Emergence of 'Hinstammungslehre' +Holistic design +Parts of the environment as external organs of man +Support of nature	+Emerging biocentric +Environment increasingly an extension of CNS +Human potentiality development +Increasing diversity and variety +New collective consciousness	+Biocentric +Intercelation of Darwinian and Lamarckian evol. theories +Accelerated biological, socio-cultural and environmental ev. +Environment replaces government +Alternative strategies for nature +Sun, earth and moon as evol. syst
+Morphodynamic structures +Recycling of building materials +Man-environment interfacing +On-line building systems +Scenarios,forecasting,simulation	+Heuristic programs +Sensing building materials +Self-positioning materials +Modified biological structures +Complex gaming +Comprehensive data base from animate and inanimate sources	+Artificial intelligence +Living environmental structures +Data generating, evaluating and decision making models

Abraham Maslow, Aristide Esser, and M. R. Rosenzweig, as well as multidisciplinary anthropologists Edward T. Hall and Robert Ardrey. Hilbertz had coauthored a report about the work ongoing at his Austin research space for the journal *Man–Environment Systems* in 1971.[38]

What held these, and many other, sources together, vis-à-vis Cybertecture, was the unified belief in the plasticity of life. Just as Hilbertz's technological ensembles blurred the distinctions between hardware and software, they also began breaking down the distinctions between technology and biology. While this was by all means a pervasive trope within the culture of responsive design, in Cybertecture it became much more explicit, and its mechanics more precisely (if erroneously) explicated. If humanity had effectively generated its own biotope, its own environment, then those dynamics inhering between the organism and its milieu were likewise artificially modified. If the environmental crisis had framed this modification as a kind of apocalyptic diversion from the natural order, those involved in design, technology, and systems thinking saw it simultaneously as a phylogenetic opportunity. Thus arose the idea and possibility not of the random evolutionary mechanics of natural selection—of the accidental compatibility between an exterior factor and a genetic mutation—but of a directed model wherein humanity gained control of both environment and organism.

At the MIT symposium Hilbertz characterized Cybertecture in the following terms:

> Evolutionary, self-organizing environmental open systems capable of forming higher orders of organization; dynamic morphological and psychological manifestations in transactional symbiotic response to continually changing interior and exterior forces. . . .
>
> Exploration of man's inner and outer self in a rapidly evolving synergistic setting with the prospect of enhancing and complementing organic and socio-cultural evolution, both being the result of organism–environment interaction.[39]

These propositions went well beyond the previous decade's desire for ergonomic, "flexible," "mobile," or otherwise transformable building systems, which were by this time a well-worn fixture of vanguard design discourse. Permutations of this idea had taken every conceivable form, from simple prefabricated components to the portable pneumatic structures proposed by young designers on both sides of the Atlantic (e.g., the work of the French group Utopie and that of the American collective Ant Farm) to kits-of-parts that could be configured at will by the inhabitant (e.g., the work of Yona Friedman) or with the help of "cybernetic" technologies (e.g., the work of Cedric Price and Nicolas Schöffer). But even though Hilbertz would have agreed that greater flexibility in architectural structures was desirable, he likely would have felt that these slightly earlier experiments lacked the level of mutual responsiveness that he felt was necessary. Indeed, soon enough, he would transcend the usage of "response" in favor of what he began to describe more universally as "evolutionary environments." He described these nuances:

> The differences between traditional, responsive and evolutionary systems are obvious. The conceptual separation of the user (stimulus) and the physical environment (response) in the responsive system implies that at best only one-sided evolution or a superficial fit between the two can be achieved. In an evolutionary environment, however, this cause-and-effect dualism is replaced by *dynamic interrelationships*. The *richness of connections* between components determines the system's performance. Whereas the responsive system produces a "mindless fit," the evolutionary system accelerates both socio-cultural and biological evolution through *purposeful stimulation*. The evolutionary system is comprised of *man, his extensions,* and *nature*; being simultaneously beginning and end, originator and result, producer and user.[40]

Hilbertz was not alone in his belief that humanity was on the verge of being able to deploy design as an evolutionary catalyst. The idea took root in many corners of scientific, artistic, spiritual, and popular thought. It was expressed increasingly as a form of human teleology via the devices of consciousness expansion and the culture of therapy and self-help that developed during these years. It was famously asserted in Pierre Teilhard de Chardin's writings, most notably *The Phenomenon of Man*.[41] Indeed, the way in which technology and culture had affected or diverted *natural* selection also became something of a leitmotif in the more popular writings of some of the world's leading geneticists, paleontologists, sociobiologists, and ethologists, including George G. Simpson, C. H. Waddington, and E. W. Sinnott. Theodosius Dobzhansky, whose works, for whatever reasons, became popular among designers, proposed what he called "cultural evolution" as "the most potent extension of biological evolution." But, he implied, the ability to control the process was not a given: "Culture does not make human environments stable and uniform; far from it," he wrote. "The tempos of environmental changes have grown and are growing."[42]

Hilbertz cited Dobzhansky's work as well as a remarkable essay by biologist John B. Calhoun titled "Space and the Strategy of Life," in which Calhoun argued that humanity was at a critical evolutionary juncture, the outcome of which would rely on environmental *design*.[43] While Calhoun is remembered primarily for his notion of the "behavioral sink" (see chapter 2), this concept became part of a much larger conceptual apparatus for thinking about the future of a highly populated planet. As humanity evolved, Calhoun asserted, the biological necessities of territoriality and resource management were replaced by a quasi-imaginary overlay—both physical and social constructions—of what he described as "conceptual space." Conceptual space was carved out any time a population increase forced certain individuals to "withdraw" from an optimum number of social interactions—that is, when crowding forced some individuals to hide. In their state of withdrawal, however, these individuals did not contribute to the impoverishment of social interactions; they postponed and subsequently enriched such interactions. This occurred because, in their state of personal, inward withdrawal, these individuals created elaborate fantasy realms wherein they related to their environments and the objects within them in a "conceptual" way rather than a physical way. This creative modality of thinking about space prepared the way for new technical and social solutions even as crowding increased. In other words, when the creative individuals emerged from their self-imposed exile, they came armed with new ideas, new designs that would allow for the reimplementation of optimum social relations for a group even of increased population in the same territory.

Thus, the "sink" was but one stage in an evolutionary process. In the short term, it proved catastrophic for many individual members of a given population, but it also created an environment from which some individuals would withdraw to create new conceptual spaces and models of interaction. Here was a sociobiological explanation of design thinking. Here, too, was a utopian escape from the neo-Malthusianism of Paul Ehrlich, for instance.[44] Calhoun understood human creativity as being intimately linked to the physical structures of space and, in a modality that Hilbertz would have sympathized with, privileged that creative, conceptual engagement as a means of implementing more beneficial environmental structures. These structures, in turn, would further spur the evolution of a humanity gaining in self-actualizing capacities.

Calhoun illustrated this concept with a small drawing of a "conceptual homunculus," a naked figure holding a rose (symbolizing his aesthetic sensitivities), whose consciousness literally expands through time, from the earliest technical achievements of early humanity through the scientific revolution of the nineteenth century to an anticipated "communication–electronic revolution" in 1988 A.D. The last of these represented a kind of McLuhanesque understanding of a "new perspective of life as an information exchange network," which would of course augment and disorganize direct physical social interactions. These could take on Orwellian proportions, or they could produce a new conceptual apparatus that would lead to the ultimate revolution in the twenty-first century: a "compassionate-systems revolution."[45] This final stage of human evolution was, for Calhoun, a direct outgrowth of cybernetics and systems theory, which posited reality as the interrelationship of dynamic systems and subsystems. "We are now," he wrote, "moving into an era when this perspective (involving

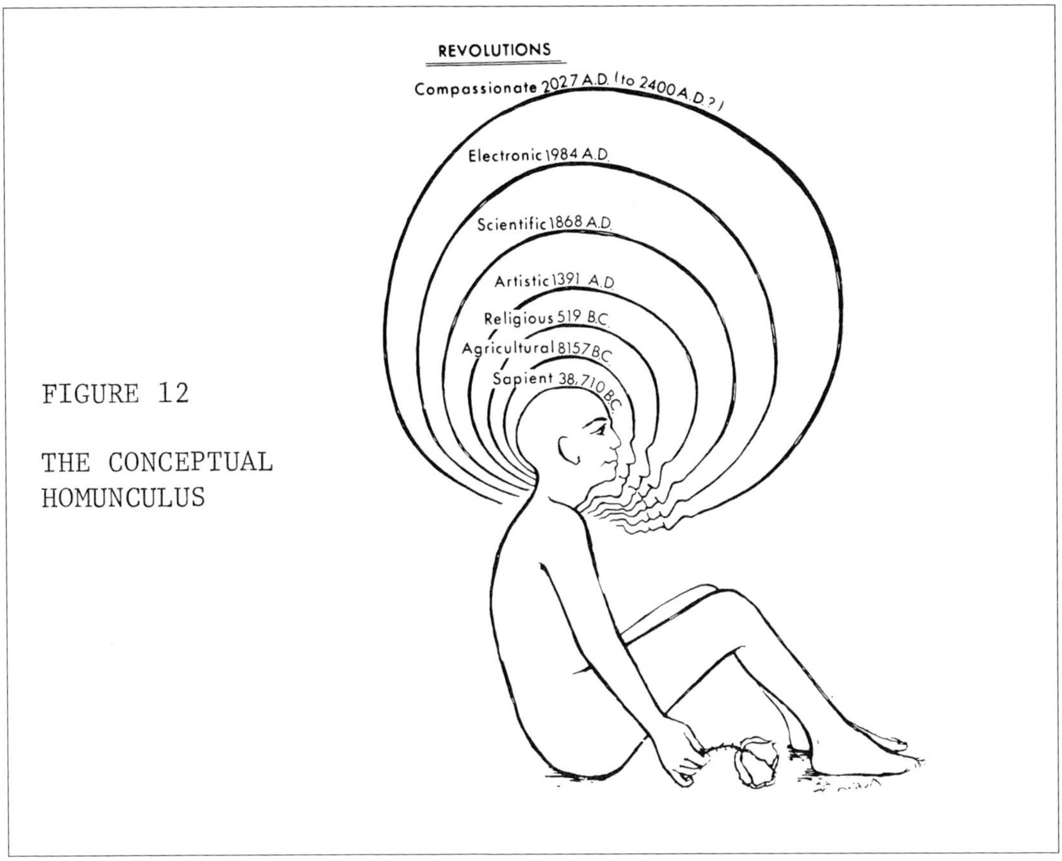

Figure 5.15. J. B. Calhoun's conceptual homunculus. With each historical "revolution" the cognitive and affective capacities of the subject continue to grow toward an immanent point at which technologies of various sorts will give way to a "compassionate-systems revolution." From J. B. Calhoun, "Space and the Strategy of Life" (1970).

the related techniques and strategies for designing and guiding interrelationships, and for permitting self-organization of subsystems) has become imperative."[46] Calhoun's homunculus was the figure of this extending and extended, evolutive subject. No longer could strict lines be drawn between the interior realm of consciousness or genetics and an exterior world of space, climate, and stimulus. Environment was now figured as an amalgam of conceptual and physical structures whose ecological interactions were increasingly subject to control. It was this upward spiral of evolutionary structures that might have appealed to Hilbertz, whose architectural systems literally allowed Calhoun's "conceptual space" to become physicalized and instrumentalized in the service of accelerating the compassionate-systems revolution.

The hinge on which these emerging ideas turned was, of course, the question of design. We see this in the call for papers discussed at the beginning of this chapter. Creating environments that were not only evolving but also capable of spurring evolution itself was becoming (for this cadre of thinkers and designers) an urgent calling. But, already, "design" had far exceeded its object-based functionalist aspect, and for Hilbertz and many others who attended his symposium, it had begun to connote the comprehension and manipulation of all the myriad systems constituting the environment in the broadest possible sense. In the wake of the conference, Hilbertz briefly published a small periodical called *Evolutionary Environments: The Symbiotic Processes Lab Forum.* Its four issues, or "editions," appeared from February 1976 to March of the following year. Instead of a "proceedings" publication, *Evolutionary Environments* served more as a vehicle to situate Hilbertz's thinking disciplinarily. Each edition of the tiny photocopied journal featured a column titled "Evolvements" that reported on the SPL's latest work.

By 1976 this work included a project that sought to stimulate growth in coral reefs off the Texas coast by running electrical current through submerged metallic structures. These experiments would lead to Hilbertz's founding of Biorock a bit later. But, while Biorock would go on to become a specific geoengineering product for the replacement of decimated coral reefs, it began as an architectural proposition that, at one point—the exact chronologies of the overlapping initiatives are vague—was called Autopia, "a place that grows itself."[47] Remarkable at this stage in Hilbertz's thinking was the way in which the conceptual aspects of Cybertecture flowed into chemical formations and processes. In one moment, Hilbertz described the "molar concentration of various ions" in different liquid solutions, and in the next he pivoted to suggesting that the products of

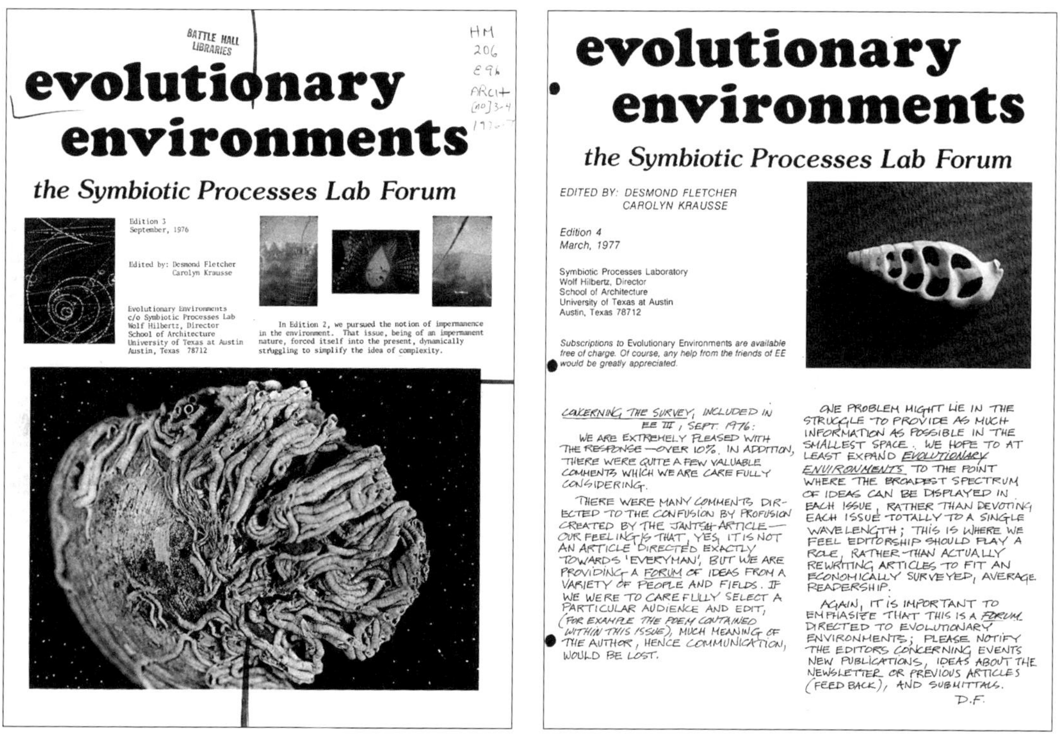

BATTLE HALL LIBRARIES

evolutionary environments

the Symbiotic Processes Lab Forum

Edition 3
September, 1976

Edited by: Desmond Fletcher
Carolyn Krausse

Evolutionary Environments
c/o Symbiotic Processes Lab
Wolf Hilbertz, Director
School of Architecture
University of Texas at Austin
Austin, Texas 78712

In Edition 2, we pursued the notion of impermanence in the environment. That issue, being of an impermanent nature, forced itself into the present, dynamically struggling to simplify the idea of complexity.

evolutionary environments

the Symbiotic Processes Lab Forum

EDITED BY: DESMOND FLETCHER
CAROLYN KRAUSSE

Edition 4
March, 1977

Symbiotic Processes Laboratory
Wolf Hilbertz, Director
School of Architecture
University of Texas at Austin
Austin, Texas 78712

Subscriptions to Evolutionary Environments are available free of charge. Of course, any help from the friends of EE would be greatly appreciated.

CONCERNING THE SURVEY, INCLUDED IN EE III, SEPT. 1976:

WE ARE EXTREMELY PLEASED WITH THE RESPONSE—OVER 10%. IN ADDITION, THERE WERE QUITE A FEW VALUABLE COMMENTS WHICH WE ARE CAREFULLY CONSIDERING.

THERE WERE MANY COMMENTS DIRECTED TO THE CONFUSION BY PROFUSION CREATED BY THE JANTSCH ARTICLE—OUR FEELING IS THAT, YES, IT IS NOT AN ARTICLE DIRECTED EXACTLY TOWARDS 'EVERYMAN', BUT WE ARE PROVIDING A FORUM OF IDEAS FROM A VARIETY OF PEOPLE AND FIELDS. IF WE WERE TO CAREFULLY SELECT A PARTICULAR AUDIENCE AND EDIT, (FOR EXAMPLE THE POEM CONTAINED WITHIN THIS ISSUE), MUCH MEANING OF THE AUTHOR, HENCE COMMUNICATION, WOULD BE LOST.

ONE PROBLEM MIGHT LIE IN THE STRUGGLE TO PROVIDE AS MUCH INFORMATION AS POSSIBLE IN THE SMALLEST SPACE. WE HOPE TO AT LEAST EXPAND EVOLUTIONARY ENVIRONMENTS TO THE POINT WHERE THE BROADEST SPECTRUM OF IDEAS CAN BE DISPLAYED IN EACH ISSUE, RATHER THAN DEVOTING EACH ISSUE TOTALLY TO A SINGLE WAVELENGTH; THIS IS WHERE WE FEEL EDITORSHIP SHOULD PLAY A ROLE, RATHER THAN ACTUALLY REWRITING ARTICLES TO FIT AN ECONOMICALLY SURVEYED, AVERAGE READERSHIP.

AGAIN, IT IS IMPORTANT TO EMPHASIZE THAT THIS IS A FORUM DIRECTED TO EVOLUTIONARY ENVIRONMENTS; PLEASE NOTIFY THE EDITORS CONCERNING EVENTS NEW PUBLICATIONS, IDEAS ABOUT THE NEWSLETTER OR PREVIOUS ARTICLES (FEED BACK), AND SUBMITTALS.

D.F.

Figure 5.16. Covers of *Evolutionary Environments* 3 and 4 (Austin: University of Texas at Austin School of Architecture Symbiotic Processes Laboratory, 1976–77). Austin Special Collections. Courtesy of Architectural and Planning Library, University of Texas at Austin.

the accretion processes possible in such solutions could be used to build "free floating or stationary city states," both of which would entail "continuous morphogenesis and evolution of all components, structures, and lifeforms involved."[48]

In the first issue of *Evolutionary Environments,* some of these experiments were reported alongside a note of encouragement from Avery R. Johnson: "Yes, count me in. I want to live in a chambered nautilus, suitably warped for filling with air and moving around in it, but capable of growing each successive room larger than the last (which then becomes my closet) before the intervening wall is dissolved away. (Maybe a loudspeaker coil could be incorporated into the apical origin of the spiral and allow one to live at the portal of a true exponential horn. Prima."[49] Other individuals were also marshaled to support the evolutionary design proposition. The architect Alton De Long (who has appeared sporadically in these pages) provided what amounted to an architectural proof of Calhoun's theory of "conceptual space," arguing that, essentially, more concentrated experiential environments could in fact speed up and direct human evolution. De Long asserted:

> 1. The reality of an environment is principally a function of the ability of the neocortex to project itself and still make reliable computations.
> 2. The purpose of the environment is to promote conceptual computation.
> 3. The value of the environment is to increase the complexity of experience through the provision of an increasingly wider array of contexts. . . .
>
> The potential role for design may strike some as unnecessarily unorthodox; but, then, man's self-actualization may require a far more radical alteration in his attitudes toward space and time than have previously been considered.[50]

But perhaps the most definitive contribution to Hilbertz's symposium and nascent journal was made by systems theorist and management guru Erich Jantsch. That year (1975) was pivotal for Jantsch, as it saw him embrace a more holistic approach to his understanding of the evolution of all systems. The paper he delivered at the conference was titled "Self Transcendence and Complexity," as was his essay in the third issue of the journal.[51] Jantsch was also in the process of publishing perhaps one of the most remarkable texts of the period that would see a synthesis of biological and cultural knowledge under the rubric of a kind of design thinking: *Design for Evolution.*[52]

Jantsch's utopian views about human systems design had been taking shape for some time, however. A couple of years before the Environmental

Evolution and Technologies symposium, Jantsch had attended Emilio Ambasz's Universitas symposium at New York's Museum of Modern Art. Here, unlike many other participants, Jantsch arrived full of optimism that an actual institution might coalesce that would address the question of "the design and management of the man-made milieu," as Ambasz's working paper put it.[53] Jantsch was open to this idea because it brought together two of his interests: expanded models of design and the "sciences" of management. He took the opportunity to redefine both fields "holistically" as a "*systems approach to total human experience and purposeful activity.*"[54] This involved a total redefinition of the human subject as it related to the systems in which it was enmeshed:

> What we are (the evolutionary aspects of bio- and sociosphere and their feedback, archetypes, and modification, possibly leading to a "quantum theory" of the psychosocial nature of man).
>
> What we feel (developing our potential to communicate—not just with our fellow human beings, but in a way also with the whole animate and inanimate world, as great artists do).
>
> What we can do (exploring possibilities to perceive and structure reality, conceptualize, develop new modes of expression and communication, etc.).
>
> What we want (exploring the potentials and imperatives of value dynamics, accepting and actively playing out the cybernetic responsibility of man in regulating a world, which, in turn, conditions him, etc.).[55]

By 1975, Jantsch had further embraced the rhetoric and potential of consciousness expansion and the model of human evolution this implied. He acknowledged that *Design for Evolution* was a departure—from his previous work, from that of most systems design theory, from social theory, and from theories of institutional organization and management. And, for that matter, it signaled Jantsch's new embrace of non-science-based knowledge.

The book's frontispiece is a photograph by Angela Maria Longo titled "Rising to the Sixth Chakra"; it depicts a swirling, rippling, narrowing form reaching—apparently upward—toward the sun, its folding rivulets becoming more complex as they climb. Jantsch had always been an aesthetically attuned person (he had written hundreds of art and music reviews in his native Austria),[56] and this proclivity seemed somehow linked to his ability to think of human systems as inherently biased or socially constructed. *Design for Evolution*, then, was his attempt to reconcile knowledge from diverse sources—scientific, spiritual, aesthetic—in

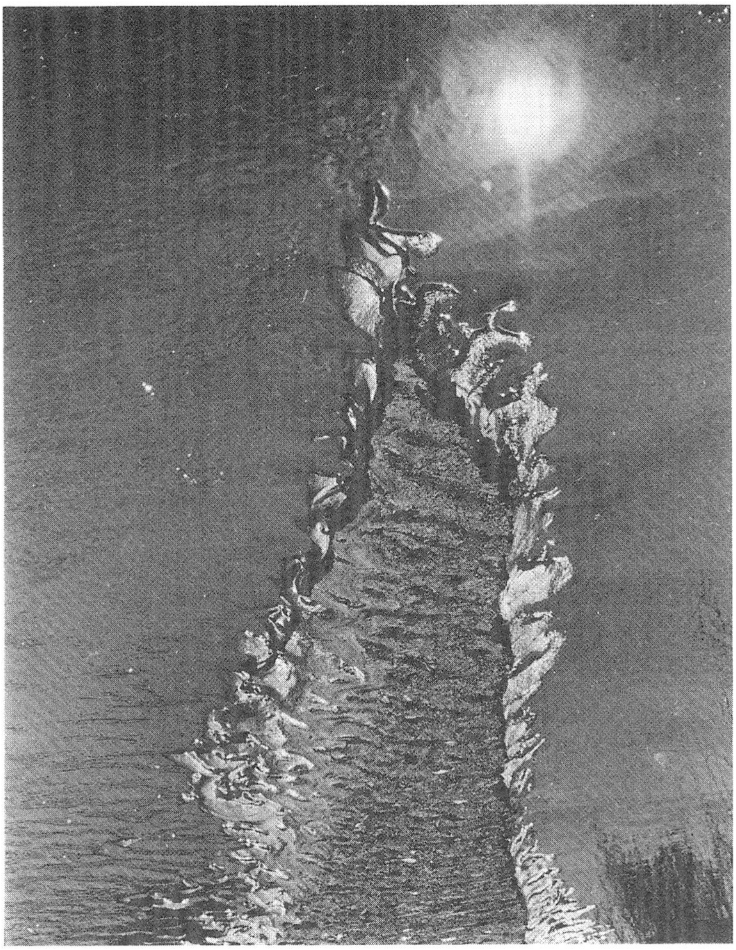

Figure 5.17. Angela Maria Longo, "Rising to the Sixth Chakra." From Erich Jantsch, *Design for Evolution* (1975).

order to advance attempts to literally intervene in the new environment of human systems to direct them toward desirable goals. Jantsch wanted to reinstantiate the teleology of Wiener's cybernetic systems with the more dynamized view of open systems being modeled simultaneously by his colleague (and friend of Hilbertz) Ilya Prigogine. Prigogine's work seemed to hold out the possibility of a resolution for the defining problem of thermodynamics—entropy. In his view, instead of being understood as futilely attempting to maintain static equilibrium in a maelstrom of chaos and entropy, systems could be seen as open and fluctuating in nonequilibrium states (while still maintaining the structure requisite to being defined as systems). Prigogine, Jantsch, and others believed that these "dissipative structures" governed the dynamic processes of life and evolution.[57] Jantsch sought to explore their potential when applied to "social and cultural systems . . . , knowledge systems, to the development of human consciousness and to the human design process."[58]

By acknowledging the productive power of entropy and the inherently open and dynamic nature of all systems constituting the universe, Jantsch believed human design agency took on a new significance and became "*an integral part of a universal evolution*."[59] He meant this quite literally, as did Hilbertz. Interestingly, too, Jantsch's broadening view of the dynamism of human systems led him to displace some hierarchies of organization while embracing others. The modern horizontal partitioning of inside and outside was fundamentally disrupted by nonequilibrium systems that were constantly exchanging massive amounts of energy with their surroundings: "Internal and external factors of selection appear here as aspects of the same process."[60] But if the horizontal/spatial realm took on a new homogeneity, Jantsch established a new regime of *vertical* distinctions or hierarchies. Even when their insides and outsides were blurred, in other words, systems could nonetheless attain ever higher levels of organizational complexity. Design activity—"the building of relations between man and his world"[61]—was the key to ensuring that powerful and complex systems could be harmonized with one another and directed toward a higher state: a teleology (in both the cybernetic and Hegelian senses).

Jantsch's view of the universal compass of design was one in which that activity mediated the relations among three realities: "man's consciousness, the reality surrounding him, and the world of ideas, models, and plans he projects onto reality."[62] Here are shades of Calhoun's conceptual space as a mediating device between the purely interior world of the subject and its ontological situation. Indeed, like Bateson and other cyberneticians before him, Jantsch situated perception and design similarly in the interstices among these processes. He evoked the complexities of environmental perception with a diagram wherein an observer relates to the "stream" of reality. The first model is that of Western science, with its rational detachment. The second—the "mythological"—is what we might describe (again, to bring these ideas into alignment with others here) as a responsive environment, an immersed subjectivity that "steers" along with the changing currents of the stream. Finally, the fully evolutionary modality of perception erases the boundary between the two.

Significantly, Jantsch situated design in the mythological phase of perception. It had to respond to a changing reality but also needed an objective bulwark from which to take rational action. Jantsch diagrammed design itself, and its mediating functions, in a deceptively complex set of drawings of a "toroidal" model. In these the plan and "cross section" are visually identical (because of the properties of the topological manifold

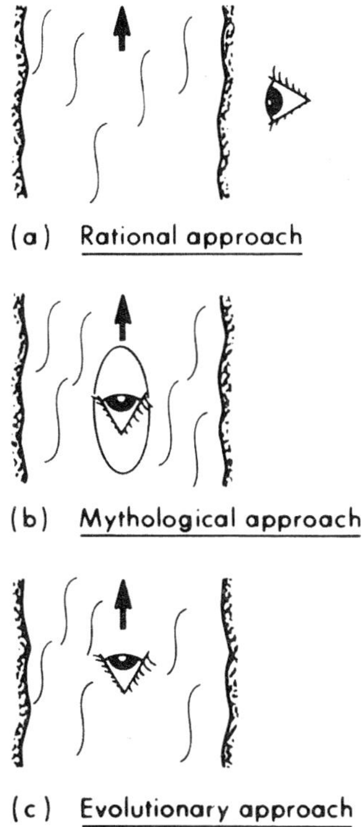

Figure 8. The three modes, or levels, of perception and inquiry illustrated by the image of a stream. At the rational level we are outside the stream, at the mythological level we try to steer our canoe in the stream, but at the evolutionary level we *are* the stream.

Figure 5.18. Erich Jantsch, "The three modes, or levels, of perception and inquiry illustrated by the image of a stream." From *Design for Evolution.*

of the torus) but describe different aspects of the design process. Here, design comes to mediate the "slabs" of elements in the dynamic systems Jantsch described, from reality to consciousness to the three different types of space inhabited by human subjects: physical, social, and spiritual. In Jantsch's worldview, these spaces and realities were always interacting, but only a concerted design could bring them into more perfect but also dynamic alignment. This would refine their relations in stages, pushing human consciousness to evolve, engendering the next state of designed patterns, and so on.

There thus emerges here a model of design not as an act that accommodates, or even adapts, but one that proactively engenders change. Calhoun and Jantsch viewed human evolution as a trade-off situation that could be directed into a complex where environmental structures would force a response in humanity, causing it to retreat or hesitate, so that it might respond to the new situation (which it had designed in the first place). This implies something like a two-steps-forward, one-step-back model, where

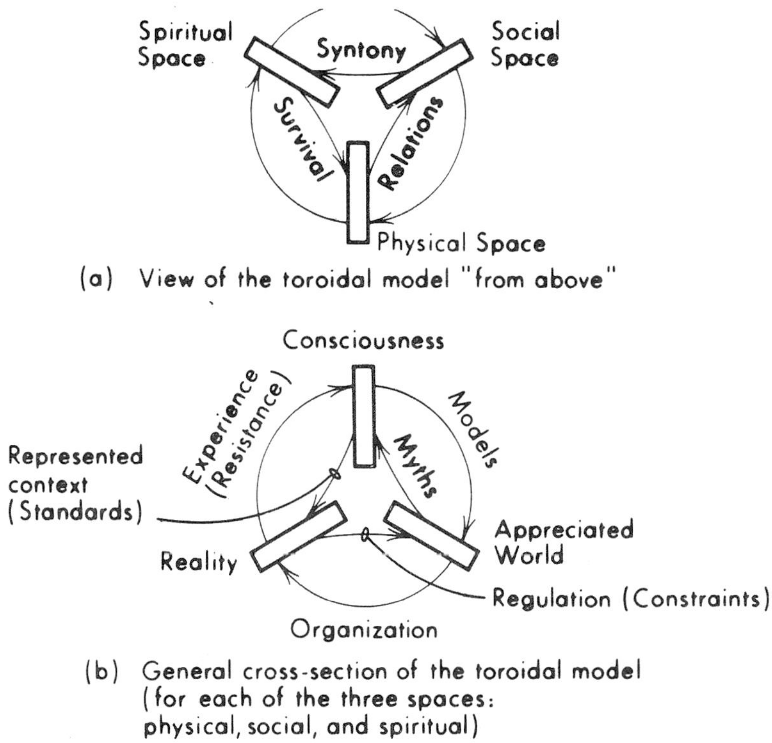

Figure 9. Two views of the toroidal model of the basic human design process.

Figure 5.19. Erich Jantsch, "Two views of the toroidal model of the basic human design process." From *Design for Evolution.*

speculative design activity deploys unexpected environments, forcing the subject to adapt, and then moves beyond them in the next evolutionary phase. In this model, equilibrium between organism and environment is cast aside in favor of dynamic forward or, really, upward movement.

This type of trade-off of physical structures and human consciousness would resonate perfectly with Cybertecture and Hilbertz's understanding of evolutionary environments. Indeed, the ways in which Hilbertz articulated these systems are worth reviewing, as they provide perhaps the most explicit evocation in this period of the ways in which responsive environments could be conceived as apparatuses (in all the critical and technical senses of this charged term).

Humanity was currently suffering, Hilbertz held, not only because of imbalances in the relationship between the human organism and the surrounding world but also because of an internal imbalance in the very structures of the brain:

> There exists an incompatibility between our limbic system (the animal brain) and the neocortex (the seat of reason and conceptual

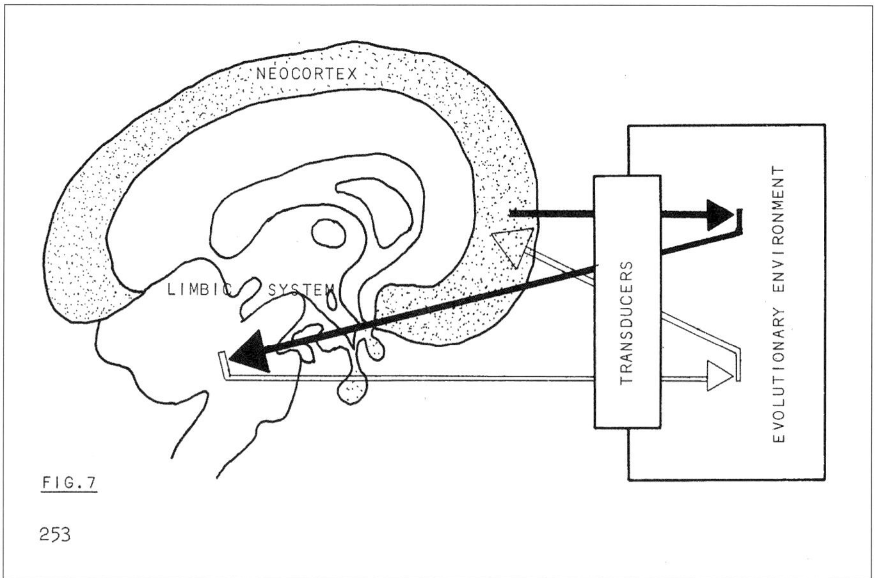

Figure 5.20. Wolf Hilbertz, relationship between the human brain and an "evolutionary environment." Courtesy of Hilbertz family.

> thought), the latest addition to our brain. The neocortex cannot successfully correct the animal drive functions of the old brain; both parts speak different languages. Considering human history and the chance of meaningful development, evolutionary environments can assume the mediating role between the two parts, and thus insure a healthy mix of reason, emotions, foresight, and instincts governing our affairs.[63]

If Hilbertz had initially inscribed Cybertecture *within* a "socio-economic milieu," soon his system had scaled up (or in) to constitute a bioevolutionary apparatus. "During the greater part of his evolution," Hilbertz wrote in a different essay, "man has had to adapt himself to his environment in order to survive. Cybertecture is a concept to reverse a historical process radically."[64] Once implemented, an evolutionary environment would not only help equilibrate the human brain torn between its ancient animal instincts and higher functions, but it might also "[induce] the further building up of neural connections between the neocortex and the limbic system at increasing rates of speed."[65] Here, both subject and object—organism and environment—are engaged in a mutual, topological inflection, teleologically taking turns at reorganizing their respective structures, gaining in organizational complexity with each successive interaction.

In these passages we can see the translation of the scientific speculation in the texts mentioned above finding its design implementation. On the one hand, these theories provided Hilbertz a scientific basis for his ultimate architectural desideratum: an environment that would not only change or respond to the demands of inhabitants but also spur their own entelechy. On the other hand, these sources cannot be viewed historiographically as simply "contextualizing" Hilbertz's work. His familiarity and relationships with these individuals and publications provides an indication of how Cybertecture might have functioned as a literal mapping and embodiment of the disciplinary connections that so many actors wished to see come to fruition at this moment. Rather than simply juxtaposing or curating essays and reviews from different disciplines, the drawings and specifications of Cybertecture, as well as its explicitly biopolitical functions, provided a hybrid platform whereupon the environmental research manifold might finally coalesce in a transdiscursive responsive structure. In this sense, the detailed technical drawings of robot arms, the beautiful renderings of organic cities, the near-nonsensical charts mapping connections between nature and culture, and Hilbertz's New Age rhetoric functioned precisely as an extradiscursive aggregator of knowledge from different disciplines—and, frankly, in a much more palpable way than a publication such as *Man–Environment Systems.*

Extensions of Man

As the evolutionary model implies, we seem to have moved on from a conception of computers aiding architectural transformation to a world in which literally everything is subject to systematic modification or design. And while biologists and systems theorists attempted to describe the exact dynamics of these processes, they never actually were able to account for perhaps the most salient mechanic of their apparatuses: How, exactly, does the exterior world relate to the interior world of the subject, so that the two might modify one another? We might return to Hilbertz's brain diagram for a clue as to his insights in this regard. Here, the "evolutionary environment" (via technical/architectural "transducers") serves as a "mediator" between the two regions of the brain. This completely literal biochemical mediation is effected through the use of the environment as a "prosthetic." This usage is equivalent to Hilbertz's descriptions of environments being modified by artifactual "extensions" of the human organism.

Indeed, the idea was, at precisely the moment Hilbertz was developing Cybertecture, undergoing an intensive discursive elaboration directly implicating design. Jantsch had signaled its significance at the Universitas meeting: "Most of the systems we are building today will be inhabited by people with *technologically extended capabilities, functions, and desires.* The modes of design, appropriate for such systems, will have to be more complex, too."[66] Certainly for Jantsch, and for any culturally aware individual after 1964, the term would have been most familiar from Marshall McLuhan's epoch-defining *Understanding Media* (1964). In this book, subtitled *The Extensions of Man,* McLuhan maintained that every new technology realigned the balance of the senses, emphasizing some while suppressing others. This realignment had direct (if unconscious) influence on the way in which subjects interacted among themselves and with the world.

As discussed in chapter 1, McLuhan was elaborating his theory of extensions and environment at the same time. The former was coming into focus for him as a quasi-invisible context for human transformation, detectable only through the "recognition" of meaningful repetitions in the media-saturated world. As it happens, McLuhan's adoption of the term was inspired by his friend the anthropologist Edward T. Hall (see chapter 2). McLuhan wrote a letter to Hall in 1964 in which he stated, "To say that any new technology or extension of man creates a new environment is a much better way of saying the medium is the message."[67] This remark was in reference to a single passage in Hall's most famous book, *The Silent Language*, which McLuhan rapturously referred to in his many letters to Hall as "your page 79," in which Hall had written:

> Occasionally organisms have developed specialized extensions of their bodies to take the place of what the body itself might do and thereby free the body for other things. Among these ingenious natural developments are the web of the spider, cocoons, nests of birds and fish. When man appeared with his specialized body, such extension activities came into their own as a means of exploiting the environment.
>
> Today man has developed extensions for practically everything he used to do with his body. The evolution of weapons begins with the teeth and the fist and ends with the atom bomb. Clothes and houses are extensions of man's biological temperature-control mechanisms. Furniture takes the place of squatting and sitting on the ground. Power tools, glasses, TV, telephones, and books which carry the voice across both time and space are examples of material extensions. Money is a way of extending and storing labor. Our transportation networks now do what we used to do with our feet and backs. In fact, all man-made material things can be treated as extensions of what man once did with his body or some specialized part of his body.[68]

It seems likely that Hall furnished McLuhan with the word *extension*, even though the latter had been working through similar ideas much earlier.[69] Hall (before bequeathing it to McLuhan) gleaned the word from R. Buckminster Fuller (another friend). Fuller had used it very early, during his years at Black Mountain, first in the 1938 *Nine Chains to the Moon* and then, much more extensively, in his *Untitled Epic Poem on the History of Industrialization* (written in 1949, but not published until 1962). In the former, Fuller wrote: "Through the leverage gained by his INANIMATE INSTRUMENT EXTENSION OF SELF, [man] has attained an extended mechanical ability far in excess of his own integral mechanical and energy content ability.'"[70] As these lines suggest, Fuller took the entirely optimistic view that technology could only be a one-way amplification of human capacity wherein the latter expanded its reach in time and space.

Nor was Fuller the first to develop the idea of extensions. Lewis Mumford had written of the history of machines and tools as so many attempts to "*extend* the powers of the otherwise unarmed [human] organism" four years before *Nine Chains to the Moon*.[71] But beyond just the word itself, the notion and general logic of extensions have been part and parcel of the cultural analysis of technology from the very beginnings of that discipline. Indeed, perhaps the founding text in the philosophy of technology—Ernst Kapp's *Philosophie der Technik* of 1877—also put forth the notion that tools are effectively morphologically and functionally linked to human body parts.[72] While Kapp did not use the term *extension*, he described these correspondences as "organ projection" and used language that uncannily predicted that of McLuhan and Hall.[73] Despite this consistency, the revival of the notion in the 1960s carried with it some distinguishing features. One of these was the newly realized potential—thanks to the cybernetic and biological theories mentioned above—to integrate technics with genetics and/or evolution. (Cybernetics, from the outset, was itself premised on an almost willful transgression of the boundaries that had traditionally separated the study of biology from technology and culture. It veritably liquidated, as Donna Haraway observed, all actions into the common currency of communication.)[74] The other feature was the totalizing, environmental component that seemed always to attend these later inscriptions of the idea of extension. Extension, once held in functional and morphological equivalence with particular organs, had now become an expression of a totalizing projection of the human organism.

While Hilbertz never referred to Fuller in particular, it is clear that his project was inscribed within this ethos of the extension as a biological amplifier and environmental modifier. Lest we reject the example of Hilbertz as an outlier, we can also find similar themes, for instance, in one of the exemplary discursive artifacts of this moment, Gyorgy Kepes's *The Man-Made Object* of 1966.[75] Even at this relatively early date we can see in this single edited volume the conflation and elision of the distinctions among natural phenomena, artifacts, and designed objects, as well as their environments. Though Kepes maintained the editorial credit in this volume, its introductory chapter was authored by Italian art critic and cultural theorist Gillo Dorfles. In defining the "man-made object," Dorfles immediately acknowledged its status as an extension: "I believe one can readily affirm that the object created by man—from the most ancient and prehistoric times—constitutes a kind of extension of man, a manifestation of his very physical, or rather physical-psychical constitution."[76] Shortly after establishing this connection, Dorfles arrived at a related observation: "If . . . at one stage the object can be considered as an instrument capable

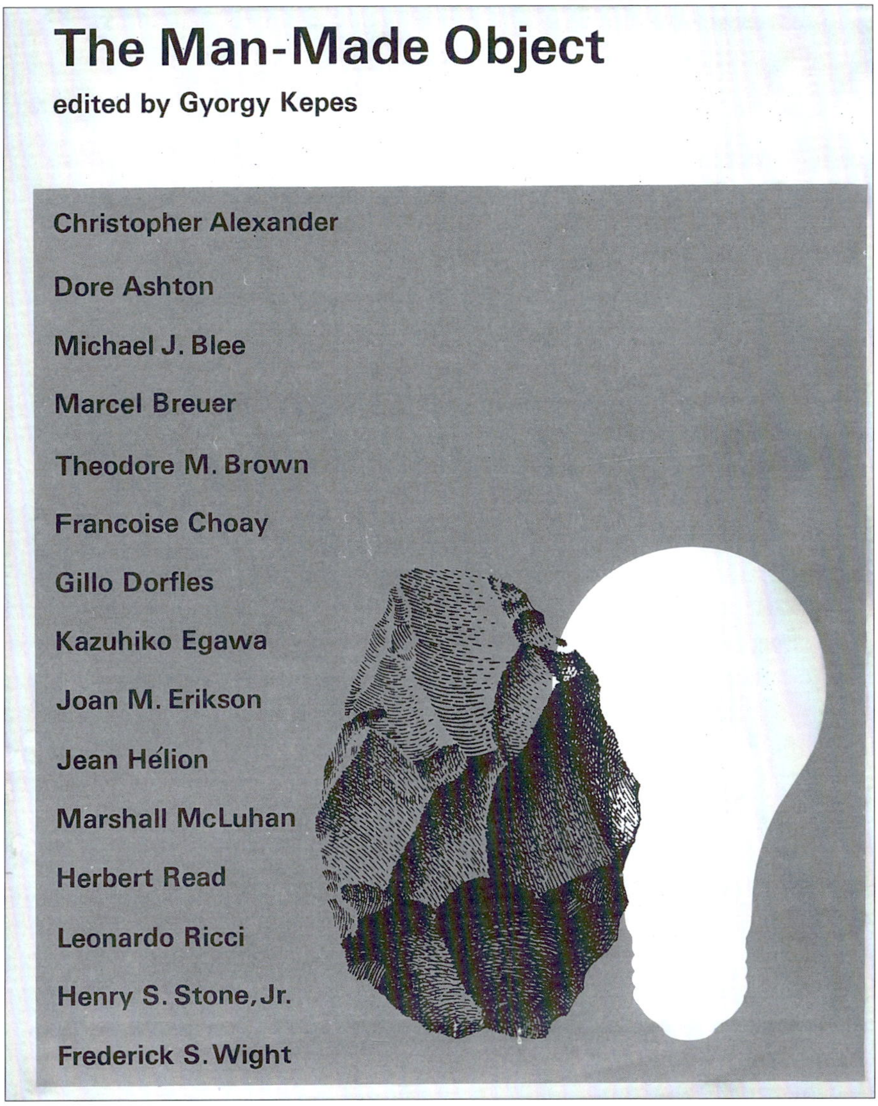

Figure 5.21. Cover of Gyorgy Kepes, editor, *The Man-Made Object* (1966). Copyright 1966 by George Braziller, Inc. Reprinted with permission of George Braziller, Inc. (New York), www.georgebraziller.com. All rights reserved.

of potentiating and prolonging the operative faculty of the individual, at a second stage the object can be understood as already being—in an autonomous and 'pre-existent' sense—part of our surrounding scene." In characterizing this surrounding scene, Dorfles wrote, "Man is constantly surrounded by an immense accumulation of 'object elements,' in large part created by himself, or created by nature but assumed as if they were 'made,' and which all together constitute an 'external world' from which we derive impulses and pretexts for our formative will."[77] In the initial formulation, the object "extends" the will of the subject. Then, magically, it becomes the background, the "pretext," the environment of that same will. Dorfles's comments were followed immediately in the publication by a photo-essay that focused first on "object forms and functions." This section's sensibility might be described as post-Bauhaus as read through the *Family of Man*. But the next section is more interesting for our purposes, as it attempted to illustrate various "communities of objects," ensembles of things generating their own ecosystems, their own social relations: a junkyard piled high with cars, a Shaker interior, an IBM 360 mainframe and console. Gone now was the operative or formative will of the subject. It had been replaced by objects relating to one another.

But before further elaborating the ramifications of these reversals, we must acknowledge that the extension gained its proper design elaboration under the aegis of contemporaneous formulations of *tools, access,* and *alternative* or "soft" technologies that found their most explicit platform in Stewart Brand's *Whole Earth Catalog*. Here, environmentally and ergonomically optimized technologies were not simply available, their adoption became apocalyptically imperative. I feel as though so much has been written about the *Whole Earth Catalog* at this point, I don't need to rehearse its significance. I will, however, point to a related development that scholars have been slow to account for: the offshoot publication *Co-Evolution Quarterly,* which took the evolutionary potentiality of tools and extensions as its raison d'être. In the second issue, for instance, Stewart Brand, borrowing concepts from biologist Paul Ehrlich, defined *tool*: "A tool consists of a use at one end and a grasp at the other. Tools, tasks, and user co-adapt and co-evolve in rich interaction."[78] While Hilbertz's work never appeared in the journal, his approach to responsive and evolutionary environments was totally consistent with its New Age aspirations.

The mystical properties of tools were celebrated in virtually every issue of *CQ*. James Tennant Baldwin, probably the most highly professionalized among the whole earth movement's designers, contributed what would become something of a regular column to the journal, beginning in 1975 with an article titled "One Highly-Evolved Toolbox."[79] This essay was really just a very practical buying guide for those looking to equip themselves—literally, with drills, saws, winches, and pliers—for the emerging culture of repair, but it concluded with this advice: "Think of tools as extensions of your hands. They should *feel* like that." Now, on the one hand, this statement simply rehearsed a very familiar modernist-Heideggerian ergonomic functionalism (that tools should be available and quasi-invisible). Nonetheless, when taken with the title of the article, it joined those two concepts that concern us here, evolution and extension. Later, in another essay, Baldwin expanded the scope and ambition of his folksy advice: "It's obvious how [tools] are extensions of your hands," he wrote. "A hammer is just a hard fist; a screwdriver, a tough fingernail. But hands usually operate according to instructions from head, so it can also be said that *tools are an extension of your mind*."[80] Here, there is a slight shift from a purely instrumental extension to the world of consciousness expansion. Baldwin also offered a bit of sociological critique: "In a modest way, you can combat the 'machines taking over' by having better control

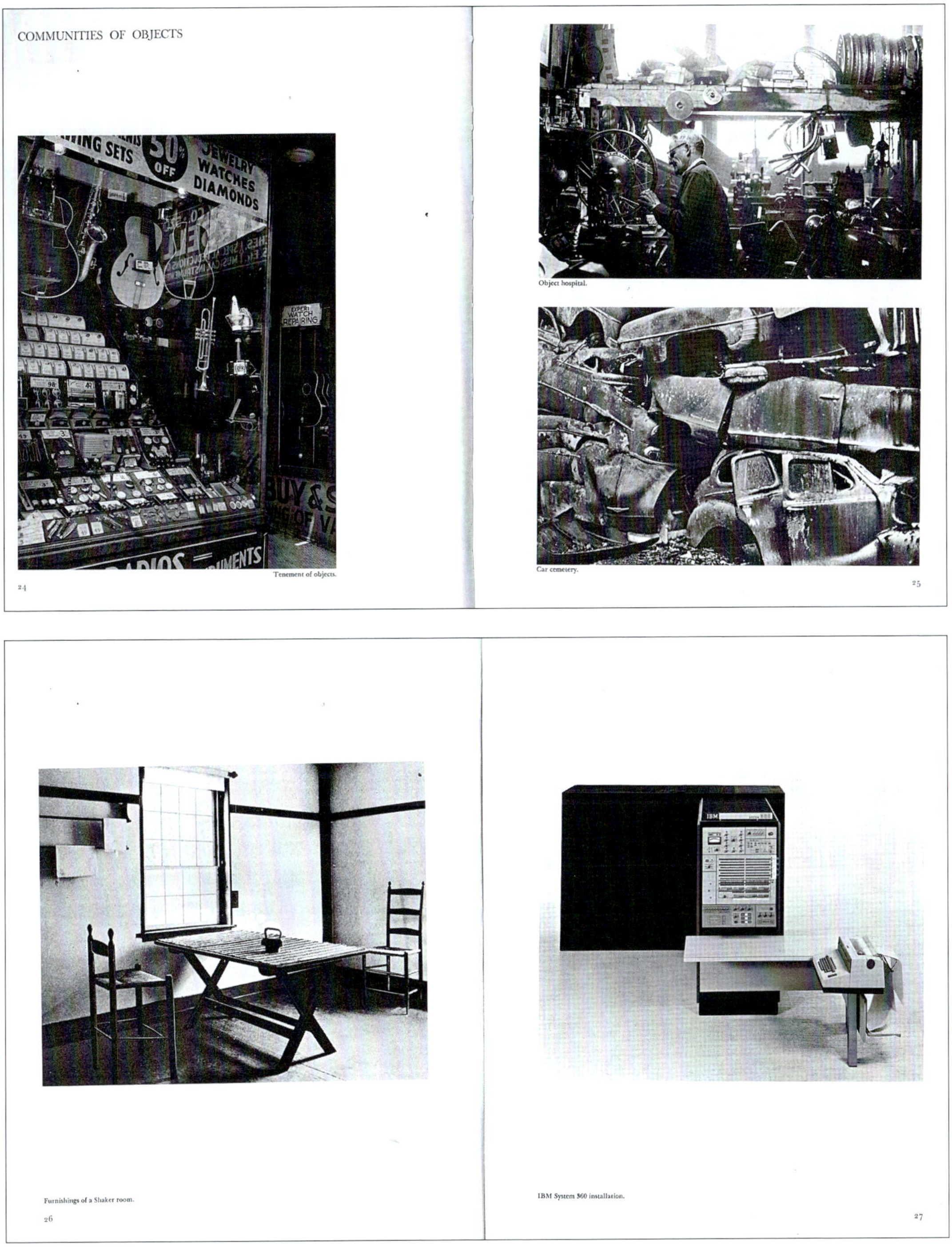

Figure 5.22. "Communities of Objects," from Gyorgy Kepes, editor, *The Man-Made Object* (1966). Copyright 1966 by George Braziller, Inc. Reprinted with permission of George Braziller, Inc. (New York), www.georgebraziller.com. All rights reserved.

of the technology you live with. It's a good feeling. And it's free."[81] In 1978, Baldwin would introduce *Soft-Tech,* part of the CoEvolution Book series, by quoting his favorite saying of his onetime professor Buckminster Fuller: "Evolution makes many starts." Baldwin then stated that he hoped that the extensions and technologies elaborated in the book would "represent beginnings that are in the process of developing into new ways of integrating us and our environment."[82]

For his part, Brand had been inspired directly by a 1964 essay by Paul Ehrlich and Peter Raven in which they discussed various species of butterflies that were not merely isolated genotypic families but actually integral parts of "community evolution" or "evolutionary interactions."[83] How, the authors asked, could biologists hope to understand the development of specific parasites, for instance, without considering the attributes and evolution of their animal hosts? They proposed instead an "examination of patterns of interaction" between given species of butterflies (in this instance) and their food sources.[84] In such patterns, chemical compatibilities or incompatibilities between butterflies and plants could cause both to enter new adaptive phases in their development. The plant species were not a stable "source" of food for any butterfly, but rather a dynamic proposition to which the butterfly had to respond. If a chemical mutation in a particular plant, for instance, protected it from a feeding butterfly larva, that chemical profile could be passed along to other similar plant species. The butterflies, in turn, would then be forced to adapt by finding another food source or selecting for a tolerance to the newly present, previously intolerable substance. These patterns could extend, Ehrlich and Raven observed, and explain, for instance, the ways in which various insects could quickly build resistances to chemical pesticides (which then must be modified in turn to regain their potency). They might also explain how "primitive" hunters selected the poisons used on their arrows.[85] In other words, coevolution included much more than direct chemical or genetic compatibilities. Such compatibilities could be seen working mechanically as well; they could be extended to virtually anything within the interactive realm, or what the authors described evocatively as "adaptive radiation."[86]

This slippage between what was proper to the "inside," or genotype, of the organism and what constituted its environment would become more pronounced in the years to follow. In what amounts to a spectacular postscript to the discourse on extensions, toward the end of the 1970s Richard Dawkins would propose his notion of the "extended phenotype," in which "the phenotypic expression of a gene may extend to inanimate objects, and it may also extend outside the body in which it sits."[87] Here, coevolution (a term Dawkins does not invoke) is itself extended. The bowerbird, for instance, externalizes its reproductive impulses in the construction of its elaborate nest. Here, there is no inherent chemical matching necessary; anything whatsoever can be considered as the extension of the internal structures of the organism. This amounts to a different frame of reference, a changed paradigm that would see organism and environment much more closely knit into a functioning unit or system.

It was precisely this adaptive radiation and the literal extension of the phenotype—the ever-changing patterns of interaction between entities once thought to have only an accidental relationship—that fueled the imaginations of Brand, Baldwin, and Hilbertz alike. This logic only intensified as the notion of extension gained traction in these years. The extension was both tool and environment. Not only did it amplify the biological capacity of the (human) organism, but it also then modified the milieu in such a way that it called forth new adaptations. Tools did not simply interact with their users—they interacted with one another in an ever-intensifying coevolutionary field.[88]

For the designers and theorists I have been discussing—Hilbertz, Fuller, Dorfles/Kepes, Baldwin—this field was the new horizon of design. It was mappable, perceivable, and, therefore, explicable, manipulable, optimizable. But others were not so sanguine. Despite their obvious debt to Fuller, for instance, both Hall and McLuhan would offer readings of extensions that diverged from the optimistic and teleological one crafted by him and his acolytes. If for Fuller an extension was considered in its most positive spatial expression as motive force or mechanical addition to a humanity that could not help but gain in self-actualizing capacity, for Hall and McLuhan extensions always had a reciprocal component. They turned back on the organisms they extended; they stunted, ablated, amputated, and distorted the senses they seemed to extend, as well as those they apparently did not affect. For every "outering," to use McLuhan's terms, there was also an "innering."[89] For his part, Hall wrote that "a species, once it begins to use the environment as a tool, sets in motion a whole series of new and often unforeseen environmental transactions that require further adjustments."[90] Relying on Freud, he essentially then pathologized this cultural and biological condition, describing it as "extension transference," a process wherein the subject attributed the powers of the extension to itself, further confusing the proper scales and domains of humanity and technology.[91]

In the formulations of both Hall and McLuhan, there is a distinct lack of clarity regarding where the various terms begin and end. At times, extensions create environments, then environments are used *as* extensions. This metonymic slippage is evident in both the formulations of the cultural theorists I have been discussing and the operative propositions of the designers. This is evident in Hilbertz's articulation of the "artifactual environment" and in Dorfles's "surrounding scene," or what he would later describe as a collapse of the two categories of "artifact and nature."[92] To list another relevant example, in the very first footnote of his *La speranza progettuale,* Tomás Maldonado—following Jakob von Uexküll and sociologist Arnold Gehlen—described a human environment that was a "system of artifacts," an "artifact-environment," and a "web of artifact-utensils and artifact-symbols."[93] Likewise, Abraham Moles was simultaneously discussing the possibility of an "ecology of objects."[94] But if the artifact environment was ostensibly conceived and analyzed through the lens of semiotics in the European context, in the Anglo-American context cybernetics and evolutionary biology remained the dominant paradigms. This means that McLuhan's statement that "any new technology or extension creates a new *environment*" should be taken quite literally. In this situation, the techno-aesthetic procedures of the discipline of *design* underwent a peculiar dilation. Design would now have to respond not to particular functional or formal problems but to the spatiotemporal relations generating environment itself.

Herein lies the distinction between the extensions of the 1960s and 1970s and those of previous generations. The industrial extension was limited to a kind of straightforward equivalence between an isolated bodily function and its direct external embodiment in a particular implement. A specific organ was "projected," to use Kapp's terminology. In the post-industrial context, the scope of the extension broadened. Communications technologies had cybernetically replicated and externalized the entirety of the circulatory and nervous systems of the subject, linking every individual into unprecedented new networks of psychical, physical, biological, and technological "elements." McLuhan was the most explicit in this regard, stating, "With circuitry we have, instead of extensions of hand or foot, or back, or arm, a kind of involvement of the whole nervous system, an extension of the nervous system itself, a most profoundly involving operation."[95]

With this, we might say that instead of being simply extended, the subject had been turned inside out; environment and organism had merged almost completely. The boundaries demarcating the human, the animal, and the technological become the most porous of membranes. Instead of a body projecting its organs into the environment, there was a kind of recognition of what Gilles Deleuze and Félix Guattari were describing at this very moment as a "body without organs," an undifferentiated haecceity that was radically open to the flows and virtualities both around it and within it. Michel Foucault, too, was beginning to imagine a radical new subjectivity—again, during the very same years that concern us here—one defined not as a classical center, as the seat of a humanistic free will, but rather as a set of effects of the environment, or *dispositifs*. In this regard, the use of the term *extension* in Anglophone theoretical and design contexts around 1970 seems a bit quaint, or naive, perhaps intentionally so. There is a certain nostalgia in the notion, the sense that design might still originate with a willful body and mind reaching out in space and evolving through time, instead of that body and mind being the by-products of so many biopolitical apparatuses—instead of, in other words, the subject itself being merely an extension.

Alternatively, Cybertecture presented the spectacle and deep structures of an ethologically driven, computer-controlled, responsive environment that extended from the primal animal brain of the subject into its surrounding milieu and was capable of altering the structures of each. Even with its mystico-utopian overtones, Cybertecture nonetheless reimagined the positionality of subject, computer, and environment. It was perhaps an early and (simultaneously, it turns out) late attempt to model architectural systems as techno-aesthetic ensembles conceived to take control of—literally, to redesign—the spatiotemporal flux of the biological and cultural development of humanity. Within these systems, the function of response radically redefined both architecture and its inhabitants. Architecture became a set of fleeting spatial structures whose actual substance could be reclaimed and recycled for succeeding iterations, determined by dynamic patterns of response with the psychic structures of the subject, which in turn became environmental material to be similarly reshaped and remolded. To alter Marx's famous phrase, all that was spatially empty became full, and all that was structurally solid became ethereal. Architecture was breathed by computers, and the human brain became an environment to be designed.

6

Arcoconsciousness

One implication of the responsive environment was that external (objective) forms, structures, and processes might interact with and change their internal (subjective) counterparts. Can it therefore be a coincidence that the design of such apparatuses overlapped historically with radically shifting models of human consciousness and subjectivity? And I do not mean here just the "expanded" model of consciousness espoused so famously by the counterculture but also its immediate progeny—the culture of consciousness design that would develop in the 1970s. This New Age scientism (or hippie postmodernism) was evident already in the work of Wolf Hilbertz and Warren Brodey, and in the pages of *CoEvolution Quarterly*. Its figureheads were those who rode the psychedelic wave well past 1968, such as cybernetician Stafford Beer, psychologist Richard Alpert (Ram Dass), and young anthropologist Carlos Castaneda, all of whom dropped out, moved to India or the American Southwest, and became yogis or shamans.[1]

This was, after all, the moment when the dashed revolutionary hopes of the protagonists of the 1960s seemed to turn inward, from the political to the personal. It was the beginning of what Tom Wolfe would so famously describe as the "Me Decade" and Christopher Lasch would characterize as "the culture of narcissism."[2] While today's readers might reflexively associate the design projects in this text with psychedelic and hippie culture, they in fact coincided more precisely with what came immediately after in the United States: the "third great awakening," as Wolfe called it; Theodore Roszak's "Aquarian frontier"; the "New Age"; consciousness manipulation via post-Freudian psychologies, group encounters, the human potential movement, est, Esalen, and so on; the peak of Scientology, yoga, meditation, dietology, jogging, and wellness.[3] In short, these projects coincided with the age of therapy, with a culture of extrareligious self-help and improvement that, sneer as we might, remains very much with us today. At the heart of all these initiatives was the thinking subject, and specifically the question of just how and where this subject was situated relative to others, to the patterns of society, the environment, and the universe. If these dynamics of inside and outside could be mapped, could they be *designed*?

The Italian architect Paolo Soleri certainly affirmed this possibility with his own unique program for responsive environments and consciousness design. Unlike the light, transparent, and digitally mediated structures we have seen thus far, Soleri's arcologies were dense, opaque, and *brut*. Their forms were possessed of a kind of structural introspection that ran counter to the open-ended, plug-in, and responsive aspirations of the time. Because of this, Soleri's work has often been maligned as representing little more than eccentric New Age utopian thinking, his realized and imagined structures disregarded as massive sculptural artifacts of an *organic* architecture parading as *ecological* design.[4] Perhaps Soleri's overt mysticism and aestheticism made it inevitable that he would be marginalized by the architecture and environmental design establishments. But the systems within which Soleri inscribed architectural form were very much in line with the models of science and aesthetics informing the design of responsive environments as I have been elaborating them here, and can be understood as part of an alternative lineage of modernist materialist and consciousness theory, including the work of Henri Bergson, Pierre Teilhard de Chardin, Ilya Prigogine, and Gilles Deleuze.

The emergence of the modern cult of therapy is strangely intertwined with the history of modern architecture and design, which sought to bring harmony to the relationship between humanity and the built environment—or, in other words, to create *outsides* that might improve human *insides*. Indeed, avant-garde design historically called for a "new man" and has frequently looked toward transcendental mysticism to define this subject, turning, for example, to Theosophy and Freemasonry, to a perennial concern with Zen Buddhism and Hindu mythology, and to Judeo-Christian belief systems and many other forms of the occult.[5]

After World War II, architecture and design extended these interconnections in a quest to "expand" consciousness, critique the Western *logos*, and orient the individual subject within the patterns of the universe itself. The design attitude corresponding to these cultural shifts is exemplified by Drop City in southern Colorado and the entire ethos of Stewart Brand's *Whole Earth Catalog*, both of which were inspired by the techno-utopian-cosmic design thinking of R. Buckminster Fuller.[6] The dominant narratives of these developments have been based on a sublimation of the mystical aspects of their discourses into a kind of technological determinism that has led to our networked, global "cyberculture" and to the current imperative for sustainable design.[7] In these accounts, the mysticism of this design moment is considered as a kind of feint. It is posed as an alibi for a technocratic optimization of global systems seeking to interface with the fear and longing of a generation disoriented by American excess and consumerism, the recession, the urban crisis, the ecological crisis, tragic political tensions with the Middle East, the rise of postmodernism, and so on.

Take, for instance, the development and subsequent appropriations of the preferred building technologies of the counterculture: *space frames* and *geodesics*. Space frames were essentially geometrical figures in material form. They were assimilated into architectural design as triangulated or polyhedral systems of interlocking and interchangeable units that promised economy, flexibility, and the potential for unprecedented aesthetic effects. They were used on playgrounds and for warehouses, and they fueled the craze for domes and zomes, which were, as Fred Turner has described, "products of technocratic industry [that] served as handy tools for transforming [a] collective mind-set."[8] In the United States, these applications were inspired by Fuller, whom Reyner Banham had famously posed as one of the only true rational functionalists of the twentieth century.[9]

But despite their ostensible function as embodiments of the morphological logics of communications networks and ultrarational and efficient building systems, during the 1970s and beyond, their metaphysical benefits were also being extolled. We can see an assumption regarding the contiguity of the geometries of geodesic domes and human consciousness in one of the most important documents of this period: *Domebook One* of 1970. While this text—like many of the other manifestations of counterculture technologies appearing at the same time—is often characterized as a hyperpragmatic ecological paean to "appropriate technology," its metaphysical content is quickly apparent.

Indeed, even the ecological situation of domes is invested with a holistic spiritual/environmental instrumentality. In one application, a circular "parasol" dome—vented at top and bottom—situates itself in the midst of grand evolutions and involutions of air currents and geothermal energies. The dome acts as a "valve" for these "atmospheric patterns," drawing them into optimized symbiotic currents.[10] This very direct climatological efficacy is mirrored by a concern with metaphysical patterns. In another section we find Swami Kriyananda and his partner photographed building and living in their new dome:

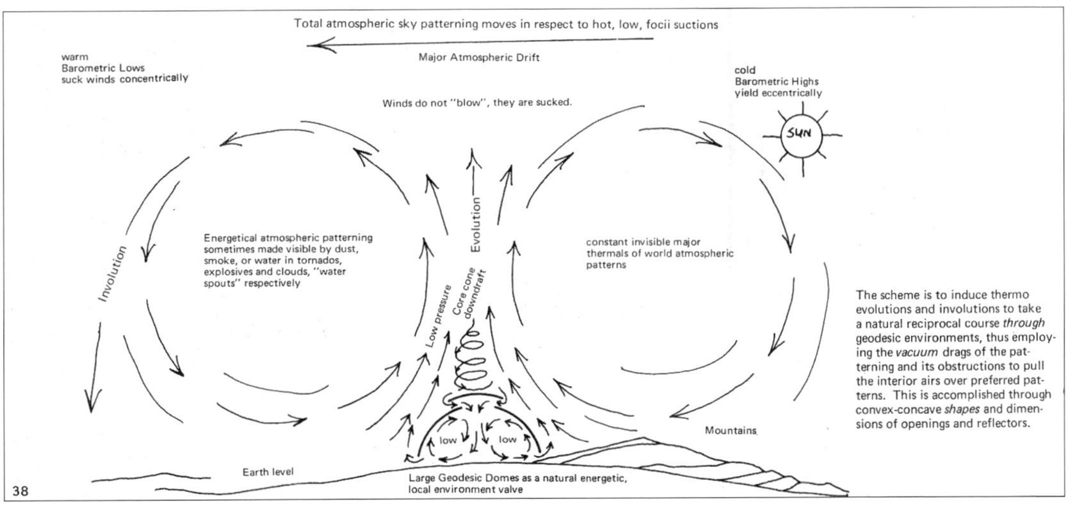

Figure 6.1. "Large Geodesic Domes as a natural energetic, local environment valve." From *Domebook One* (Los Gatos, Calif.: Pacific Domes, 1970), 38.

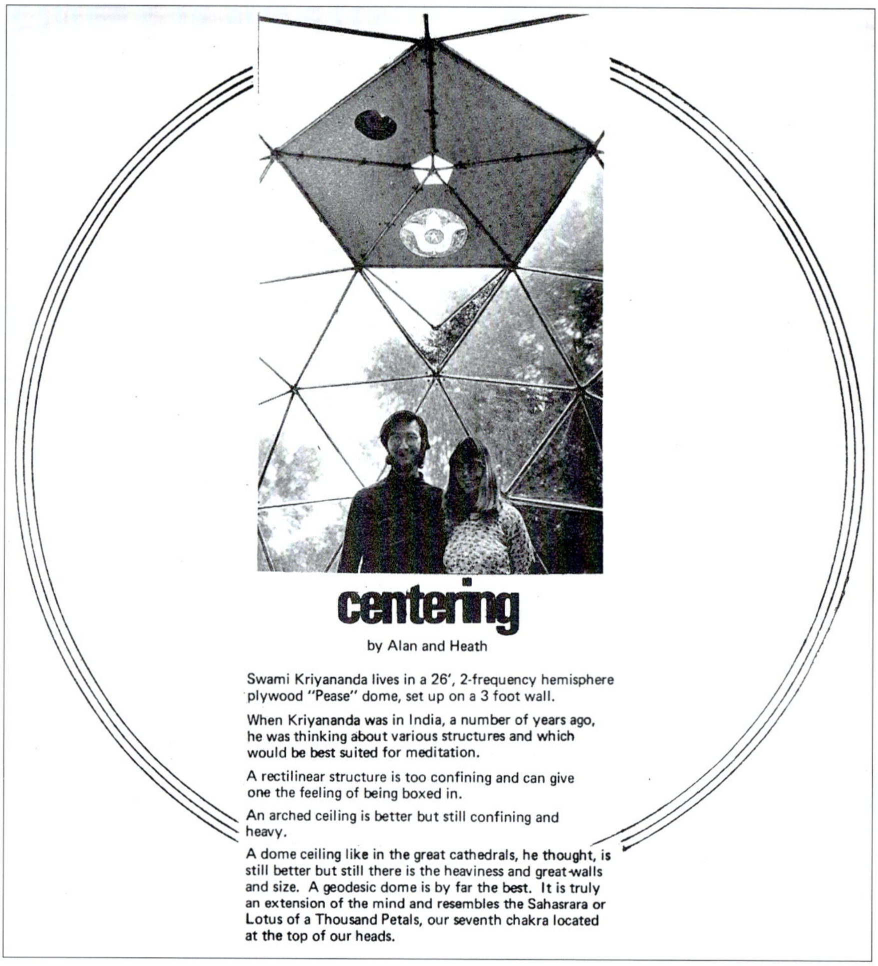

Figure 6.2. "Living in a spherical single unit home makes us wholer people. We feel more whole and have our whole trip around us." From *Domebook One* (Los Gatos, Calif.: Pacific Domes, 1970), 47.

> When Kriyananda was in India, a number of years ago, he was thinking about various structures and which would be best suited for meditation.
>
> A rectilinear structure is too confining and can give one the feeling of being boxed in. . . .
>
> A geodesic dome is by far the best. It is truly an extension of the mind and resembles the Sahasrara or Lotus of a Thousand Petals, our seventh chakra located at the top of our heads.[11]

The phrase "truly an extension of the mind" is interesting, as it resonates with the human extensions discussed in chapter 5. Nonetheless, it also seems more abstracted, more formalized, or more patterned. Regardless, his type of extension was also a significant part of design discourse during these years. Architecture was seen as a kind of mental projection whose structures would find isomorphic models in both the consciousness of the subject and the external environment. Indeed, these complex, topological structures, most of which were arrived at through intuitive mathematics, entered into a mutually affirmative relationship with cybernetics and systems theory that culminated most spectacularly in Buckminster Fuller's 1975 magnum opus *Synergetics,* the subtitle of which was *Explorations in the Geometry of Thinking*—which I believe should be taken as literally as possible.[12]

In other words, the historiography surrounding Fuller and countercultural design has demonstrated a certain amnesia about their consciousness metaphysics, whereas Soleri's mysticism has remained firmly in the foreground. If Fuller managed to cast himself as a designer who saw the geopolitical and technological reality of the world clearly, Soleri increasingly looked like a mythical figure—the prophet in the desert digging around in the dirt with no shirt on.

The Vise of the Universe

Soleri appeared more like Carlos Castaneda, seeking a desert-situated spiritual fulfillment through an ethnopsychedelic escape into other, higher, states of awareness. (Ironically, Castaneda identified more powerfully with Fuller.)[13] In the early 1970s, such comparisons became unavoidable journalistic glosses. The 1977 *Psychology Today Omnibook of Personal Development* included detailed (and very incisive) entries on both Castaneda's system of "nonordinary reality" and Soleri's arcology as a metaphysical system of human–environment integration.[14] (We can also note that the entry on Marshall McLuhan was followed by one titled "Meditation," and that the entry on Edward T. Hall preceded "High-Fiber Diet" and "Homeopathy.") But not everyone would accept the easy compatibility between Castaneda's cultic discourse and Soleri's work in Arizona. William Irwin Thompson, one of the best-known ecological humanists of the time, drew a distinction between the two:

> When Carlos Castaneda goes into the desert, he tries to move away from the heritage of his Italian father to discover the older heritage of the grandfather of the race, the shaman, Don Juan. For Castaneda isolation in the desert is a psychedelic technique for projecting the unconscious, but for Soleri, the desert is the Archimedean place to stand to move the cities of the earth. Soleri does not indulge in youth-culture fantasies about mysticism and nature; for him human nature is the only nature possible to us.[15]

Soleri's version of conscious clarity was emphatically not the type of self-dissolution promoted by Castaneda.[16] It was earthier, literally more material, more solid, structured, and, indeed, more *formed.* Moreover, unlike Fuller's architecture of lightness and expansive tension (or Castaneda's somatic regime of dissolution), Soleri's architecture was opaque and crystalline, thick and encrusted with the traces of its own fabrication.

Arcology was an evolutionary engine for pressing the subject in on herself, transforming consciousness by infolding it into ever more tightly packed and complex structures. Architecture was not a physical impediment to be removed from the path of the consciousness expanding out into the environment and cosmos. According to Soleri's own metaphor, it was a "vise." In "Esthetogenesis of the Universe"—a drawing from one of Soleri's sketchbooks, which are philosophical journals as much as collections of architectural renderings—the concept of esthetogenesis is depicted through images of a clawlike cosmos squeezing and extruding the energies of "the cultural world" into more specific, sharper forms (Plate 9). In other words, Soleri did not want to expand human consciousness (a term he used interchangeably with *conscience, logos, spirit,* and *mind*) so much as he wanted to concentrate it.

"Consciousness is like a membrane interposed between the inner mystery and the outer mystery," Soleri wrote. "Architecture as environment is the man-made conscience-maker."[17] Here, the human subject is not figured as a woefully earthbound animal seeking metaphysical transcendence. She is a physical filter between two parallel realities—the pincers, as it were, of a vise. Accordingly, Soleri never advocated for a model of consciousness that had transcended the "illusion" of matter, or that called for a relinquishing of earthly possessions or the alienating trappings of human culture. Soleri may not have been materialistic, but he was most certainly a materialist.[18] His "membrane" was precisely that—a porous border between two (material) realities:

> If our existence can be described as the reality of a membrane of consciousness interposed between two universes equally unknowable (the inner universe is complex, durational, imploded; the outer universe, spatiotemporal, expanding), then the degree of consciousness inherent in the sensitized membrane depends upon the flow, quality, and quantity of information traversing through and apprehended by the membrane. This situation entails the desirability of an environment surrounding the membrane as rich as circumstances allow, and it is entirely up to the membrane, us, to see that such richness is made, nurtured, maintained, accrued, and transfigured for the sake of the beholder.[19]

This quite remarkable passage might read at first like a typical New Age meditation on alienated subjects lost in the world, subjects who require a ready-made belief system to lead them to the light of transcendence, where their worldly burdens might be lifted and their consciousness freed. But nothing could be further from the truth. Rather, Soleri was saying that only the world can provide the raw material from which subjects can reorganize their environment, which, in turn, might help to reorganize their consciousness. He wrote: "The physical world is the world of objectified information in which we are immersed as on an all-enveloping continuum, a continuum sensitive to our responses as much as we are sensitive to its challenges."[20]

Arcology

Soleri first came to architectural prominence in the context of an international network of utopian designers in the early 1960s, when his richly detailed renderings of Mesa City (begun 1958) were first published (Plate 10).[21] The appeal of the project's monumental, organic forms was only enhanced by the already eventful life of the young Italian, who had received an architectural degree at the Turin Polytechnic and then traveled to the Sonoran Desert for an apprenticeship at Frank Lloyd Wright's Taliesin West in 1947–48. Despite a falling out between Soleri and Wright, the desert landscape was to have a profound appeal for the Italian, who returned to Arizona in the mid-1950s and settled in Scottsdale, where he began work on the so-called Dome House and then the Cosanti compound.[22] The 1969 publication of his book *Arcology: The City in the Image of Man,* followed the next year by a major exhibition of his work at the Corcoran Gallery (an exhibition that subsequently traveled), secured his fame and his connection to environmental design.[23] Thereafter, a series of published writings, speaking engagements, and exhibitions kept Soleri—in ebbs and flows—in the public eye.[24]

The concept of arcology, a conjunction of architecture and ecology, would constitute one of the centerpieces of Soleri's comprehensive philosophical and operative worldview. It was, in a sense, the most concrete of his proposals and took shape as thirty individual arcologies rendered in the large drawings and intricate models he published and displayed in 1969 and 1970. In the parlance of the time, the arcologies were megastructures: massive city-scale buildings incorporating advanced structural technologies.[25] The scale of these projects derived in part from their environmental function: they constituted urban ecosystems designed specifically for various types of sites. Some arcologies would spread across plains, others would perch on cliffs, and still others would float on the open sea. Some were designed specifically for tropical, arctic, or desert conditions or conceived typologically as agricultural, metropolitan, or research centers. Soleri rendered arcologies that were anchored deep underground and others that were suspended on massive *pilotis*; one project was even meant to float through the "black void of space."[26]

Another aspect of arcology that set it apart from other visionary schemes of the 1960s was its ostensible immanence. Instead of climaxing with the largest and most extravagant design, the final project featured in the 1969 edition of *Arcology* was on a much more modest scale. It was called Arcosanti, and it was an urban complex specified for "mesa topography" and destined to house just fifteen hundred people (compared with the tens or hundreds of thousands projected for many other arcologies). Arcosanti's footprint was a simple rectangle covering seven acres and incised on three

Figure 6.3. Paolo Soleri, Hexahedron, Arcology 28 from *Arcology: The City in the Image of Man* (1969), partial section. Photograph by Cosanti Foundation.

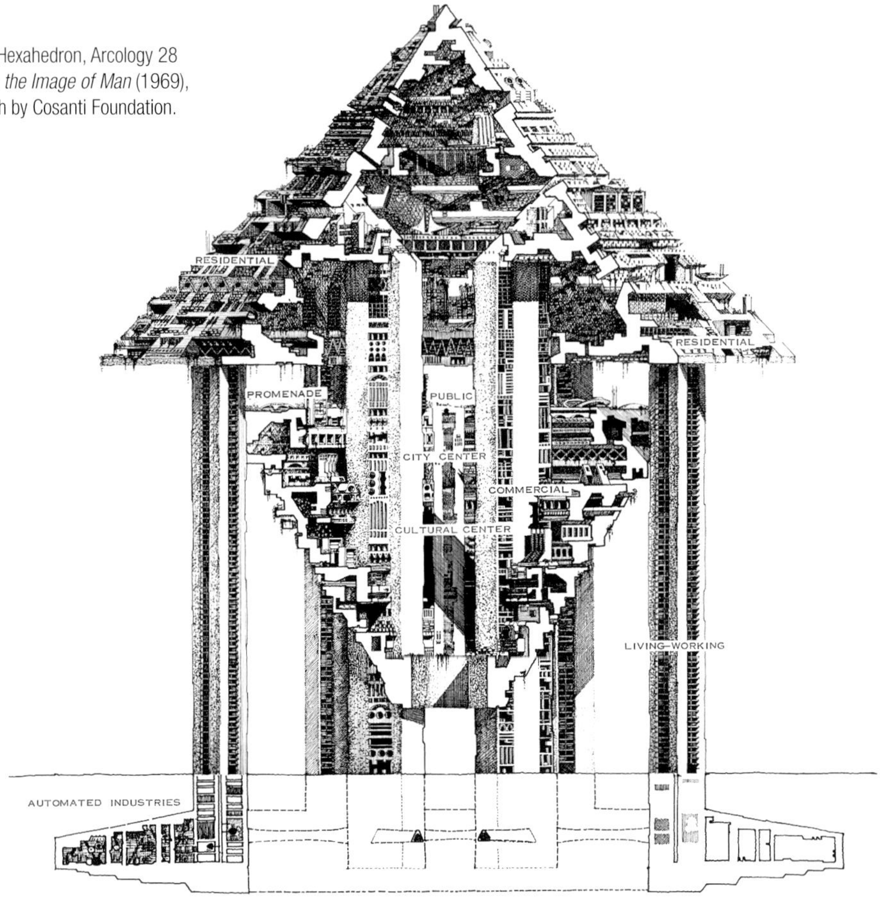

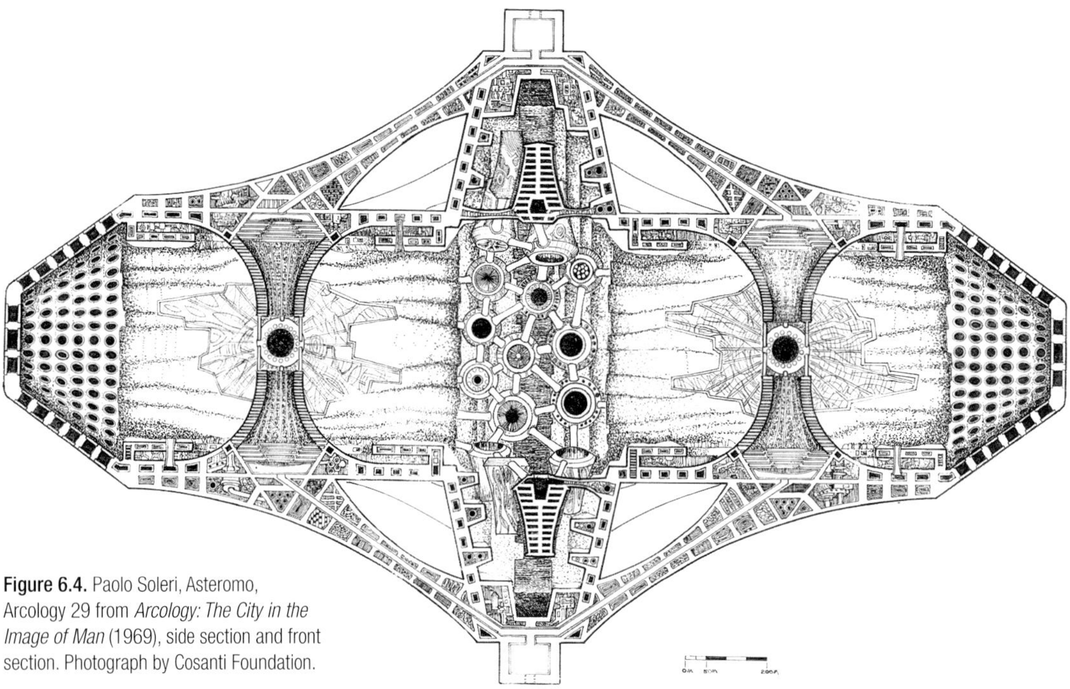

Figure 6.4. Paolo Soleri, Asteromo, Arcology 29 from *Arcology: The City in the Image of Man* (1969), side section and front section. Photograph by Cosanti Foundation.

sides by sectioned domes whose openings faced outward. The volume into which these pantheon-like forms were set was thick with towers and terraces containing residential and work spaces. The roof of the complex was likewise articulated by a landscape of sculptural towers constructed from the juxtaposition of half squares and circles, which formed shaded plazas and a platform from which the surrounding desert could be surveyed. Arcosanti was not merely a distant and visionary projection; it was on the verge of becoming reality. Referring to his home in Scottsdale, Soleri said of this initial scheme for Arcosanti: "I am urbanizing the Cosanti Foundation. [Arcosanti] will be a macro-Cosanti."[27] To illustrate this principle, one remarkable axonometric section of Arcosanti showed the complex literally interfacing with, or plugging into, a minuscule Cosanti site: the tiny, handcrafted domes of the extant project thus extended and grew spatially and temporally into the new, macroscale configuration. As Soleri wrote:

> There is a structure of things that must be sought in a degree directly proportional to the degree of complexity of such things. The avalanche of life and "goods" that is cascading on us is begging for a structure. Meaningfulness is not something that extravagantly comes into being. Nothing in the universe has such kindness in store for man, nor can we seriously desire such casual demiurgy.
>
> If it is true that there are structural priorities that every civilization must define for itself, then to make sense out of our physical environment has a very urgent call for priority. Macro-Cosanti will be a testing ground for environmental concepts that seek coherence between aims and ends. Macro-Cosanti will apply arcological concepts. I call it Arcosanti, and we are now actively working at the initial phase.[28]

Ground was broken on Arcosanti in August 1970, some seventy miles away from Cosanti, in Cordes Junction, Arizona. Its name derived from a loose conjunction of several Italian and Latinate words roughly meaning "coming before arcology," Arcosanti was a metropolitan vision realized with archaic techniques by a rotating workforce of counterculture dropouts and architecture students. Arcosanti rose up (and continues to rise) on the walls of a small desert valley. In contrast to the symmetricality of the renderings of the final project, the massing and footprint of the complex as it exists now are less formal and schematic (the master plan has been altered to accommodate current constructions and has changed several times in the intervening decades). Interestingly, the first structure erected was monumental in nature: a large barrel vault made of reinforced concrete, open at either end (1971–72). This structure established a kind of agora (just one of many indicators of Soleri's classicism) at the heart of Arcosanti, and it serves to visually frame the surrounding desert landscape.

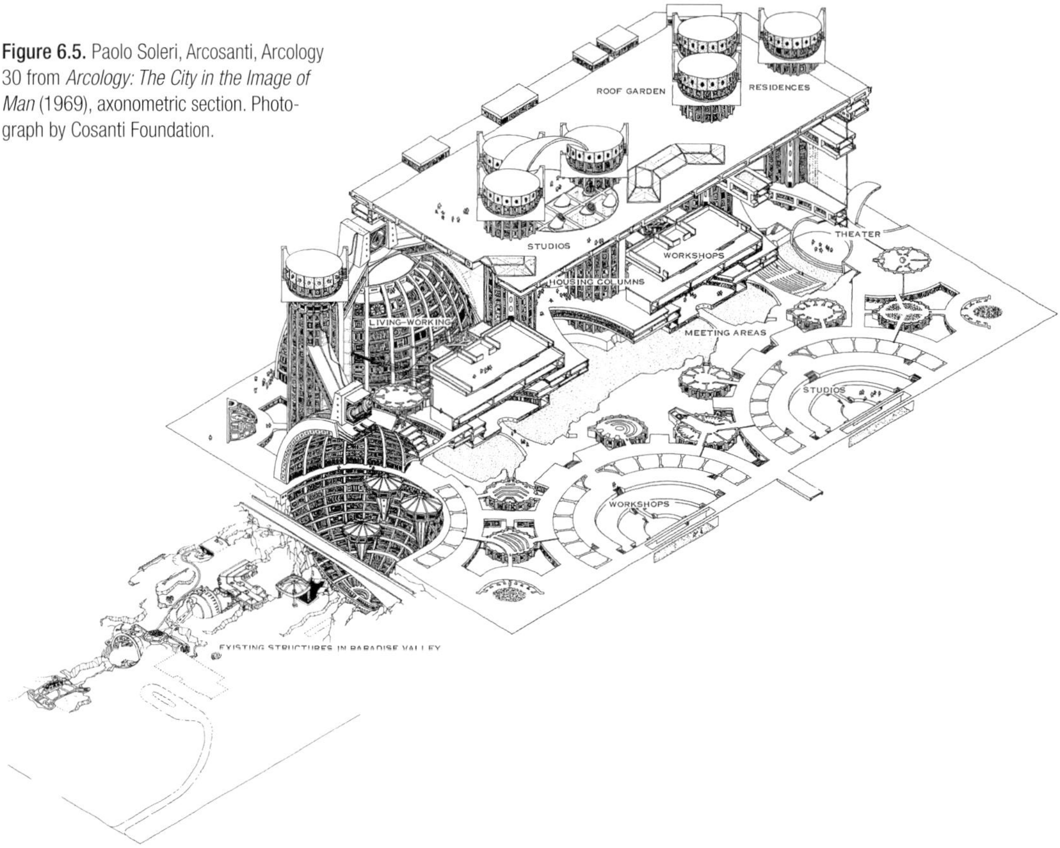

Figure 6.5. Paolo Soleri, Arcosanti, Arcology 30 from *Arcology: The City in the Image of Man* (1969), axonometric section. Photograph by Cosanti Foundation.

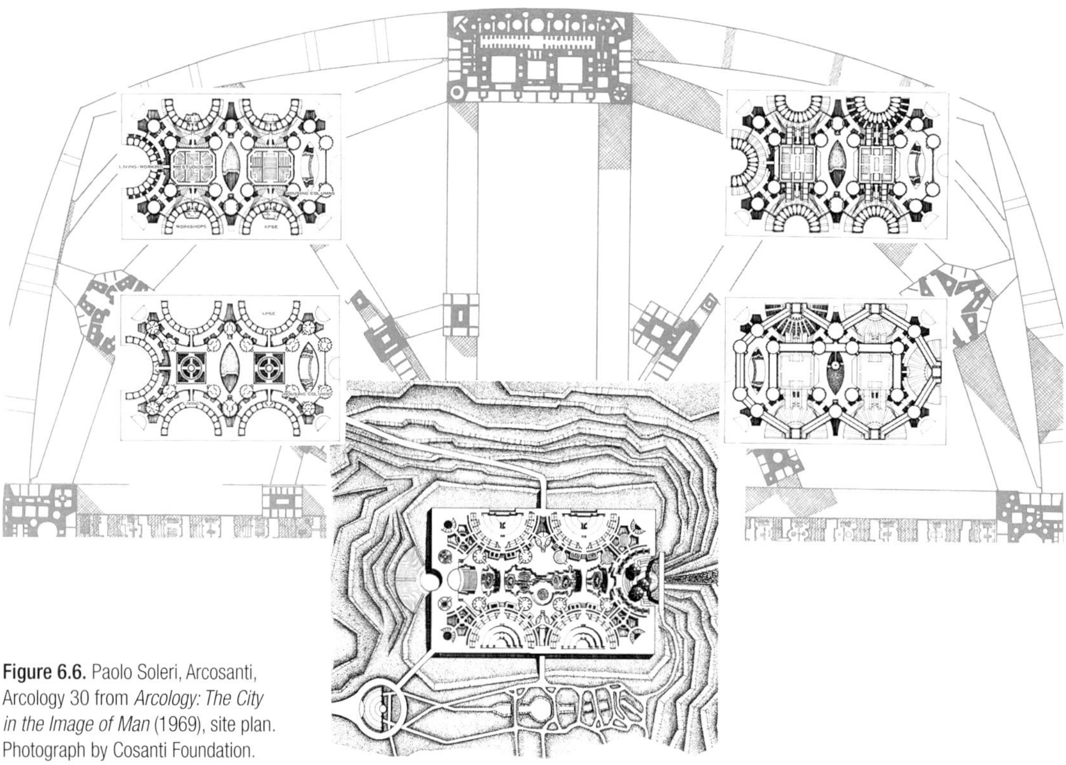

Figure 6.6. Paolo Soleri, Arcosanti, Arcology 30 from *Arcology: The City in the Image of Man* (1969), site plan. Photograph by Cosanti Foundation.

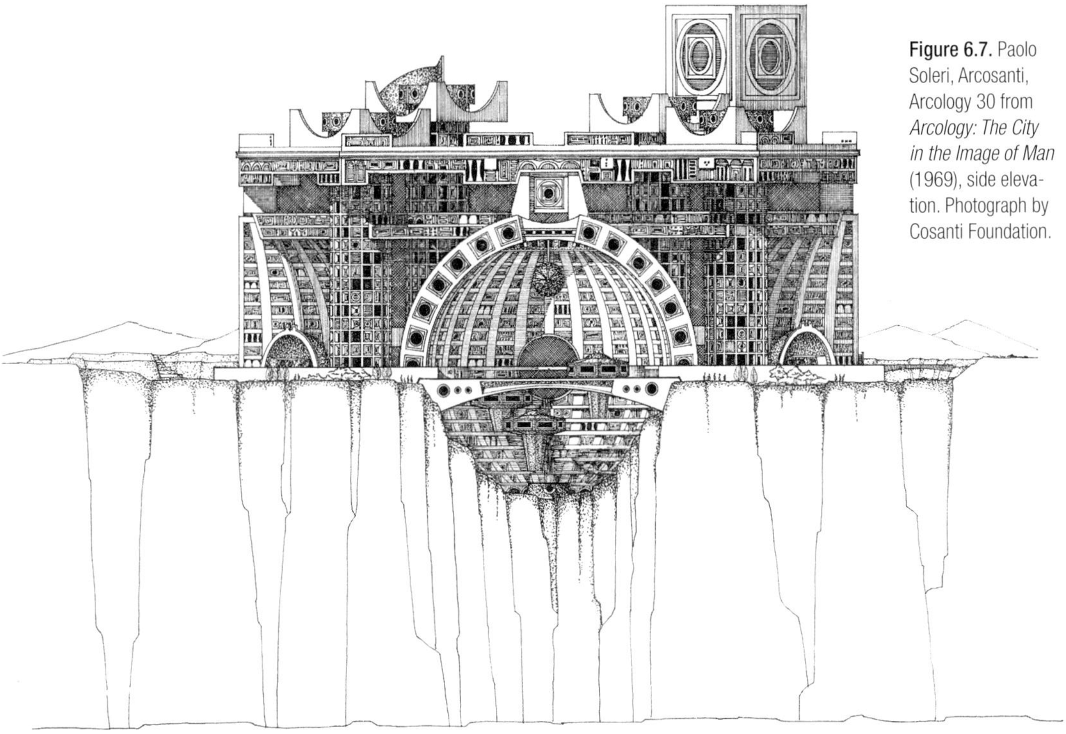

Figure 6.7. Paolo Soleri, Arcosanti, Arcology 30 from *Arcology: The City in the Image of Man* (1969), side elevation. Photograph by Cosanti Foundation.

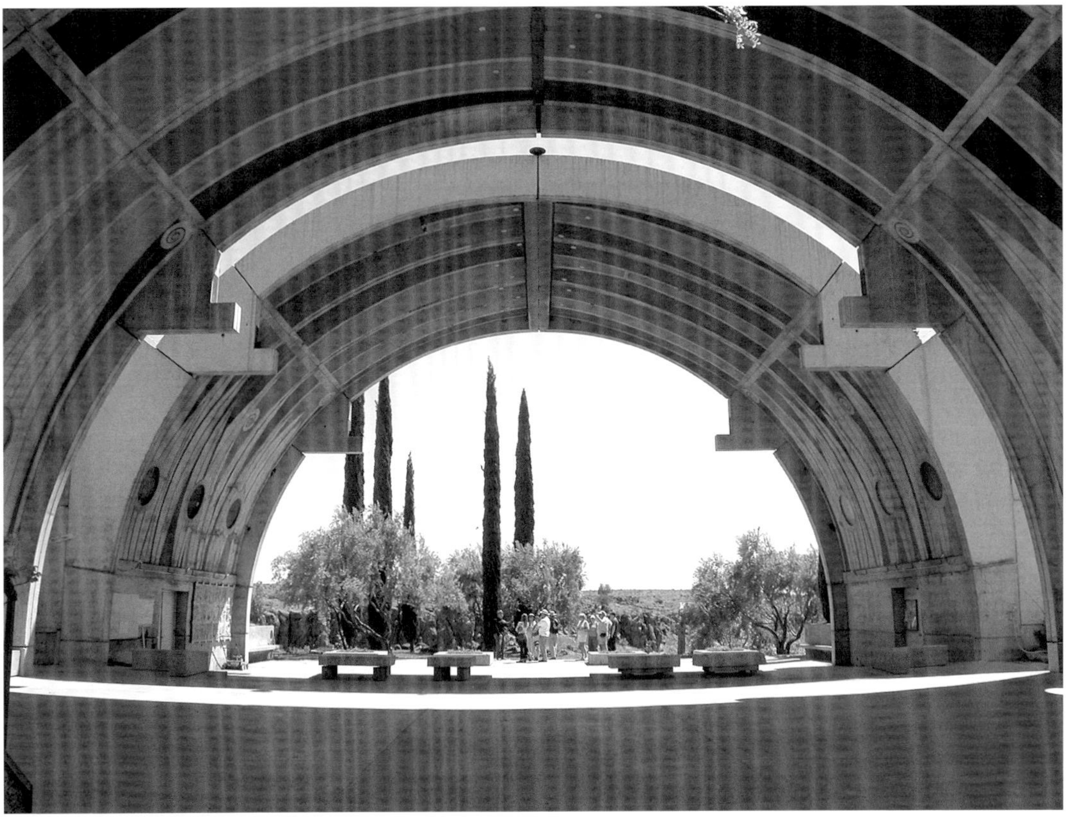

Figure 6.8. Paolo Soleri, Arcosanti Vaults (1971/1975). Photograph by Yuki Yanagimoto.

The choice of reinforced concrete (almost the exclusive tectonic solution here) had some interesting implications. Foremost among these were its economy and flexibility. Soleri had developed a unique casting technique at Cosanti, in which large piles of silt were built up by hand or heavy equipment, and concrete was poured over them. Then, when the concrete set, the dirt was excavated, leaving an open space covered by a canopy. Soleri was able to achieve complex and dramatic forms using this rudimentary method. Thus utilized, the concrete suggested something in between the organic and the synthetic, and the physical process of arresting a liquid substance into a more solid form would prove particularly compelling for Soleri's philosophy of architectural aesthetics. Furthermore, Soleri found that he could etch decorative patterns and mix pigment into his silt forms, both of which would transfer and bond to the concrete, turning even the most mundane of surfaces into something of an artistic synthesis—a polychromed and sculptural shell. The patterns Soleri devised were also syntheses of organic and synthetic, of art nouveau fantasy and the geometrical restraint of Wright, filtered through a keen awareness of modern masters such as Henri Matisse, Joan Miró, and one of Soleri's heroes, Le Corbusier.

By 1974, Soleri had added two more open-air structures—apses for the production of ceramics and the famous windbells that are sold to tourists—that incorporated the first apartments for residents.[29] He had also begun one of the most iconic of the buildings at the site, a structure called Crafts III, which would become the social heart of Arcosanti (it currently houses the visitors' center, an art gallery, and a café). This building, which also utilizes reinforced concrete, did not, however, employ the silt casting method—it was far too large. Instead, Soleri adopted a more systematic approach to the forms, constructing cubic modules from concrete slabs. Each slab was five meters square, and many had circular voids (such slabs, usually smaller, are ubiquitous at the site), a format that was employed as window opening, threshold, and belfry. The building's massing and elevation resembled some of the earlier arcological types, such as Arckibuz. The design also betrayed Soleri's formal debt to Brutalist contemporaries Louis Kahn, Paul Rudolph, and Moshe Safdie. Accordingly, Crafts III connoted a more institutional ethos for Arcosanti, one that would carry over to an ensemble begun in 1980 called the East Crescent, which included housing and a large amphitheater that hosted performances of modern music and dance, all of which were a part of Soleri's ambitious cultural program. Construction at Arcosanti continues to this day, executed (and funded) by participants in semiannual workshop programs.[30]

From the outset, Arcosanti and Soleri's other designs occupied an ambiguous position in public and professional discourse. They gained great purchase in the public imagination. In a 1976 article in *Newsweek*, art and technology futurist Douglas Davis hyperbolically claimed, "As urban architecture, Arcosanti is probably the most important experiment

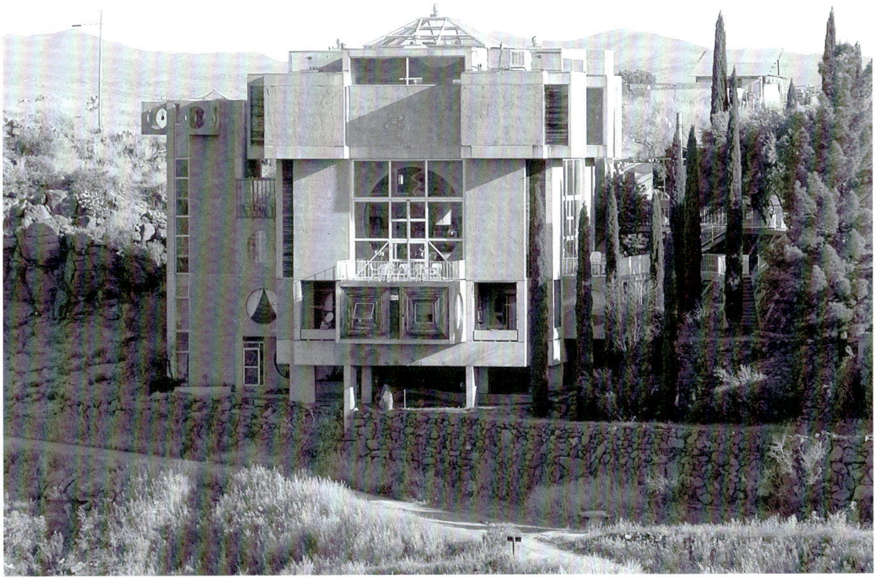

Figure 6.9. Paolo Soleri, Arcosanti, Crafts III (1972–77). Photograph by Yuki Yanagimoto.

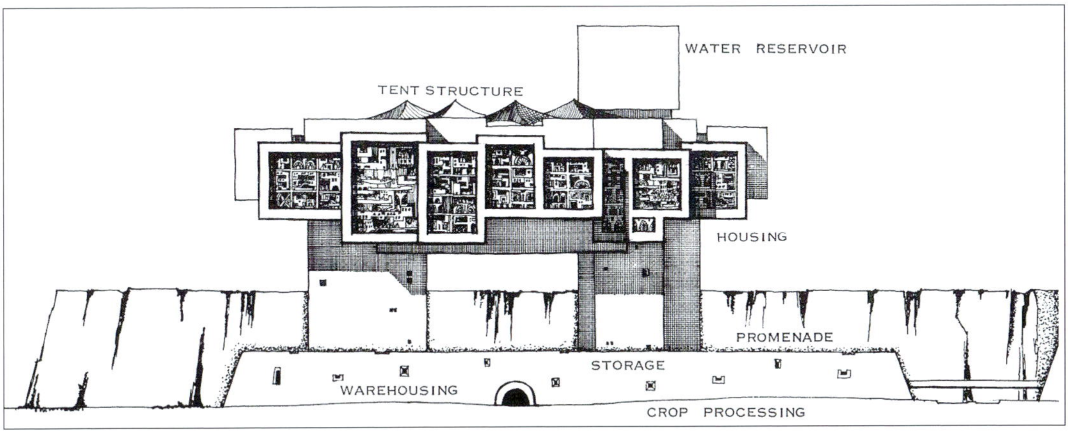

Figure 6.10. Paolo Soleri, Arckibuz, Arcology 15 from *Arcology: The City in the Image of Man* (1969), elevation. Photograph by Cosanti Foundation.

undertaken in our lifetime."[31] Accordingly, Soleri found himself becoming something of a public intellectual in the fashion of Buckminster Fuller.[32] Indeed, the former was possessed of a certain scientific pragmatism and "cool" demeanor that seemed to ground his otherwise fanciful propositions (his famously obtuse prose notwithstanding).[33] According to one observer at the time: "[Soleri] eschews, on the one hand, the shrill claims and messianic preachments of a Buckminster Fuller, and, on the other, the pseudo-scientific posturing and Madison Avenue soft-soaping of a Constantinos Doxiadis."[34] And, unlike these other visionary advocates of modern design, Soleri insisted on the primacy of aesthetic form and the need for cultural as well as instrumental sophistication.

Also in distinction to Fuller, Soleri largely rejected the connections to the so-called counterculture that were often thrust upon him. He distanced himself from these and from Fuller as well by invoking the common ecological trope of the world's limited resources. In his view, the hippies, in their quest to simplify existence and eliminate all forms of alienation from one another, had inadvertently gotten rid of all the good things about culture as well, becoming, in his words (and those of Desmond Morris), little more than "naked apes."[35] Soleri contrasted himself to Fuller in analogous terms: "Even though Fuller may tell us we will never run out of resources, we must now accept frugality. What I am advocating is not squalid *survival,* but a rich life."[36] (For his part, Fuller once paid Soleri the backhanded compliment of calling him "one of the greatest of the dreaming strategists.")[37] Nonetheless, Soleri attracted many counterculture adherents to Arcosanti, many of whom left after becoming disillusioned by what they felt was a lack of democratic openness in the social structure there.[38] Apparently, it was difficult to escape the messianic undertones of leading a group of disciples out into the desert to build a new civilization.[39]

Despite Soleri's public relations successes, the professional—even the vanguard—stance on his work was one of extreme skepticism. At the same moment as the *Newsweek* article, Reyner Banham mused, "Yet one still has to wonder if it is not the sheer physical exhaustion brought on by all that hand-labour that prevents his loyal students asking themselves what they are doing working for such a thoroughly old-fashioned and Establishment figure."[40] As Banham noted, despite their radical elevations, the arcologies did little to transform Athens Charter urban segregation.[41] Archigram's David Greene echoed Banham's sentiments when he visited Wright's Taliesin West and Soleri's compounds in 1971. In a mythologized report of his trip that conflated the sentiments of Robert Venturi and Denise Scott Brown's expedition to Las Vegas and a prose style strongly reminiscent of Tom Wolfe, Greene described his journey from San Diego:

> I can remember a burnt August afternoon on mission beach, and as the day cooled, gassing up and winding into the hills leaving the surf behind searching out the road to Phoenix through a bug-splashed windscreen, not knowing then that it was to be Phoenix that would really blow the mind—suburban Phoenix and air-conditioned Chevrolet faces behind green glass and boxes astride dayglo grass spray, hosed into life out of the sand against the cactus.
>
> Both pads, Wright's and Soleri's seemed only an extension of suburban Phoenix, except made from stone and wood instead of plastic and aluminum, the sources Navaho and Wagner not Hollywood and Mantovani, the techniques of the frontiersman rather than scotch tape.[42]

Of course, it comes as no surprise that Banham and Greene, originators of the very idea of a systems architecture—a plug-in conception of design—would fail to see in Soleri's obdurate, neo-Gothic forms a viable engagement with the technological environment. What they saw instead was art—sculpture, to be precise.[43] Greene summed up Arcosanti thus: "Soleri merely has a passionate desire to make the city a sculptural object with reference to his own styling preferences."[44] And Banham commented a bit later that Arcosanti's real power was not as serious urbanism; rather, its strength was more like that of "a desert earth sculpture by someone like Robert Smithson."[45] Indeed, Arcosanti was sculptural, expressionistic, emphatically handmade, ornate even.[46]

Complexity–Miniaturization–Duration

It was not ignorance of systems theory and cybernetics that inspired Soleri to craft individuated architectural objects, but rather the radical philosophical and spiritual inflection of those discourses. Soleri was not making forms against systems; he had come to understand aesthetic form as a very particular kind of system in its own right. "A technological environment is a nonhuman environment," Soleri wrote, "and the question is not of adapting man to it but of investing *[sic]* a lean system of not purely instrumental flesh on its skeletal structure."[47] This "not purely instrumental flesh" was to be aesthetic form integrated into a technical structure at the deepest levels (despite the spatial implications of the flesh metaphor). In comparison, Banham's and Greene's understanding of technological systems and the design style (or lack thereof) appropriate to them seemed somewhat dated, a product of the euphoria of the immediate postwar years instead of later developments in second-order cybernetics, general systems theory, and the environmental research manifold as they were developing in the Anglo-American context. Soleri himself acknowledged this on one occasion by distinguishing between two types of information transmission (and reception). "Synthetic information" was the exclusive product of rationality and a purely scientific approach to the world, while "environmental information" was a true, organic, and experiential mode of being in the world:

> After being debugged, sterilized and catalogued, synthetic information is communicated through the many channels invented by the mind. Environmental information is impervious to such treatment because it is an evolving situation more than a packaged set of data. The channels in which this information travels are the facets of the environment itself, and are ever-changing and dynamic. It is received bodily as much as mentally. . . . Abstract informations, chained to one another, tend to produce abstract

> world. Given the chance to operate, such worlds tend toward the nonhuman.[48]

Soleri was not designing for equilibrium, which would imply a stable and resolved situation. He viewed the human–environment system as being in a state of teleological transformation. His model of a system, and of the urban effect in general, did not derive from classical cybernetics (as had that of Kepes, for instance) but correlated more closely with contemporaneous models of *irreversible processes* introduced into scientific and popular discourse by Russian physicist and Nobel laureate Ilya Prigogine.[49] Since the late 1940s Prigogine had been elaborating theories of asymmetrical, directional temporalities as a corrective to classical thermodynamics (a category in which he included not only Newtonian physics but relativity and quantum mechanics as well), which was limited to considerations of equilibrium states within isolated or closed systems.[50] The major advantage of the science of irreversible processes, for Prigogine, was that it could potentially account for the behaviors of open systems operating "far from equilibrium," in which massive influxes of energy from exterior sources could change chemical and material configurations of elements over time. Surprisingly, open systems were not purely combustible and entropic. They could give rise to surprising new types of organization; entropy itself could become an organizing force.[51] The results of these processes were termed *dissipative structures*: entities arising out of open systems that move and maintain stable morphological and behavioral attributes. Naturally occurring examples would be a stable wave, such as a tsunami, and the formation of a hurricane.

For Soleri, architectural form was just such a structure: solid material imbued with a temporal impetus, an élan vital that could effect transactions between the built environment and its inhabitants.[52] Of course, Prigogine never suggested such a profoundly personified or operative model. Of far more importance to Soleri's understanding of an evolutionarily purposive urban design was the work of Jesuit priest, naturalist, and philosopher Pierre Teilhard de Chardin.[53] Man of both faith and science, a missionary who was present at the discoveries of both Piltdown Man (a famous paleontological hoax) and Peking Man in the early twentieth century, Teilhard was devoted to the centrality of the human spirit in a world of material reality. Consciousness became, for Teilhard, the highest expression of evolution. So profound were the transformations in the organization of the world since the appearance of humankind that a new spatiotemporal descriptor was needed: the noosphere, a term Teilhard adapted from the work of Russian geologist Vladimir Vernadsky.

As unlikely as it seems, Teilhard's posthumously published theories were received directly into the polemics around networks and systems in the 1950s–70s and had a discernible impact on the artistic vanguard.[54]

The salutary result of Teilhard's *mythos* within the *logos* of cybernetics was that it provided the possibility of resisting, and possibly reversing, that destructive and inevitable by-product of all networks and systems, entropy. Degradation of structure and homogeneity of form were anathema in Teilhard's theistic cosmogony. As he explained regarding the structure of matter:

> If one says fabric or network, one thinks of a homogeneous plexus of similar units which it may indeed be impossible to section, but of which it is sufficient to have recognised the basic unit and to have defined the law to be able to understand the whole by repetition: a crystal or arabesque whose laws are valid for whatever space it fills, but which is wholly contained in a single mesh.
>
> Between such a structure and the structure of matter there is nothing in common. . . .
>
> The stuff of the universe, woven in a single piece according to one and the same system, but never repeating itself from one point to another, represents a single figure. Structurally, it forms a Whole.[55]

Teilhard envisioned the universe not as a homogeneous network of even dispersal of interchangeable elements but as a vast multitude of centers, a series of discrete identities atomically organizing to attain higher levels of self-awareness. This last statement should be taken in the most literal sense. For Teilhard (and for Soleri subsequently), organization equaled consciousness. Mind and matter were no longer placed at the opposite ends of a philosophical polarity, but were comingled and profoundly interactive. Rocks were conscious, animals more so, and the human mind represented the apex of organizational complexity. This complexity expressed itself temporally through evolution. Evolution, for Teilhard, was not a lurching and random adaptive mechanism but a spiritual striving, the attainment by material structures of ever-higher states of organizational complexity and consciousness. Teilhard found it necessary to differentiate his theories from those of other scientists who would maintain that evolution was a directionless mechanism of a chaotic biosphere. In a passage that must have reverberated strongly for Soleri, Teilhard lamented the skepticism of his colleagues: "Men's minds are reluctant to recognize that evolution has a precise *orientation* and a privileged *axis*. Weakened by this fundamental doubt, the forces of research are scattered, and there is no determination to build the earth."[56]

Teilhard's appeal to directionality and intentionality in evolution led him (in a manner not unlike that of Prigogine) to reject the second law of thermodynamics, which he concluded was a "mathematical trick."[57] In his view, instead of entropically being thrown off by physical and chemical organizational processes in the form of useless "heat," energy was in fact *lost,* burned up into nothingness, and not simply converted to a different, simpler form. So, as evolutionary time passed, consciousness had progressively less raw material with which to work but was still bound to become progressively more complex. Interestingly, this evolutionarily driven complexification expressed itself (literally and metaphorically) spatially: in the refinement of *interiors.* By interiority, Teilhard meant the literal "arrangement" of organic nervous systems inside of bodies as well as their reflective or conscious potential: an "arrangement whose successive advances are inwardly reinforced . . . by a continual expansion and deepening of consciousness."[58]

The impact of Teilhard's thought on Soleri is well known and nicely captured by the catchphrase that began to circulate in the first workshops at Cosanti and Arcosanti, where every student was encouraged to read *The Phenomenon of Man* and other works: "Work hard, play hard, Teilhard."[59] More specifically, Soleri adapted Teilhard's model of expansion within contraction to his theories of architecture and ecology, insisting that, much like organic and mineral structures, human establishments were capable of undergoing a process of refinement, of complexification of form and function (as well as consciousness). The goal, therefore, was not dynamic equilibrium but material and spiritual *irreversibility.* Thus, distinct models of materialism and spatiotemporality became integral to Soleri's conception of ecological design. He began to speak of intensities, concentrations, and singularities rather than evenly distributed nodes and their balanced interconnections.

These considerations help to explain Soleri's core imperative of complexity–miniaturization–duration.[60] The first term in this chain, taken straight from Teilhard, refers to the literal complexity of organizational structures, which Soleri conceived as adhering at the atomic level and the cosmic scale alike. For Soleri, beyond mere survival, human life was complex. It involved myriad activities that were, conventionally speaking, nonproductive: scientific and artistic experimentation, enterprise, reflection, and so on. Cities, therefore, needed to be complex in both form and function, "membranes" that would facilitate rather than hinder humanity's poetic and instrumental relationship with the world. In *Arcology,* Soleri called for a "three-dimensional" city, a structure that would extend itself, not just vertically like the historical megalopolis or horizontally like suburban development, but in all directions simultaneously in a complex pattern of interconnecting and interweaving spaces and forms.

To use the word *extension* in this context is misleading, as Soleri's next design imperative was miniaturization, which demanded less an additive notion of building than an implosive force of urban energies. "The liveliness of man's world is hindered by the physical extension of his shelter and the spatial dilution of his institutions," Soleri wrote.[61] Arcology, therefore, entailed the enfolding of matter *into* itself, an elaboration of the interior of things (*pace* Teilhard) to their most highly developed state. Thus, in the case of cities, more and more functions and forms are contained in a single building or structure. Complexity plus miniaturization meant that cities could continue to grow, but their growth would be inward, not expansive. So, too, the humanity living in such structures would expand their consciousness by refining their interiors, allowing them to accommodate ever more complex patterns of mental and material interactions.

Duration, finally, was the evolutionary arc of these developments, the time it took for these material and spiritual elaborations to play out. For Soleri, duration was abstract time enlivened or given texture by human activity, urban activity.[62] Though Soleri discussed duration less than he did his other "imperatives," it seems fundamental to his ontology. Time is irreversible and almost immeasurable. It is possessed of a certain qualitative character that makes life fundamentally different from one moment to the next. Here, Soleri seemed to follow Henri Bergson, who, early in the century, wrote the following: "For our duration is not merely one instant replacing another; if it were, there would never be anything but the present—no prolonging of the past into the actual, no evolution, no concrete duration. Duration is the continuous progress of the past which gnaws into the future and which swells as it advances."[63] For Bergson, as for Teilhard, and then Prigogine after him (though in different ways), time was an irreversible material reality, something woven into the very fabric of existence.[64] In the case of living beings, it had a definite direction, which could yet never be determined, since the very consciousness that might describe it was itself caught up in its uneven flow. "The more we study the nature of time," Bergson continued, "the more we shall comprehend that duration means invention, *the creation of forms*, the continual elaboration of the absolutely new."[65]

Synthesizing Bergson's understanding of duration with Teilhard's cosmic teleology of complexity and miniaturization (or interiorization), Soleri posited the city as an eschatological instrument, an Apollonian technology producing temporary congelations in the reciprocal interplay of the vital and material forces shaping life itself.[66] As such, even though they were massive and obdurate things, his buildings were not static. They were understood rather as evolutionary waypoints, architecture in a state not of being but of becoming. Soleri thus reversed the typical utopian chronology: where many designers had opted to be prospective with their designs, to leave their structures open and modifiable with an eye to future developments, he envisioned his cities as the end point of a teleological sequence of the coevolution of natural systems and consciousness itself. This is why his arcologies seem to rise from the earth in a Heideggerian fashion, striving upward, only to involute upon themselves, dividing and individuating into complex interiors.

Esthetogenesis

These architectural/urban dynamics would have been inconceivable without the aesthetic impulse. Esthetogenesis, as Soleri termed it, was the conscious shaping of simple material structures into more complex ones; it represented will, discernment, and intentionality in man's relationship to his environment.[67]

Esthetogenesis was the infusion of spirit into matter and vice versa, in an ongoing process of volitional creation. It was the guiding principle that would lead to a more evolutionarily productive relationship between mind and matter. For Soleri, form was an embodiment of will in an antientropic structure, the conscious creation of forms that would, when interacted with or inhabited, induce human consciousness to evolve (enabling it to produce more refined forms, and so on). Soleri wrote his most sustained explication of esthetogenesis in 1970, while Arcosanti was just getting under way. He invoked the concept of duration to distinguish properly aesthetic creation from simple mechanical transformation:

> Process is the producer of change, but this is only half of the story, and not the most important, the instrumental half. I see change as of two kinds. The first kind is the change brought about by what I call "process." Process is the transformation of the inanimate world, the mineral and the technological world. . . . The most crucial character of process is that it is reversible. . . . The second kind of change is that brought about by what I call becoming. Becoming is irreversible and qualifies and is qualified by duration, the biopsychological time by whose beats life develops. . . .
>
> It is only in the esthetic phenomenon, the esthetogenesis of things, that process and becoming can come into fusion. There is where life must tend toward, to make full use of the energetic universe without itself being distracted from the tide of evolution and into a mechano-deterministic event, durationally indifferent, that is to say, reversible, ethically nil.[68]

For Soleri, aesthetic creation was born out of humanity's alienation from its environment and its "anguished" attempts to reinstantiate a motivated connection to the natural rhythms of the cosmos (not cyclical, but teleological). To consciously form matter was, in turn, to allow matter to form consciousness. Taking a position that seemed to synthesize (or forcibly suture) the aesthetic philosophies of Hegel and Nietzsche, Soleri stated emphatically, "If the origin was the indifferentiate, then one must move away from it by the creation of the differentiate."[69] As Spiro Kostof summarized, "To Soleri the ultimate role of man is that of an artist; the ultimate character of a city is to be a work of art."[70] But Soleri did not view the aesthetic as a defined set of practices or techniques resulting in a singular stylistic product. Rather, the aesthetic defined a charged field of the interactions of mind and matter. It was a zone wherein the structures of the human psyche pushed against the obdurate structures of matter like microtectonic plates, an "agonized" movement whose friction threw out new and complex structures that were natural and cultural simultaneously. Aesthetic intention imbued this laborious activity with a temporal impetus, an irreversibility that dictated ever more complex structures and, in so doing, chided both mind and matter into new evolutionary forms.

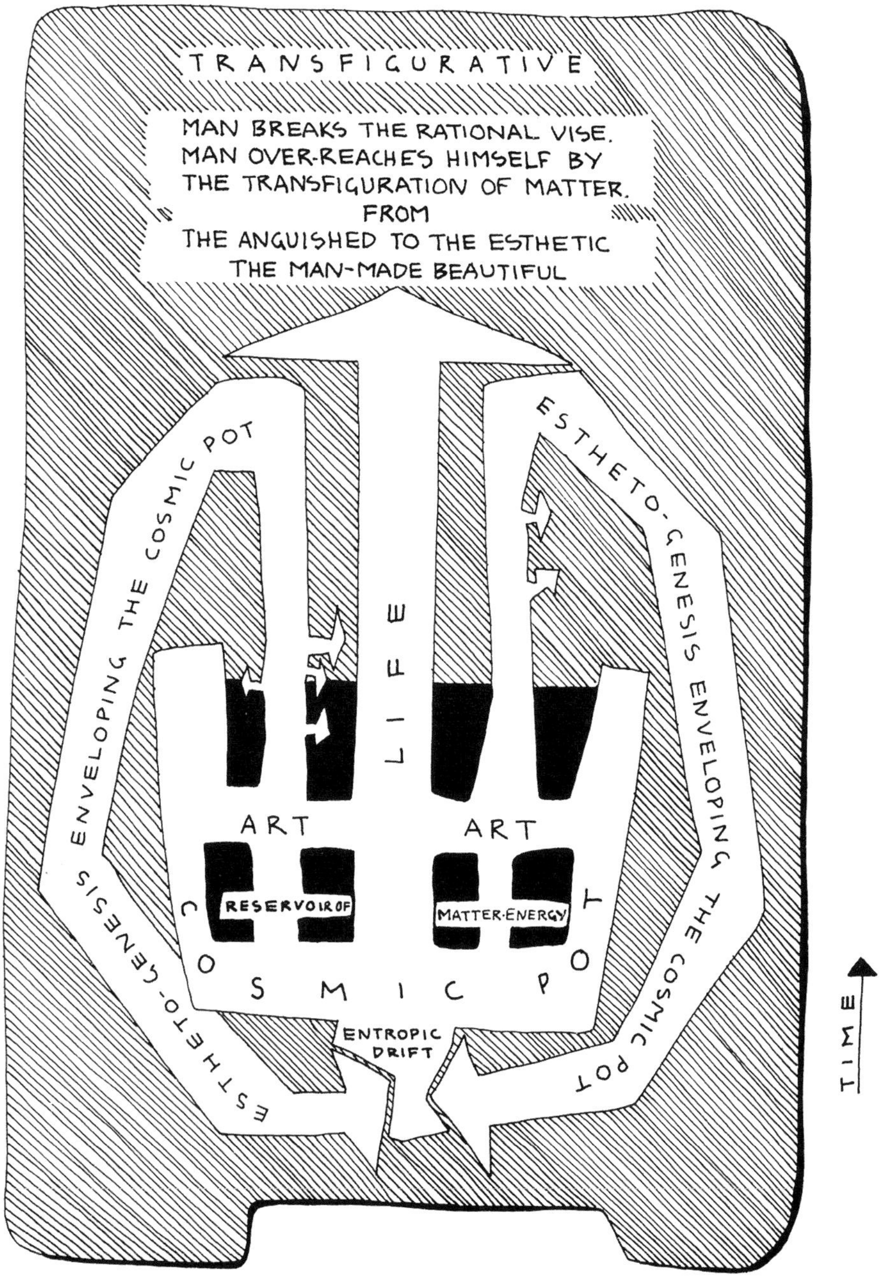

Figure 6.11. Paolo Soleri, Esthetogenesis. Figure 33 from *Arcology: The City in the Image of Man* (1969). Photograph by Cosanti Foundation.

But what of Soleri's aesthetic? It is remarkable the degree to which the style of his architecture and design objects has been ignored. As we have seen, commentators like David Greene found them, frankly, repugnant—outmoded and romantic, a rehashing of art nouveau serpentine lines and crusty organic forms. But these surface effects, if you will, belie a profound classicism wherein the Vitruvian motifs of circle and square dominate building modules as well as the plans and elevations of Soleri's largest and most complex designs. The impression one gets at both Cosanti and Arcosanti is of a kind of *modular organicism.* One is uncertain if the materials and techniques Soleri used imposed a kind of organic finish on his classical forms, or if he was instead bending the silt, cement, and bronze to his classicizing will.

He was distinctly aware of surface—the apses constructed from the silt casting method are almost pneumatic; one feels the tension of the bubble having had its solid insides sucked out to create not just a simple void but a vacuum. These skins then reveal their other function: they are pages, surfaces filled with signifiers etched into the mold and transferred to the taut cement. But the meaning of these symbols is murky at best. Soleri developed his own symbolic repertoire, including primitivizing male and female figures, fishes, and branch and leaf motifs, as well as abstract geometries that conform to the shape of the structure of which they are a part. Often, Soleri allowed the students working on-site to develop their own designs, so the ornamental programs lack the coherence of Le Corbusier's symbology, which they superficially resemble.

Much of Soleri's ornamental design is to be found in the famous windbells he began producing at Cosanti in the mid-1950s, initially in ceramic, and then in bronze. These were first molded in holes dug into the ground, and then with simple two-piece mold forms. The bells themselves are only part of the design; the elaborate armatures that support them are equally significant. These armatures often include a large horizontally oriented "yoke" that suggests an animal or vegetal form. To this are attached vertically hung armatures, decorative plates that catch the wind, and smaller chain-like forms that suggest vertebrae dangling from these various levels of support. There is a fusion in these forms between the synthetic and the organic—futurist lines of force culminate in "vortices" that suggest eyes, limbs, or sinews. There is something distinctly Gothic, or even Scythian, about them as they vacillate between the geometric and the animalian. Soleri himself and his foundation more generally tended to minimize the importance of the bells, describing them as a mere expedient for financial support and public outreach. As Elissa Auther has shown, however, the conception and aesthetic of the bells resonate with the idea of arcology at the largest scale.[71]

It is difficult to see the bells and the *brut* surfaces of Soleri's buildings as anything other than out of step with the technocratic ethos of the moment, as anything other than a countercultural response to the sleekness

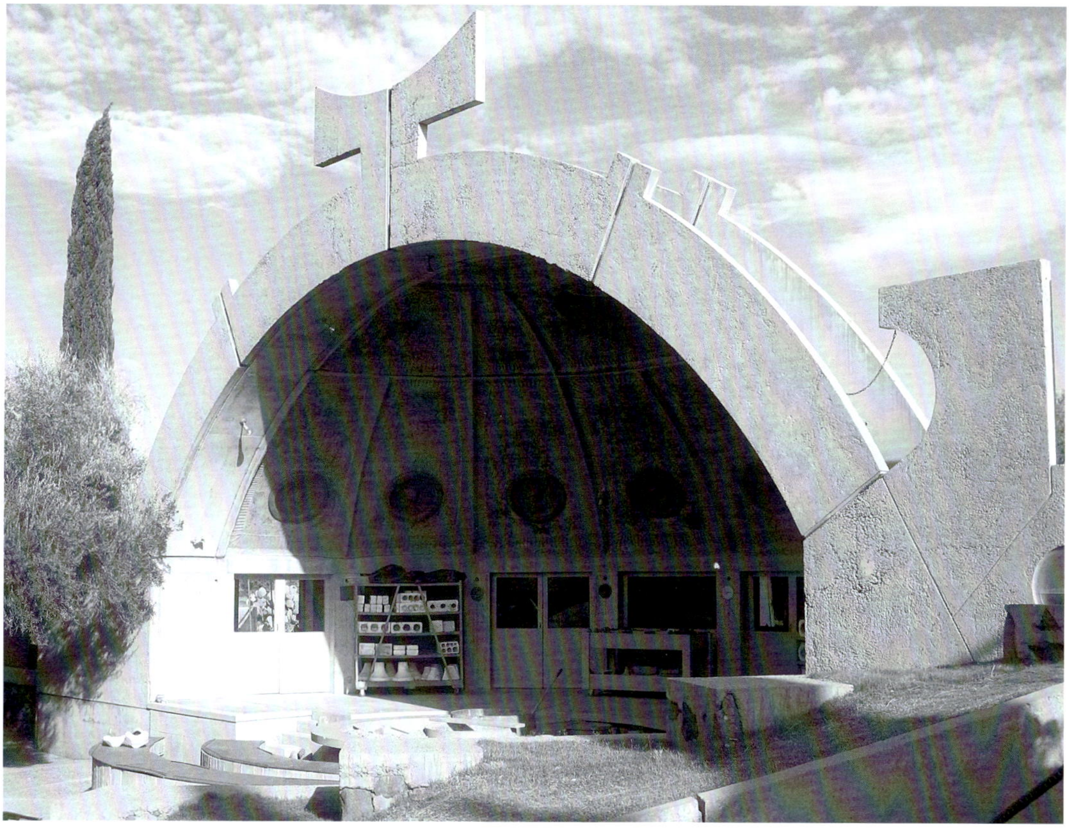

Figure 6.12. Paolo Soleri, Arcosanti, Ceramics Apse (1971–73). Photograph by Tomiaki Tamura.

of glass, steel, and silk screens. Banham himself had hinted at another reading, though, which was to connect Soleri to the materialist current in contemporary art—earthworks, for instance. There was a certain superficial resemblance, after all, between Soleri's apses rising up from the desert floor and Smithson's mounds and spirals scraped up from the earth. This reading would place Soleri and Smithson together at odds with the technological functionalism in design evident at this moment, opposite the systems aesthetic of Burnham, Fuller, and Kepes, for instance. Reinhold Martin has described this distance vis-à-vis the relationship between Kepes and Smithson.[72] In that instance, the modernist trope of organicism itself was the index of the antithetical orientations of the utopian modernist, on the one hand, and the artist who was "interested in collaborating with entropy," on the other.[73] Alessandra Ponte has pointed out the ironic proximity of Soleri's actual constructions to Smithson's entropic ideal.[74]

As we have seen, however, Soleri's stated understanding of the cosmic system could not have been further from Smithson's nonorganicism. It was likewise opposed to the cybernetically equilibrated organic systems proposed by Kepes. Soleri saw aesthetics as the surge of energy that could be introduced into a system, pushing it "far beyond equilibrium" to become an evolutionary catalyst, to produce entirely new formations of matter and consciousness.[75] His was a different kind of organicism altogether, one that recognized a vital impulse in even the basest material, and one that unified everything in the cosmos, not through a balanced net of interconnections but through a great, upward-turning and irreversible spiral. In this sense, Soleri's aesthetic organicism resembled that described by Henri Focillon, who took up Bergson's philosophy and likewise insisted on dismantling the mind/matter and form/content dualities that had informed Western art and science since the Renaissance.[76] Interestingly, Focillon's interest in identifying this aesthetic vitalism in ornament could have underwritten Soleri's willingness to modify his functionalist sentiments. For instance, in early Christian Irish manuscript illumination, Focillon wrote, "the interlace appears as a transitory, but endlessly renewed meditation on a chaotic universe that deep within itself clasps and conceals the debris or the seeds of humankind."[77]

Such a conception of vivified and aestheticized matter had also been described in *A Thousand Plateaus,* the landmark text by Gilles Deleuze and Félix Guattari, who, like their forebears Bergson and Focillon, sought to challenge the dichotomies fundamental to Western metaphysics.[78] *A Thousand Plateaus* was perhaps one of the last great holistic statements of the late twentieth century, compiled and written in France during the precise time span covered in this book. It contained the seeds of contemporary critical theory as well as vestiges of the formal structures of the counterculture. Indeed, Carlos Castaneda featured quite prominently in Deleuze and Guattari's formulations, where his ideas were often used to articulate the formal patterns constituting the deterritorialized subject the authors were attempting to describe. "In the course of Castaneda's books," they wrote, "the reader may begin to doubt the existence of the Indian Don Juan, and many other things besides. But that has no importance. So much the better if the books are a syncretism rather than an ethnographical study, and the protocol of an experiment rather than an account of an initiation."[79] They further noted:

> Castaneda illustrates, for example, the existence of a molecular perception to which drugs give us access (but so many things can be drugs): we attain a visual and sonorous microperception revealing spaces and voids, like holes in the molar structure. That is precisely what clarity is: the distinctions that appear in what used to seem full, the holes in what used to be compact; and conversely, where just before we saw end points of clear-cut segments, now there are indistinct fringes. . . . Everything now appears supple, with holes in fullness, nebulas in forms, and flutter in lines.[80]

Deleuze and Guattari eradicated distinctions between the organic and the synthetic, between form and substance, understanding these categories instead as intrinsic to dynamic organizational principles, which were

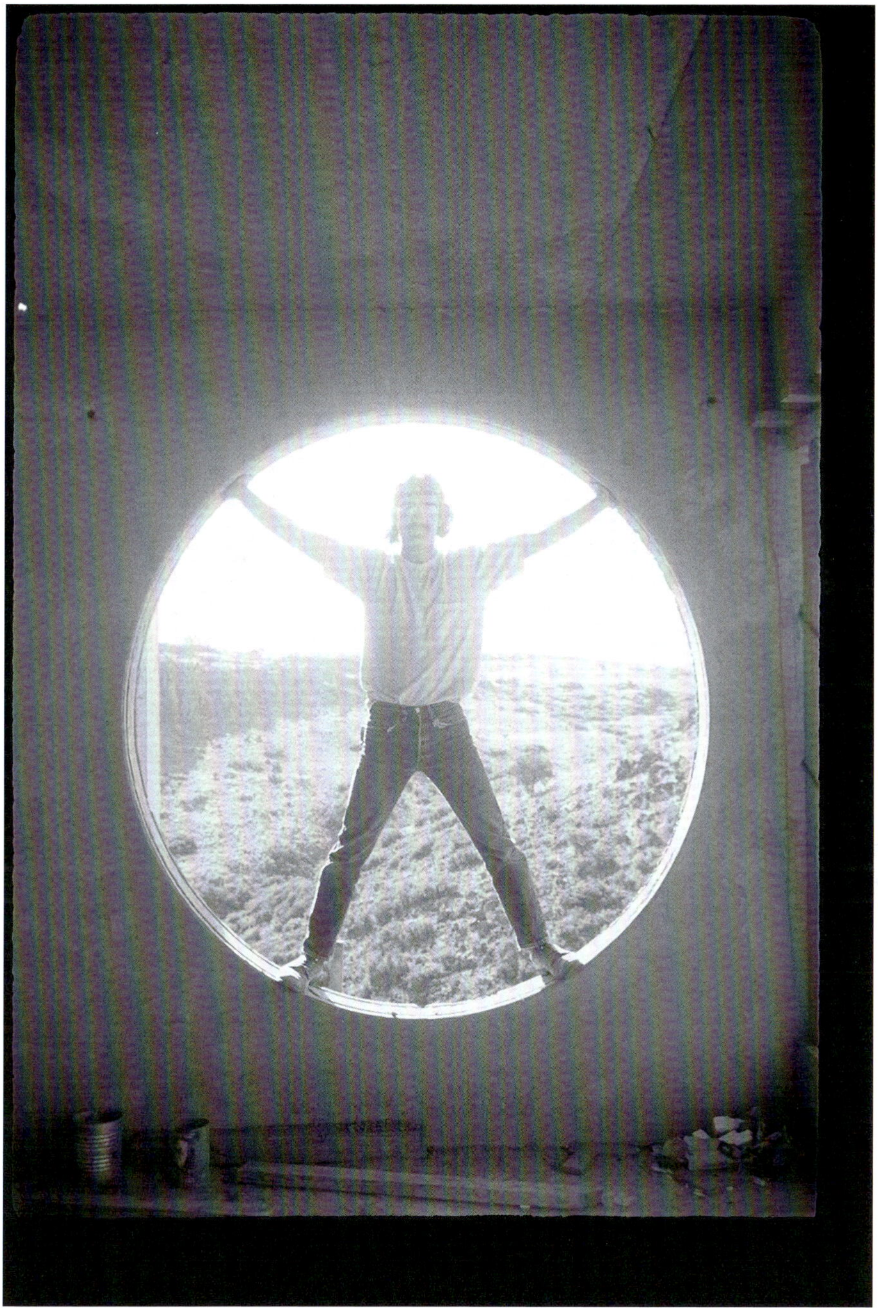

Figure 6.13. Arcosanti, December 1973. Copyright James Carnahan.

equal parts historical and material. Like Soleri, Deleuze and Guattari saw the cosmos as a complex series of patterns that comingled matter and mind, space and time, in never-ending flows and striations. Their view of the physical world also resembled that of Prigogine.[81] Like him, they saw life not as the exclusive domain of the organism but as a series of qualities that could manifest in various kinds of systemic organization. The patterns described by Deleuze and Guattari were both expansive and implosive; they had a temporality but not a teleology. And perhaps most important, their patterns offer us a view of a composite humanity, no longer whole and autonomous but perforated by ethereal energies and the flows of matter. In this view—and in contradistinction to Soleri—the subject is no longer at the center of the natural and technical systems surrounding her, and she thereby may be freed from the impossible task of balancing the energetic and spiritual dynamics of those systems, as well as from the imperative of never-ending (self) design.

Conclusion

A conclusion is a temporal device. Its utility here is as suspect as my synecdochic evocation of "the 1970s." All the more so as this has been a text about space, about a lifeworld advancing and retreating not by turns or diachronically but experientially. Change (ruptural, evolutionary, and teleological) was perceived and implemented in the preceding examples, but it felt here-and-there more than now-and-then. Nonetheless, periodization is demanded by both historical method and the conventions of academic writing. Can we place chronological brackets around the responsive environment? Yes, but the primary benefit of doing so would seem to be that such brackets allow us to perceive a spatial expansion and contraction of environmental response from the first years of modernity to our own moment. Rather than an origin, a maturity, and a dissipation, there is an eternal recurrence of environmental response as transcendentalism, positivism, vitalism, existentialism, determinism, constructionism, and the strange admixture of interpellation and self-actualization that we are currently experiencing.

Nonetheless, the 1970s seem worth dwelling on for several reasons. Heretofore, these years have been viewed as transitional at best. Thus, the radical technological ideas of the 1960s are seen as a prelude to the coalescing of our current network culture.[1] Further, the topological spaces of the visionary architecture of the postwar period are divested of their political contingency and understood as evolutionary forerunners to, and legitimators of, a new digital atmospherics.[2] Only recently have the years in between been given much critical attention, and even in these instances, the seventies have been marked by latencies, repressions, and uncanny foreshadowings rather than any exclusive qualities. The significance of these aporia has been suppressed in favor of a simplified narrative in which architecture was able to escape the reductive, behavioristic, and bureaucratic tendencies of design methods, environmental design, and social design by returning to its own semantic and cultural forms under the intellectual banners of theoretical formalism and postmodernism.[3] Here, I have lingered over these latencies and repressions in order to consider not only their temporal ramifications but their spatial ones.

But the point has not been to recuperate some exclusive or canonical importance for an arbitrarily chosen ten-year period. The point, rather, has been to locate its hinge. The hinge of the 1970s is precisely design itself, as the historically locatable emergence of a perceived ability to instrumentalize the conditioning mechanisms of environment. This was a moment at which the vast amounts of human data thrown out by the environmental research manifold seemed aggregable and deployable as so many responsive interfaces. "We are talking about man's environment," George Litwin, president of Intermedia Systems, Inc., said in 1974. "It's been here all along. It's been influencing us all along. What we are saying is: we can begin to have some control over the environmental influences on our behavior, attitudes, and motivation."[4] Contained in this single, rather trite corporate pitch is the entire ethos I have been evoking here—that some form of "control" could be woven into the fabric of environment itself. The implementation of this control was premised on design, a modality of design that required not an object to draft, form, and produce but an entire encompassing field of action. In this field were walls, ceilings, furniture, and apertures opening to endless exteriors that were equally structured by human contrivances. Further, this field required equipmental atmospheric conditioners such as light sources, sound filters, and air vents. Increasingly, this immersive field was crossed by wires carrying electronic impulses, by the sounds and sights of new media broadcasting new (and old) messages. And there was the computer interface, slowly integrating itself into the most intimate spaces of the human lifeworld. But equally present here was that other apparatus, the human organism, perceptually and cognitively probing its surroundings, grasping for the ergonomic surfaces of its environmental affordances, extending its innermost capacities, seeking out meaningful symbols, and testing the surface tension of its invisible yet obdurate culturally patterned bubbles.

The naïveté of the historical attempts on the part of the various (*pace* Sloterdijk and Sontag) TV technicians, electronics engineers, media theorists, architects, sculptors, psychologists, anthropologists, air and mood phenomenologists, neurologists, and relationship therapists to design such a thing as a responsive environment—their awkward literalness and inevitable essentialism—might be amusing were it not for their political, technical, and aesthetic valences. For who alive today does not feel newly opened, exposed, porous—more immersed in, and penetrated by, systems not entirely perceptible and even less controllable than ever before?

People are looking for environment now in ways they haven't for decades.[5] Their methods have constituted a (partial) repetition of the strategies of environmental explication that emerged circa 1970. In modes reminiscent of those of McLuhan and Kepes, implements, objects, extensions, tools, and, simply, things are once again being brought forth as indices of our relationship with the surrounding world. This has taken the form of granting agency to those things as *actors* alongside human subjects, for instance, in the work of Bruno Latour.[6] It has taken the form of granting to the very mechanisms of worldly invisibility and "withdrawal" a new ontological weight, as in the works of Graham Harman and other "speculative realists."[7] New materialisms—always forms of grappling with environmental response—are rampant.[8] To wit, there is a totally new conception of "correlationism" that has no apparent memory of the origins of that term in the postsurrealist techno-aesthetics of Frederick Kiesler![9] And perhaps the flip side of these models of nonhuman entities coacting in our world is the understanding that human activity is so unprecedentedly substantial as to have literally *covered* everything else, leaving its own stratum on the surface of the earth.[10]

It becomes apparent in these contemporary iterations (whether they are new or revivalist) that the romantic or phenomenological self—at the center of a private universe of unimpeded action—is compromised. Instead, we emerge, we interface, we become entangled, we concresce, we traject.[11] We are, to render these processes in a different discursive register, interpellated.[12] We are recognized as being immersed in formative processes instigated by various ideological or institutional apparatuses. By aggregating these theoretical terms here, I do not wish to efface their critical differences; rather, I want to draw attention to a series of patterns that are beginning to orient us once again toward various models of environmental response. Indeed, pattern itself has reentered the critical consciousness of various researchers as part of a new kind of formalism dealing with the virtual structures that exist in the space between subject and object. The literary critic Caroline Levine has even recently appropriated the notion of *affordances* in her work: "Let's now use affordances to think about form," she writes. "The advantage of this perspective is that it allows us to grasp both the specificity and generality of forms—both the constraints and possibilities that different forms afford, and the fact that those patterns and arrangements carry their affordances with them as they move across time and space."[13]

These philosophical and ecological elaborations are taking place alongside—or forming a ready-made foil for—emerging designerly approaches to human environment, in which new hardware and software insinuate themselves into our surroundings in ever-novel modalities of response. I have not attempted here to catalog or analyze these contemporary developments with the same sense of obsessiveness that has guided my overview of the historical instances. Perhaps I can't yet see them. Or perhaps they remain too "object oriented" (to borrow a phrase from Serge Boutourline) for my sensibilities. For no matter how ubiquitous they become—or fast, or miniaturized, or ethereal—they are nonetheless overly delimited by function, on the one hand, and by their placement in the network, on the other. They rhetorically insist on their utility. They strain toward the extremities of spectacle and disappearance.[14] They remain *applications* through and through.

We have also entered into a relationship with these applications that is based not on revelation but on a more problematic dialectic of appearance and strategic invisibility. If fifty years ago the patterns of environment seemed within the perceptual grasp of an extended humanity, today our extensions seem complicit in effacing their own conditioning mechanisms. They become so ubiquitous that they disappear. They are "spatialized" to such an extent that they seem to recede into an ideological ground rather than advance as objects of critical perception and interaction.[15] The endgame of what Sloterdijk described as modernist explication is not a form of complete technical accessibility but a kind of aesthetic elision. Unlike Vladimir Nabokov's son looking for the port in Saint-Nazaire in 1940, who becomes, once he catches sight of the ship's funnel, "the finder" who "cannot unsee what has been seen," not only can we unsee the "stratagems" of environment, we can do little else.[16]

My attempt to track a similar series of figure/ground reversals from half a century ago has therefore not seen me dwell on the hardware, the digitality, or the aesthetic effects of the various design proposals I historicize here. Nor have I made too many categorical statements about the nature of the responses or the positionality of the human subjects implicated in their systems. I have lingered instead, insofar as possible, in the spaces between these two—object and subject. This is the space of extension, affordance, and pattern. It is a space in which human possibility is facilitated or thwarted, drawn out or turned away, magnified or elided. This is the space of environment. It is a space in which politics and aesthetics are forever coforming.

In such a situation, design appears not as a means to introduce new objects into the world but rather as a *subtractive* activity. It becomes a method of removing blockages, reorienting relations, and understanding virtually everything as a dynamic interface between subject and surroundings. Here, design is a form of "environmental management," as Boutourline would suggest, the microadjustment of perceptual encounters, or the "programming of sensations," as Susan Sontag described. The failure of this project was not a technical one. It is not just a matter of time. It is not just a matter of technology becoming smart enough, physical enough, or malleable enough to allow the subject to pass through it unmolested, unmolded. Such a project negates the subject, as that entity is itself the by-product of scraping, of stoppage, of the slowing, congelation, and friction that produce it for the world.

"Each apparatus," Gilles Deleuze wrote of Michel Foucault's concerns in his late work, "has its way of structuring light, the way in which it falls, blurs and disperses, distributing the visible and the invisible, giving birth to objects which are dependent on it for their existence, and causing them to disappear." "Could this be," he asked, "the intrinsic aesthetic of modes of existence as the ultimate dimension of social apparatuses *[dispositifs]*?"[17] Far from being a reduction of Foucault's modeling of the apparatus to mere surface effects, such a formulation prods us to consider not just the political contents or outcomes of its procedures but the way these procedures are *formed*. Another way to approach this insidious problem is to ask: Is it possible to imagine an art history of the apparatus? A formal/critical narrative of the sensory regimes that allowed environment to come forward as a perceptible material—not only as a set of systemic forces or particles or ecological dependencies but as a suite of conditioning devices in culture as much as in nature? Such an art history would not have its traditional icons; it would have to content itself with virtual objects, with patterns whose rhythms and symmetries might be at least partially traced through various discursive and physical configurations, with shifting models or diagrams of response.

Such is the provisional project of this book: to trace the shifting forms of a newfound perceptual and technical capability and its friction with a new understanding of the environmental limits placed on human action. In this sense, the projects—intellectual and designerly—covered in the preceding chapters are therefore not designed things; they are not reducible to their materials, their structures, sensors, processors, or algorithmic operations. I have had no choice here other than to take up the diction of the 1970s, to use "environment" not as a stable ground or as a description of a circumscribed form but as a specific designation for a profoundly existential class of interactions. For there can be no environment without the subject to call *it* into being, to topologically confirm its manifold structures, outlines, textures, smells, pheromones, switches, track pads, and touch screens. There is no such thing as a subject free from these interactions. There is no humanity without them. Just as much as they are obviously collapsing in on one another at all times, they are the very basis of describing a difference, a distance, a border that is as liberating as it is constraining. Environment is not a monolithic imposition. It is something that rises up to meet us, to challenge us to push against it, resist its contingencies, and embrace its autonomies. This is the subject that has emerged here and there in the preceding study—not a centered, classical, free subject, but a dense and capable subject nonetheless: a subject who makes up in discernment what she lacks in absolute freedom of choice, a subject equipped with environmental capacities that allow her to distinguish sight from touch, an affordance from an obstacle, life from automation.

Notes

Introduction

1. Edward T. Hall, *The Hidden Dimension* (Garden City, N.Y.: Doubleday, 1966), 4.
2. Noortje Marres, *Material Participation: Technology, the Environment and Everyday Publics* (New York: Palgrave Macmillan, 2015), ix.
3. Lucy Bullivant, *Responsive Environments: Architecture, Art and Design* (London: Victoria and Albert Museum, 2006), 9.
4. Matt Shaw, "Interaction Packed: How Interaction Design and Immersive Environments Are Changing How We Relate to Architecture and Ourselves," *Architect's Newspaper,* November 4, 2015, 25, 29.
5. Alberto Pérez-Gómez, *Attunement: Architectural Meaning after the Crisis of Modern Science* (Cambridge: MIT Press, 2016), 7, 20. Another text that examines the ramifications of these issues is Ariane Lourie Harrison, ed., *Architectural Theories of the Environment: Posthuman Territory* (London: Routledge, 2013).
6. On connections between postwar design and the internet of things, see Justin McGuirk, "Honeywell, I'm Home! The Internet of Things and the New Domestic Landscape," *e-flux Journal,* no. 64 (April 2015), https://www.e-flux.com.
7. See "About," Morphocode, accessed June 18, 2017, https://morphocode.com; Data Walking, accessed June 18, 2017, http://datawalking.com; "Overview," Responsive Environments, MIT Media Lab, accessed June 18, 2017, https://www.media.mit.edu/groups/responsive-environments; "The Lab," Responsive Environments and Artifacts Lab, Harvard Graduate School of Design, accessed June 18, 2017, http://research.gsd.harvard.edu/real.
8. Sha Xin Wei, *Poiesis and Enchantment in Topological Matter* (Cambridge: MIT Press, 2013), 257.
9. Marshall McLuhan, "The Emperor's Old Clothes," in *The Man-Made Object,* ed. Gyorgy Kepes (New York: George Braziller, 1966), 94–95.
10. Gyorgy Kepes, "Art and Ecological Consciousness," in *Arts of the Environment,* ed. Gyorgy Kepes (New York: George Braziller, 1972), 11.
11. Jack Burnham, *Beyond Modern Sculpture: The Effects of Science and Technology on the Sculpture of This Century* (New York: George Braziller, 1968), 363.
12. Sean Wellesley-Miller, "Work Notes on the Need for a New Building Technology," in *The Responsive House,* ed. Edward Allen (Cambridge: MIT Press, 1974), 19, 21.
13. Myron W. Krueger, *Artificial Reality* (Reading, Mass.: Addison-Wesley, 1983), 43–44.
14. Beatriz Colomina and Mark Wigley, *Are We Human? Notes on an Archaeology of Design* (Zurich: Lars Müller, 2016), 103. See also Nick Axel, Beatriz

Colomina, Nikolaus Hirsch, Anton Vidokle, and Mark Wigley, eds., *Superhumanity: Design of the Self* (New York: e-flux Architecture, 2018).

15. These functions are nicely synthesized in an almost normative document titled *Responsive Environments: A Manual for Designers.* Although this book was published quite late (1985), it demonstrates the admixture of social and formal concerns that had been animating and disrupting design practice for the previous twenty years. Here, *responsiveness* is defined in a multifaceted way that draws on both the expertise of the professional architect/planner and the qualitative needs of end users, as those had been defined since the landmark publications of Jane Jacobs and Kevin Lynch, for instance. Or, in the words of the book's authors, "the idea that the built environment should provide its users with an essentially *democratic* setting, enriching their opportunities by maximising the degree of *choice* available to them. We call such places *responsive.*" Ian Bentley, Alan Alcock, Paul Murrain, Sue McGlynn, and Graham Smith, *Responsive Environments: A Manual for Designers* (London: Architectural Press, 1985), 9.
16. See Theodora Vardouli, "Who Designs? Technological Mediation in Participatory Design," in *Empowering Users through Design: Interdisciplinary Studies and Combined Approaches for Technological Products and Services,* ed. David Bihanic (Cham, Switzerland: Springer International, 2015), 13–41.
17. Trevor Pearce, "From 'Circumstances' to 'Environment': Herbert Spencer and the Origins of the Idea of Organism–Environment Interaction," *Studies in History and Philosophy of Biological and Biomedical Sciences* 41 (2010): 241–52.
18. Leo Spitzer, *Essays in Historical Semantics* (1948; repr., New York: Russell & Russell, 1968), 232–33.
19. One of the most seminal historical and philosophical treatments of these developments is Georges Canguilhem's "The Living and Its Milieu," in *Knowledge of Life,* ed. Paola Marrati and Todd Meyers, trans. Stefanos Geroulanos and Daniela Ginsburg (New York: Fordham University Press, 2008). See also Jakob von Uexküll, *A Foray into the Worlds of Animals and Humans,* trans. Joseph D. O'Neil (Minneapolis: University of Minnesota Press, 2010).
20. Peter Sloterdijk, *Foams: Spheres III,* trans. Wieland Hoban (London: Semiotext[e], 2016). While Sloterdijk's work uncannily evokes the spirit of the ways environment has been culturally elaborated, I do not mean here to assign to his oeuvre the status of singular explanatory cipher. Rather, Sloterdijk seems able to synthesize many of the materialist and ideological concerns of recent critical theory. I will cite examples as required in the following chapters, but here I signal several key sources, some of which will be upheld here, and some challenged: Jane Bennett, *Vibrant Matter: A Political Economy of Things* (Durham, N.C.: Duke University Press, 2010); Manuel De Landa, *A Thousand Years of Nonlinear History* (New York: Zone Books, 1997); Félix Guattari, *The Three Ecologies,* trans. Ian Pindar and Paul Sutton (London: Continuum, 2008); Timothy Ingold, *The Perception of the Environment: Essays on Livelihood, Dwelling and Skill* (London: Routledge, 2000); Caroline Levine, *Forms: Whole, Rhythm, Hierarchy, Network* (Princeton, N.J.: Princeton University Press, 2015); Timothy Morton, *Ecology without Nature: Rethinking Environmental Aesthetics* (Cambridge, Mass.: Harvard University Press, 2007).

21. See, for instance, Eugene P. Odum, *Ecology: The Link between the Natural and the Social Sciences* (New York: Holt, Rinehart and Winston, 1975).
22. This ambiguity fueled much of the foundational ecological writing of this period, including Murray Bookchin, *Our Synthetic Environment* (New York: Alfred A. Knopf, 1962); Rachel Carson, *Silent Spring* (Boston: Houghton Mifflin, 1962).
23. On environmental psychology, see William Ittelson, "Environmental Psychology and Architectural Planning" (paper presented at the American Hospital Association Conference on Hospital Planning, New York, 1964); Daniel Stokols, ed., *Perspectives on Environment and Behavior: Theory, Research, and Applications* (New York: Plenum Press, 1977). On ecological psychology, see Roger Barker, *Ecological Psychology* (Stanford, Calif.: Stanford University Press, 1968). On the interwar origins of "human ecology," see Jennifer S. Light, *The Nature of Cities: Ecological Visions and the American Urban Professions, 1920–1960* (Baltimore: Johns Hopkins University Press, 2009).
24. See Geoffrey Broadbent and Anthony Ward, eds., *Design Methods in Architecture* (London: Architectural Association, 1969); S. A. Gregory, ed., *The Design Method* (London: Butterworths, 1966); Gary T. Moore, ed., *Emerging Methods in Environmental Planning and Design* (Cambridge: MIT Press, 1970).
25. The Environmental Design Research Association (EDRA) was founded in 1968 and had its inaugural conference the following year in Chapel Hill, North Carolina. It was organized along with the Design Methods Group and Man–Environment Systems, a manifestation of ASMER, mentioned below. Henry Sanoff and Sidney Cohn, eds., *EDRA 1: Proceedings of the 1st Annual Environmental Design Research Association Conference* (Stroudsburg, Penn.: Dowden, Hutchinson & Ross, 1970). According to Henry Sanoff, one of EDRA's original protagonists, the association's founding arose from the very aesthetic and philosophical impulses of many of the other manifestations recorded here. "Although we believed in something that was not perceptible at the time," he wrote, "we had no illusions." Henry Sanoff, "EDRA: The Beginnings," excerpted in "About," Environmental Design Research Association, accessed December 15, 2016, http://www.edra.org.
26. The history of environmental design and these related institutional transformations has only recently coalesced, and only in piecemeal fashion. See, for instance, Arindam Dutta, ed., *A Second Modernism: MIT, Architecture, and the "Techno-Social" Moment* (Cambridge: MIT School of Architecture and Planning/MIT Press, 2013); Waverly Lowell, Elizabeth Byrne, and Betsy Frederick-Rothwell, *Design on the Edge: A Century of Teaching Architecture at the University of California, Berkeley, 1903–2003* (Berkeley: College of Environmental Design, University of California, 2009); Joanna Merwood-Salisbury, "Interior Design as Environmental Design: The Parsons Program in the 1960s," in *After Taste: Expanded Practice in Interior Design*, ed. Kent Kleinman, Joanna Merwood-Salisbury, and Lois Weinthal (New York: Princeton Architectural Press, 2012), 110–29; Kenny Cupers, ed., *Use Matters: An Alternative History of Architecture* (New York: Routledge, 2013); Anthony Raynsford, "Simulating Spatial Experience in the People's Berkeley: The Urban Design Experiments of Donald Appleyard and Kenneth Craik," *Design and Culture* 6, no. 1 (2014): 45–64.

27. On the Hochshule für Gestaltung, see Tomás Maldonado, "How to Fight Complacency in Design Education," *Ulm* 17–18 (1966): 14–20; Tomás Maldonado, *Design, Nature, and Revolution: Toward a Critical Ecology*, trans. Mario Domandi (Minneapolis: University of Minnesota Press, 2019). On the Institut de l'Environnement, see Tony Côme, *L'Institut de l'environnement: Une école décloisonnée* (Paris: Éditions B42, 2017).
28. On the role of the United Nations and the Ford Foundation in the consolidation of environmental research, see Felicity Scott, *Outlaw Territories: Environments of Insecurity/Architectures of Counterinsurgency* (New York: Zone Books, 2016).
29. ASMER was founded after discussions held at a meeting of the American Association for the Advancement of Science. The first chair of the new association was social psychologist Irwin Altman, and founding members included cultural geographer David Lowenthal and pioneer of environmental design Raymond Studer.
30. Emilio Ambasz, "Project Working Paper," in *The Universitas Project: Solutions for a Post-technological Society*, ed. Emilio Ambasz (New York: Museum of Modern Art, 2006), 23.
31. One of the foundational projects of environmental design resulted in Alexander Kira's book *The Bathroom: Criteria for Environmental Design* (Ithaca, N.Y.: Center for Housing and Environmental Studies, Cornell University, 1966).
32. Cary Wolfe has acknowledged the complex interplay of interior/exterior dynamics in several iterations of this theoretical history. Cary Wolfe, *Critical Environments: Postmodern Theory and the Pragmatics of the "Outside"* (Minneapolis: University of Minnesota Press, 1998).
33. For one example of the use of the phrase *environmental response* in psychology, see Brian Wells, "Individual Difference and Environmental Response," in *Environmental Psychology: Man and His Physical Setting*, ed. Harold M. Proshansky, William H. Ittelson, and Leanne G. Rivlin (New York: Holt McDougal, 1970), 483–92.
34. Jim Burns, *Arthropods: New Design Futures* (New York: Praeger, 1972), 7.
35. Susan Sontag, "One Culture and the New Sensibility," in *Against Interpretation* (1966; repr., New York: Anchor Books & Doubleday, 1990), 298.
36. Henry Sanoff and Sidney Cohn, preface to Sanoff and Cohn, *EDRA 1*, v.
37. Sontag, "One Culture," 301, emphasis added.
38. Sontag, "One Culture," 301–2.
39. Gyorgy Kepes, "The Artist's Role in Environmental Self-Regulation," in Kepes, *Arts of the Environment*, 184–85.

1. Invisible Environments

1. Ina Blom, *The Autobiography of Video: The Life and Times of a Memory Technology* (Berlin: Sternberg Press, 2016), 80.
2. One of the protagonists in this chapter, Erwin Straus, was instrumental in the late 1960s in reviving the Platonic notion of aisthesis, which entails a processual and mutually generative model of the object and act of perception "in which two very distinct potentialities are simultaneously actualized, the sensible (active) qualities of the world and the sensing (passive) powers of the sentient body." Harmon Chapman, "Aisthesis," in

Aisthesis and Aesthetics: The Fourth Lexington Conference on Pure and Applied Phenomenology, ed. Erwin W. Straus and Richard M. Griffith (Pittsburgh: Duquesne University Press, 1970), 7–8. Straus's own contribution on this occasion was an analysis of the phenomenon of the "phantom limb" and its invocation of a particular model of aisthesis. Both psychological and physiological explanations of this problem were lacking, for Straus, precisely because they misunderstood the relations among self, body, and environment, in which "the animal is in an open relation, in a contraposition, facing its environment, meaningfully responding to its structure and events." Erwin W. Straus, "The Phantom Limb," in Straus and Griffith, *Aisthesis and Aesthetics*, 144. Present-day readers will think immediately of Jacques Rancière's *Aisthesis: Scenes from the Aesthetic Regime of Art* (London: Verso, 2013).

3. Announcement pamphlet for the exhibition *TV as a Creative Medium*, Howard Wise Gallery, New York, 1969, n.p.
4. Serge Boutourline, "The Concept of Environmental Management," *Dot Zero* 4 (September 1967): 11.
5. Serge Boutourline Jr. to Edward T. Hall, January 9, 1964, box 1, folder 18, Edward T. Hall Papers, Special Collections, University of Arizona Libraries (hereafter ETH Papers).
6. Boutourline to Hall, January 9, 1964.
7. Serge Boutourline Jr., Michel A. Carré, Michel François-Poncet, Peter S. Miller, Clifford D. Oldham, Paul B. Rosenberg, and William M. Twaddle, *Individual Creativity and the Corporation* (Boston: Manufacturing Group 25 and Institute of Contemporary Art, 1959). Although this was a group project, Boutourline and Rosenberg maintained the copyright on the publication, indicating perhaps that they were the primary contributors.
8. Boutourline et al., *Individual Creativity*, 3.
9. John Harwood, *The Interface: IBM and the Transformation of Corporate Design, 1945–1976* (Minneapolis: University of Minnesota Press, 2011), 197.
10. Robert S. Weiss and Serge Boutourline Jr., *Fairs, Pavilions, Exhibits, and Their Audiences* (1962). This bound booklet was, according to its introduction, commissioned by David Holzman and Robert S. Lee of IBM Communications Research as part of that firm's interest in public outreach and education. It was never widely distributed.
11. Susan Buirge, *Une vie dans l'espace de la danse* (L'Isle-sur-la-Sorgue: Le Bois d'Orion, 2012), 43.
12. John Harwood, "Early Computer Interface Design: Two Archival Documents," *Design Issues* 31, no. 2 (Spring 2015): 44.
13. Harwood, *The Interface*, 197–98.
14. Harwood, "Early Computer Interface Design," 44.
15. Serge Boutourline Jr. to Robert S. Lee, memo, November 24, 1964, reprinted in Harwood, "Early Computer Interface Design," 45–54.
16. Boutourline to Lee, memo, November 24, 1964, 48–49.
17. Serge Boutourline, "Some Notes on the World's Fair," unpublished manuscript, circa 1962, n.p., box 1, folder 18, ETH Papers.
18. Boutourline, "Some Notes on the World's Fair," n.p.
19. Boutourline, "Some Notes on the World's Fair," n.p.
20. Yalkut includes an interview with Susan Buirge and Boutourline in his paper "Electronic Zen: The Alternate Video Generation" (unpublished

manuscript, 1984), pt. 2, p. 1, accessed April 20, 2016, http://vasulka.org/archive/Artists10/Yalkut,Jud/ElectronicZen.pdf.

21. Announcement pamphlet for *TV as a Creative Medium.*
22. Jud Yalkut, "Interview with Eric Siegel," *Radical Software* 1, no. 2 (Autumn 1970): 21.
23. Marita Sturken, "TV as a Creative Medium: Howard Wise and Video Art," *Afterimage* 11, no. 10 (May 1984): 7.
24. Howard Wise to Richard Deagen, April 28, 1969, Howard Wise Papers, Special Collections, Harvard Art Museums.
25. Yalkut, "Electronic Zen," pt. 2, p. 4.
26. "An outgrowth of the early happenings, [this type of 'humanistic theater'] is headed, through psychology, movement exploration, and group interaction, toward a greater consciousness of self—in relation to the world, not in isolation from it. The extent of the audience's or the performer's participation depends more on what he gives to the other elements of his environment than on what he takes from them." Marcia B. Siegel, "Televanilla: Theater in Two Flavors," *New York,* June 10, 1968, 57–58.
27. Yalkut, "Electronic Zen," pt. 2, p. 3. The quote in this passage is taken from a review of *Televanilla* published in the *Village Voice.*
28. Yalkut, "Electronic Zen," pt. 2, p. 6.
29. "The Concept of Environmental Management" was reprinted in 1970 in the first real textbook of environmental psychology, Proshansky et al.'s *Environmental Psychology,* 496–500. The page numbers in subsequent citations of the essay refer to the original publication in *Dot Zero.*
30. Boutourline, "Concept of Environmental Management," 11.
31. Boutourline, "Concept of Environmental Management," 11.
32. Boutourline, "Concept of Environmental Management," 12.
33. Serge Boutourline Jr., "Notes on 'Object-Oriented' and 'Signal-Oriented' Approaches to the Definition of the Physical World Which Surrounds Individual Human Beings," unpublished typescript, circa 1968, Howard Wise Papers, Special Collections, Harvard Art Museums.
34. Boutourline, "Notes on 'Object-Oriented' and 'Signal-Oriented' Approaches," 3.
35. Yalkut, "Electronic Zen," pt. 1, pp. 12–14.
36. Boutourline, "Notes on 'Object-Oriented' and 'Signal-Oriented' Approaches," 3.
37. See Hashim Sarkis, "Disoriented: Kevin Lynch, around 1960," in Dutta, *Second Modernism,* 408–10.
38. James J. Gibson, *The Perception of the Visual World* (Boston: Houghton Mifflin, 1950); James J. Gibson, *The Senses Considered as Perceptual Systems* (Boston: Houghton Mifflin, 1966); James J. Gibson, *The Ecological Approach to Visual Perception* (Boston: Houghton Mifflin, 1979).
39. Gibson, *Perception of the Visual World,* 2.
40. On Gibson's sources and the development of his thought, see Edward S. Reed, *James J. Gibson and the Psychology of Perception* (New Haven, Conn.: Yale University Press, 1988); Thomas Lombardo, *The Reciprocity of Perceiver and Environment: The Evolution of James J. Gibson's Ecological Psychology* (Hillsdale, N.J.: Lawrence Erlbaum, 1987).
41. Gibson, *Perception of the Visual World,* 43.
42. Gibson, *Perception of the Visual World,* 55.

43. Gibson, *Perception of the Visual World,* 56.
44. "Visual space perception, Gibson argued from 1950 onward, does not consist of seeing the third dimension, but of seeing a laid-out environment, cluttered with objects above and along the ground surface." Reed, *James J. Gibson,* 141.
45. Gibson, *Senses Considered as Perceptual Systems,* 4.
46. Gibson, *Senses Considered as Perceptual Systems,* 5.
47. Michael James Braund, "The Structures of Perception," *Kritike* 2, no. 1 (June 2008): 124.
48. The nature of this "structure" is developed in Braund, "Structures of Perception."
49. Gibson, *Ecological Approach,* 3.
50. Gibson, *Ecological Approach,* 116, 118.
51. Gibson, *Ecological Approach,* 138.
52. Don Norman, *The Psychology of Everyday Things* (New York: Basic Books, 1988). Much like the scientists Gibson was criticizing, Norman locates the success or failure of interactions in the design of exterior objects, and not in the processes of interaction that take place among emergent entities. Nonetheless, the concept has become fundamental to human–machine interface design.
53. Gibson, *Ecological Approach,* 40.
54. Gibson, *Ecological Approach,* 138.
55. Gibson, *Ecological Approach,* 138
56. James J. Gibson, "Notes on Affordances," in *Reasons for Realism: Selected Essays of James J. Gibson,* ed. Edward Reed and Rebecca Jones (Hillsdale, N.J.: Lawrence Erlbaum, 1982), 411. As Amanda Boetzkes has recently written, linking Gibson's theories to both a Heideggerian understanding of the *thing* and Graham Harman's contemporary elaborations on it, "The concept of affordance walks the line between an objective perception as such and the possibilities of uncovering new meanings, sensations, and interpretive reactions." Amanda Boetzkes, "Interpretation and the Affordance of Things," in *Heidegger and the Work of Art History,* ed. Amanda Boetzkes and Aron Vinegar (Surrey: Ashgate, 2014), 275.
57. In this sense, it is instructive to compare Merleau-Ponty's and Gibson's respective approaches to images: Maurice Merleau-Ponty, "Cézanne's Doubt," in *The Merleau-Ponty Aesthetics Reader: Philosophy and Painting,* ed. Galen A. Johnson (Evanston, Ill.: Northwestern University Press, 1993), 59–75; James J. Gibson, "The Ecological Approach to the Visual Perception of Pictures," *Leonardo* 11, no. 3 (1978): 227–35. See also Ingold, *Perception of the Environment.* Ingold cross-references Gibson's perceptual models with Bateson's epistemological ones.
58. Erwin Straus, *The Primary World of Senses: A Vindication of Sensory Experience* (New York: Free Press, 1963), 24.
59. Straus, *Primary World of Senses,* 33.
60. Straus, *Primary World of Senses,* 43–44.
61. Straus, *Primary World of Senses,* 243–45.
62. Straus, *Primary World of Senses,* 243.
63. Straus, *Primary World of Senses,* 244–47.
64. Erwin Straus, "The Forms of Spatiality," in *Phenomenological Psychology: Background, Foreground, and Influences* (New York: Basic Books, 1966), 4.

65. Straus, "Forms of Spatiality," 4.
66. Straus, "Forms of Spatiality," 5–6.
67. Straus, "Forms of Spatiality," 7.
68. Straus, "Forms of Spatiality," 16.
69. Gregory Bateson, *Steps to an Ecology of Mind* (New York: Ballantine Books, 1972).
70. Bateson, *Steps to an Ecology of Mind,* xxv.
71. Bateson, *Steps to an Ecology of Mind,* xxii.
72. Bateson, *Steps to an Ecology of Mind,* xxv.
73. Bateson, *Steps to an Ecology of Mind,* 271.
74. Bateson, *Steps to an Ecology of Mind,* 275.
75. Bateson, *Steps to an Ecology of Mind,* 276.
76. Bateson, *Steps to an Ecology of Mind,* 276.
77. See Bernard Dionysius Geoghegan, "Editor's Introduction: What Bound the Double Bind?," *Grey Room,* no. 66 (Winter 2017): 103–9.
78. Bateson, *Steps to an Ecology of Mind,* 206–7.
79. Bateson, *Steps to an Ecology of Mind,* 211.
80. G. Spencer-Brown, *Laws of Form* (London: Allen & Unwin, 1969), v.
81. Bateson, *Steps to an Ecology of Mind,* xii.
82. R. G. Collingwood, *The Idea of Nature* (Oxford: Oxford University Press, 1945); R. G. Collingwood, *The Principles of Art* (Oxford: Oxford University Press, 1938).
83. Collingwood, *Principles of Art,* 109–11.
84. Collingwood, *Principles of Art,* 109.
85. Collingwood, *Idea of Nature,* 133–34.
86. Collingwood, *Idea of Nature,* 135.
87. Collingwood, *Idea of Nature,* 146–47.
88. Alfred North Whitehead, *Process and Reality* (Cambridge: Cambridge University Press, 1929); Samuel Alexander, *Space, Time, and Deity,* 2 vols. (London: Macmillan, 1920).
89. Bateson, *Steps to an Ecology of Mind,* 451.
90. Bateson, *Steps to an Ecology of Mind,* 458–59. Bateson gave another nice example in a 1964 letter: "Is the efficiency of the windshield in the system, me-plus-automobile, to be measured in terms of its contribution to gas mileage? Or in terms of its contribution to my metabolism?" Gregory Bateson to Charles D. Michener, June 11, 1964, box 11, folder 463, Gregory Bateson Papers, Special Collections and Archives, University of California, Santa Cruz (hereafter Bateson Papers).
91. On Bateson and art, see William Kaizen, "Steps to an Ecology of Communication: *Radical Software,* Dan Graham, and the Legacy of Gregory Bateson," *Art Journal* 67, no. 3 (2008): 86–106.
92. Stephen Nachmanovitch, "Bateson and the Arts," *Kybernetes* 36, nos. 7–8 (2007): 1122.
93. Gregory Bateson, call for papers sent as a letter to select individuals, November 5, 1968, box 36, folder 1480, Bateson Papers.
94. Bateson's lack of exposure to architectural culture was signaled by the fact that he had just gotten his hands on a copy of Christopher Alexander's *Notes on the Synthesis of Form* and concluded that Alexander "might have things to say to us." See box 36, Bateson Papers.
95. Gregory Bateson to Jaquelin Robertson (architect running the New York

Office of Mid-Town Planning and Development), June 18, 1970, document B5-65, p. a, box 39, Bateson Papers.

96. Gregory Bateson, position paper, 1970, document B5-10, pp. B5–10d, box 39, binder 5, Bateson Papers.
97. Gregory Bateson, "Restructuring the Ecology of a Great City," *Radical Software* 1, no. 3 (Spring 1971): 2–3; Gregory Bateson, "Ecology and Flexibility in Urban Civilization," in *Steps to an Ecology of Mind*, 494–505.
98. Ronald Kline, *The Cybernetics Moment* (Baltimore: Johns Hopkins University Press, 2015), 233.
99. Bateson, "Ecology and Flexibility," 494.
100. Simon Sadler, "The Bateson Building, Sacramento, California, 1977–81, and the Design of a New Age State" *Journal of the Society of Architectural Historians* 75, no. 4 (December 2016): 469–89.
101. Sim Van der Ryn, quoted in Sadler, "The Bateson Building," 473.
102. Gregory Bateson, *Mind and Nature: A Necessary Unity* (1979; repr., Cresskill, N.J.: Hampton Press, 2002).
103. Bateson, *Mind and Nature*, 7.
104. Bateson, *Mind and Nature*, 7.
105. Bateson, *Mind and Nature*, 14.
106. Bateson, *Mind and Nature*, 7. The allusion to the primrose was a famous motif for Bateson and derived from William Wordsworth's *Peter Bell*: "A primrose by a river's brim; / A yellow primrose was to him; / And it was nothing more." Bateson invoked this quote to characterize the attitude of modern science.
107. Bateson, *Mind and Nature*, 5.
108. Bateson, *Mind and Nature*, 11.
109. Bateson, *Mind and Nature*, 14.
110. Marshall McLuhan, "Address at Vision 65," *American Scholar* 35, no. 2 (Spring 1966): 201.
111. Marshall McLuhan, *Understanding Media: The Extensions of Man* (New York: McGraw-Hill, 1964).
112. Alton J. De Long, "Physical and Conceptual Space: The Value of Simultaneous Involvement and Detachment—A Review of *The Medium Is the Rear View Mirror*," *Man–Environment Systems* 1, no. 5 (May 1971): 13.
113. Marshall McLuhan, *The Gutenberg Galaxy: The Making of Typographic Man* (Toronto: University of Toronto Press, 1962), 1.
114. Marshall McLuhan to Edward T. Hall, September 16, 1964, box 8, folder 28, ETH Papers.
115. McLuhan, "Address at Vision 65," 201. McLuhan disseminated his thoughts on environment through several different publications in the period 1966–68. According to Richard Cavell, McLuhan's ideas on the topic began to take shape in the paper he presented at the Vision 65 conference. Richard Cavell, *McLuhan in Space: A Cultural Geography* (Toronto: University of Toronto Press, 2002), 174. McLuhan's works addressing environment include the following: "Art as Anti-environment," *Art News Annual* 31 (1966): 55–57 (this version was written at the behest of Harold Rosenberg); "Emperor's Old Clothes"; "The Relation of Environment to Anti-environment," in *The Human Dialogue: Perspectives on Communication*, ed. Floyd W. Matson and Ashley Montagu (New York: Free Press, 1967), 39–47; "The Invisible Environment: The Future of an Erosion," *Perspecta* 11 (1967): 162–67;

and "Environment as Programmed Happening," in *Knowledge and the Future of Man,* ed. Walter J. Ong (New York: Holt, Rinehart and Winston, 1968), 113–24.

116. Cavell, *McLuhan in Space,* 52.
117. McLuhan, "Invisible Environment," 166.
118. McLuhan, "Invisible Environment," 164.
119. Marshall McLuhan to Edward T. Hall, June 22, 1965, box 8, folder 28, ETH Papers.
120. McLuhan, "Relation of Environment to Anti-environment." See also Kenneth R. Allan, "Marshall McLuhan and the Counterenvironment: The Medium Is the Massage," *Art Journal* 73, no. 4 (Winter 2014): 22–45.
121. Marshall McLuhan, "A Dialogue," in *McLuhan: Hot and Cool,* ed. Gerald Stearn (New York: Signet Books, 1969), 263. McLuhan was referring to Sigfried Giedion, *Space, Time and Architecture: The Growth of a New Tradition* (Cambridge, Mass.: Harvard University Press, 1941).
122. McLuhan, "Environment as Programmed Happening," 124.
123. For an overview of the interactions of Tyrwhitt, McLuhan, and Giedion, see Michael Darroch, "Bridging Urban and Media Studies: Jaqueline Tyrwhitt and the Explorations Group, 1951–1957," *Canadian Journal of Communication* 33 (2008): 147–69. See also Mark Wigley, "Network Fever," *Grey Room,* no. 4 (Summer 2001): 95–96.
124. Edmund Carpenter and Marshall McLuhan, "Acoustic Space," in *Explorations in Communication,* ed. Edmund Carpenter and Marshall McLuhan (Boston: Beacon Press, 1966), 67. Another source for McLuhan was Rudolf Arnheim's description of "spatial resonance" in his book *Radio,* trans. Margaret Ludwig and Herbert Read (London: Faber & Faber, 1936). My thanks to John Harwood for this reference. See also Emily Thompson, *The Soundscape of Modernity* (Cambridge: MIT Press, 2002); Carlotta Daro, *Avant-garde sonores en architecture* (Dijon: Presses du Réel, 2013).
125. For more on McLuhan's and Carpenter's conceptions of acoustic space and actual spatial experience (in this case, of the vast spaces of Northern Canada), see Alessandra Ponte, *The House of Light and Entropy* (London: Architectural Association, 2014), 135–68.
126. Sigfried Giedion, "Space Conception in Prehistoric Art," in Carpenter and McLuhan, *Explorations in Communication,* 86.
127. Sigfried Giedion, *Mechanization Takes Command* (Oxford: Oxford University Press, 1948); Sigfried Giedion, *Architecture, You, and Me: The Diary of a Development* (Cambridge, Mass.: Harvard University Press, 1958); Sigfried Giedion, *The Eternal Present,* vol. 1, *The Beginnings of Art* (New York: Bollingen Foundation, 1962); Sigfried Giedion, *The Eternal Present,* vol. 2, *The Beginnings of Architecture* (New York: Bollingen Foundation, 1964).
128. Spyros Papapetros, "Modern Architecture and Prehistory: Retracing *The Eternal Present* (Sigfried Giedion and André Leroi-Gourhan)," *RES: Anthropology and Aesthetics,* nos. 63/64 (Spring/Autumn 2013): 185. Papapetros is speaking here of the first volume of *The Eternal Present,* but his characterization applies generally to the first sections of the second volume as well.
129. Papapetros, "Modern Architecture and Prehistory," 189. In the long run, however, Giedion resisted the most radical implications of acoustic space. According to Michael Darroch, when Giedion was in Toronto in 1955 he

was reticent about engaging McLuhan on the subject. Tyrwhitt was likewise hesitant, telling McLuhan that "the only space architects can handle is physical space, which is basically visual space." Jaqueline Tyrwhitt, quoted in Darroch, "Bridging Urban and Media Studies," 166. When broaching the subject in *The Beginnings of Art,* the first volume of *The Eternal Present,* Giedion acknowledged that caves were in fact structured as acoustic spaces, but his contemporary correlative example was not McLuhan's acoustic environment, but rather Le Corbusier's *éspace indicible,* with its reverberating "plastic acoustics." Giedion, *Eternal Present,* 1:526–28.

130. McLuhan, "Environment as Programmed Happening," 118.
131. Giedion, *Eternal Present,* 2:525.
132. I discuss the specifics of McLuhan's engagement with *The Eternal Present* in another version of this section, published as Larry Busbea, "McLuhan's Environment: The End (and *The Beginnings*) of Architecture," *Aggregate,* December 11, 2015, http://www.we-aggregate.org.
133. Henri Lefebvre, *The Production of Space,* trans. Donald Nicholson-Smith (Oxford: Blackwell, 1991), 127.
134. McLuhan, "Invisible Environment," 164, 165.
135. I use this litany of older and newer critical terms to indicate the futility of precisely identifying McLuhan's intellectual sources. Certainly, phenomenology was operative in his understanding of environment. He granted art a revelatory role very similar to the one Heidegger recognized (as an entity that might make a "world" available from the brute and inaccessible "earth"). Like Merleau-Ponty, he sought a reunification of the senses that scientific method and Cartesian thought had alienated from one another. But his understanding of the human sensorium vis-à-vis environment was equally informed by a certain positivism: the idea that certain social and natural "climates" would be determinative for different peoples. Given McLuhan's antipathy toward Marxism, it is not surprising that he sought out other models for accounting for the ideological mechanisms of this relationship, from the American transcendentalists to the biological theory of milieu as described by Claude Bernard. The postwar period provided a plethora of models for describing the ways in which human perception is shaped from "outside," from the writings on scientific method by Thomas Kuhn to the cultural economics of McLuhan's colleague Harold Innis to B. F. Skinner's behaviorism to the social linguistics of Benjamin Lee Whorf.
136. Marshall McLuhan, "An Interview with Marshall McLuhan," by Eli Bornstein, *Structurist,* no. 6 (January 1966), 61.
137. Peter Sloterdijk, *Terror from the Air,* trans. Amy Patton and Steve Corcoran (Los Angeles, Semiotext[e], 2009).
138. McLuhan, "Environment as Programmed Happening," 118.
139. McLuhan, "Environment as Programmed Happening," 113, 124.
140. McLuhan, "Environment as Programmed Happening," 115.
141. McLuhan, "Invisible Environment," 167, emphasis added. Even into the next decade, McLuhan continued to have enthusiasm for the types of experiences provided by cities: "The city is a place for the heightening of human awareness by providing the greatest possible range and diversity of space for dialogue." Marshall McLuhan and Barrington Nevitt, *Take Today: The Executive as Dropout* (New York: Harcourt Brace Jovanovich, 1972), 29.
142. Marshall McLuhan to Edward T. Hall, August 24, 1964, box 8, folder 28,

ETH Papers. McLuhan was likely gearing this description toward Hall, as he was obsessed with culturally contingent patterns of environmental interaction—patterns that were, unsurprisingly, invisible to those caught within them. See Edward T. Hall, *The Silent Language* (1959; repr., New York: Anchor Books, 1973); Hall, *Hidden Dimension.*

143. Marshall McLuhan to Jaqueline Tyrwhitt, May 11, 1964, in Marshall McLuhan, *Letters of Marshall McLuhan,* ed. Matie Molinaro, Corinne McLuhan, and William Toye (New York: Oxford University Press, 1987), 298–99. This thesis was most rigorously (if obtusely) explored in the image/text juxtapositions of McLuhan's collaboration with Harley Parker, *Through the Vanishing Point: Space in Poetry and Painting* (New York: Harper & Row, 1968). See also the 1973 film *Picnic in Space,* in which McLuhan and Parker have a dialogue over a jazz sound track and montaged images of Piet Mondrian's *Broadway Boogie Woogie.*

144. McLuhan, "Emperor's Old Clothes," 94–95.

2. Pattern Watchers

1. For more on the specific ways in which patterns and environment were connected for designers at this moment, see Larry Busbea, "Pattern Watchers I: Environmental Seeing, c. 1970," in *The Culture of Nature in the History of Design,* ed. Kjetil Fallan (London: Routledge, 2019), 31–43.
2. Christopher Alexander to Edward T. Hall, April 30, 1970, box 1, folder 4, ETH Papers.
3. Brockman wrote to Hall of his new book: "Manuscript is on the way—would appreciate any comments—the 'inspiration' for the book was [a] story you related the evening we met 2 yrs ago—about the cave man saying 'we're talking'—its an attempt to kill off 'man' and deal with the operant transactional level." John Brockman to Edward T. Hall, February 15, 1969, box 2, folder 4, ETH Papers. Hall responded: "I really do think the fact that man was not aware that he talked for up to half a million years is extraordinarily important and that just the mere realization was the crossing of a kind of boundary. It's this realization that I've tried to communicate in *The Silent Language* and *The Hidden Dimension.*" Edward T. Hall to John Brockman, February 20, 1969, box 2, folder 4, ETH Papers. Brockman also acknowledges Hall as his source of inspiration in the publication; see John Brockman, *By the Late John Brockman* (Toronto: Macmillan, 1969), 21.
4. We might in this sense draw a connection between Hall's thought and Bruno Latour's actor-network-theory, which sees a kind of radical leveling of interacting elements within dynamic systems. See Bruno Latour, *Reassembling the Social: An Introduction to Actor-Network-Theory* (Oxford: Oxford University Press, 2005).
5. Edward T. Hall and George L. Trager, *The Analysis of Culture* (Washington, D.C.: Foreign Service Institute, 1953).
6. Ray L. Birdwhistell, *Kinesics and Context: Essays on Body Motion Communication* (Philadelphia: University of Pennsylvania Press, 1970), 5.
7. Edward T. Hall, *An Anthropology of Everyday Life: An Autobiography* (New York: Doubleday, 1992), 211.
8. Hall, *Silent Language,* 10.
9. Hall, *Silent Language,* 12, 13.

10. Edward T. Hall, "Patterns and Systems in Communication: A Plea to Anthropologists," undated abstract, box 43, folder 23, ETH Papers.
11. Hall, *Silent Language,* 111
12. See Peter L. Berger and Thomas Luckmann, *The Social Construction of Reality: A Treatise in the Sociology of Knowledge* (New York: Anchor Books, 1966).
13. Hall, *Silent Language,* 111, 113.
14. Hall, *Silent Language,* 114–15. Hall's use of the idea of sets here can be traced to his earliest anthropological publications. See Hall and Trager, *Analysis of Culture,* 46.
15. Hall, *Silent Language,* 124.
16. Hall, *Silent Language,* 124.
17. Jane Jacobs, *The Death and Life of Great American Cities* (New York: Random House, 1961); Kevin Lynch, *The Image of the City* (Cambridge: MIT Press, 1960). Interestingly, Hall and his friend McLuhan were both critical of Lynch for his exclusive emphasis on vision as the primary orienting faculty in the urban environment.
18. The first publication to describe proxemics systematically was Edward T. Hall, "A System for the Notation of Proxemic Behavior," *American Anthropologist* 65, no. 5 (October 1963): 1003–26. Hall then published *The Hidden Dimension* (1966), which was about the cultural implications of proxemics but did little to advance it methodologically. Finally, a more or less complete notation system, designed for computer processing, was published in 1974: Edward T. Hall, *Handbook for Proxemic Research* (Washington, D.C.: Society for the Anthropology of Visual Communication, 1974).
19. Hall, "System for the Notation of Proxemic Behavior," 1003. By 1966, Hall defined proxemics as "the interrelated observations and theories of man's use of space as a specialized elaboration of culture." Hall, *Hidden Dimension,* 1.
20. Hall, "System for the Notation of Proxemic Behavior," 1022.
21. Maurice Grosser, *The Painter's Eye* (New York: Rinehart, 1951); Alexander Dorner, *The Way beyond "Art"* (1947; repr., New York: New York University Press, 1958); Ernö Goldfinger, "The Sensation of Space," *Architectural Review* 90 (November 1941): 128–31; Ernö Goldfinger, "Urbanism and Spatial Order," *Architectural Review* 90 (December 1941): 163–66; Ernö Goldfinger, "The Elements of Enclosed Space," *Architectural Review* 91 (January 1942): 5–8.
22. Hall, *Anthropology of Everyday Life,* 187–89.
23. Hall, *Hidden Dimension,* xi. I will return to Hall's use of the term "extension" below.
24. Hall, *Hidden Dimension,* 2.
25. Hall, *Hidden Dimension,* 4.
26. John J. Christian, Vagn Flyger, and David E. Davis, "Factors in the Mass Mortality of a Herd of Sika Deer, *Cervus nippon,*" *Chesapeake Science* 1, no. 2 (June 1960): 79–95; John B. Calhoun, "Population Density and Social Pathology," *Scientific American* 206, no. 2 (February 1962): 139–48.
27. John B. Calhoun, quoted in Hall, *Hidden Dimension,* 24.
28. Tom Wolfe, "O Rotten Gotham—Sliding Down into the Behavioral Sink," *New York,* supplement to the *World Journal Tribune* (1966), reprinted in Tom Wolfe, *The Pump House Gang* (New York: Bantam Books, 1968), 233.

"If I remember that day," Wolfe recalled, "we first went to Grand Central. We did all that, went down in the subways, walked around in the middle of Manhattan a bit; then *New York* magazine hired a car. We got in the car. There was a driver so we could both talk and look at things, and we went all through Harlem and all over the place." Tom Wolfe, "'Tom Wolfe' by David Bellamy," in *Conversations with Tom Wolfe*, ed. Dorothy Scura (Jackson: University Press of Mississippi, 1990), 54.

29. Wolfe, "O Rotten Gotham," 233–34. For more on the popular reception of "the sink," see Edmund Ramsden and John Adams, "Escaping the Laboratory: The Rodent Experiments of John B. Calhoun and Their Cultural Influence," *Journal of Social History* 42, no. 3 (Spring 2009): 761–97.
30. Hall, *Hidden Dimension*, 105.
31. Hall, "System for the Notation of Proxemic Behavior," 1005. Hall credited Goffman's description of "the stuff of encounters" from Erving Goffman, "Alienation from Interaction," *Human Relations* 10, no. 1 (February 1957): 47–60, though that exact phrase is never used in that source. Goffman and Hall were friends whose work would intersect in many ways. Goffman, however, was interested more in the "stagecraft" of human interaction (its presumably conscious aspects), while Hall's focus was on those factors below the threshold of cognizance.
32. Hall, "System for the Notation of Proxemic Behavior," 1006–7. Later, this list of proxemic dimensions would expand to nineteen. See Hall, *Handbook for Proxemic Research*, 3.
33. Hall, *Handbook for Proxemic Research*, 3.
34. Despite Hall's efforts, few others were interested in adopting proxemics as a science. One exception was O. Michael Watson, who published *Proxemic Behavior: A Cross-Cultural Study* (The Hague: Mouton, 1970).
35. Hall, *Handbook for Proxemic Research*, 14.
36. Edward T. Hall to Marshall McLuhan, February 8, 1971, box 8, folder 29, ETH Papers.
37. Hall, *Handbook for Proxemic Research*, 6.
38. Hall, *Handbook for Proxemic Research*, 27.
39. Hall, *Handbook for Proxemic Research*, 12.
40. Edward T. Hall to Kevin Lynch, November 7, 1961, box 8, folder 18, ETH Papers.
41. Phillip Thiel, "A Sequence-Experience Notation for Architectural and Urban Spaces," *Town Planning Review* 32, no. 1 (April 1961): 33.
42. Goldfinger, "Elements of Enclosed Space," 5.
43. Goldfinger, "Sensation of Space," 130.
44. Hall, *Hidden Dimension*, 108.
45. Hall, *Silent Language*, 146–47.
46. Hall, *Hidden Dimension*, 77.
47. The term *spherological* comes from Sloterdijk, *Foams*.
48. Hall, *Hidden Dimension*, 121.
49. Hall himself cautioned, however, that proxemics "can never tell the designer how to design, only some of the things he should consider." Edward T. Hall, "Proxemics and Design," *Design & Environment* 2, no. 4 (Winter 1971): 58.
50. Edward T. Hall to John Entenza, February 10, 1964, box 5, folder 23, ETH Papers.

51. Mildred Hall and Edward Hall, *The Fourth Dimension in Architecture: The Impact of Building on Man's Behavior* (Santa Fe, N.M.: Sunstone Press, 1975), 7.
52. Hall and Hall, *Fourth Dimension in Architecture,* 21.
53. Hall and Hall, *Fourth Dimension in Architecture,* 8.
54. For a contemporary echo of these concerns, see Galen Cranz, *Ethnography for Designers* (London: Routledge, 2016).
55. Sam A. Sloan, "Translating Psycho-Social Criteria into Design Determinants," in *Environmental Design: Research and Practice,* proceedings of EDRA 3/AR8 conference, ed. William J. Mitchell (1972), 14.5.1–14.5.10.
56. Sloan, "Translating Psycho-Social Criteria," 14.5.1.
57. Sloan, "Translating Psycho-Social Criteria," 14.5.10.
58. Sloan, "Translating Psycho-Social Criteria," 14.5.1.
59. Sloan, "Translating Psycho-Social Criteria," 14.5.4.
60. Sloan, "Translating Psycho-Social Criteria," 14.5.1.
61. Sloan, "Translating Psycho-Social Criteria," 14.5.9.
62. Sloan, "Translating Psycho-Social Criteria," 14.5.10.
63. "Alexander and his group studied the transit systems of New York, Chicago, Philadelphia and Toronto; talked with a cross section of those involved in transit, from administrators to janitors to passengers; consulted a number of behavioral scientists; and fed their findings through computers." "BART: The Bay Area Takes a Billion Dollar Ride," *Architectural Forum* 124, no. 6 (June 1966): 49.
64. Christopher Alexander, *Notes on the Synthesis of Form* (Cambridge, Mass.: Harvard University Press, 1964); Christopher Alexander, "From a Set of Forces to a Form," in Kepes, *Man-Made Object*; Christopher Alexander and Barry Poyner, "The Atoms of Environmental Structure" (working paper no. 42, Center for Planning and Development Research, Institute of Urban and Regional Development, University of California, Berkeley, 1966); Christopher Alexander, "A City Is Not a Tree," *Architectural Forum* 122, no. 1 (April 1965): 58–62; Christopher Alexander, "A City Is Not a Tree, Part 2," *Architectural Forum* 122, no. 2 (May 1965): 58–61.
65. Alexander and Poyner, "Atoms of Environmental Structure," 1.
66. Molly Steenson, *Architectural Intelligence: How Designers and Architects Created the Digital Landscape* (Cambridge: MIT Press, 2017), 36–37.
67. Alexander, "From a Set of Forces."
68. Alexander, *Notes on the Synthesis of Form,* 16.
69. Alexander, *Notes on the Synthesis of Form,* 18.
70. Alexander, *Notes on the Synthesis of Form,* 19.
71. Alexander, *Notes on the Synthesis of Form,* 19.
72. See Kimberly Dovey, "The Pattern Language and Its Enemies," *Design Studies* 11, no. 1 (January 1990): 3–9.
73. All quotes in the preceding paragraph are from Alexander, "From a Set of Forces," 96.
74. Alexander, "From a Set of Forces," 100.
75. Christopher Alexander and Marvin Manheim, *The Use of Diagrams in Highway Route Location* (Research Report R62–3, Civil Engineering Systems Laboratory) (Cambridge: School of Engineering, MIT, 1962). He noted that on this occasion, the authors preferred the term "requirement" to "force."

76. See Steenson, *Architectural Intelligence,* 21–76; Mary Louise Lobsinger, "Two Cambridges: Models, Methods, Systems, and Expertise," in Dutta, *Second Modernism,* 652–85; Alise Upitis, "Alexander's Choice: How Architecture Avoided Computer-Aided Design c. 1962," in Dutta, *Second Modernism,* 474–505; Sean Keller, "Fenland Tech: Architectural Science in Postwar Cambridge," *Grey Room,* no. 23 (Spring 2006): 40–65; Philip Steadman, "Research in Architecture and Urban Studies in Cambridge in the 1960s and 1970s: What Really Happened," *Journal of Architecture* 21, no. 2 (2016): 291–306.
77. Christopher Alexander, Sara Ishikawa, and Murray Silverstein, with Max Jacobson, Ingrid Fiksdahl-King, and Shlomo Angel, *A Pattern Language: Towns, Buildings, Construction* (New York: Oxford University Press, 1977), xxxvii.
78. Christopher Alexander, *The Timeless Way of Building* (New York: Oxford University Press, 1979), 83.
79. Alexander, *Timeless Way of Building,* 19–40. "There is a central quality which is the root criterion of life and spirit in a man, a town, a building, or a wilderness. This quality is objective and precise, but it cannot be named" (19).
80. Alexander, *Timeless Way of Building,* 84.
81. Alexander, *Timeless Way of Building,* 89–90
82. Alexander, *Timeless Way of Building,* 91.
83. Alexander, *Timeless Way of Building,* 94.
84. Hall, *Handbook for Proxemic Research,* 79.
85. Hall, *Handbook for Proxemic Research,* 14.
86. This is not to say that Alexander was totally insensitive to cultural patterns. He acknowledged, for instance, that a "Chinese kitchen" was a different pattern than a Western kitchen. Alexander, *Timeless Way of Building,* 94.

3. Responsive Environments

1. "Elytra Filament Pavilion, Victoria and Albert Museum, 2016," Institute for Computational Design and Construction, University of Stuttgart, accessed October 13, 2016, http://icd.uni-stuttgart.de/?p=16443.
2. Menges's work is discussed further in Mario Carpo, *The Second Digital Turn: Design beyond Intelligence* (Cambridge: MIT Press, 2017), 40–54.
3. Chris Salter offers a larger historical overview of "responsive environments" under the heading of "performance." Salter's work is incredibly helpful in mapping this entire field, however. Chris Salter, *Entangled: Technology and the Transformation of Performance* (Cambridge: MIT Press, 2010), 303–48.
4. See Lisa Tilder and Beth Blostein, eds., *Design Ecologies: Essays on the Nature of Design* (New York: Princeton Architectural Press, 2010).
5. James Nisbet, *Ecologies, Environments, and Energy Systems in Art of the 1960s and 1970s* (Cambridge: MIT Press, 2014). See also Mark Crinson, *Nothing Less Than Literal: Architecture after Minimalism* (Cambridge: MIT Press, 2004); Hal Foster, *The Art–Architecture Complex* (London: Verso, 2011).
6. See Bullivant, *Responsive Environments.* The work of Branko Kolarevic is especially helpful for its chronicling of both the historical and contempo-

rary architectural works in this vein: Branko Kolarevic and Ali Malkawi, eds., *Performative Architectures: Beyond Instrumentality* (London: Routledge, 2005); Branko Kolarevic, "Exploring Architecture of Change," in *ACADIA 09: ReForm—Proceedings of the 29th Annual Symposium of the Association for Computer Aided Design in Architecture,* ed. Tristan d'Estree Sterk and Russell Loveridge (Fargo, N.D.: ACADIA, 2009). See also Anthony Burke and Therese Tierney, eds., *Network Practices: New Strategies in Architecture and Design* (New York: Princeton Architectural Press, 2007); Michael Fox and Miles Kemp, *Interactive Architecture* (New York: Princeton Architectural Press, 2009). Laurent Stalder has chronicled some of the key moments in the history of responsive architecture. See Laurent Stalder, "Air, Light, and Air-Conditioning," *Grey Room,* no. 40 (Summer 2010): 84–99; Laurent Stalder, "François Dallegret's Machine World," in *God & Co.: François Dallegret beyond the Bubble,* ed. Alessandra Ponte, Laurent Stalder, and Thomas Weaver (London: Architectural Association, 2011), n.p.

7. See Jonathan Hill, "The Edison Responsive Environment: Its Development and Its Use," *Innovations in Education and Training International* 7, no. 1 (1970): 29–42.
8. Alan Anderson and Omar K. Moore, "Autotelic Folk Models," *Sociological Quarterly* 1 (1959): 204–16.
9. For some basic details regarding early experiments, see "Education: O.K.'s Children," *Time,* November 7, 1960. See also Omar Khayyam Moore, "Autotelic Responsive Environments and Exceptional Children," in *Experience Structure and Adaptability,* ed. O. J. Harvey (New York: Springer, 1966), 169–216; Omar Khayyam Moore and Alan R. Anderson, *Environment and Exceptional Children* (Hamden, Conn.: Responsive Environments Foundation, 1962).
10. Barbara Sanderson and Daniel Kratochvil, *The Edison Responsive Environment Learning System; or, The Talking Typewriter* (Palo Alto, Calif.: American Institutes for Research, 1972).
11. Richard Kobler and Omar K. Moore, Educational System and Apparatus, U.S. Patent 3,281,959, filed April 6, 1962; issued November 1, 1966.
12. Moore, "Autotelic Responsive Environments," 172.
13. For a history and critique of environmental determinism in architecture, see Simon Richards, *Architect Knows Best: Environmental Determinism in Architecture Culture from 1956 to the Present* (London: Routledge, 2012).
14. See, for instance, Dean Hawkes, *The Environmental Imagination: Techniques and Poetics of the Architectural Environment* (New York: Taylor & Francis, 2007).
15. Reyner Banham, *The Architecture of the Well-Tempered Environment* (Chicago: University of Chicago Press, 1966).
16. Banham distinguishes three types of architectural environmental control: "selective" control, which attempts to keep unwanted environmental exigencies outside; "conservative" control, which attempts to keep desirable exigencies inside; and "regenerative" control, which overrides the inside/outside dichotomy through active mechanics. Banham, *Architecture of the Well-Tempered Environment,* 22–25.
17. Michael Osman provides a contemporary take on this type of architectural technology in *Architecture's Visible Hand: Architecture and Regulation in America* (Minneapolis: University of Minnesota Press, 2018). See also Luis

Fernández-Galiano, *Fire and Memory: On Architecture and Energy,* trans. Gina Cariño (Cambridge: MIT Press, 2000).

18. Banham, *Architecture of the Well-Tempered Environment,* 277.
19. Reyner Banham, *The Architecture of the Well-Tempered Environment,* 2nd ed. (Chicago: University of Chicago Press, 1984), 292.
20. Banham, *Architecture of the Well-Tempered Environment,* 2nd ed., 292.
21. Richard Neutra, *Survival through Design* (New York: Oxford University Press, 1954), 4.
22. Banham, *Architecture of the Well-Tempered Environment,* 208; Neutra, *Survival through Design,* 5.
23. Neutra, *Survival through Design,* 202.
24. Furthermore, Lavin tells us, these contrasting emphases would go on to characterize the diverging paths of architecture as a discipline at this historical juncture, with a technoscientific branch moving toward environmental design even as a new emphasis on the internal codes of architectural meaning was producing the first "autonomous" monuments of postmodernism. Sylvia Lavin, *Form Follows Libido: Architecture and Richard Neutra in a Psychoanalytic Culture* (Cambridge: MIT Press, 2004), 139–44.
25. This despite the fact that he was present at one of the most significant design methods symposia of the period. See Nigel Cross, ed., *Design Participation: Proceedings of the Design Research Society's Conference, Manchester, September 1971* (London: Academy Editions, 1972).
26. McLuhan, "Environment as Programmed Happening," 115.
27. Umberto Boccioni, "Technical Manifesto of Futurist Sculpture" (1912), trans. Richard Chase, in *Futurism,* ed. Joshua C. Taylor (New York: Museum of Modern Art, 1961), 131; Italian text from Umberto Boccioni, "La scultura futurista," in *I manifesti del futurismo,* ed. F. T. Marinetti (Florence: Edizione di Lacerba, 1914), 79–80.
28. Nancy J. Troy, *The De Stijl Environment* (Cambridge: MIT Press, 1983), 3.
29. Victor Papanek, "A Bridge in Time: An Attempt at Non-Euclidean Aesthetics," in Marshall McLuhan, *Verbi-Voco-Visual Explorations* (New York: Something Else Press, 1967), 1–10 (pagination is nontraditional). Richard Cavell has noted that Papanek later renounced the content of this article as mostly inspired by McLuhan and not representative of his own views. Cavell, *McLuhan in Space,* 113.
30. Alexander Dorner, quoted in Papanek, "Bridge in Time," 8.
31. Dorner, *Way beyond "Art,"* 103–5.
32. Papanek, "Bridge in Time," 8.
33. Wolfgang Paalen (1939), quoted in Papanek, "Bridge in Time," 9.
34. Papanek, "Bridge in Time," 9; Cavell, *McLuhan in Space,* 173–74.
35. Alberto Pérez-Gómez has recently characterized it as an example of an "embodied" model of architectural space and sensorial user engagement. See Pérez-Gómez, *Attunement,* 104–5.
36. Frederick J. Kiesler, "On Correalism and Biotechnique: A Definition and Test of a New Approach to Building Design," *Architectural Record* 86, no. 3 (September 1939): 60–75.
37. Kiesler, "On Correalism and Biotechnique," 61. Kiesler's elaboration of correalism would span thirty years. See Frederick Kiesler, "Notes on Architecture: The Space House," *Hound & Horn* 7, no. 2 (January–March

1934), 293–97; Frederick Kiesler, "Manifeste du corréalisme," *L'Architecture d'Aujourd'hui* (June 1949); Frederick Kiesler, "Second Manifesto of Correalism," *Art International* 9, no. 2 (March 1965): 16–17; Frederick Kiesler, *Inside the Endless House* (New York: Simon & Schuster, 1966).

38. On the connections between Kiesler's work and the larger discourse of biomimetics and technology, see Marie-Pier Boucher, "Architectures of Aliveness: Building beyond Gravity," in *The Routledge Companion to Biology in Art and Architecture*, ed. Charissa Terranova and Meredith Tromble (New York: Routledge, 2017), 177–78.
39. Kiesler, "On Correalism and Biotechnique," 64–65.
40. Stephen Phillips, "Toward a Research Practice: Frederick Kiesler's Design Correlation Laboratory," *Grey Room*, no. 38 (Winter 2010): 103.
41. Though the emphasis in this essay was very technical and objective rhetorically, Kiesler never let go of the fundamental belief in aesthetic experience as one of the unifying forces of the environments he described. See, for instance, Frederick Kiesler, "Design-Correlation: Marcel Duchamp's 'Big-Glass,'" in *Frederick J. Kiesler: Selected Writings*, ed. Siegfried Gohr and Gunda Luyken (Stuttgart: Verlag Gerd Hatje, 1996), 38–41.
42. Kiesler, "On Correalism and Biotechnique," 61.
43. Kiesler, "On Correalism and Biotechnique," 65.
44. Kiesler, "On Correalism and Biotechnique," 67.
45. On the psychosexual aspects of the Space House, see Beatriz Colomina, "La Space House et la psyche de la construction," in *Frederick Kiesler: Artiste-architecte* (Paris: Centre Georges Pompidou, 1996), 67–76.
46. As Phillips writes, "Kiesler endeavored to create more socially conscious and economically viable building environments that might ensure the ease and fluidity of human interactions within their evolving technological surroundings." Stephen J. Phillips, *Elastic Architecture: Frederick Kiesler and Design Research in the First Age of Robotic Culture* (Cambridge: MIT Press, 2017), 4.
47. "The reason for this superficial interpretation of reality [of acknowledging matter alone] lies in the limitation of man's senses in relation to the forces of the universe." Kiesler, "On Correalism and Biotechnique," 61. "Nature is so compact and so condensed that each innermost particle would open an endless world to us if we had strong enough lenses in our eyes and enough cells in our frontal lobes to see and grasp it. We don't. But the artists present us that world outright." Kiesler, *Inside the Endless House*, 18.
48. Reinhold Martin, *The Organizational Complex* (Cambridge: MIT Press, 2003), 46.
49. Gyorgy Kepes, *The Language of Vision* (Chicago: Paul Theobold, 1944); Gyorgy Kepes, ed., *The New Landscape in Art and Science* (Chicago: Paul Theobold, 1956); Gyorgy Kepes, ed., *Arts of the Environment* (New York: George Braziller, 1972).
50. Kepes, *Language of Vision*, 30.
51. See Martin, *Organizational Complex*; Orit Halpern, *Beautiful Data: A History of Vision and Reason since 1945* (Durham, N.C.: Duke University Press, 2014), 79–144; Christopher Hight, *Architectural Principles in the Age of Cybernetics* (New York: Routledge, 2008); John R. Blakinger, "Artist under Technocracy: Gyorgy Kepes and the Cold War Avant-Garde" (PhD diss., Stanford University, 2016); Anna Vallye, "The Middle Man: Kepes's Instruments," in Dutta, *Second Modernism*, 144–85.

52. Gyorgy Kepes, quoted in Martin, *Organizational Complex*, 67.
53. Martin, *Organizational Complex*, 66.
54. As Bill Arning puts it, for Kepes "there exists immediately before us hard-to-fathom reality of order and meanings. Our blindness to this reality is a result of improper training. To see it, we need a special perception that can be learned. Once we can see this new reality, a plethora of seemingly intractable world problems and risks to the survival of humankind become solvable." Bill Arning, "Gyorgy Kepes' Vision + Value, 1965–1972" (master's thesis, Tufts University, 2008), 9.
55. McLuhan, "Emperor's Old Clothes."
56. Arning, "Gyorgy Kepes' Vision + Value," 138–39.
57. Kepes, "Art and Ecological Consciousness," 1.
58. Kepes, "Art and Ecological Consciousness," 3.
59. Kepes, "Art and Ecological Consciousness," 11.
60. See Judith Wechsler, "Gyorgy Kepes," in *Gyorgy Kepes: The MIT Years: 1945–1977* (Cambridge: MIT Press, 1978), 7–19.
61. Typescripts of these essays, some of which are undated but seem to share the diction and style of Kepes's writing circa 1969, are preserved in microfilm reel 5313, Gyorgy Kepes Papers, 1925–89, Archives of American Art, Washington, D.C. (hereafter Kepes Papers).
62. Gyorgy Kepes, untitled manuscript, undated, n.p., reel 5313, Kepes Papers.
63. Gyorgy Kepes, "Responding to the Impacts of Environment" (1969–70), 3, reel 5313, Kepes Papers.
64. Gyorgy Kepes, "Man-Made Environment," undated, 3, emphasis added, reel 5313, Kepes Papers.
65. Gyorgy Kepes, "The Lost Pageantry of Nature," *ArtsCanada*, December 1968, 33.
66. Kepes, "Art and Ecological Consciousness," 11.
67. Kepes, "Artist's Role in Environmental Self-Regulation," 167.
68. Kepes, "Artist's Role in Environmental Self-Regulation," 171.
69. Kepes, "Artist's Role in Environmental Self-Regulation," 178.
70. Kepes, "Artist's Role in Environmental Self-Regulation," 184.
71. Kepes, "Artist's Role in Environmental Self-Regulation," 184–85.
72. Caroline Jones, "Artist/System," in Dutta, *Second Modernism*, 506–49.
73. On the postwar development of constructivism, see Benjamin Buchloh, "Cold War Constructivism," in *Reconstructing Modernism: Art in New York, Paris, and Montreal 1945–1964*, ed. Serge Guilbaut (Cambridge: MIT Press, 1990), 85–110. On the environmental implications of kinetic art during this period, see Larry Busbea, "Kineticism–Spectacle–Environment," *October*, no. 144 (Spring 2013): 92–114.
74. See Margit Rosen, ed., *A Little Known Story about a Movement, a Magazine, and the Computer's Arrival in Art: New Tendencies and Bit International, 1961–1973* (Cambridge: MIT Press, 2011).
75. Nicolas Schöffer, *La ville cybernétique* (Paris: Tchou, 1969). See also Larry Busbea, *Topologies: The Urban Utopia in France, 1960–1970* (Cambridge: MIT Press, 2007).
76. Jennifer Licht, *Spaces* (New York: Museum of Modern Art, 1969), n.p.
77. Licht, *Spaces*, n.p.
78. See Mackenzie Wark, "The Public Sensoriums of Pulsa: Cybernetic Abstraction and the Biopolitics of Urban Survival," *Art Journal* 67, no. 3 (Fall 2008): 47–67.

79. Felicity Scott, "Vanguards," *e-flux Journal,* no. 64 (April 2015), https://www.e-flux.com.
80. Pulsa, "The City as an Artwork," in Kepes, *Arts of the Environment,* 208–21.
81. Pulsa, "City as an Artwork," 210.
82. Licht, *Spaces,* n.p.
83. Foster, *Art–Architecture Complex,* 204.
84. See Benjamin H. D. Buchloh, *Neo-Avantgarde and Culture Industry: Essays on European and American Art from 1955 to 1975* (Cambridge: MIT Press, 2000).
85. Zabet Patterson, *Peripheral Vision: Bell Labs, the S-C 4020, and the Origins of Computer Art* (Cambridge: MIT Press, 2015).
86. Willoughby Sharp, *Air Art* (New York: Kineticism Press, 1969), 11.
87. Jack Burnham, "Systems Aesthetics," *Artforum* 7, no. 1 (September 1968): 30.
88. Burnham, *Beyond Modern Sculpture,* 363.
89. Roy D. Chapin Jr., sponsor's statement in *Software: Information Technology: Its New Meaning for Art* (New York: Jewish Museum, 1970), 5. Chapin was chairman of American Motors Corporation.
90. Burnham, "Notes on Art and Information Programming," in *Software,* 12.
91. Burnham, "Notes on Art and Information Programming," 14. Burnham was an alumnus of the Center for Advanced Visual Studies.
92. Similar contemporary (and contemporaneous) attempts to capture some of these interactions in art are chronicled in Caroline Jones, David Mather, and Rebecca Uchill, eds., *Experience* (Cambridge: Center for Art, Science & Technology at MIT, 2016).
93. John Goodyear, "*Level of Heat,*" in *Software,* 25.
94. Robert Barry, "*Ultrasonic Wave Piece,*" in *Software,* 37.
95. Douglas Davis, *Art and the Future: A History/Prophecy of the Collaboration between Science, Technology and Art* (New York: Praeger, 1973), 94–95.
96. Burns, *Arthropods,* 9.
97. Burns, *Arthropods,* 9.
98. Jim Burns, "Social and Psychological Implications of Megastructures," in Kepes, *Arts of the Environment,* 135–51.
99. Nisbet, *Ecologies, Environments,* 1–66.
100. Fred Turner, *The Democratic Surround: Multimedia and American Liberalism from World War II to the Psychedelic Sixties* (Chicago: University of Chicago Press, 2013), 276.
101. John Brockman, quoted in Elenore Lester, "So What Happens after Happenings?," *New York Times,* September 4, 1966, D9. As an example of the types of work Brockman had in mind, we might think of Robert Whitman's productions around this time. See Branden Joseph, "Plastic Empathy: The Ghost of Robert Whitman," *Grey Room,* no. 25 (Fall 2006): 64–91.
102. See Pamela M. Lee, *Chronophobia: On Time in the Art of the 1960s* (Cambridge: MIT Press, 2004).
103. Stewart Kranz, *Science and Technology in the Arts: A Tour through the Realm of Science/Art* (New York: Van Nostrand Reinhold, 1974), 214. On USCO, see Michel Oren, "Getting Out of Your Mind to Use Your Head," *Art Journal* 69, no. 4 (Winter 2010): 76–95.
104. George Litwin, in Kranz, *Science and Technology in the Arts,* 261. Litwin's remarkable description appeared in Stewart Kranz's large tome about a fairly hypostasized movement he referred to as "science-art." Here, Kranz spelled out a narrative in which the attitudes of the 1960s paved the way

for the responsive environments immediately following: "The idea of 'Art as Object' was rejected; the significant part of the aesthetic experience became the moment when the spectator came in contact with the work of 'art.' With this new art, spectator involvement took on the characteristics of a partnership between artist and participant" (16). He surveyed a broad range of practices engaging all of the senses, works that utilized film, animation, "light sculptures," and interactive environments. These works were produced not only by artists but also by engineers, sound specialists, educators, and managers.

105. Harwood, *The Interface.*
106. Nicholas Negroponte, *Soft Architecture Machines* (Cambridge: MIT Press, 1975), preface (n.p.), 5.
107. Georges Teyssot, "Responsive Envelopes: The Fabric of Climatic Islands," *Appareil* 11 (2013), 2, https://journals.openedition.org/appareil/1748.
108. Mary Louise Lobsinger, "Cybernetic Theory and the Architecture of Performance," in *Anxious Modernisms: Experimentation in Postwar Architectural Culture,* ed. Sarah Williams Goldhagen and Réjean Legault (Cambridge: MIT Press, 2001), 119–39.
109. Stanley Mathews, *From Agit-Prop to Free Space: The Architecture of Cedric Price* (London: Black Dog Publishing, 2007), 195.
110. Steenson elaborates on this: "Generator marked a point of emergence of important factors for responsive architecture: embedded, distributed, electronic intelligence; active computer-aided design tools; the correspondence of the model to the design tool; and questions of machine intelligence." Steenson, *Architectural Intelligence,* 162.
111. Krueger, *Artificial Reality.* This book was based on Krueger's 1974 dissertation, which he struggled to get published—due to conceptual and disciplinary misunderstandings—until the following decade. Myron Krueger, telephone conversation with author, May 14, 2014.
112. Krueger, *Artificial Reality,* xi.
113. Krueger, *Artificial Reality,* xii.
114. Katja Kwastek, *Aesthetics of Interaction in Digital Art* (Cambridge: MIT Press, 2013).
115. Salter, *Entangled,* 320.
116. Krueger, *Artificial Reality,* 207.
117. For a historical overview of such projects, see Vardouli, "Who Designs?"
118. Felicity Scott thoroughly explores the ramifications of the Architecture Machine Group's implication in the military–industrial complex in *Outlaw Territories,* 339–429.
119. Nicholas Negroponte, "Discussion Following Blair Hamilton's Presentation," in Allen, *Responsive House,* 243.
120. The term *symbiosis* here is in reference to J. C. R. Licklider's influential text "Man–Computer Symbiosis," *IRE Transactions on Human Factors in Electronics* HFE-1, no. 1 (March 1960): 4–11. Negroponte would reformulate this as an "architect–machine symbiosis" that could lead to an "environmental humanism." Nicholas Negroponte, *The Architecture Machine: Toward a More Human Environment* (Cambridge: MIT Press, 1970), 5–9.
121. Negroponte dedicated *The Architecture Machine,* in anticipation, no doubt, "to the first machine that can appreciate the gesture."
122. Negroponte, *Soft Architecture Machines,* 39.

123. Negroponte, *Soft Architecture Machines,* 41.
124. See Salter, *Entangled,* 97.
125. Sean Wellesley-Miller, "Intelligent Environments," in Negroponte, *Soft Architecture Machines,* 125.
126. Wellesley-Miller, "Intelligent Environments," 127. This, of course, echoes the classic cybernetic emphasis on teleology.
127. Wellesley-Miller, "Intelligent Environments," 127.
128. Wellesley-Miller, "Intelligent Environments," 129.
129. Negroponte, *Soft Architecture Machines,* 133.
130. Negroponte, *Soft Architecture Machines,* 135.
131. Charles Eastman wrote one of the more systematic statements regarding a programmable architecture at this time, elaborating especially on the metaphor and precedent of the thermostat as a regulative environmental technology whose functions begged to be expanded. But he also acknowledged the nontechnical components of architectural responsiveness: "It is important to recognize that an adaptive mechanism may be mechanical in nature, as in the thermostat. For example, activity 'pods' may be relocated automatically in a building structure, lighting or acoustics automatically adjusted. Just as important are social mechanisms for adaptation. An example of a social mechanism would be a yearly survey to determine the services to be provided in a community center. In this case the survey is a sensing mechanism, the control mechanism is the governing board of the center, and the change mechanism is the staff running the different activities. Equipment locations, room scheduling, and other spatial adjustments are part of the outcome. Similarly, feedback processes may include combinations of mechanical and social adaptation mechanisms." Charles Eastman, *Adaptive Conditional Architecture* (Pittsburgh: Institute of Physical Planning, Carnegie-Mellon University School of Urban and Public Affairs, 1972), 8–9.
132. Negroponte, *Soft Architecture Machines,* 134.
133. Negroponte, *Soft Architecture Machines,* 134.
134. Negroponte made the connection between Chomsky and Alexander in *Soft Architecture Machines,* 39.
135. Edward Allen, introduction to Allen, *Responsive House,* x.
136. Wellesley-Miller would go on to be an advocate of sustainable architecture and a symbiotic model of human–environment interaction. See Sean Wellesley-Miller, Day Charoudi, and Marguerite Villecco, "Bio Shelter," *Architecture Plus* 4, no. 6 (November/December 1974): 90–95.
137. Wellesley-Miller, "Work Notes," 11.
138. Wellesley-Miller, "Work Notes," 12.
139. Wellesley-Miller, "Work Notes," 13.
140. Wellesley-Miller, "Work Notes," 19–21.

4. Soft Control Material

1. Avery R. Johnson to Gregory Bateson, October 7, 1973, box 17, folder 728, Bateson Papers.
2. The work was funded by Peter Oser. According to Brodey: "The lab was located in a beautiful old long-vacant warehouse on the Boston waterfront and then kept secret for the first 6 months . . . so we could develop the lab

in our own way. Peter Oser chose that location so we could have a view of the sea from our windows. The ocean environment, he felt, allowed us to keep in touch with the raw environmental reality. Peter felt that was important. He did not want us to be limited by traditional ways and surrounds." Warren Brodey, e-mail correspondence with author, January 4, 2017.

3. Warren Brodey, e-mail correspondence with author, January 2, 2017.
4. Warren Brodey, "Recycling Biotopology 1972: Notes from Ecology Tool and Toy," *Radical Software* 1, no. 5 (Spring 1972): 35.
5. W. Brodey and A. R. Johnson, Soft Control Material, U.S. Patent 3,818,487, filed April 24, 1972; issued June 18, 1974.
6. Brodey and Johnson, U.S. Patent 3,818,487, sec. 24.
7. C. P. Hall, Liquid Support for Human Bodies, U.S. Patent 3,585,356, filed July 27, 1970; issued June 15, 1971. Hall was a graduate student in art and design at the University of California, San Francisco.
8. Brodey, "Recycling Biotopology," 34–36.
9. Negroponte, *Soft Architecture Machines,* preface (n.p.). Negroponte's preface is dated 1972.
10. Negroponte, *Soft Architecture Machines,* preface (n.p.).
11. Negroponte, *Soft Architecture Machines,* 38.
12. See Marc Dessauce, ed., *The Inflatable Moment: Pneumatics and Protest in '68* (New York: Princeton Architectural Press, 1999). See also James Baldwin and Stewart Brand, eds., *Soft-Tech* (New York: Penguin, 1978); Ralph Pomeroy, *Soft Art* (Trenton: New Jersey State Museum, 1969).
13. Accordingly, SCM can also be situated within the much larger field of intersections between the counterculture and cybernetic discourse. See, for instance, Fred Turner, *From Counterculture to Cyberculture: Stewart Brand, the Whole Earth Network, and the Rise of Digital Utopianism* (Chicago: University of Chicago Press, 2006). For a recent overview of some of these cross-pollinations, see Andrew Blauvelt, ed., *Hippie Modernism: The Struggle for Utopia* (Minneapolis: Walker Art Center, 2015). The rhetoric of "soft" technology also developed as an adjunct to the notions of "alternative" and "appropriate" technologies in the British context. These are discussed by David Dickson in *The Politics of Alternative Technology* (New York: Universe Books, 1975). In this volume, Dickson reproduces Robin Clark's "Some Utopian Characteristics of Soft Technology," a list opposing the properties of a "hard" technology society and those of its "soft" counterpart. Needless to say, the term *soft* never achieved anything like stability in all of these different sources and instances of use.
14. Negroponte actually stated, as he was warning of "soft Soleris," that Brodey and Johnson were capable of taking the term *soft* too literally, "often transposing it from a computational paradigm to a building technology." Negroponte, *Soft Architecture Machines,* 147.
15. Georges Teyssot invokes Brodey's concept of "biotopology" to reflect on the genesis of responsive environments. Teyssot, "Responsive Envelopes," 1.
16. While I am attempting to stress the specificity of the provenance of the term *soft* in the case of Negroponte's close relationship with Brodey and Johnson, the usage was just as certainly in the air (as they say). See, for instance, that early genealogical entry into what is now known as "design thinking," Don Koberg and Jim Bagnall, *The Universal Traveler: A Soft*

Systems Guide to Creativity, Problem-Solving and the Process of Reaching Goals (New York: W. Kaufmann, 1971).

17. Warren Brodey, "Soft Architecture: The Design of Intelligent Environments," *Landscape* 17, no. 1 (1967): 8–12.
18. Gilbert Simondon, *Du mode d'existence des objets techniques* (Paris: Aubier, Éditions Montaigne, 1958). See also Larry Busbea, "Metadesign: Object and Environment in France, c. 1970," *Design Issues* 25, no. 4 (Autumn 2009): 103–19.
19. Brodey, "Soft Architecture," 8–9.
20. Martin Heidegger, "The Question Concerning Technology," in *Basic Writings: From "Being and Time" (1927) to "The Task of Thinking" (1964)*, rev. ed., ed. David Farrell Krell (New York: HarperCollins, 1993), 307–42.
21. Brodey, "Soft Architecture," 10.
22. Brodey, "Soft Architecture," 11.
23. Dutta, *Second Modernism.*
24. Norbert Wiener, *Cybernetics; or, Control and Communication in the Animal and the Machine* (Cambridge: MIT Press, 1948).
25. Arturo Rosenblueth, Norbert Wiener, and Julian Bigelow, "Behavior, Purpose, Teleology," *Philosophy of Science* 10, no. 1 (1943): 18–24; Warren S. McCulloch and Walter H. Pitts, "A Logical Calculus of the Ideas Immanent in Nervous Activity" (1943), in Warren S. McCulloch, *Embodiments of Mind* (Cambridge: MIT Press, 1965), 19–39.
26. Rosenblueth et al., "Behavior, Purpose, Teleology," 18.
27. Rosenblueth et al., "Behavior, Purpose, Teleology," 23, emphasis added.
28. McCulloch and Pitts, "Logical Calculus," 19.
29. Halpern, *Beautiful Data,* 154.
30. "At any instant a neuron has some threshold, which excitation must exceed to initiate an impulse. This, except for the fact and time of its occurrence, is determined by the neuron, not by the excitation." McCulloch and Pitts, "Logical Calculus," 19.
31. Halpern, *Beautiful Data,* 157.
32. McCulloch and Pitts, "Logical Calculus," 37.
33. McCulloch and Pitts, "Logical Calculus," 35.
34. Warren M. Brodey and Nilo Lindgren, "Human Enhancement through Evolutionary Technology," *IEEE Spectrum* 4, no. 9 (September 1967): 94.
35. Warren Brodey, "Experiments in Evolutionary Environmental Ecology," in *Computer Graphics in Architecture and Design,* ed. Murray Milne (New Haven, Conn.: Yale School of Art and Architecture, 1969).
36. Andrew Pickering, *The Cybernetic Brain: Sketches of Another Future* (Chicago: University of Chicago Press, 2010), 337–38.
37. Pask mentioned Brodey's work on responsive systems in Gordon Pask, "The Architectural Relevance of Cybernetics," *Architectural Design* 39 (September 1969): 495.
38. See Warren M. Brodey and Nilo Lindgren, "Human Enhancement: Beyond the Machine Age," *IEEE Spectrum* 5, no. 2 (February 1968), 79–93. This essay was the second in a two-part series. The first, cited above in note 33, was titled "Human Enhancement through Evolutionary Technology."
39. Brodey, "Soft Architecture," 11.
40. Avery R. Johnson, "The Three Little Pigs," in Allen, *Responsive House,* 284.
41. Negroponte, *Soft Architecture Machines,* 35.

42. Negroponte, *Soft Architecture Machines,* 37–38.
43. Brodey, "Soft Architecture," 10.
44. Warren M. Brodey, "Unlearning the Obsolescent," *Architectural Design* 39 (September 1969): 484.
45. Avery R. Johnson, "Organization, Perception, and Control in Living Systems," *Industrial Management Review* 10, no. 2 (Winter 1969): 1–15.
46. Johnson, "Organization, Perception, and Control," 1.
47. Johnson, "Organization, Perception, and Control," 2.
48. Johnson, "Organization, Perception, and Control," 5.
49. Johnson, "Organization, Perception, and Control," 7.
50. Johnson, "Organization, Perception, and Control," 9.
51. Johnson, "Organization, Perception, and Control," 9, emphasis added.
52. John Harwood, "The Interface: Ergonomics and the Aesthetics of Survival," in *Governing by Design: Architecture, Economy, and Politics in the Twentieth Century,* ed. Aggregate (Pittsburgh: University of Pittsburgh Press, 2012), 83.
53. SCM was also open source. From the patent: "The invention is therefore limited only by the scope of the claims attached hereto, since variations of the invention therewithin will become immediately apparent to one skilled in the art." Brodey and Johnson, U.S. Patent 3,818,487, sec. 25.
54. Johnson, "Three Little Pigs," 290–91.
55. Brodey, "Recycling Biotopology," 36.
56. Johnson, "Three Little Pigs," 290.
57. Brodey and Johnson, U.S. Patent 3,818,487, abstract.
58. They mentioned that the Raytheon Corporation had recently (1964) trademarked the Raysistor, which was typically used as a switching device (commonly in electrical musical equipment). Because the Raysistor used light, no physical circuit was required.
59. In a sense, the story of SCM presents something of an alternative to other cultural analyses of the cybernetic ethos that have stressed its deployment of virtuality or its qualities of disembodiment. See, for instance, N. Katherine Hayles, *How We Became Posthuman: Virtual Bodies in Cybernetics, Literature, and Informatics* (Chicago: University of Chicago Press, 1999).
60. Brodey and Johnson, U.S. Patent 3,818,487, secs. 23–24.
61. Canguilhem, "Living and Its Milieu."
62. Bateson, *Steps to an Ecology of Mind,* 155.
63. Brodey, "Recycling Biotopology," 34.
64. Brodey and Lindgren, "Human Enhancement through Evolutionary Technology," 90.
65. Brodey and Johnson, U.S. Patent 3,818,487, sec. 14.
66. Paul Ryan, "Cybernetic Guerrilla Warfare," *Radical Software* 1, no. 3 (1971): 1.
67. For more on Ryan, *Radical Software,* and topology, see Kaizen, "Steps to an Ecology of Communication"; Eric de Bruyn, "Topological Pathways of Post-minimalism," *Grey Room,* no. 25 (Fall 2006): 32–63.
68. Ryan, "Cybernetic Guerrilla Warfare," 1.
69. For more on the biological and ecological aspects of video practices (and Johnson and Brodey's relation to them), see Blom, *Autobiography of Video,* 69–97.

70. Warren Brodey, "Biotopology 1972," *Radical Software* 1, no. 4 (Summer 1971): 4–7.
71. Brodey, "Biotopology 1972," 4.
72. Brodey, "Biotopology 1972," 6.

5. Cybertecture

1. Call for papers poster for the conference Environmental Evolution and Technologies, 1975.
2. Joseph Mathis, conversation with author, December 4, 2015.
3. I have assembled this roster with the aid of the anonymous "Summary Report to the President 1974–75," 4, Alexander Architectural Archives, University of Texas at Austin. Pliny Fisk III, e-mail correspondence with author, July 25, 2016.
4. Erich Jantsch, *Design for Evolution: Self-Organization and Planning in the Life of Human Systems* (New York: George Braziller, 1975); Erich Jantsch and Conrad H. Waddington, eds., *Evolution and Consciousness: Human Systems in Transition* (London: Addison-Wesley, 1976).
5. Fisk, e-mail, July 25, 2016.
6. We could in this sense link Cybertecture to the emerging field of "object-oriented ontology," but I think it might be more useful to think about it as what Zeynep Çelik Alexander has called "neo-naturalism": Zeynep Çelik Alexander, "Neo-naturalism," *Log*, no. 31 (Spring/Summer 2014): 23–30.
7. As is well known, Reyner Banham had, in the middle of the decade, relegated such projects to the realm of history. Reyner Banham, *Megastructure: Urban Futures of the Recent Past* (London: Thames and Hudson, 1976).
8. Wolf Hilbertz, "Toward Cybertecture," *Progressive Architecture*, May 1970, 98–103. Hilbertz also penned a feature article in *Architectural Design* about a student workshop conducted in Minnesota in January 1973 that involved the construction of ice and snow structures: Wolf Hilbertz, "Ice City," *Architectural Design* 43 (April 1973): 213–15. He also reported on this project in "Ice City," *Man–Environment Systems* 3, no. 2 (March 1973): 129–36.
9. Wolf Hilbertz, Mineral Accretion of Large Surface Structures, Building Components and Elements, U.S. Patent 4,246,075, filed March 19, 1979; issued January 20, 1981. For more on the philosophical and technical evolution from Cybertecture to Biorock, see Paul Cureton, "Videre: Drawing and Evolutionary Architectures," *Materials Architecture Design Environment (MADE)* 7 (October 2013): 18–27.
10. Both Cybertecture and Biorock were featured in the 2009 Barbican exhibition *Radical Nature*. See Francesco Manacorda et al., *Radical Nature: Art and Architecture for a Changing Planet, 1969–2009* (Cologne: Walther König, 2010). See also Lydia Kallipoliti, ed., "Ecoredux: Design Remedies for an Ailing Planet," special issue, *Architectural Design* 80 (November/December 2010); Lydia Kallipoliti, "Ecoredux: Environmental Architecture from 'Object' to 'System' to 'Cloud,'" *Praxis* 13 (2011): 5–17.
11. Poster for Ice City, 1975.
12. Hilbertz, "Ice City," *Architectural Design*; Hilbertz, "Ice City," *Man–Environment Systems*. See also Wolf Hilbertz, "Eis-City," *Deutsche Bauzeitung* 107, no. 6 (1973): 632–34.

13. Hilbertz, "Ice City," *Architectural Design,* 214.
14. Hilbertz, "Ice City," *Architectural Design,* 215.
15. Hilbertz, "Ice City," *Architectural Design,* 213.
16. John J. Allan, Wolf Hilbertz, and Alton J. De Long, "Symbiotic Processes Laboratory—University of Texas School of Architecture," *Man–Environment Systems* 1, no. 6 (September 1971): S60–S61.
17. Newton Fallis, a student of Hilbertz at the time, recalls a humorously botched experiment involving a machine that was constructed to extrude clay bricks and then "bake" them with high-voltage electricity—it did not work. Newton Fallis, conversation with author, December 4, 2015.
18. Mathis, conversation with author.
19. Michael Kennedy, ed., *Proceedings of the Kentucky Workshop on Computer Applications to Environmental Design* (independently published, 1971).
20. Wolf Hilbertz, "Cybernetic Architecture: A Teleological Process," in Kennedy, *Proceedings,* 95.
21. Here and in the description that follows I rely primarily on Hilbertz, "Cybernetic Architecture"; and Hilbertz, "Toward Cybertecture." These two sources are largely redundant, with slightly different emphases.
22. Hilbertz, "Toward Cybertecture," 99.
23. See, for instance, Fabio Gramazio, Matthias Kohler, and Jan Willmann, eds., *The Robotic Touch: How Robots Change Architecture* (Zurich: Park Books, 2014).
24. Hilbertz, "Toward Cybertecture," 99, 100.
25. Wolf Hilbertz and R. Mather, "Grant Application: Materials Distribution and Reclamation," November 23, 1970, Alexander Architectural Archives, University of Texas at Austin.
26. Hilbertz and Mather, "Grant Application," n.p.
27. Fallis, conversation with author.
28. Appropriately, perhaps, CT was being developed at exactly the moment Reyner Banham was producing his historical overview of such projects, *Megastructure* (1976).
29. Hilbertz, "Toward Cybertecture," 100.
30. Hilbertz, "Toward Cybertecture," 103.
31. The presentations were by Hilbertz, Robert E. Lucas, Joseph Mathis, and Forrest Higgs, respectively. See Edward Allen, ed., *The Responsive House* (Cambridge: MIT Press, 1974), 247–67.
32. Allen, *Responsive House,* 268–75. These pages also included an expanded selection of images.
33. One attendee apparently said, "You've got a magic carpet here, but you're trying to nail it to the floor." For the full discussion, see Allen, *Responsive House,* 268–70.
34. That digitality demanded the separation of information from its embodied vessels forms one of the key arguments, for instance, in N. Katherine Hayles's classic book *How We Became Posthuman.*
35. Wolf Hilbertz, "Colloquium: Adaptive Architecture," unpublished typescript, circa 1974, courtesy Desmond Fletcher.
36. Wolf Hilbertz, "Strategies for Evolutionary Environments," in Allen, *Responsive House,* 255. The Maldonado reference was to the latter's seminal *Design, Nature, and Revolution.*
37. For a brief contextualization of Hartley's place in modern perceptual aes-

thetic theory, see Anthony Enns and Shelley Trower, introduction to *Vibratory Modernism*, ed. Anthony Enns and Shelley Trower (London: Palgrave Macmillan, 2013), 6. As Enns and Trower state, by augmenting Newton's theories of perception, "Hartley thereby constructed a scientific argument to show how humans vibrate in sympathy with the cosmos."

38. Allan et al., "Symbiotic Processes Laboratory."
39. Hilbertz, "Strategies for Evolutionary Environments," 247–48.
40. Hilbertz, "Strategies for Evolutionary Environments," 251.
41. Pierre Teilhard de Chardin, *The Phenomenon of Man*, trans. Bernard Wall (New York: Harper & Row, 1959).
42. Theodosius Dobzhansky, *Mankind Evolving* (New Haven, Conn.: Yale University Press, 1962), 319, 321.
43. John B. Calhoun, "Space and the Strategy of Life," in *Behavior and Environment*, ed. Aristide H. Esser (New York: Plenum Press, 1971), 329–87. The impressive volume in which Calhoun's essay appears, edited by one of the founding members of the Association for the Study of Man–Environment Relations, represents the apex of that group's activities.
44. Paul Ehrlich, *The Population Bomb* (New York: Ballantine Books, 1968).
45. Calhoun, "Space and the Strategy of Life," 372–74.
46. Calhoun, "Space and the Strategy of Life," 374.
47. Wolf Hilbertz, Desmond Fletcher, and Carolyn Krausse, "Mineral Accretion Technology: Applications for Architecture and Aquaculture," *Industrialization Forum* 8, nos. 4–5 (1977): 84.
48. Wolf Hilbertz, "On Growing Evolutionary Marine Structures," *Evolutionary Environments*, no. 1 (February 1976): n.p.
49. Avery R. Johnson, "Why Wasn't It Obvious Before? (excerpts from a letter by Avery Johnson, Milford, N.H.)," *Evolutionary Environments*, no. 1 (February 1976): n.p.
50. Alton De Long, "Conceptual Evolution and Design: The Potential Manipulation of Spatial Scale and Time-Frames," *Evolutionary Environments*, no. 4 (March 1977): 7.
51. Erich Jantsch, "Self Transcendence and Complexity," *Evolutionary Environments*, no. 3 (September 1976): 2–3.
52. Jantsch, *Design for Evolution*. The book was part of a series titled the International Library of Systems Theory and Philosophy, which was edited by Ervin László.
53. Ambasz, "Project Working Paper," 23.
54. Erich Jantsch, "Education for Design: Preliminary Notes on a Systems Approach to Total Human Experience and Purposeful Activity," in Ambasz, *The Universitas Project*, 111–41.
55. Jantsch, "Education for Design," 115.
56. Leah McVie, "Erich Jantsch Biography," accessed February 28, 2017, http://leahmacvie.com/blog/erichjantsch.
57. See, for instance, Ilya Prigogine, "Order through Fluctuation: Self-Organization and Social System," in Jantsch and Waddington, *Evolution and Consciousness*, 93–127.
58. Jantsch, *Design for Evolution*, xvi.
59. Jantsch, *Design for Evolution*, xvi.
60. Jantsch, *Design for Evolution*, xvii.
61. Jantsch, *Design for Evolution*, 101.

62. Jantsch, *Design for Evolution,* 101.
63. Hilbertz, "Strategies for Evolutionary Environments," 252.
64. Hilbertz, "Toward Cybertecture," 103.
65. Hilbertz, "Strategies for Evolutionary Environments," 252.
66. Jantsch, "Education for Design," 122, emphasis added.
67. McLuhan to Hall, September 16, 1964.
68. Hall, *Silent Language,* 79.
69. Indeed, the provenance of this word would prove contentious when, in 1977, Hall mentioned that McLuhan "borrowed" the term from his *Silent Language* (79). I go into some detail here about these exchanges not to establish who has a claim to primacy in the matter but to demonstrate the interesting way in which extension and its various synonymic formulations were inextricably bound to environment. For an excellent account of McLuhan's other sources for the term, see Cavell, *McLuhan in Space,* 256–57n52.
70. R. Buckminster Fuller, *Nine Chains to the Moon* (Philadelphia: J. B. Lippincott, 1938), 68. This passage is also quoted in Mark Byers, "Environmental Pedagogues: Charles Olson and R. Buckminster Fuller," *English* 62, no. 238 (2013): 253.
71. Lewis Mumford, *Techniques and Civilization* (1934; repr., New York: Harcourt, Brace & World, 1963), 10, emphasis added.
72. For a comparison of Kapp's and McLuhan's respective theories, see Philip Brey, "Theories of Technology as Extension of Human Faculties," in *Metaphysics, Epistemology, and Technology,* ed. Carl Mitcham (Bingley, England: Emerald, 2000), 59–78.
73. Ernst Kapp, quoted in Carl Mitcham, *Thinking through Technology: The Path between Engineering and Philosophy* (Chicago: University of Chicago Press, 1994), 24.
74. Donna J. Haraway, "The High Cost of Information in Post–World War II Evolutionary Biology: Ergonomics, Semiotics, and the Sociobiology of Communications Systems," *Philosophical Forum* 13, nos. 2–3 (Winter–Spring 1981–82): 244–78.
75. Gyorgy Kepes, ed., *The Man-Made Object* (New York: George Braziller, 1966).
76. Gillo Dorfles, "The Man-Made Object," in Kepes, *Man-Made Object,* 1.
77. Dorfles, "Man-Made Object," 2.
78. Stewart Brand, "Some Cybernetic Words," *CoEvolution Quarterly,* no. 2 (Summer 1974): 69.
79. James Baldwin, "One Highly-Evolved Toolbox," *CoEvolution Quarterly,* no. 5 (Spring 1975): 80–85.
80. James Baldwin, "More Highly-Evolved Toolbox," *CoEvolution Quarterly,* no. 9 (Spring 1976): 100.
81. Baldwin, "More Highly-Evolved Toolbox," 104. This idea accords with Andrew Kirk's observation that Baldwin, Steve Baer, and others associated with the Alloy group wished "to remake, literally remake with their brains and hands, the material world into a place that balanced nature and culture." Andrew Kirk, "Alloyed: Countercultural Bricoleurs and the Design Science Revival," in *Groovy Science: Knowledge, Innovation and American Counterculture,* ed. David Kaiser and W. Patrick McCray (Chicago: University of Chicago Press, 2016), 307.

82. James Baldwin, introduction to Baldwin and Brand, *Soft-Tech,* 4.
83. Paul Ehrlich and Peter Raven, "Butterflies and Plants: A Study in Coevolution," *Evolution* 18, no. 4 (December 1964): 586.
84. Ehrlich and Raven, "Butterflies and Plants," 586.
85. Ehrlich and Raven, "Butterflies and Plants," 598.
86. Ehrlich and Raven, "Butterflies and Plants."
87. Richard Dawkins, "Replicator Selection and the Extended Phenotype," *Ethology* 47, no. 1 (January–December 1978): 71. See also Richard Dawkins, *The Extended Phenotype* (Oxford: Oxford University Press, 1982).
88. There is also the evolution of tools themselves to consider (though I cannot account for that discourse fully here). See Philip Steadman, *The Evolution of Designs: Biological Analogy in Architecture and the Applied Arts* (Cambridge: Cambridge University Press, 1979). Steadman's text followed in the footsteps of philosophical considerations such as Gilbert Simondon's landmark 1958 work *Du mode d'existence des objets techniques,* published in English as *On the Mode of Existence of Technical Objects,* trans. Cecile Malaspina and John Rogove (Minneapolis: University of Minnesota Press, 2016).
89. McLuhan, *Understanding Media.*
90. Edward T. Hall, *Beyond Culture* (New York: Anchor Books, 1976), 25.
91. Hall, *Beyond Culture,* 25–40.
92. Gillo Dorfles, *Artificio e natura* (Turin: Einaudi, 1968).
93. Maldonado, *Design, Nature, and Revolution,* 79.
94. Abraham Moles, *Théorie des objets* (Paris: Éditions Universitaires, 1972), 22.
95. McLuhan, "Invisible Environment," 166.

6. Arcoconsciousness

1. For a compelling account of this ethos within the physics community, see David Kaiser, *How the Hippies Saved Physics: Science, Counterculture, and the Quantum Revival* (New York: W. W. Norton, 2011). On Beer, see Pickering, *Cybernetic Brain.*
2. Tom Wolfe, "The 'Me' Decade and the Third Great Awakening," *New York,* August 23, 1976; Christopher Lasch, *The Culture of Narcissism: American Life in an Age of Diminishing Expectations* (New York: W. W. Norton, 1979).
3. See Theodore Roszak, *Unfinished Animal: The Aquarian Frontier and the Evolution of Consciousness* (New York: Harper & Row, 1977); Wouter J. Hanegraaff, *New Age Religion and Western Culture: Esotericism in the Mirror of Secular Thought* (Albany: State University of New York Press, 1998); Peter Sloterdijk, *You Must Change Your Life,* trans. Wieland Hoban (Cambridge: Polity Press, 2013).
4. Soleri's work continues to be placed in this marginal category. See Alastair Gordon, *Spaced Out: Crash Pads, Hippie Communes, Infinity Machines, and Other Radical Environments of the Psychedelic Sixties* (New York: Rizzoli, 2008), 11–13. Otherwise, the literature on Soleri is paradoxical. It constitutes a massive body of writing with virtually no critical or interpretive content. Many of the articles on his work comprise journalistic accounts of visits to Soleri's two sites in Arizona. See, for instance, J.M.D., "Job Site for Utopia," *Progressive Architecture* 54 (April 1973): 76–81; James Shipsky, "Diary of an Arcosanti Experience," *AIA Journal* 71, no. 5 (May 1982): 30–39; François

Burckhardt, "Thirty-Five Years After: A Visit to Cosanti," *Domus*, no. 812 (February 1999): 44–47. The major exception is the monograph by Antonietta Iolanda Lima, *Soleri: Architecture as Human Ecology* (New York: Monacelli Press, 2003). This volume also contains a comprehensive bibliography of Soleri's writings and secondary sources. The 2017 exhibition *Repositioning Paolo Soleri: The City Is Nature* at the Scottsdale Museum of Contemporary Art provided valuable critical insight as well. See the exhibition's catalog: Claire Carter, ed., *Repositioning Paolo Soleri: The City Is Nature* (Scottsdale: Scottsdale Museum of Contemporary Art, 2017).

5. The spiritual and religious aspects of modernist architecture and contemporary practice are reviewed in several recent volumes: Renata Hejduk and Jim Williamson, eds., *The Religious Imagination in Modern and Contemporary Architecture* (London: Routledge, 2011); Thomas Barrie, Julio Bermudez, and Phillip James Tabb, eds., *Architecture, Culture, and Spirituality* (Surrey: Ashgate, 2015); J. K. Birksted, *Le Corbusier and the Occult* (Cambridge: MIT Press, 2009).
6. Even though Soleri has languished in the shadow of Fuller's ostensible digital oracularism, it is certainly not because the latter was in fact more rational or realistic. To be blunt, Fuller believed in extrasensory perception and telepathy and felt that "thinking" itself had form or geometry. See Lloyd Steven Sieden, *Buckminster Fuller's Universe* (New York: Basic Books, 1989), 72–73. See also R. Buckminster Fuller with E. J. Applewhite, *Synergetics: Explorations in the Geometry of Thinking*, 2 vols. (New York: Macmillan, 1975–79).
7. On the counterculture and its impact on art and architecture, see Felicity Scott, *Architecture or Techno-utopia* (Cambridge: MIT Press, 2007); Caroline Maniaque-Benton, *French Encounters with the American Counterculture, 1960–1980* (London: Ashgate, 2011); Elissa Auther and Adam Lerner, eds., *West of Center: Art and the Counterculture Experiment in America, 1965–1977* (Minneapolis: University of Minnesota Press, 2012); Turner, *From Counterculture to Cyberculture.* See also Blauvelt, *Hippie Modernism*; Wigley, "Network Fever," 96–97.
8. Turner, *From Counterculture to Cyberculture*, 49.
9. Reyner Banham, *Theory and Design in the First Machine Age* (Cambridge: MIT Press, 1960).
10. "Vents," in *Domebook One* (Los Gatos, Calif.: Pacific Domes, 1970), 38.
11. Alan and Heath, "Centering," in *Domebook One*, 46.
12. Fuller, *Synergetics.*
13. "Carlos Castaneda found this process . . . to be a perfect energetic description of the modern practice of Don Juan's teachings: In the case of the magical passes, *Tensegrity®* practice refers to the interplay of tensing and relaxing the tendons and muscles, and their energetic counterparts, in a way that enhances the overall integrity of the body as a physical and an energetic unit, and promotes a conscious awareness of how all the parts of our being—tendon, muscle, bone, nervous systems, organs, etc. work together, integrated by a healthy flow of energy." Carlos Castaneda website, accessed February 8, 2012, https://castaneda.com. See also Carlos Castaneda, *The Magical Passes* (New York: Harper Perennial, 1998).
14. Katinka Matson, *Psychology Today Omnibook of Personal Development* (New York: William Morrow, 1977), 122–25, 432–36.

15. William Irwin Thompson, *Passages about Earth: An Exploration of the New Planetary Culture* (New York: Harper & Row, 1973), 38.
16. Carlos Castaneda, *The Teachings of Don Juan: A Yaqui Way of Knowledge* (Berkeley: University of California Press, 1968).
17. Paolo Soleri, *The Omega Seed: An Eschatological Hypothesis* (Garden City, N.Y.: Anchor Books, 1981), 216.
18. Here, we might refer to the current reprise of materiality in philosophy, which draws on a certain lineage stretching from Henri Bergson and Alfred North Whitehead through Gilles Deleuze and up through Manuel De Landa. See, for instance, Bennett, *Vibrant Matter.*
19. Soleri, *Omega Seed,* 251.
20. Soleri, *Omega Seed,* 250.
21. See, for instance, Peter Blake, "Paolo Soleri's Visionary City," *Architectural Forum* 114, no. 3 (March 1961): 111–18; "Projet de ville idéale, Mesa City," *L'Architecture d'Aujourd'hui* 102 (June/July 1962): 64–73.
22. For a chronology of the complex construction history at Cosanti, see Roger Tomalty, *Cosanti: The Studios of Paolo Soleri—Walk-Through Guide* (Mayer, Ariz.: Cosanti Press, 2012).
23. Paolo Soleri, *Arcology: The City in the Image of Man* (Cambridge: MIT Press, 1969). This massive folio volume saw several different print runs and new editions over the years. Most of my citations are to the 1970 second printing of this first edition and the newer Cosanti Press edition: Paolo Soleri, *Arcology: The City in the Image of Man* (Phoenix: Cosanti Press, 2006); the editions are distinguished in the cites by their dates. The catalog for the Corcoran show was produced by Donald Wall, *Paolo Soleri Documenta* (Washington, D.C., Corcoran Gallery of Art, 1970). Wall also published a separate monograph that year, no less remarkable for its graphic design than for its content: Donald Wall, *Visionary Cities: The Arcology of Paolo Soleri* (New York: Praeger, 1970).
24. After *Arcology,* Soleri began to publish images and texts from his famous sketchbooks and notebooks. The former were large folios with cast metal covers, filled with Leonardoesque scribbles, images, and text. These were captured in another volume issued by MIT Press: *The Sketchbooks of Paolo Soleri* (Cambridge: MIT Press, 1971). Collections of essays were also forthcoming: Paolo Soleri, *The Bridge between Matter and Spirit Is Matter Becoming Spirit* (Garden City, N.Y.: Anchor Books, 1973); Paolo Soleri, *Fragments: A Selection from the Sketchbooks of Paolo Soleri* (New York: Harper & Row, 1980); Soleri, *Omega Seed*; Paolo Soleri, *Arcosanti: An Urban Laboratory?* (Scottsdale: Cosanti Press, 1983); Paolo Soleri, *Technology and Cosmogenesis* (New York: Paragon House, 1985); Paolo Soleri, *Conversations with Paolo Soleri,* ed. Lissa McCullough (New York: Princeton Architectural Press, 2012).
25. Banham, *Megastructure.*
26. Soleri, *Arcology* (2006), 127.
27. Soleri, *Arcology* (1969), 120.
28. Soleri, *Arcology* (1969), 120. Initially, Soleri had planned, as an intermediate step, a smaller version of Arcosanti that might house just two hundred or so residents—a more direct extension of the craft and pedagogical activities of Cosanti. At some point in the late 1960s, he decided to skip this intermediate phase and move to establish Arcosanti as a larger arcology. Roger Tomalty, conversation with author, October 16, 2012.

29. On the windbells, see below and, especially, Elissa Auther, "Craft and the Handmade at Paolo Soleri's Communal Settlements," in Auther and Lerner, *West of Center,* 110–27.
30. For more on the institutional organization of Arcosanti, see http://www.arcosanti.org.
31. Douglas Davis, "Arcosanti: Dream City," *Newsweek,* August 16, 1976, 78.
32. One index of this was the traction his work gained outside the architectural field proper among philosophers like Henryk Skolimowski, several of whose essays are cited here. (Skolimowski went on to become one of the key protagonists in the field of "eco-philosophy.") The geographer Edward Higbee wrote one of the more thoughtful essays on Soleri when the Corcoran exhibition opened: Edward Higbee, "Soleri: Plumber with the Mind of Saint Augustine," *AIA Journal* 55 (February 1971): 17–22.
33. "*What is [Soleri] trying to say?*" Peter Blake asked rhetorically in his foreword to *Arcology.* "Answer: I am not completely sure, because this is a very difficult book to read. Like many so-called visionary types, Soleri has invented his own language, and some of the words in that language won't be found in any English dictionary." Blake, foreword to Soleri, *Arcology* (1969), n.p. John Elkington likened Soleri's use of language to that of Fuller in that both were "given to piling one word upon the next until the very structure of language seems to be on the verge of collapse." John Elkington, "Paolo Soleri: Flight from Flatness," *Architectural Association Quarterly* 6, no. 1 (1974): 60. Skolimowski offered his attempt to translate Soleri's core neologisms in his foreword to Soleri's *Fragments.*
34. Dana F. White, "The Apocalyptic Vision of Paolo Soleri," *Technology and Culture* 12, no. 1 (January 1971): 87.
35. Soleri, *Bridge between Matter and Spirit,* 127–28.
36. Paolo Soleri, quoted in J.M.D., "Job Site for Utopia," 79. See also Paolo Soleri, "Relative Poverty and Frugality," *CoEvolution Quarterly,* no. 6 (Summer 1975): 118–21.
37. R. Buckminster Fuller, quoted in Henryk Skolimowski, "Paolo Soleri: The Philosophy of Urban Life," *Architectural Association Quarterly* 3 (1970): 40.
38. See Robert Jensen, "The Arcosanti Antithesis: Paolo Soleri and the Counter Culture," *Architectural Record* 156 (August 1974): 121–26.
39. See Ada Louise Huxtable, "Prophet in the Desert," *New York Times,* March 15, 1970.
40. Banham, *Megastructure,* 202.
41. Spiro Kostof offered a more nuanced comparative reading of Soleri's approach to urban design in "Soleri's Arcology: A New Design for the City?," *Art in America* 59, no. 2 (1970): 90–95.
42. David Greene, "A Blast from the Past," *Architectural Design* 41 (July 1971): 433–34.
43. They were not alone. A fairly typical response was offered in *Progressive Architecture*: "With their grand scale and intricate detail, [the models at the Corcoran exhibition] were among the finest sculpture we have seen in recent years, but all of us who saw them wondered whether any would ever be built." J.M.D., "Job Site for Utopia," 76.
44. Greene, "Blast from the Past," 434.
45. Reyner Banham, *Scenes in America Deserta* (Salt Lake City: Peregrine Smith, 1982), 86. On Banham's fascination with the desert and Soleri's con-

nections to Smithson, see Alessandra Ponte, "The House of Light and Entropy: Inhabiting the American Desert," *Assemblage,* no. 30 (August 1996): 12–31. In 1972, Soleri sat down with artists Walter De Maria and Michael Heizer (both of whom had also worked in the Southwest) for a dialogue in a television documentary produced by Stewart Udall: *Paolo Soleri: Work and Ideas* (Creative Arts Television, 1972).

46. Paradoxically, though, at least one observer attributed Soleri's success to the advent of new communications technologies: "The young generation, particularly in the United States, is a visual generation, *brought up on TV,* with a highly developed pictorial sensitivity; hence the impact of Soleri's forms." Skolimowski, "Paolo Soleri," 41.
47. Soleri, *Arcology* (1969), 29.
48. Paolo Soleri, "The New Environments," in *Environment, the University, and the Welfare of Man,* ed. Billy Ray Wilson (Philadelphia: J. B. Lippincott, 1969), 56–57. This essay was reproduced, somewhat altered, in Soleri, *Bridge between Matter and Spirit,* 27–39.
49. Certainly, Soleri was familiar with Prigogine's work, but I would not want to imply that Soleri's theories were derived directly from it. Rather, Soleri integrated Prigogine's ideas about thermodynamics into his own understanding of Teilhard. See Soleri, *Technology and Cosmogenesis,* 108.
50. See Ilya Prigogine, *Introduction to Thermodynamics of Irreversible Processes* (Springfield, Ill.: Charles C. Thomas, 1955). It is worth noting that Prigogine was also interested in the urban application of these theories. See Ilya Prigogine and Robert Herman, *Kinetic Theory of Vehicular Traffic* (New York: American Elsevier, 1971).
51. See Ilya Prigogine and Isabelle Stengers, *Order out of Chaos: Man's New Dialogue with Nature* (New York: Bantam Books, 1984); Ilya Prigogine, *The End of Certainty* (New York: Free Press, 1997).
52. Sibyl Moholy-Nagy was one of the first to identify in Soleri's philosophy a Bergsonian vitalism. See Sibyl Moholy-Nagy, "The Arcology of Paolo Soleri," *Architectural Forum* 132, no. 4 (May 1975): 74. Though he did not use the term *dissipative structure,* Soleri did in his later writings refer to his urban forms and the urban effect in general as a metaphorical "tsunami" and also as what he described as a nonorganic "hyperorganism." See Soleri, *Conversations with Paolo Soleri,* 37.
53. Interestingly, Soleri and Prigogine met at a symposium held to honor the centennial of the birth of Teilhard at Georgetown University on May 1, 1981. On that occasion, the two men's ideas did not really seem to mesh—Soleri asked about the place of God and the directionality of Prigogine's chaotic and random systemic operations, while Prigogine suggested that Soleri's urban designs might "impose an enormous structure on the people who would live [in them]." Thomas M. King and James F. Salmon, eds., *Teilhard and the Unity of Knowledge* (New York: Paulist Press, 1983), 46, 82.
54. In developing his idea of an "expanded cinema," Gene Youngblood relied on Teilhard as one of his fundamental sources. See Gene Youngblood, *Expanded Cinema* (New York: E. P. Dutton, 1970).
55. Teilhard, *Phenomenon of Man,* 44–45.
56. Teilhard, *Phenomenon of Man,* 142.
57. "In every physico-chemical change, adds thermodynamics, a fraction of the available energy is irrecoverably 'entropised,' lost, that is to say, in

the form of heat. Doubtless it is possible to retain this degraded fraction symbolically in equations, so as to express that in the operations of matter nothing is lost any more than anything is created, but that is merely a mathematical trick. As a matter of fact, from the real evolutionary standpoint, something is finally burned in the course of every synthesis in order to pay for that synthesis." Teilhard, *Phenomenon of Man,* 51. For a critique of Teilhard's scientific suppositions, see Peter Medawar, *The Art of the Soluble* (London: Methuen, 1967).

58. Teilhard, *Phenomenon of Man,* 143.
59. I learned of this endearing phrase from Mary Hoadley during a small gathering at Arcosanti on April 29, 2010. For a more extensive reading of the influence of Teilhard on Soleri, see Henryk Skolimowski, "Teilhard, Soleri, and Evolution," *Eco-Logos* 22, no. 79 (1976): 3–10.
60. MCD, as Soleri came to abbreviate it, is a principle that he discussed constantly, from *Arcology* to his most recent publications.
61. Soleri, *Arcology* (1969), 9.
62. "Temporal extension is warped by living stuff into acts of duration." Soleri, *Arcosanti,* 15.
63. Henri Bergson, *Creative Evolution,* trans. Arthur Mitchell (New York: Henry Holt, 1913), 4.
64. For Teilhard, Bergson's *Creative Evolution* was a pivotal part of his intellectual development. He read the book at the precise moment that he was doing paleontological fieldwork in England. See Robert Speaight, *The Life of Teilhard de Chardin* (New York: Collins, 1967), 45. Prigogine was drawn to Bergson's critique of the abstracting tendencies of classical science, but he largely saw his own descriptions of dissipative structures as addressing many of the elusive aspects of duration as defined by Bergson. See Prigogine and Stengers, *Order out of Chaos,* 94.
65. Bergson, *Creative Evolution,* 11, emphasis added.
66. On the eschatological logic of modernist discourse, see Colin Rowe, *The Architecture of Good Intentions: Towards a Possible Retrospect* (London: Academy Editions, 1994), 30–43.
67. Along with MCD, esthetogenesis (or aesthetogenesis) is a constant in Soleri's thought. Its fundaments can be found in Soleri, *Arcology* (1969), 19–20; Soleri, *Technology and Cosmogenesis,* 105–11; Soleri, *Bridge between Matter and Spirit,* 114–20.
68. Soleri, *Bridge between Matter and Spirit,* 117. This collection of essays was published in 1973 but includes content dating back to 1961 (see p. 255).
69. Soleri, *Bridge between Matter and Spirit,* 148. Indeed, Soleri would effectively posit the eventual triumph of "spirit" over all space, time, and matter. See Soleri, *Omega Seed.* As regards the influence of Nietzsche on Soleri, we can see many parallels, but they ultimately diverge. Nietzsche had considered the Dionysian impulse, or the will to return to a "primal unity," of utmost importance to the realization of human potential. See Friedrich Nietzsche, *The Birth of Tragedy and The Case of Wagner,* trans. Walter Kaufmann (New York: Vintage Books, 1967). Later, he would even describe life's return to inorganic matter as a kind of "celebration." See Spyros Papapetros, *On the Animation of the Inorganic: Art, Architecture, and the Extension of Life* (Chicago: University of Chicago Press, 2012), 146.
70. Kostof, "Soleri's Arcology," 95.

71. Auther, "Craft and the Handmade."
72. Reinhold Martin, "Organicism's Other," *Grey Room*, no. 4 (Summer 2001): 34–51.
73. Robert Smithson, ". . . The Earth, Subject to Cataclysms, Is a Cruel Master," interview by Gregoire Miller, in *Robert Smithson: The Collected Writings*, ed. Jack Flam (Berkeley: University of California Press, 1996), 256. Smithson was contrasting himself in this context to Buckminster Fuller. For more on Smithson's understanding of time and entropy, see Lee, *Chronophobia*.
74. Ponte, "House of Light and Entropy," 29–30. That the actual conditions at the Arcosanti site are "entropic," as Ponte points out, is a fact not lost on its inhabitants and the "workshoppers" who keep the activity (marginally) progressing; see, for instance, Robert Jensen, "Arcosanti as a Practical Place," *Arts+Architecture* 2, no. 4 (1983): 60–63.
75. As Martin explains, Kepes, too, was interested in furthering human evolution (he cited Julian Huxley) through a greater integration between natural and artificial systems. Martin, "Organicism's Other," 40.
76. Henri Focillon, *The Life of Forms in Art*, trans. Charles Hogan and George Kubler (New York: Zone Books, 1989). Focillon's *La Vie des formes* was first published in 1934, and Kubler's translation first appeared in 1948.
77. Focillon, *Life of Forms in Art*, 38.
78. Gilles Deleuze and Félix Guattari, *A Thousand Plateaus: Capitalism and Schizophrenia*, trans. Brian Massumi (Minneapolis: University of Minnesota Press, 1987). On the connections between Deleuze and Focillon, see Tom Conley, "Translator's Foreword: A Plea for Leibniz," in Gilles Deleuze, *The Fold: Leibniz and the Baroque*, trans. Tom Conley (Minneapolis: University of Minnesota Press, 1993), ix–xx.
79. Deleuze and Guattari, *Thousand Plateaus*, 161–62.
80. Deleuze and Guattari, *Thousand Plateaus*, 227–28.
81. Manuel De Landa has described some of the possible connections between the work of Prigogine and that of Deleuze and Guattari. See Manuel De Landa, "Nonorganic Life," in *Incorporations*, ed. Jonathan Crary and Sanford Kwinter (New York: Zone Books, 1992), 128–67. De Landa writes, "Matter, it turns out, can 'express' itself in complex and creative ways, and our awareness of this must be incorporated into any future materialist philosophy" (133). See also De Landa, *A Thousand Years of Nonlinear History*.

Conclusion

1. Turner, *From Counterculture to Cyberculture*. See also Blauvelt, *Hippie Modernism*.
2. See, for instance, Harrison, *Architectural Theories of the Environment*.
3. Reinhold Martin, *Utopia's Ghost: Architecture and Postmodernism, Again* (Minneapolis: University of Minnesota Press, 2010); K. Michael Hays, *Architecture's Desire: Reading the Late Avant-Garde* (Cambridge: MIT Press, 2009); Sean Keller, *Automatic Architecture: Motivating Form after Modernism* (Chicago: University of Chicago Press, 2017). See also Jorge Otero-Pailos's intriguing discussion of Charles Moore on the borders of environmental phenomenology and architectural semiotics: Jorge Otero-Pailos, *Architecture's Historical Turn: Phenomenology and the Rise of the*

Postmodern (Minneapolis: University of Minnesota Press, 2010), 100–45. Two documents that seem indexical vis-à-vis these shifts are Charles W. Moore, "Plug It in Ramses, and See if It Lights Up, Because We Aren't Going to Keep It Unless It Works," *Perspecta* 11 (1967): 33–43; and James Wines, *De-Architecture* (New York: Rizzoli, 1987).

4. Litwin, in Kranz, *Science and Technology in the Arts,* 261.
5. Sarah Williams Goldhagen, *Welcome to Your World: How the Built Environment Shapes Our Lives* (New York: Harper, 2017).
6. Latour, *Reassembling the Social.*
7. Graham Harman, *Tool Being: Heidegger and the Metaphysics of Objects* (Chicago: Open Court, 2002).
8. Bennett, *Vibrant Matter*; Karen Barad, *Meeting the Universe Halfway: Quantum Physics and the Entanglement of Matter and Meaning* (Durham, N.C.: Duke University Press, 2007).
9. Quentin Meillassoux, *After Finitude: An Essay on the Necessity of Contingency,* trans. Ray Brassier (London: Continuum, 2008).
10. T. J. Demos, *Against the Anthropocene: Visual Culture and Environment Today* (Berlin: Sternberg Press, 2017).
11. See Branden Hookway, *Interface* (Cambridge: MIT Press, 2014); Harwood, *The Interface*; Ian Hodder, *Entangled: An Archaeology of the Relationships between Humans and Things* (London: Wiley-Blackwell, 2012); Whitehead, *Process and Reality*; Jennifer Gabrys, *Program Earth: Environmental Sensing Technology and the Making of a Computational Planet* (Minneapolis: University of Minnesota Press, 2016); Augustin Berque, *Écoumène: Introduction à l'étude des milieux humains* (Paris: Belin, 2000).
12. Louis Althusser, *Ideology and Ideological State Apparatuses* (1970; repr., New York: Verso, 2014).
13. Levine, *Forms,* 6. Landscape designers Karen M'Closkey and Keith VanDerSys have invoked the patterning ethos of Gyorgy Kepes as one source of new ways of visualizing our contemporary environment. See Karen M'Closkey and Keith VanDerSys, *Dynamic Patterns: Visualizing Landscapes in a Digital Age* (London: Routledge, 2017).
14. Paul Virilio, *The Lost Dimension,* trans Daniel Moshenberg (Cambridge: MIT Press, 1991).
15. I am thinking here of what Antoine Picon has described as "the spatialisation of intelligence" in the so-called smart city. Antoine Picon, *Smart Cities: A Spatialised Intelligence* (West Sussex: John Wiley, 2015).
16. Vladimir Nabokov, *Speak, Memory: An Autobiography Revisited* (1947; repr., New York: Vintage Books, 1989), 310.
17. Gilles Deleuze, "What Is a *Dispositif*?," in Michel Foucault, *Michel Foucault: Philosopher,* trans. Timothy J. Armstrong (New York: Routledge, 1992), 160, 163.

Index

acoustics / acoustic space, 26–27, 32, 39–40, 42, 96, 99, 173, 250nn124–25, 250n129, 263n131
adaptation / adaptive design, xxv, 34, 46, 80, 139, 145, 152, 175, 183–84, 204–5, 225, 263n131
aesthetics, iii–iv, xiii–xv, xviii–xix, xxiii–xxv, 2, 4–5, 8, 23, 27–28, 30, 34–36, 41, 43–44, 46, 79, 81, 84, 87, 90–91, 96–98, 103–5, 107, 109, 111, 114–17, 120–21, 125, 127, 129, 131, 137, 139, 173, 188, 192, 206–7, 210–11, 220–21, 223, 228–32, 236–38, 243n25, 244n2, 247n57, 259n41, 261n104
affordance, xiv, xviii, xxiv, 16, 21–23, 65, 132, 236–39, 247n56
Agam, Yaacov, 116
aisthesis, 2, 244n2
Alexander, Christopher, xxiv, 32, 45–46, 52, 68, 78–87, 98, 135–36, 183, 248n94, 255n64, 263n134
Allen, Edward, 134–37, 182
Althusser, Louis, xxi
Altman, Irwin, 244n29
Ambasz, Emilio, xx, 192
ambience, xiv, xix, 12, 18, 89, 94, 96, 111, 118, 125–26, 140, 142, 159
anthropocene, 278n10
anthropology: cultural, xviii, 40, 48–50, 103, 135, 161; ecological, xx
apparatus, xvii, xxiv, xxvi, 2–3, 14–15, 17, 25, 28, 38, 42, 57, 60, 62–64, 72, 87, 91–92, 129, 139, 141, 157, 187–88, 197, 236, 238; *appareil*, xxi; dispositif, xxi, 206, 238
Aquarian frontier, 209
Archigram, 95, 170, 181, 222
Ardrey, Robert, 186
Arnheim, Rudolf, 250n124
Arning, Bill, 105, 260n54
Artaud, Antonin, xxii
artificial intelligence, 114, 126–27, 131, 144, 151, 153
Association of Man Environment Relations (ASMER), xix–xx, 243n25, 244n29
atmosphere/atmospheric, xiii–xiv, xvi, xix, xxiv, 24, 41, 48, 58, 76, 89, 97, 115, 129, 140, 211, 235–36. *See also* ambience
Auer, Thomas, 89

Baer, Steve, 135–36, 183, 270n81
Bagnall, Jim, 264n16
Baldwin, James, 202, 204–5, 270n81
Banham, Reyner, 93–96, 133, 211, 222–23, 231, 257n16, 267n7, 268n28, 274n45
Barker, Roger, 8
Barron, R. L., 160
Barry, Robert, 118, 120
Barthes, Roland, xxii
Bateson, Gregory, xxiv, 2, 28–36, 131, 141, 156, 161–62, 194, 247n57, 248n90, 249n106; double bind, 29–39
Bauhaus, 97–98, 103, 111, 202
Bay Area Regional Transit (BART), 68, 78, 255n63
Beer, Stafford, 152, 209
Benjamin, Walter, 38
Bennett, Jane, 242n20
Bennington College, 52–53
Bergson, Henri, 24, 210, 227, 232, 273n18, 275n52, 276n64
Bernard, Claude, xviii, 251n135
Berque, Augustin, 278n11
Bigelow, Julian, 147
biomimesis/biomimetic, xvi, 140, 144–45, 151, 161, 259n38
biopolitics, 42, 198, 206
biotechnology, 99–102, 106, 138
Birdwhistell, Ray, 48, 52
Blake, Peter, 274n33

Blake, William, 34
Blom, Ina, 2
Boccioni, Umberto, 97
Boetzkes, Amanda, 247n56
Boutourline, Serge, Jr., xvi, xxiv, 2–16, 18, 37, 123, 237–38, 245n7
Brand, Stewart, 35, 202, 210
Breton, André, xxii, 97
Brockman, John, 45, 47–48, 123, 252n3, 261n101
Brodey, Warren, x, xvi, xxv, 34, 134, 142–47, 150–51, 153–55, 157–66, 169, 209, 263n2, 264n16, 265n37, 266n69
Brown, Denise Scott, 222
Brown, Normon O., xxii
Bueno, Mauricio, 110–11
Buirge, Susan, 8, 10, 123
Bullivant, Lucy, xiv
Burnham, Jack, xv, 117–20, 231
Burns, Jim, xxii, 121–23
Burtin, Will, 36

Cage, John, xxii
Calhoun, James B., 54, 185, 187–89, 191, 194–95, 269n43
Cambridge University, xx, 96, 136
Canguilhem, Georges, 242n19
Castaneda, Carlos, 209, 213, 232, 272n13
Cavell, Richard, 38
Çelik Alexander, Zeynep, 267n6
Chamberlain, Wynn, 9, 12
Collingwood, R. G., 31–33
Colomina, Beatriz, xvii
computers/computation, ix, xv–xvi, xxv, 2–3, 5–7, 15, 38, 44, 47, 58, 60, 84, 86, 91, 96, 111–12, 114, 116, 120, 124–27, 129–31, 135–36, 141, 145, 147, 150–55, 170–71, 174–76, 179–80, 191, 198, 207, 236, 253n18, 255n63, 262n110, 264n14; digitality, xiv–xvi, xxv, 84, 90, 94, 96, 115, 117, 124, 126–27, 137, 142, 151, 154, 167, 170, 174, 176, 184, 210, 235, 238, 268n34, 272n6
Comte, Auguste, xviii
constructivism, 97, 111, 260n73
context, xviii, xxi, 28–36, 48–51, 53, 62, 80–81, 86–87, 105, 114, 131–35, 144–45, 150, 155–56, 162, 166
cybernetics, xvi, xxiv–xxvi, 2, 28, 30, 33–35, 82, 85, 103, 111, 115, 125–27, 131, 139, 141–42, 146–47, 149, 152, 155–56, 161–62, 164–65, 170, 184, 186, 188, 192–94, 200, 206, 209, 213, 223–25, 231, 266n59; communication, 6, 29–30, 48–49, 52–53, 60, 75, 85, 91, 108, 115, 127, 131, 133, 138, 141, 144, 146, 159, 188, 192, 200, 206, 211; feedback and feedback loops, 8, 10, 30, 36, 68, 107, 109, 111, 114, 129, 138, 144, 147, 149–50, 156, 174, 192

Dada, 111, 123
Darling, Candy, 9
Dass, Ram, 209
Deleuze, Gilles, xxi, 206, 210, 232–34, 238, 273n18, 277n78, 277n81
Descartes, René: Cartesianism, 21, 23–24, 32, 42, 105, 113, 117, 150, 155, 166, 251n35
Design Methods, xx, 52, 72–73, 79, 235
Design Thinking, xx, 15, 188, 191, 210, 264n16
determinism, xx, xxiii, 93, 210, 235, 257n13
Diller, Elizabeth, 90
disco, xvi
dissipative structures, xxv, 194, 224, 275n52, 276n64
Dobzhansky, Theodosius, 185, 187
domes, design of, 68, 211–12, 215, 217
Dorfles, Gillo, 200–201, 205
Dorner, Alexander, 52, 98
Doxiadis, Constantinos, xx, 221; ekistics, xx
drugs / drug culture, 110, 232
Drury, Felix, 114
Dubos, René, 105

Eames, Charles, 6
Eames, Ray, 6
earthworks, 231
Eastman, Charles, 90, 134, 263n131
ecology / ecosystems, xx, 28, 33–35, 90, 105, 137, 141–42, 144, 150–51, 162, 164, 166, 172, 202, 206, 215, 226
Ehrlich, Paul, 188, 202, 204
ekistics, xx

embedded technologies, 89, 94, 108, 109, 125, 127, 130, 176, 181, 262n110
emergence, xv, 24, 32, 145
Engelbart, Douglas, 153
entangled/entanglement, xxi, 116, 237
Entenza, John, 69
entropy, 106, 193–94, 224–25, 231, 250, 277n74
Environmental Design, discipline of, xix–xx, xxiii, xxiv, 11, 37, 78–79, 169, 174, 185, 210, 215, 235, 243nn25–26, 244nn29–31, 258n24
Environmental Design Research Association (EDRA), 73, 243n25
epistemology, ix, 4, 12, 16, 24–25, 28, 30, 32, 34–35, 79, 84, 98, 131, 247n50
ergonomics, xxi, 81, 142, 160–61, 202, 236
Erikson, Erik, 105
Esalen Institute, 209
eschatology, 227
Esser, Aristide, 69, 186
ether/aether, 32, 43, 49, 131, 185
ethnicity and race, 49–62
ethology, xviii, 54, 74, 95, 103
Euclidean, xxi, 16, 27, 42
evolution, xvi, xxv, 5, 45, 48, 90, 101, 114, 126, 137, 139, 144, 153, 157, 162, 167–72, 180, 183–84, 186–89, 191–97, 199–200, 202, 204, 211, 224–25, 227–28; coevolution, 202, 204–5, 209, 227, 270n81, 271n88
evolutive design, 93, 189
Experiments in Art and Technology, 123–24
extensions, theory of, xviii, xxv, 21, 23, 38, 41–42, 47–48, 68, 105, 166–67, 170, 187, 198–206, 212, 236
extrusion, 137, 144, 170, 173, 178–79

Fallis, Newton, 268n17
Fisk, Daria Bolton, 169
Fisk, Pliny, 169
foam, 125, 137, 139, 142, 145, 159–60, 162–63, 173
Focillon, Henri, 232
form, 27–35, 78–85, 87, 89–90, 93, 105–7, 158, 220–30, 232, 237; formalism, 145, 235, 237; formlessness, 32, 80
Foucault, Michel, xxi, 206, 238
Freud, Sigmund, xxi, 205
Friedman, Yona, 129–30, 132, 186
Fromm, Erich, 52
Fuller, R. Buckminster, xxii, xxv, 1, 52–53, 95, 120, 199–200, 204–5, 210–11, 213, 221–22, 231
functionalism, 52, 96, 98, 147, 170, 202, 231
furniture, 56, 78, 82, 134, 142, 144, 199, 236

Gabo, Naum, 97
Gabor, Dennis, 105
Gehlen, Arnold, 205
Geiger, H. R., 89
general systems theory, xx, 188, 223
generative design, 80, 142
genotype, 204
geography, xx, 115
Gesamtkunstwerk, 96, 111, 113
Gibson, James J., xxiv, 2, 15–25, 27–28, 52, 141
Giedion, Sigfried, xxii, 39–42, 52, 68, 250n129
Gillette, Frank, 9, 34
Glass, Philip, 10
Goffman, Irving, 52, 56
Goldberg, Bertrand, 69
Goldfinger, Ernö, 52, 65–67, 69
Graham Foundation, 69
Grosser, Maurice, 52
Guattari, Félix, 206, 232–34, 242n20, 277n81

Haacke, Hans, 111, 116
habitus, 52
Habraken, N. J., 135
Hall, Edward T., xiii–xiv, xxiv, xxv, 3, 12, 38, 44, 45–87, 105, 186, 199, 205, 213, 270; proxemics, xxiv, 47, 50, 52, 56, 60–62, 68–72, 76–78, 87, 253n18, 254n49
Halpern, Orit, 147, 149
Halprin, Anna, 121
Halprin, Lawrence, 65, 69, 121
happening(s), 39, 43, 114, 123, 133
Haraway, Donna, 200
hardware, 91, 114, 125, 134, 153, 159, 174, 176, 182, 186, 237–38. *See also* software

Hardy, Holzman & Pfeiffer, 121
Harrison, Newton, 90
Harvard University, 2, 4; Graduate School of Design, xv
Harwood, John, 5–6
Hediger, Heini, 52
Heidegger, Martin, 23–24, 145
Higgins, Dick, 123
Hilbertz, Wolf, xvi, xxv, 135, 167, 169–91, 193–94, 196–98, 200, 202, 205, 209
hippie, 209, 222
Hochschule fur Gestaltung (Ulm), xx
Hockett, Charles, 52
Hoffman, Abbie, 9
hologram, 180
homeostat, 152
human, conceptions of the, xiii, xv–xvi, xix, xxii, xxiv, 2, 15, 25, 35–36, 38, 40–41, 43, 52–55, 67, 98, 101, 104–5, 118, 144, 154–55, 166, 186–88, 195–96, 205, 207, 210, 224, 226–28, 232, 234, 237, 239
human environment, concept of, xx, 3, 100, 117, 205
Hunter, David, xv

immersion, 44, 53, 62–64, 116
individuation, 31, 223, 227
Ingold, Timothy, 242n20, 247n57
innerspace, 143
Institut de l'environnement (Paris), xx
interaction, xiv–xix, xxiv, xxvi, 2–3, 6–8, 10–12, 14–16, 21–25, 29–30, 36, 43–44, 47, 56, 58, 60, 64, 73–74, 77, 79, 87, 93–94, 97, 99–101, 103, 105, 107, 110–11, 117–18, 124, 127, 129, 131, 134, 139–41, 145–46, 150–51, 155, 160, 163–64, 166–67, 174, 185–86, 188, 197, 202, 204–5, 227, 229, 238–39
interface, xiii–xv, xviii, 6, 21, 47, 72, 82, 90, 93, 109, 124–32, 140–41, 144–46, 153, 156–57, 162–63, 166, 173–74, 210, 217, 236–38
intermedia, 3, 8, 10, 34, 47, 114, 116, 118, 123–24, 130, 133, 236
International Business Machines (IBM), 3, 5–8, 10–11, 202
interval, 14, 42–43, 53
Ittelson, William, 243–44

Jantsch, Erich, 169, 191–96, 198
Johnson, Avery, xvi, xxv, 131–36, 141–42, 153, 157, 165, 169, 191

Kahn, Louis, 220
Kapp, Ernst, 200, 206
Kaprow, Allan, 123
Kepes, Gyorgy, xv–xvi, xxii–xxiii, xxv, 65, 103–11, 113–14, 117, 120, 123, 130, 140, 200–201, 203, 205, 224, 231, 236
Kiesler, Frederick, xxv, 67, 98–106, 117, 237
kinesics, 52, 252
kineticism, 116
Klee, Paul, 184–85
Knowles, Ralph, 169
Koberg, Don, 264n16
Kobler, Richard, 91
Koffka, Kurt, 21
Kostof, Spiro, 228
Kriyananda, Swami, 211–12
Krueger, Myron, x, xvi, xxiv, 126–29

Labrouste, Henri, 89
Latour, Bruno, 236, 252n4
Lavin, Sylvia, 95–96, 258n24
Lee, Robert S., 3, 6, 245n10
Lefebvre, Henri, 42
Levine, Caroline, 237
Lévi-Strauss, Claude, xxii
Lewin, Kurt, 21
Licht, Jennifer, 113–15
lifeworld, 87, 235–36
Litwin, George, 124, 236, 261n104
Longo, Angela Maria, 192
Lynch, Kevin, 52, 65, 242, 253n17

Maldonado, Tomás, 185, 205, 268n36
Man–Environment Systems, group and publication, xx, 37, 173, 186, 198, 243n25
Martin, Reinhold, 103
Marx, Karl: Marxism, xxi, 105–6, 145, 207
Maslow, Abraham, 186
Massachusetts Institute of Technology: Architecture Machine Group, 130; Center for Advanced Visual Studies, 108–11, 117, 123; Media Lab, xv, 130, 141

materialism/ materiality, 16, 87, 170, 210, 214, 226, 231, 236
McCulloch, Warren, xxv, 28, 131, 142, 147–50, 153–55, 164
McHarg, Ian, 69
McLuhan, Marshall, xv, xxii, xxiv–xxv, 1–2, 26, 36–45, 48, 52, 65, 93, 96, 98–99, 104, 117, 123, 198–200, 205–6, 213, 236
Mead, Taylor, 9
Medalla, David, 116
Menges, Achim, 89, 256n2
Meyer Harrison, Helen, 90
milieu, xiii–xiv, xvi–xvii, xix, xxiv, 4, 10, 47, 96, 101, 103–4, 114, 118, 131, 137–38, 144, 169–70, 174, 186, 192, 197, 205, 207, 251n135
minimalism, 90
Minsky, Marvin, 144, 151
mobility in design, 46, 102, 125, 186
Moles, Abraham, 206
Moore, Charles, 1, 114
Moorman, Charlotte, 9
Morphocode, xv
Mumford, Lewis, 200
Museum of Modern Art (MoMA), 115, 123
mysticism, xxvi, 210, 213

Nabokov, Vladimir, 238
nature, xix, 23, 32, 162, 166–67, 213
Negroponte, Nicholas, xxv, 124–25, 130–35, 140, 144–45, 154, 173, 183
Nelson, George, 1
neuroaesthetics, 1
Neutra, Richard, 95–96, 258n24
New Age culture, xxv, 28, 35, 170, 198, 202, 209–14
Newton, Sir Isaac: Newtonian conceptions of space, 14, 105, 185, 224, 269n37
Nicoletti, Manfredi, 69
Nietzsche, Friedrich, xxi–xxii, 228, 276n69
Nisbet, James, 90
noosphere, 224

ontology, 3, 14, 16–18, 23, 25, 28, 30, 46, 86, 100, 149, 166, 194, 227, 236, 267n6
organicism, 170, 184, 230–32; non-organic life, 156, 161, 166, 275n52, 277n81; inorganic, theories of the, 173, 176, 276n69
organisms, natural and artificial: relation to environment, xiv, xix, xxiv, 21–22, 24–26, 31–33, 45, 54, 68, 80, 82, 94–95, 99, 101, 103, 107–8, 147, 149–50, 153, 155–56, 158, 161–62, 167, 169, 176, 186, 196, 198–200, 204–6, 233, 236
ornament, 230, 232
Osmond, Humphrey, 52

Paalen, Wolfgang, 98
Paik, Nam Jun, 9
Pailos, Jorge Otero, 277n3
Papanek, Victor, 98–99
Papapetros, Spyros, 41, 250n128
Papert, Seymour, 144
participation: participatory design, xv, xvii–xviii, 44, 97, 107–9, 113–14, 123, 127–29, 135, 156–57
Pask, Gordon, 90, 125, 152–54
pattern, v, vii, xv, xvii–xix, xxi–xxii, xxiv–xxv, 2, 10, 14, 17–18, 29, 31–39, 42–43, 45–56, 58, 60, 62, 64–65, 67–70, 72–76, 78–87, 89–90, 95, 104–5, 107–8, 113, 118, 124–25, 131, 133–34, 136, 139, 145–46, 151, 155, 161–62, 171, 174, 176, 179–80, 184, 195, 204–5, 207, 209–11, 220, 226–27, 232–34, 237–39, 252n142, 256n86, 278n13; interference, 49, 56, 78, 174, 179–80; phasing, 45, 87; recognition, 38, 42, 47, 51, 60, 113, 124, 131, 155, 199
Pavlov, Ivan: Pavlovian response, xvii, 24–25, 37
Pennsylvania State University, xx
perception, xv, xviii, xxiii, 1–3, 7, 10–12, 14–16, 18–25, 27–28, 30, 40, 42–45, 49, 51–52, 54, 57, 65, 69, 98, 107, 114, 123, 131, 141, 149–50, 155–57, 185, 194–95, 232, 238
Pérez-Gómez, Alberto, xv
performativity in design, 123, 129
Pevsner, Antoine, 97
phenomenology, 3, 8, 14, 16, 23, 25, 27, 245n2, 277n3
phenotype, 204–5
photopolymerization, 174

phylogenetic, 68, 186
physiology, 17, 24, 26, 65, 95, 149
Pickering, Andrew, 152
Piene, Otto, 111, 116
Piltdown Man, 224
Pitts, Walter, 147
plastic, 109, 125, 137, 142, 160, 163, 173, 176, 222. *See also* foam
plasticity, literal and metaphorical, xxiii, 173, 186
pneumatic design, xvi, 137, 186, 230
polyurethane, 158. *See also* foam; plastic
Ponte, Alessandra, 231
Ponty, Maurice Merleau, 23
positivism, xvii–xviii, 235, 251n135
posthumanism, 48
postindustrialism, 43, 184
postminimalism, 115–17
postmodernism, xxi, 209–10, 235
prefabrication and design, 92, 129, 137–38, 186
Prigogine, Ilya, 169, 193–94, 210, 224–25, 227, 233
programming, xviii, 72, 107, 133, 138, 145, 153, 158, 238
prosthetic, 198
proxemics, xxiv, 47, 50, 52–54, 56–58, 60–65, 67–69, 72, 74–78, 86–87
Pruitt Igoe Housing, 69
psychedelics, 124, 209, 213
psychology, ix–x, xviii–xx, 1, 3, 6, 12, 16, 22, 30, 40, 46, 52, 65, 69, 78, 81, 95, 103, 105, 135, 137, 141, 161, 185, 209, 213, 246n26; behavioral/ behaviorism, xvii, xxiv–xxv, 5, 16, 23, 28, 37, 48, 54, 56, 60, 62, 69, 72, 87, 91, 113, 139, 147, 154, 173–74, 187, 224, 235, 251, 253, 255; environmental, x, xx, 1, 46, 81, 243n23; perceptual, 12, 15–19, 40, 52, 141; transactional, 52
Pulsa, 105, 111, 113–15, 123

quantum physics/mechanics, 98, 192, 224

Radical Software journal, 34, 163–66
Rancière, Jacques, 245n2
recycling, 182, 207
regenerative design, 94
regulation: self-regulating mechanisms, 90, 108, 147, 192
robots: robotic construction, xvi, 89, 140, 142, 144, 147, 154, 170, 175–76, 178–83, 198
Rosenblueth, Arturo, 147
Rosenzweig, M. R., 186
Roszak, Theodore, 209
rubber, 145. *See also* foam; plastic
Rudolph, Paul, 220
Ryan, Paul, 9, 163–65

Saarinen, Eero, 69–70
Sadler, Simon, 35
Safdie, Moshe, 220
Salter, Chris, 129, 256n3
Sanoff, Henry, 243n25
Saussure, Ferdinand de, xxi
Scheerbart, Paul, 95
schizophrenia, 29–30, 36, 147
Schneider, Ira, 9
Schöffer, Nicolas, 111–12, 125, 129, 186
Schrödinger, Erwin, 98
Schwitters, Kurt, 97
scientology, 209
Scofidio, Ricardo, 90
sculpture, xvi, 9, 41, 97, 109, 113–17, 223
Seattle World's Fair, 3, 5, 7–8, 12
semiconductors, 160
sensing, xv, xxv, 8, 24–27, 90, 108, 118, 134, 146, 150, 159, 166, 175–76, 180, 244n2; sensation, xxiii, 1, 6, 14, 19, 26, 42, 65–66, 114, 117, 148, 185, 238; sensor, xv, 89, 109, 111, 125, 134–35, 153, 156, 174, 239; sensorium, 2, 15–16, 23, 39, 41, 44, 87; sensory apparatus, xvi, 8, 24, 42–44, 54, 57; sensory deprivation, 113, 115
servomechanisms, 151
shamanism, 209, 213
Sharp, Willoughby, 89, 116–17
Shepard, Sam, 9
Sherrington, C. S., xxii
Siegel, Eric, 9
Simondon, Gilbert, 145
Sinnott, E. W., 187
Skinner, B. F., 251

Skolimowski, Henryk, 274n32
Sloan, Sam A., 72–77
Sloterdijk, Peter, xiii–xiv, xix, xxii, 8, 236, 238, 242n20
Smithson, Robert, 105, 111, 223, 231, 275n45, 277n73
Snow, C. P., xxii
social construction: constructionism, xvi, xx, xxiii, xxv, 42, 47, 50, 60, 100, 136–38, 170, 235
sociobiology, 187–88
sociology, xviii, 3
sociopetal/sociofugal space, 52, 56, 75–76
softness, 144–46, 173
software, 114, 117–20, 124, 134, 153, 159, 176, 182, 186, 237. *See also* hardware
Soleri, Paolo, iv, x, xvi, xxv, 145, 169, 209–10, 213–34, 264n14, 271n4, 273n28, 274n32, 274n45, 276n69; arcology, 210, 213–19, 221–22, 226–27, 229–30; Arcosanti, x, 215, 217–23, 226, 228, 230–31, 233
Sontag, Susan, xxii–xxiii, 236, 238
Spencer, Herbert, xix
Spencer-Brown, George, 30–31
Spitzer, Leo, xix
Spivack, Meyer, 46
Steenson, Molly, 79
St. Florian, Friedrich, 169
Straus, Erwin, xxiv, 2, 23–28, 37, 40, 244n1, 245n2
subjectivity, 80, 194, 206, 209
Superstudio, 121
surrealism, 97–99
sustainability, design, 90, 166, 171, 210
symbiosis, 131, 170, 173–74, 186, 190, 211

Teilhard de Chardin, Pierre, 187, 210, 224–27
territoriality, 54, 68, 188
Teyssot, Georges, 125, 264n15
theosophy, 210
thermodynamics, xix, 100, 193, 225
thermostat, 14, 133–34, 173, 263n131
Thompson, D'Arcy Wentworth, 36
Thompson, William Irwin, 213
topology, 52, 85, 144, 149, 161, 163–64
transactional processes, 45, 60, 106, 118, 156, 205, 224. *See also* interface
transducers, 198
Troy, Nancy, 97
Turing test, 160
Turner, Fred, 123, 211
Tyrwhitt, Jaqueline, 39–40, 44

Uecker, Günther, 116
Uexküll, Jakob von, 23, 25, 205; Umwelt, 24
Universitas, xx, 192, 198
University of California, Berkeley, xx
University of Texas, Austin, xi, xx, 96, 167, 169–70, 186, 190
University of Utah, xx
University of Wisconsin–Madison, 127
USCO, 124
utopianism, xx, xxvi, 47, 53, 103–6, 111, 115, 130, 170, 184, 188, 191, 210, 215, 227, 231
Utopie, 186

van der Ryn, Sim, 35, 135, 183
Vernadsky, Vladimir, 224
Vignelli, Massimo, 3
von Foerster, Heinz, 153

Waddington, C. H., 187
Wei, Sha Xin, xv
Wellesley–Miller, Sean, xvi, 133, 135, 137–40, 183
Wenner-Gren Foundation, 34
Whitehead, Alfred North, 32, 100, 273n18
Whorf, Benjamin Lee, 52, 251
Wiener, Norbert, 146–47, 149, 156, 193
Wigley, Mark, xvii
Wittgenstein, Ludwig, xxii
Wolfe, Cary, 244
Wolfe, Tom, 55, 209, 222, 254n28
Wright, Frank Lloyd, 215, 220, 222

Yale University, 114, 151
Yalkut, Jud, 8, 10, 14
Youngblood, Gene, 119, 275n54

Larry D. Busbea is associate professor of art history at the University of Arizona, Tucson. He is author of *Topologies: The Urban Utopia in France, 1960–1970* and *Proxemics: Social Construction/Environmental Design.*